Rationality

The study of rationality is one of the most exciting and important areas of contemporary cognitive science: recent research has involved collaborations across disciplinary boundaries, and theoretical progress has been rapid and profound. *Rationality: Psychological and Philosophical Perspectives* gathers together leading researchers in Europe and the United States to survey these developments and present them in an accessible and interesting form. While the emphasis of the book is primarily psychological, the contributors also consider arguments from philosophy, logic and computational theory.

Several major themes emerge: the two views of rationality as logical power and as the ability to do the right thing; the relation between normative (logical) and descriptive (psychological) accounts of human reason; the need to be cautious both in interpreting the dictates of logic and in the conclusions we draw from experiments; arguments for and against the theory of 'mental logic'; and the bounds of rationality itself. In addition, theoretical arguments are also directed at the kinds of problems for rationality which are found in the real world.

K.I. Manktelow is Principal Lecturer in Psychology at the University of Wolverhampton, and **D.E. Over** is Principal Lecturer in Philosophy at the University of Sunderland. They are the authors of *Inference and Understanding* (Routledge, 1990).

International Library of Psychology

Rationality

Psychological and philosophical perspectives

Edited by K.I. Manktelow and D.E. Over

London and New York

First published in 1993
by Routledge
11 New Fetter Lane, London EC4P 4EE

Simultaneously published in the USA and Canada
by Routledge
29 West 35th Street, New York, NY 10001

Typeset in Times by J&L Composition Ltd, Filey, North
Yorkshire.

Printed and bound in Great Britain by
Mackays of Chatham PLC, Chatham, Kent.

British Library Cataloguing in Publication Data
A catalogue record for this book is available from the British
Library

Library of Congress Cataloging in Publication Data
Rationality: psychological and philosophical perspectives /
edited by K.I. Manktelow and D.E. Over.
   p.   cm. – (International library of psychology)
   Includes bibliographical references and index.
   1. Reasoning (Psychology).   2. Cognitive psychology.
   3. Logic.   4. Psychology and philosophy.
   I. Manktelow, K.I., 1952–   . II. Over, D.E., 1946–   .
   III. Series.
BF442.R38   1993
153.4′3–dc20   92–47072
                                                          CIP

ISBN 0–415–06955–6

Contents

Figures

Contributors

R.M.J. Byrne, Department of Psychology, Trinity College Dublin, Dublin 2, Ireland.

N. Chater, Department of Psychology, University of Edinburgh, 7 George Square, Edinburgh, EH8 9JZ, UK.

J. St B.T. Evans. Department of Psychology, University of Plymouth, Drake Circus, Plymouth PL4 8AA, UK.

G. Gigerenzer, Department of Psychology, University of Chicago, 5848 South University Avenue, Chicago, IL 60637, USA.

P.N. Johnson-Laird, Department of Psychology, Princeton University, Green Hall, Princeton, NJ 08544–1010, USA.

E.J. Lowe, Department of Philosophy, University of Durham, 50 Old Elvet, Durham, DH1 3HN, UK.

K.I. Manktelow, School of Health Sciences, University of Wolverhampton, 62–68 Lichfield St, Woverhampton, WV1 1DJ, UK.

M.R. Oaksford, Department of Psychology, University College of North Wales, Bangor, Gwynedd, LL57 2DG, UK.

D.P. O'Brien, Baruch College and University Graduate Center, City University of New York, 17 Lexington Ave, New York, NY 10010, USA.

D.E. Over, School of Social and International Studies, University of Sunderland, Forester Building, Chester Road, Sunderland, SR1 3SD, UK.

E. Shafir, Department of Pyschology, Princeton University, Green Hall, Princeton, NJ 08544–1010, USA.

K. Stenning, Human Communication Research Centre, University of Edinburgh, 8 Buccleuch Place, Edinburgh, EH8 9LW, UK.

R.J. Stevenson, Department of Psychology, University of Durham, Science Laboratories, South Road, Durham, DH1 3LE, UK.

N.E. Wetherick, Department of Psychology, King's College, University of Aberdeen, Aberdeen, AB9 2UB, UK.

Acknowledgements

Naturally, we must first express our thanks to the contributors to this volume for all their efforts. All of these people have influenced and inspired our own work. In addition, we would like to acknowledge the debt we owe to those whose names do not appear on the contents page, principally: Pat Cheng, Leda Cosmides, Dorothy Edgington, Vittorio Girotto, Richard Griggs, Keith Holyoak, Maria and Paolo Legrenzi, Guy Politzer and Peter Wason.

Our appreciation also goes to David Stonestreet and Bradley Scott at Routledge for their unfailing positivity.

Lastly, we must also say 'thanks' to our families: Alice and Edward, and Marilyn and Harriet.

Introduction
The study of rationality

K.I. Manktelow and D.E. Over

This book is concerned with one of the most active areas of interest in contemporary cognitive science; human rationality. Why should rationality be such a 'hot' topic? After all, it is a concept that has probably been employed ever since people first started to think about thinking. There are several reasons. One is the historical and continuing influence in cognitive science of formal systems for generating valid arguments: logic, in other words. As a way of assessing the rationality of reasoning, logic has been with us for over two thousand years, in the legacy of Aristotle's great works, but most of what we now know as formal logic is a product only of the last century or so. Even more recent has been the claim, most famously put forward by Piaget and his followers, that there is a kind of natural formal logic in the minds of human beings for generating their reasoning. This theory of the natural programming of the mind has obvious implications for cognitive science, and the testable consequence that people should tend to be rational in their ordinary deductive reasoning.

A second current is the tremendous increase in interest in human reasoning on the part of cognitive psychology. Again, we have some pioneers, followed by a recent explosion of effort. These psychologists, of course, are interested in how people actually reason, as opposed to reasoning in some ideal sense. However, in describing ordinary reasoning, they have often invoked formal systems as standards against which to assess their subjects' performance. For this purpose, they have used not just logic, but also the probability calculus and decision theory. Some psychologists have claimed to find that ordinary people tend to be irrational by these standards. Clearly, this opposing view also has serious implications for any theory of the mind, and for accounts of human behaviour generally in the social sciences.

This relation between *descriptive* accounts of reasoning, primarily the object of psychologists, and *normative* ones, philosophers' main concern, gives us a third source of impetus for the current upsurge of interest in the area. While psychologists have felt obliged to look to normative theories to evaluate subjects' behaviour, philosophers have begun to pay heed to the psychologists' findings and to incorporate them into their own theorizing. Two extreme examples from the recent literature are the papers by Cohen (1981) and Stich (1985), who came to directly opposite conclusions about rationality. Cohen posed the question of whether human irrationality could be experimentally demonstrated and concluded that it could not, in principle. His point was that people, including psychologists and their subjects, have to be rational in order to communicate with each other.

Another type of general argument for human rationality has been based on evolutionary principles. In simple terms, the claim is that we could not have evolved to the level at which we could study our own rationality without being rational. On the other hand, Stich asked whether humans could be an irrational species and concluded that they could be. He rejected the general arguments for rationality, and appealed to the psychological literature for evidence of widespread irrationality. This, then, is where the *rationality debate* is situated: to what extent can people be described, in principle or in practice, as rational? That is the question addressed by the eleven contributions to this volume.

What is it to be rational? Standard dictionaries use a number of concepts in the attempt to define 'rational', but leave it unclear how these are related to each other. We learn that being rational is having the ability to be logical, to reason, or to draw conclusions properly. We learn as well that to be rational is to be reasonable, sensible, and judicious. Now can we distinguish between the power of drawing conclusions logically and the extent to which exercising this power is reasonable, and between the exercise of reason and acting in a sensible or judicious way? The fact that these distinctions do not come to the same thing is one of the main themes of this book.

The distinction between rationality as the ability to do the right thing and as logical power is the focus of our first chapter, by Jonathan Evans, who urges that the two notions should be kept separate. Evans thus distinguishes between rationality of purpose, which yields adaptive behaviour, and rationality of process, for which formal logic has been taken as the standard. He argues that the former should be the primary concept, and that much work in cognitive psychology on reasoning has drawn the wrong conclusions because this fact has not been recognized. He concludes from this thesis that the import of most psychological work on reason is largely for the *bounds* of rationality.

The concept of bounded rationality was first clearly advanced by Herbert Simon, and it is a basic notion for several of the other contributors here. It is the central concern of the chapter by Mike Oaksford and Nick Chater (Chapter 2). Like Simon, they affirm that rationality must be bounded because of the real constraints on cognitive processing which psychological research has revealed: in particular, the restrictions on working memory, and the 'frame problem' revealed by work in artificial intelligence. The frame problem is not often invoked in this field, but Oaksford and Chater argue strongly that it should be: it concerns the search and selection process of relevant information from long-term memory, a process which is central to many contemporary accounts of content-dependent reasoning.

Content-dependence in reasoning is addressed by Rosemary Stevenson (Chapter 3), who argues that logical, content-independent reasoning cannot guarantee us knowledge of the world or the ability to act successfully in it. She contends that many apparent errors in reasoning arise from the content-dependent nature of inductive reasoning and learning in the real world. She considers the developmental consequence of this view, by proposing that children's task in acquiring reason lies in the integration of the inductive and deductive components of thought. Her approach is thus compatible with a Piagetian viewpoint, and also with Evans' scheme of two kinds of rationality.

Stevenson makes an assumption which is shared by other contributors, especially Norman Wetherick (Chapter 4) and David O'Brien (Chapter 5): that of an 'underlying abstract logical competence'. Wetherick presents a detailed argument for inherent rationality, based on his study of syllogistic inference. He suggests, along with Oaksford and Chater, that much of the observed error in psychological experiments on reasoning have to do with the unrepresentative nature of laboratory problems. O'Brien agrees with this, and also makes the point that theories of mental logic are not 'monolithic' – what is evidence against one is not necessarily evidence against another, and they do not all imply that people are more logical than properly interpreted experiments reveal. He sets out a three-part theory of reasoning, which contains a set of restricted inference schemas (with 'feeder' and 'core' elements), a reasoning programme that implements these rules, and a set of pragmatic principles which promote or inhibit certain inferences. In this type of bounded mental logic, the set of inference rules is constrained in its application both by pragmatic considerations and by its implementation in the mind.

The question of how implementation affects rationality benefits particularly from work in the computational modelling of thought, and is the focus of Keith Stenning and Mike Oaksford in Chapter 6. They ask what kind of computational architecture supports human deductive capacities. After all, even the logic programming language Prolog has to contain non-logical implementation devices such as backward chaining and the 'cut' operator to make it functional. This view leads them to regard traditional mental-logic theories as 'anachronistic', in that they only describe sets of consequence relations, and we are not told how they might be implemented in the mind.

This is not, of course, the only critique of mental-logic theories. The most well-known comes from the theory of mental models, which is represented here in Chapter 7 by Phil Johnson-Laird and Ruth Byrne. Concentrating on deductive rationality, they set out their definition, which has two components: to believe what is true (rational belief), and to infer what is true (rational thinking). They reject the idea that people have in their minds systematic inferential principles or rules of inference, on the grounds that the deductive mechanism is fundamentally semantic rather than syntactic. Thus, reasoning is inseparable from its content, and hence people will not be either impeccably rational – they make mistakes – or wholly irrational – they make valid inferences. We are rational in principle, but err in practice.

The theories of mental models and mental logic are often regarded as polar opposites, but this notion is attacked by Jonathan Lowe (Chapter 8), from a philosophical perspective. For one thing, logic, he contends, is an artificial system for extending our inferential powers beyond their normal range, just as mathematics is for calculation, or a telescope is for vision. For another, mental models require a 'quasi-mechanical procedure', which he argues is superfluous to an account of ordinary human reason. Further-more, both semantic and syntactic approaches are equally formal. Lowe detects little more than notational differences between systems of mental models and proposed mental logics, and suggests instead a connectionist approach as a proper alternative, something advocated by some of the other authors, for example, Oaksford and his colleagues.

Much of this debate concerns what Evans has characterized as rationality of process. We should recall that his other category is rationality of purpose. This has traditionally been the domain of research on decision making, and Evans has for a long time bemoaned the unnecessary division between the fields of reasoning and decision making. The crossing of this border is explicitly addressed by David Over and Ken Manktelow (Chapter 9). They look at deontic reasoning, which appeals to rules and regulations about which actions ought to be, or may be, performed. It is ultimately founded, they hold, on the concept of preference, and is a rich mix of moral, prudential, probabilistic, and social cognitions. They advocate an account of these cognitions, at the basic semantic level, in terms of mental models. They also argue that there are many unanswered normative as well as descriptive questions about deontic reasoning, and that deontic conflicts and dilemmas are a serious challenge to both normative and descriptive theories of human rationality.

Rational decision making is explored in detail by Eldar Shafir (Chapter 10). He addresses the relation between normative and descriptive accounts of human decision making: whether these can be expected to coincide depends on the assumed underlying cognitive processes. Shafir takes as his case study recent work by himself and others on Savage's 'Sure-thing principle' and Simpson's paradox. He argues that a tendency to violate the former, and to fall into the latter, can reveal something important about our cognitive processes for making decisions. He further concludes that 'both normative and descriptive accounts capture important aspects of human experience', on the grounds that normative principles which are violated when their relevance is unclear become satisfied by people when their application is 'transparent'.

Decision making calls for probabilistic reasoning, and this is the topic of Chapter 11 by Gerd Gigerenzer. He criticizes, on both methodological and theoretical grounds, past characterizations of ordinary probability judgements as irrational, as committing errors, and displaying biases. He makes his empirical case using examples from work on apparent failures of rationality, such as the conjunction fallacy. He points out that research going back to Tversky and Kahneman (1983) shows how this fallacy can be avoided by presenting the problems in 'frequentist' rather than Bayesian or single-event format – using Shafir's term, we might say that the former makes the problems 'transparent'. The mind, Gigerenzer argues, naturally computes frequencies efficiently, and this is only to be expected on evolutionary grounds. Once again, then, we are urged to consider rationality as bounded, and to be cautious in relating psychological research to what people think and do in the real world.

REFERENCES

Cohen, L.J. (1981) 'Can human irrationality be experimentally demonstrated?' *Behavioral and Brain Sciences* 4: 317–70.

Stich, S.P. (1985) 'Could man be an irrational animal?' *Synthese* 64: 115–35.

Tversky, A. and Kahneman, D. (1983) 'Extensional versus intuitive reasoning: the conjunction fallacy in probability judgment', *Psychological Review* 90: 293–315.

Chapter 1

Bias and rationality

J. St B.T. Evans

Here is a paradox. The human species is evidently highly intelligent. We have not merely adapted to our environment but have shown the ability to control it and alter it in many ways to suit our purposes. We have developed the extraordinarily complex and powerful system of natural language which in itself gives us powers of cognitive representation and communication which far exceed those of any other species on Earth. We store vast amounts of information from which – in contrast with existing computer systems – we can access with the greatest of ease just those parts relevant to our current situation. Our perceptual abilities are perhaps even more astounding, far exceeding those of the most skilfully programmed super-computer.

But what happens when the owner of this remarkable brain is taken into the pyschological laboratory and asked to perform apparently straight-forward tasks requiring reasoning or judgement? The answer is that a whole range of systematic errors and biases is produced. People ignore relevant information or attend to irrelevant features of the tasks and their performance is highly dependent upon the precise content and context in which a logical problem is presented (see Evans, 1989, 1992).

So, human beings are highly intelligent on the one hand and chronically biased in their reasoning and judgement on the other. This paradox has gripped and perplexed a number of authors in the recent psychological literature. Bias researchers such as myself have been forced, however reluctantly, to consider what implications our research findings and their interpretation have for the notion of human rationality. In particular, the research fields have come under attack by those who appear to regard rationality as axiomatic. Criticisms of bias research and researchers include the following claims:

1 Authors selectively cite evidence of bias and ignore studies reporting good reasoning (Christensen-Szalanski and Beach, 1984).
2 Errors are judged relative to an arbitrary normative system such as standard logic or probability theory, whereas subjects may use some alternative system (Cohen, 1981, 1982).

3 Rationality is bounded by cognitive-processing constraints. Norm reference systems such as logic and probability theory are irrelevant since it is computationally impossible for a human being to apply these principles to problems of real-world complexity (Oaksford and Chater, 1992).
4 Psychological experiments are arbitrary and unrepresentative of the real world. They produce 'cognitive illusions' similar to visual illusions (Cohen, 1981).
5 Psychological experiments which induce errors are designed to be informative about the cognitive processes involved but do not support extrapolations about likely erroneous performance in the real world (Lopes, 1991; Funder, 1987).
6 Apparent errors of reasoning reflect subjects' personalized representation of the problem information (Henle, 1962).
7 There is a circular relation between logic and understanding, and the only consistent position possible is to assume logical reasoning (Smedslund, 1990).

Argument (1) – the citation bias – I have dealt with elsewhere (Evans, 1984) and it will not be discussed in this chapter. The fact is that experimental evidence of biases abounds – whether excessively cited or not – and these findings must somehow be resolved in the rationality debate. Arguments (2) and (3) are cases of normative-system problem; (4) and (5) are examples of the external-validity problem; and (6) and (7) can be described as the interpretation problem. I will discuss these three major problems for bias research in due course, but first I wish to examine carefully the notion of rationality itself. I will argue that the resolution of the paradox rests upon a realization that there are not one but two concepts of rationality hiding in the literature.

THE CONCEPT OF RATIONALITY

Bias research – and arguments about rationality – span two major fields of psychological research. The first is the area of decision making and judgement and the second is the study of deductive and inductive reasoning. Two different conceptions of rationality emerge from these areas. The first which I shall call rationality$_1$ is rationality of purpose, whereas the second – rationality$_2$ – is rationality of process. I will discuss the development of these notions in each of the main fields.

Rationality in behavioural decision making

Normative decision theory derives from economic game theory (von Neuman and Morgenstern, 1947). The basic principle which drives this theory is the assumption that people choose in such a way as to maximize expected utility – in other words to maximize the benefit or minimize the cost to themselves. Specifically, the theory proposes that all decision acts are subject to outcomes, and that each outcome is associated with a utility for the decision maker. The choice situation which most interests psychologists is decision making under uncertainty, or risky choice. The decision maker has a number of alternative acts to choose between. Each choice is associated with one or more possible outcomes which will occur with a given probability and which have a utility for the decision maker. The theory assumes that the expected utility of each action is computed by the following equation:

$$EU = \sum p_i.U_i$$

The action with the highest expected utility is the one chosen. In other situations, such as that of competition with another rational decision maker, an alternative rule known as maximin is applied. In this case you choose the action with the best security level, i.e. the one that maximizes the minimum loss. For example, chess players are taught to choose the move with the best outcome on the assumption that the opponent makes the best possible reply from their point of view.

The notion of maximizing utility is clearly a case of rationality$_1$ and a number of apparent exceptions to this principle can be dealt with easily. People give money to charities because they have a utility for altruism or to avoid a negative utility for guilt; some people avoid favourable gambles because they have a negative utility for gambling; we buy insurance because our utility for the potential loss is disproportional to the utility for the payment. Decision theory is unashamedly subjective not only in terms of the utilities of outcomes but also with regard to their prospective probabilities. Indeed the approach is often known as SEU – the principle of maximizing *subjective* expected utility. Behavioural decision theory also has a field of application known as decision analysis (see von Winterfeldt and Edwards, 1986, for a textbook). In decision analysis, a consultant helps decision makers to structure their problems which involves developing decision trees and associating projected outcomes with probabilities and utilities so that decisions may be made in line with the SEU principle.

Although behavioural decision theory is founded on the notion of rationality$_1$, the approach also has implications for rationality$_2$ – rationality of process as opposed to purpose. Consider for example, the case of a weary traveller stopping for a meal at a franchised restaurant and choosing from the menu. What determines the choice made? A learning theorist might argue that the person would generalize from previous experience in other restaurants of the same franchise and thus be likely to choose a meal that was previously enjoyed and avoid any that were disliked. Thus the choice is seen to be driven by past experience. The decision theorist on the other hand would argue that the traveller would attempt to calculate which of the various options is most likely to maximize his utility and choose accordingly. If you ask how this calculation would be made, then, of course, it would be by recalling experiences in similar restaurants and choosing meals they had previously enjoyed.

This example is interesting because both learning and decision theory predict the same choices and each respect the principle of rationality$_1$. However, the decision theorist's account appears more rational and hence tells us something about the nature of rationality$_2$. The learning theorist's decision maker is seen to be the unthinking captive of his or her past reinforcement history, whereas the decision theorist portrays someone who thinks explicitly about the options and chooses freely according to a rational principle. Hence, components of the rationality$_2$ concept are seen to include conscious thought, free will, and logicality. The first two aspects relate to the problem of self-knowledge (see Evans, 1989, Ch. 5). In this chapter I will focus on the notion of logicality.

The history of research in behavioural decision theory reveals that much argument has surrounded the concept of rationality$_2$ and especially the assumption that the process of human choice is based upon the principles of economic game theory. One of the major controversies surrounded the question of whether people's choices actually respect the principle of SEU. Although the provision for both probabilities and utilities to be subjective makes the theory hard to refute, ingenious methods were devised and by the late 1970s many leading researchers considered the theory to be inadequate as a descriptive model (see Slovic *et al.*, 1977) and alternatives were attempted, most notably prospect theory (Kahneman and Tversky, 1979).

The other major difficulty for the notion of rational decision making under uncertainty concerns people's ability to assess probabilities and understand uncertainty. Decision analysts favour the Bayesian view that a probability is a number which represents the degree of belief that an event will occur. However, if decision making is to be seen as rational, most authors would expect these beliefs to be reasonably accurate in terms of formal probability theory. At one time 'man' was indeed judged to be a good intuitive statistician (Peterson and Beach, 1967). In the past twenty years or so, however, evidence has accumulated that the way in which subjective probabilities are formed is apparently subject to a wide variety of biases, a comprehensive listing of which is attempted by Evans (1992, Table 1). For example, subjects appear to give insufficient weight to the size and representativeness of samples, often to ignore key information such as base-rate statistics, to be biased by information which is vivid or easier to retrieve from memory, to perceive patterns in random variation, and so on.

Much of this assault on rationality$_2$ in the field of judgement under uncertainty is associated with the work of Amos Tversky and Daniel

Kahneman on judgemental heuristics. In a series of very influential papers dating from the early 1970s, these authors have argued that probability judgements are based upon the application of heuristics such as anchoring, availability, and representativeness (see Tversky and Kahneman, 1974; Kahneman *et al.*, 1982) and this application of these heuristics often leads to error and bias. Tversky and Kahneman's work has been read widely and cited beyond the bounds of experimental psychology and has led to the widespread notion of irrational human decision making which so concerns the various defenders of rationality cited above.

If we leave aside the external-validity problem for the moment, it is surely *not* the case that the heuristics approach was devised to demonstrate irrationality. The objective of psychological theory is to describe and predict what people actually do. Kahneman, Slovic and Tversky comment that:

> much of the early work used the normative model to explain human performance and introduced separate processes to explain departures from optimality. In contrast, research on judgemental heuristics seeks to explain both correct and erroneous judgements in terms of the same psychological processes.
>
> (Kahneman *et al.*, 1982, Preface)

By 'correct' and 'erroneous' Kahneman *et al.* clearly refer to classification by the normative model. They go on to acknowledge a debt to Bruner and Simon for use of the notion of 'bounded rationality'. For example, Newell and Simon (1972) developed the notion of heuristic strategies in problem solving precisely in order to be able to account for intelligent (rationality$_1$) behaviour in the face of the computational intractability of approaching complex problems with logical algorithms. We need, therefore, to restate our principle of rationality$_1$ to include the bounded-rationality principle as follows: 'People act in such a way as to maximise benefit to themselves, *within the constraints of their cognitive processing capacity.*'

A little reflection will reveal that the bounded-rationality qualification is essential. Without it, we would have to consider people irrational because they cannot compute large sums in their heads or reason out problems involving hundreds of premises. This notion is implicit in most bias research, since we are most interested in problems which are comparatively simple in form although still inducing errors in the subjects. However, if you accept the argument that application of normative theories to problems of real-world complexity far exceeds the processing capacity of the human brain, then it would be pointless to try to base a descriptive psychological theory on such theories – the basic tenet of belief in rationality$_2$. It is arguable, at least, that human intelligence must rely on the kind of heuristics that Kahneman and Tversky propose – unreliable and error prone though they may be – given our cognitive restraints.

Rationality in deductive reasoning

In the field of behavioural decision theory, as we have seen, the notion of rationality was founded in rationality$_1$ – purposive, adaptive behaviour – even though most of the argument has surrounded rationality$_2$, particularly the extent to which judgemental processes conform to normative principles. In the psychology of reasoning, by contrast, the prevailing concept has been rationality$_2$ and awareness of the importance of rationality$_1$ is comparatively recent (see for example Cosmides' (1989) discussion of Darwinian algorithms).

Historically, rationality$_2$ has been equated with logicality in the study of reasoning in both philosophy and psychology (see Henle, 1962). To say that someone does not reason logically is to say that they are irrational. Logic is a subdiscipline of philosophy concerned with formal systems for deductive reasoning. A logically valid argument is one whose conclusion can be shown necessarily to follow from its premises. If human beings reason illogically then they will commit fallacies – draw inferences which do not follow. Hence, it is argued, rational thought requires the application of deductive logic. The belief that people have a logic in the mind with which they reason is one with deep philosophical and psychological roots. Particularly influential in psychology was Piaget's theory of formal operations (Inhelder and Piaget, 1958) and the majority of modern authors studying the development of reasoning adhere to the mental-logic position (see Overton, 1990).

The study of adult deductive reasoning is comparatively recent and following the pioneering work of Peter Wason and his colleagues in the 1960s (see Wason and Johnson-Laird, 1972) has developed a tradition which in many ways parallels the work on statistical judgement inspired by Tversky and Kahneman. That is to say, many authors have focused on tasks which produce errors and biases of reasoning with numerous experiments and theoretical explanations being produced. Particular attention has been given to two tasks devised by Wason: the 2 4 6 problem (Wason, 1960), and the four-card selection task (Wason, 1966) which have in common an apparent simplicity of structure and the tendency to invoke almost universal error in the subjects who attempt them. The extensive research in these fields (reviewed by Evans, 1982, 1989) has created an apparent mass of evidence for bias and illogicality in human reasoning. Advocates of mental logic persist, however, and contemporary formulations envisage a cognitive system consisting of a set of abstract logical rules together with an inferential mechanism for applying them to particular premises in order to draw conclusions (e.g. Rips, 1983; Braine and O'Brien, 1991).

Put simply, there is a strong tradition which equates logicality with rationality$_2$ and which presumes that this is a necessary condition for rationality₁. People reason logically because this is necessary for rational actions, i.e. those which achieve the goals of the reasoner. In this article, I intend to challenge both component assumptions and show that not only are there a number of reasons why we should not regard logic as the mechanism for human reasoning but also that logic does not form an adequate basis for achieving rationality₂. In other words, logicality is not required for intelligent behaviour. The problems for the rationality = logicality view include the following:

1 Formal logic is an inaccurate and unnatural representation of reasoning involving natural language and real-world concepts.
2 Mental logic is computationally intractable: mental-proof procedures suffer from combinational explosion as the number of premises to be considered increases.
3 Psychological experiments show that people's reasoning is influenced (biased?) by many factors in the form and content of problems which are independent of their logical construction.
4 Logical competence, where it is observed, can be accounted for by reasoning mechanisms other than mental logic, for example, on the assumption that people manipulate mental models or that they use content-dependent rules or schemas.
5 Inductive inferences are inherently illogical, but vitally necessary for intelligent behaviour.

The first three issues will be discussed in the following section where I consider the problems which rational theorists pose for bias researchers and vice versa. The argument that a mental logic is not required for logical competence is central to the theory of reasoning by mental models (Johnson-Laird, 1983; Johnson-Laird and Byrne, 1991). In common with mental-logic theorists, mental modellers presume that deductive competence is central to human intelligence, but that this can be achieved without the possession and application of a set of logical rules. The theory develops from semantic or model-based approaches to logic and essentially proposes the following method of reasoning:

1 The reasoner inspects the premises of the problem and devises a mental model to represent a possible world state in which the premises are true.
2 The reasoner draws a provisional conclusion which is true in the model and non-trivial (for example, not explicit in the premises given).
3 The reasoner attempts to refute the conclusion by seeking counter-examples, i.e. alternative mental models in which the premises but not the conclusion would hold true. If no such counterexamples are found then the inference is deemed valid.

This procedure would appear to ensure logically valid reasoning, but its authors propose some intrinsic causes of error and bias: for example, subjects may fail to find counterexamples where there are several possible models due to working-memory constraints. The theory also appears to deal better with the problem of computational complexity than that of mental logic. This is because Johnson-Laird and Byrne (1991) have tackled the problem of restricting the number of possible deductive inferences that people may draw. They argue that subjects only consider putative conclusions which are semantically informative. For example, they would not restate information explicit in the premises or which is clearly less informative. This enables them to explain reasoning on open-ended problems where a conclusion is not presented in advance for evaluation.

Whilst mental-models theory offers a different mechanism of reasoning from that of mental logic it can still be seen as placing great emphasis on logicality. All research on mental-models theory to date, for example, has been concerned with explanations of deductive rather than inductive reasoning (see below). Hence, at a general level, mental-model theorists also can be seen as subscribers to the logicality = rationality equation, albeit one which shows more respect for the notion that rationality is bounded by cognitive-processing constraints. This is not the case with theorists who argue that competent reasoning is achieved by the possession of domain-specific rules or context-sensitive reasoning schemas (e.g. Cheng and Holyoak, 1985). For example, a car mechanic who systematically diagnoses the cause of a car not starting by a series of tests gives the appearance of logical reasoning but is in fact following a set of specific rules that he has learned. Many examples of competent reasoning and expert judgement in the real world might be explained in this way, without proposing any general-purpose mechanism for deductive competence. We turn now to the problem of induction.

Rationality in inductive reasoning

Deductive inferences can only draw out information which is already implicit in the premises: nothing new is added. For example, if I tell you that Jane is taller than Sally and that Mary is shorter than Sally you can infer by a deductive inference that Jane is taller than Mary. To the premises supplied you must add your knowledge that height is a transitive dimension, i.e. that by definition whenever A is taller than B and B is taller than C then A must be taller than C. Contrast this with the problem of predicting the outcome of a sporting encounter, say a rugby match between France and Scotland. If you know that in recent games France beat England and England beat Scotland you might well be inclined to bet on France. There is, of course, no logical necessity that France will win: 'beating' in sport is not a transitive dimension.

Your prediction of a French win is an inductive inference: one which is probabilistic and beyond logical necessity. Such an inference is dependent upon not just the observations of the recent results but upon other beliefs. For example, you would not make the forecast if you believed that the outcome of all rugby matches was a chance event but you might well if you believed that results depend upon the current 'form' of the teams. The point I wish to make is that inductive inferences of this kind which are used to forecast uncertain events are not only commonplace but essential for rational behaviour. It may not be important to forecast the outcome of sporting events (unless you are a gambler) but it is necessary to anticipate the reaction of other people when engaging in social interactions and it may be a matter of life and death to predict the behaviour of other road users when driving your car.

The most obvious way in which inductive inference is vital to our intelligence is through concept learning and empirical generalization. From the viewpoint of logic, a universal statement of the form 'All A are B' can never be verified, no matter how many times you observe an A that is a B, but can be disconfirmed by one single instance of an A that is not a B. If in practice we were to reason logically in this regard, intelligence would be effectively impossible. Given the vast amount of information with which we are confronted in the real world, the ability to induce concepts, categories, and general rules is absolutely vital. Consider, for example, a belief such as 'All cats have tails'. Logic tells us that we have no right to form such a belief no matter how many cats we observe that have tails. Moreover, logic tells us that should we hold this belief as a working hypothesis then we must abandon it upon observing a single tailless cat, for example, a Manx breed or one that lost its tail in an accident.

In order to be intelligent we have to do the exact opposite to what logic tells us. We need to form general beliefs in order to organize our knowledge of the world and to predict the nature of objects and events. Moreover, we should not necessarily abandon our beliefs when isolated or rare falsifying instances are encountered. It is effective to hold to general rules and store exceptions in what Holland *et al.* (1986) describe as 'default hierarchies'. Thus we hold as a general rule that 'All birds can fly' and store the exceptionality of the ostrich as part of its specific concept.

What I am arguing here is that inductive inference, including probabilistic forecasting and empirical generalization, is both essential for rationality₁ and also inherently illogical. Hence, we cannot justify the equation of logicality with rationality. This in turn shows a serious limitation of theories of human reasoning which specify mechanisms of deductive competence, whether based upon mental logic or mental models. The mental-model theory would seem to have more potential application to the problem of inductive inference, but this is yet to be developed.

It is of interest to consider briefly how the notion of rationality has been treated in psychological studies of inductive inference. Cognitive studies of inductive inference focus on hypothesis-testing behaviour. Authors have been much influenced by the writings of Karl Popper (1959, 1962) who attempted to replace a philosophy of science based upon (illogical) inductive generalization with one based upon deductive reasoning. In order to achieve this, one must think of the object of scientific research to be falsification rather than verification. A theory makes predictions which can be confirmed or refuted by observation. A confirmatory finding does not prove the theory true, but a disconfirmatory finding can refute it. Thus, scientists should make every effort to formulate and test their theories in such a way as to maximize the chances of falsification. Strong theories with high predictive power will thus evolve by a kind of natural selection.

In inductive-reasoning research, particularly in the line of studies started by Wason (1960), Popperianism has been regarded as the standard of rationality. Many authors, following Wason, have claimed that humans are prone to a 'confirmation bias', that is, they tend to seek evidence which supports their hypothesis. Confirmation bias has been widely regarded as providing major evidence of human irrationality, although this is highly questionable. Closer examination of the research literature reveals that subjects actually have a bias to test hypotheses by positive rather than negative predictions which leads to confirmatory behaviour on these particular tasks, but which could often lead to falsification in other situations. Arguments have been made that positive testing reflects a cognitive constraint (Evans, 1989) which can be regarded as a bounded-rationality argument, and that positive testing is normally effective in most situations (Klayman and Ha, 1987) which can be seen as an external validity argument. There are, of course, alternative philosophies of science and it is also perfectly possible to question whether the falsification strategy is a good model for science, let alone everyday life, but we will let that pass.

The interesting point here is that the criterion of rationality in the study of inductive inference is based not upon rationality$_1$ – as in my argument for the necessity of inductive generalization above – but upon a prior notion that rationality$_2$ must equate with logicality.

RATIONALITY AND BIAS RESEARCH

So far I have tried to elucidate the concept of rationality as it appears in the research literature. I have suggested that preconceptions about the rationality of process, or rationality$_2$, and especially its equation with logicality may be unjustified. I have, however, not questioned the principle of rationality$_1$, that people reason in such a way as to achieve intelligent (i.e. goal-seeking) actions, within the constraints of their cognitive capacity. Indeed, I am willing to accept (bounded) rationality$_1$ as axiomatic. Human intelligence must have evolved in the species and must be developed in the life of an individual in such a way as to maximize the achievement of goals.

This may seem a surprising statement from one who has spent twenty years studying reasoning biases, especially since these kinds of study appear to provide evidence against rationality$_1$. This brings us back to the paradox presented at the start of this chapter. Can we resolve the proven intelligence of the human species with its apparent stupidity in the psychological laboratory? In addressing this question as a committed bias researcher, I must set a constraint not placed upon those commenting from the outside (such as Cohen, 1981). I cannot resolve the paradox simply by assuming that the psychological experiments are unsound and unimportant.

As indicated at the outset, arguments about rationality in bias research have focused around three major issues which I have called the 'normative-system problem', the 'interpretation problem', and the 'external validity problem'. We will consider each in turn.

The normative-system problem

To talk of 'error' or 'bias' implies deviation from some standard of correctness. In most areas of cognitive research this is not a problem. In a signal-detection experiment it is clearly an error to miss a signal which is present or to respond when no signal is given. In memory research, a subject who recalls a word you did not present or omits one which was given is equally obviously in error. Even in problem-solving research, it is simple to decide whether a well-defined problem has been solved or not. In each of these areas there is generally no problem with the criteria of accuracy. There is also no rationality debate. No-one, for example, is accused of bias or irrationality for having a limited short-term memory span. It is simply accepted as an indicator of the processing capacity of the human brain – a cognitive constraint.

In decision and reasoning research, however, the situation is very different. The question of cognitive constraint is for the most part implicit, although some authors refer to the distinction between 'competence' and 'performance'. Interest focuses on tasks which are normally sufficiently simple in structure that there is a tacit agreement that subjects 'ought' to be able to solve them. When subjects' responses deviate from the answer which is prescribed by standard logic or by some other normative system, for example, Bayes' rule, then subjects are typically reported as making errors. A 'bias' is usually defined as systematic attention to some logically irrelevant features of the task, or systematic neglect of a relevant feature. Such research findings often then give rise to claims that people are inherently irrational decision makers in the real world to the consternation of those authors who regard human rationality as axiomatic.

The normative-system problem is that of deciding whether responses to reasoning problems should be considered right or wrong. This problem has to be addressed even by those who accept the strictures of Funder (1987) and Lopes (1991) to the effect that errors observed in the laboratory are of interest for the study of the cognitive processes involved and not for their possible extrapolation to real-world rationality. Critics of bias research such as Cohen (1981, 1982) have also suggested that application of standard normative systems may be an inappropriate way of judging error, since the subject may be using some alternative system and must be judged rational only to the extent to which they follow their own principles. Normative systems may also be regarded as inadequate criteria for judging human reasoning since they are computationally unrealistic for human subjects (Oaksford and Chater, 1992: 225–30; Baron, 1985) or because they do not adequately map on to the real-world problems.

I believe that my distinction between rationality$_1$ and rationality$_2$ ought to be helpful here. I have already argued, in the discussion of induction, that illogicality does not necessarily equate with irrationality in the sense of real-world goal-achieving intelligence. To say that someone has made a logical error should not in itself be a matter of controversy. The argument lies in the interpretation of that result. For example, in a reasoning experiment you may ask subjects to draw inferences which follow necessarily from the information given. Consider, for example, the following problem presented to subjects in a study reported by Ellis:

> Susan's mother wanted her to stay in on Saturday night to keep her company. She told her
> 'If you stay in on Saturday night
> then I'll take you sailing on Sunday'
> Susan did not stay in on Saturday night.
> Therefore, her mother did not take her sailing.
>
> (Ellis, 1991, Experiment 5)

Subjects were asked to indicate whether or not the conclusion followed. Most said that it did. The inference concerned – denial of the antecedent (DA) – is a well-known 'fallacy' and therefore an error in standard logic. So did Ellis's subjects reason irrationally? Of course not, quite the reverse.

It is clear from the linguistic context that when a conditional promise is made, then the DA inference is implied pragmatically, though not logically. It would be clear violation of relevance (as defined by Sperber and Wilson, 1986) to make the promise 'I'll take you sailing' conditional when you mean to fulfil it anyway. Of course, Susan's mother *might* actually intend to take her sailing anyway but that is not what she intends Susan to think, since she is clearly trying to influence her behaviour on the Saturday night.

Ellis (1991) embedded conditional sentences in a whole range of contexts, the great majority of which – temporal, causal, promise, threat, tip and warning – induced most subjects to endorse the DA inference. Now, you might say that this is not a logical error because in Ellis's task subjects are really judging what is meant by the speaker of the utterance who they assume to be conforming to the principle of relevance, i.e. not stating relevant conditions. However, suppose subjects are presented with a task which is specified as one of logical reasoning, in which they should only endorse conclusions which necessarily follow. They are then given some abstract problem such as:

> If the letter is an A, then the number is a 4
> The letter is not an A,
> Therefore the number is not a 4

To endorse this inference now would clearly appear to be a logical error. A number of such studies have been reported and all find high rates of endorsement of the DA inference. For example, experiments reported by Evans (1977), Wildman and Fletcher (1977) and Markovits (1988) all reported DA rates of over 50 per cent.

It seems to me that subjects in these experiments are clearly making logical errors, but are not being irrational. Whilst the 'If . . . then . . .' syntax does not appear to a logician to convey more than the relation 'p implies q', how is a subject to understand the meaning of an utterance in an artificial context such as this, except by reference to its normal everyday usage? As Ellis and others have demonstrated, the DA inference is reasonably to be made in most real-world contexts in which it appears. This is why in my own experimental reports of reasoning over the years I have never endorsed the common practice of reporting data in terms of logical 'errors'. Instead, I report what inferences subjects do and do not make, and which factors affect their frequency. Although it may be technically correct to describe certain reasoning patterns as logical errors, the practice imbues logic with an unjustified importance and tempts both author and readers to adopt a judgemental view of the subjects' behaviour.

From the viewpoint of a reasoning researcher, the value of logic lies not so much in the ability to classify subjects as 'right' or 'wrong' as to provide a control for structure. For example, the demonstration of biases requires that we introduce factors which influence reasoning whilst holding the logical structure constant. Much can be made of the fact that logic is content independent, so that the conclusion which follows in logic depends only on the syntax. Thus the syllogism:

> No C are B
> Some A are B
> Therefore, some C are not A

is always valid, no matter what you substitute for A, B, and C. The judgement that a subject gives you, however, is highly dependent upon the problem content, as demonstrated by the 'belief bias' effect. For example, Evans *et al.* (1983) presented the above syllogism with different content, including the following two versions:

A No nutritional things are inexpensive
   Some vitamin tablets are inexpensive
   Therefore, some nutritional things are not vitamin tablets

B No police dogs are vicious
   Some highly trained dogs are vicious
   Therefore, some police dogs are not highly trained

With problem A most subjects reject the conclusion as invalid and thus appear to be logically correct in their assessment. However, the majority of subjects endorse the inference when it is presented in form B. The difference is that in A the conclusion is unbelievable on *a priori* grounds, whereas in B it is believable. Despite the fact that the instructions to the subjects tell them to disregard their prior beliefs and judge only whether the conclusions follow from the premises, they are generally unable to do so.

What findings such as the belief bias effect (and many other examples of reasoning bias that I could quote) show us is that logical structure is insufficient to account for our subjects' behaviour. Extra-logical or non-logical factors are clearly at work. Does this mean that subjects are inherently irrational? If you believe in rationality$_2$ then the answer would appear to be yes, since the process of reasoning cannot be deemed logical. However, believers in mental logic can argue that beliefs inhibit reasoning and that subjects are 'failing to accept the logical task' (Henle, 1962). That way lies a dangerous circularity, however. Whenever subjects' responses are logical they are reasoning, and when they are illogical they are not reasoning.

If you believe in rationality$_1$, on the other hand, you can attempt to explain phenomena such as belief bias on the argument that it is symptomatic of processes that are adaptive in everyday life (see, for example, Pollard, 1982). As Evans *et al.* (1983) and others have shown, logic and belief interact such that there is more belief bias on invalid problems. One interpretation of this is that subjects tend to accept believable conclusions uncritically but selectively examine the logic of arguments with unbelievable conclusions (see Barston, 1986; Evans, 1989). You can make a bounded-rationality argument for this. We have too many beliefs constantly to be questioning evidence which confirms them; it is when our beliefs are disconfirmed that we need to give the matter careful thought. Of course, we must also assume that one of the bounds on our rationality is that we cannot abandon easily habitual methods of reasoning in order to obey the instructions of a psychological experiment.

Whilst logic provides a dubious criterion for the assessment of deductive-reasoning performance, some stronger evidence for genuine fallacies in probabilistic reasoning exists (see Kahneman *et al.*, 1982; Evans, 1989). Probability theory seems to me to make stronger contact with the real world than does logic. You can demonstrate empirically (e.g. by computer simulations) that statistical phenomena obey the laws of probability. For instance, larger samples do estimate population parameters more accurately and base-rate statistics do affect the posterior likelihood of events which are judged by imperfectly diagnostic evidence. An interesting example is the sample-to population-size fallacy demonstrated by Bar-Hillel (1979) and Evans and Bradshaw (1986). You can show theoretically and empiric-ally that the predictive power of a sample depends upon its absolute size and is independent of the size of the population. Yet, when information about population size is made available, experimental subjects act as though the value of the sample depends upon the proportion of the population for which it accounts. For example, they are more confident of a sample of given size on problems where the population size is smaller. No rational basis for this intuition is apparent.

If judgements under uncertainty respect the principle of rationality$_1$, then one is forced to the conclusion that the rationality is very bounded indeed. Why should this be? The answer probably lies in the consideration that the laws of probability are such that it is extremely difficult to learn them inductively, by observation of the outcome of probabilistic processes (see Einhorn (1980), for a very interesting discussion of this problem). However, some hope for rationality$_1$ is provided in the work of Nisbett and colleagues who have shown that everyday reasoning is more likely to respect statistical principles in domains where people have more expertise (Nisbett *et al.*, 1983) and that formal training in statistical principles can provide some transfer to real-world reasoning (Fong *et al.*, 1986).

The interpretation problem

The 'interpretation problem' is a particular favourite of defenders of rationality$_2$ who believe that human reasoning is invariably logical. The purpose of the argument is to explain away apparent observation of logical errors and fallacies. The argument in essence is this: experimental subjects often interpret or represent the problem presented in a different way than the experimenter intended. Whilst the conclusions they draw follow logically from the premises on which they are based, these premises are not those of the experimenter. Thus the illusion of logical error is created.

The most influential paper to argue this view was that of Henle (1962).

Citing protocols from a reasoning experiment, she attempted to demonstrate that her subjects were wont to restate, add, or omit premises, and that their conclusions were logically valid from their reformulated problem. When all else failed, she resorted to the 'failure to accept the logical task' explanation mentioned earlier. The interpretation problem need not rely on empirical evidence such as protocol analysis, however, and can be stated in purely logical terms. This has been done most forcefully by Smedslund in his argument of the 'circular relation between logic and understanding'. This was first published by Smedslund (1970) and has been updated and elaborated several times, most recently by Smedslund (1990).

Smedslund's basic argument goes as follows. Suppose you give someone some premises and ask them to deduce or evaluate a conclusion. If we assume that they have understood the premises as we intended them to, then we can judge the logicality of their reasoning from the answer that they give. If, for example, they propose an invalid conclusion then we can infer that they are reasoning illogically. Conversely, let us suppose that the subject reasons logically. Now, the conclusion they provide can tell us whether or not they understood the premises as we intended or expected them to. On this assumption, a fallacious conclusion would indicate misunderstanding (or a different understanding) of the premises. Smedslund (1990) develops the argument by equating the understanding of a statement with the ability to deduce its implications. (But which implications? All statements provide an infinite number in logic.)

Smedslund (1990) discusses the example of the conjunction fallacy (Tversky and Kahneman, 1983). In one of their problems subjects are given a brief character description of 'Linda' and asked to judge the relative probability of the following three statements:

1 Linda is a bank teller
2 Linda is active in the feminist movement
3 Linda is a bank teller who is active in the feminist movement

The description given is more representative (i.e. stereotypical) of (2) than (1). The conjunction fallacy is that subjects judge statement (3) to be more likely than (1), which is statistically impossible. The probability of the conjunction of two events cannot be greater than that of either of its components.

How, Smedslund asks, can we be sure this is a fallacy? Only by checking that subjects understood the statements correctly. For example, if subjects interpret statement (1) as 'Linda is a bank teller who is not active in the feminist movement' then it would not be a fallacy. But how can we tell whether subjects have interpreted statement (1) in this way? Only by checking what implications they would draw from the statement. But this presumes they can reason logically and so on. Smedslund ends with the rather startling conclusion that: 'the only possible coherent strategy is always to presuppose logicality and regard understanding as a variable'. Smedslund squares his circle, but at what seems to me to be an unacceptable price: the assumption of invariant logicality.

Whilst the interpretation argument for logicality appears a strong one at first sight, there are great practical problems with it for those wishing to interpret the psychological literature on deductive reasoning. The essential difficulty for interpretational explanations of reasoning biases is inconsistency on the part of the subjects. Subjects do not consistently reason with a given statement on different inferences, and nor do they always reason in a manner which could be logically consistent with any truth functional interpretation of the statement. This can be illustrated by reference to problems in conditional logic. There are four basic inferences associated with conditional statements as follows:

Modus ponens (MP)	If p then q, p therefore q
Denial of the antecedent (DA)	If p then q, not-p therefore not-q
Affirmation of the consequent (AC)	If p then q, q therefore p
Modus tollens (MT)	If p then q, not-q therefore not-p

If we assume that the conditional represents the logician's rule of material implication ($p \rightarrow q$) then the MP and MT inferences are valid, and the DA and AC inferences are fallacies. On the other hand if we assume that people take the rule to be a biconditional ($p \leftrightarrow q$) so that q also implies p, then all four inferences would follow.

On an interpretational argument all subjects should make MP and MT and some (those interpreting the statement as biconditional) should also make DA and AC. The evidence is not compatible with this. MP is almost invariably made, but subjects frequently fail to endorse MT. Acceptance rates of DA and AC are approximately equal across studies, but vary quite widely from each other within particular studies (see Evans, 1977; Wildman and Fletcher, 1977; Rumain et al., 1983; and Markovits, 1988, for typical experiments).

The failure to make modus tollens is not compatible with any sensible interpretation of a conditional statement that one can think of, and nor is the analogous failure to investigate the not-q card when testing the truth value of a conditional statement in the famous and much investigated Wason selection task (Wason, 1966; see Evans, 1982, 1989 for a review of relevant studies). Moreover when attempts have been made to infer conditional or biconditional readings on the basis of subjects' reasoning, many are classified as inconsistent (see Evans, 1982). Worse still, subjects' inference rates can be manipulated by syntactic variations in the presentation of the conditional statements. For example, if the antecedent of the statement is negated then a modus tollens argument looks like this:

If not-p then q; not-q therefore p

Far fewer subjects endorse the MT inferences in this case than when the antecedent is affirmative. How could the negative change the interpretation of the conditional such that the MT implication would be less likely to follow? In fact, it is implausible that it has anything to do with interpretation at all, since it can be demonstrated that when negative components are introduced any of the four inferences will be drawn more often when the conclusion is negative rather than affirmative (see Evans, 1977; Pollard and Evans, 1980; and the data of Wildman and Fletcher, 1977). Surely subjects are being biased in some way to prefer negative conclusions?

Smedslund's assertion of the circularity of logic and understanding has force to it, but his conclusion that one should treat logicality as axiomatic and deal only with interpretational variables is hopelessly impractical as the above brief discussion of conditional inference should illustrate. Certainly subjects' interpretation of statements is of great importance, and I have argued elsewhere that heuristics which determine representations of problem information are of great importance in the determination of biases (Evans, 1984, 1989). However, the notion that all variables are interpretational and that the process of reasoning is invariably logical is simply not sustainable in the light of experimental evidence.

How, then, should we deal with the interpretation problem? Before I answer I should explain that there are really two ways of looking at what the problem is. From the viewpoint of defenders of rationality$_2$ the problem is one for bias researchers who – the critics appear to believe – wish to describe their subjects as illogical. From the viewpoint of a researcher such as myself, however, the problem is rather different. My research is not motivated by concern about rationality or logicality at all, but rather by a desire to understand the process of human reasoning. Also, I am not so much concerned to explain logical 'errors' as inconsistencies: why do variables irrelevant to the logical structure of a problem affect the answers that the subjects give? My version of the interpretation problem then is this: do subjects' responses reflect variation in their representation of a problem or in the process of reasoning or both?

This problem is genuinely difficult. Take, for example, the oft-demonstrated claim that performance on the Wason selection task – logically poor in its standard abstract form – is greatly 'facilitated' in certain realistic contexts, i.e. subjects' answers are more likely to conform to those indicated by logical analysis of the problem. Is this because the content changes subjects' mental representation of the conditional statement or because it changes the method of reasoning by subjects? Both types of explanation have been offered in the literature. For example, Cheng and Holyoak (1985) argue that certain thematic contexts evoke pragmatic reasoning schemas which allow subjects to reason in ways which extrapolate experience; such reasoning methods are not available in the abstract formulation. An interpretational account is offered by Johnson-Laird and Byrne (1991) who argue that subjects will only solve the problem if their mental representation of the conditional statement is fleshed out to include mental models of situations in which the antecedent of the rule does not hold – something which can be determined by context. My own account based on relevance is also interpretational but actually assumes that no reasoning as such is taking place at all on this particular task (Evans, 1989).

Smedslund's circle is not really specific to reasoning research at all, but is an argument similar to that of Anderson (1978) that all cognitive theories are representation-process pairs. The main lesson to draw from Smedslund's argument is that interpretation of reasoning data is difficult and cannot be achieved by inspection of isolated results. Certainly the presence or absence of logical errors does not in itself inform us as to whether or not people are reasoning by a logical process. We need much converging evidence from a range of studies to begin to decide on how the nature of the representations and processes that underlie performance interact. However, Smedslund's proposal of invariable logicality is, as indicated above, empirically refutable on existing evidence. The circle does not confirm rationality$_2$.

The external-validity problem

Now we come perhaps to the crux of the rationality debate – what really upsets the critics of bias research. Because we observe errors and fallacies in the laboratory we are not entitled to claim that people will be irrational decision makers in the real world (Cohen, 1981; Funder, 1987; Lopes, 1991). Psychologists are criticized for extrapolating far too freely from their findings and creating a fashionable view outside of the psychological world – in business schools, for example – that people are irrational. In this part of the argument we are clearly talking about rationality$_1$ – behaving in such a way as to maximize utility or achieve one's desired goals. I cannot, as above, rely on the misplaced faith in rationality$_2$ to resolve the problem.

I have stated above that I am willing to accept rationality$_1$ as axiomatic. Does this mean that I believe that people do not make important mistakes in their real-world decision making and that laboratory experiments are of no relevance? Of course not! Rationality$_1$, remember, is bounded. We are rational within our cognitive constraints. These constraints, however, may lead us to make serious mistakes. The constraints in turn are understood, at least in part, by studying reasoning and decision making in the laboratory. However, the critics are correct in one respect: extrapolation from laboratory studies is both difficult and dangerous.

The distinction between the laboratory and the real world is an odd one. Laboratory experiments are part of the real-world experience of the subjects and their behaviour in them must tell us something. No-one suggests in the science of metallurgy, for example, that the properties of metals studied in the laboratory will have no relevance when the same substances are used in the 'real world', for example, as a component in a machine or as a structural support on a bridge. The laboratory is part of the universe in which the laws of physics and chemistry apply. Similarly, subjects of psychological experiments use the same brain in the laboratory as they do elsewhere. Psychologists would have to be very clever indeed to succeed constantly in contriving situations wholly unrepresentative of those outside. If biases, errors, and mistakes are so easy to produce in laboratory reasoning tasks, it beggars belief to suppose that these are easily avoided at all other times. Moreover, we are surrounded by evidence of bias, error, and misjudgement in the real world.

Let us think for a moment of the strengths and weaknesses of cognition in the real world. We are incredibly good at a range of activities that can be broadly defined as pattern recognition. We can perceive and categorize the complexities of our surrounding world with astonishing ease and speed. Much implicit inferencing is involved in this as in our other area of phenomenal intelligence – natural language. But our capacity for explicit, conscious forms of cognition is very much weaker. We can remember relatively few items of arbitrary information and can perform very little arithmetical calculation with any great reliability. Nowadays, we make extensive use of computers to compensate for these deficiencies. Our inability to explicate, however, means that we cannot at present program computers efficiently to perform the kinds of tasks – pattern recognition, natural language processing – that we ourselves are best at. Most progress in this area is being made currently by use of implicit models, based on parallel distributed processing (PDP). Indeed, one view which makes sense of our capabilities is that the brain is a connectionist machine: highly suited to parallel computation but not to explicit sequential reasoning processes which are very difficult to simulate in a PDP model (see Rumelhart *et al.*, 1986, for an attempt).

Induction – the formation and identification of concepts and schemas – is precisely the kind of pattern-recognition task which connectionist systems are very good at performing. Deduction, however, is another matter. It is not simply that our brains did not happen to evolve as efficient deductive reasoning machines, but that such machines *cannot* exist. Logic problems belong to that set of problems known as NP-complete in complexity theory – the most difficult problems known. In essence the number of logical checks required to determine the consistency (or infer the consequences) of any set of statements increases exponentially with the number of such statements you need to consider. This is why, as observed earlier, psychological theories of reasoning based on deductive competence – mental logic and mental-model theory – are applicable only to very small-scale problems. For example, the number of mental models to be considered will grow exponentially with the number of premises. It is a logical and practical impossibility for such theories to account for the way in which we draw inferences from a large body of beliefs. This certainly constitutes a major external validity problem for these theories.

These considerations provide us with a new paradox. It is precisely those theories which give the most rational sounding account of subjects' thought processes in the laboratory which are least able to account for rational behaviour in the outside world. Conversely, the theorists who would provide our experimental subjects with crude and error-prone heuristics with which to face the psychologists' problems are best placed to imbue subjects with some real-world reasoning competence. Heuristics, by definition, are short-cut methods which avoid the problem of combinational explosion by allowing us to search only very small and selected parts of the potential problem space (Newell and Simon, 1972).

We have, then, established one dimension – problem complexity – which may affect the external validity of the interpretations we give to our laboratory experiments. The other obvious consideration is knowledge. In the outside world (outside of that part of the real world which is the laboratory) we normally operate in contexts where we have large numbers of prior beliefs. The role of knowledge is therefore of great importance and has by no means been neglected in experimental research. For example, the fact that prior belief can bias reasoning even when subjects are explicitly instructed to reason logically (see earlier discussion of 'belief bias') suggests that the beliefs will have a major influence in real-world reasoning. There are more beliefs, more strongly held and no instructions. Research in the area of statistical judgement also provides evidence that knowledge can be a cause rather than a cure for bias. For example, subjects are prone to 'illusory correlations' – the perception of patterns in random data that conform with *a priori* theories (Chapman, 1967; Chapman and Chapman, 1971). Other biases have been shown to apply equally to expert and novice groups, for example, overconfidence in judgement (see Lichtenstein *et al.*, 1982).

The external-validity problem in bias research is discussed in some detail by Evans (1992). The conclusion presented there can be summarized as follows. Bias in laboratory experiments is indicative of mistakes in the real world and suggestive of their nature. However, subjects' performance in the laboratory is so dependent upon the precise presentation of the tasks, that extrapolation to any given situation in the outside world is virtually impossible. Hence, applied research in the situations of interest is required. The design and interpretation of such applied research should, however, benefit greatly from the knowledge acquired in the reasoning laboratory.

CONCLUSIONS

I started this chapter with the statement of a paradox – human beings of proven real-world intelligence exhibiting errors and biases in relatively simple laboratory tasks. In order to explicate this paradox – and the rationality debate which it has evoked – I have argued that the term 'rationality' has two separate meanings which the literature has generally failed to distinguish. It seems axiomatic that human beings must be rational but only in the sense that I have called rationality$_1$ – behaviour must be intelligent in the sense of being adaptive, serving to achieve goals. However, a number of authors use the term in a second sense – rationality$_2$ – which presumes rationality of process, most usually to equate it with logicality.

This confusion lies at the heart of the rationality debate. Many experiments demonstrate illogicality which their authors assume – or so their critics allege – to be evidence for irrationality. It is not. It is evidence only against rationality$_2$. In the course of this chapter I have presented a number of arguments against the equation of logic and rationality. Logical reasoning – including deductive competence achieved by manipulation of mental models – cannot be the (sole) mechanism of human reasoning since logical proof is computationally intractable for problems with more than a small number of premises. Logical reasoning would prevent induction – a process essential for human intelligence, i.e. rationality$_1$. Logic is a poor and misleading normative system against which to evaluate verbal reasoning because it cannot account for the ways in which we understand statements in natural language, the influence of pragmatics, relevance and so on. The argument that we must assume reasoning to be logical in order to avoid circularity with interpretation has also been examined and refuted.

If we dispense with rationality$_2$ and abandon the belief that rationality is based on logicality, then how does reasoning research bear upon rationality$_1$? The accumulated evidence of laboratory studies still seems to imply that subjects will make many mistakes in their reasoning and decision making. This, however, is no more than evidence for the obvious: rationality$_1$ is bounded by cognitive constraints. By studying 'biases' in the laboratory, psychologists are discovering the nature of reasoning processes and the cognitive constraints that bear upon them. This in turn will help us to explain, predict, and perhaps remedy errors of reasoning and judgement that occur in the real world.

In essence, my argument is that bias research has no implications for rationality, only for the bounds that are placed upon it. It is the study of cognitive constraints with all the theoretical and practical implications that flow from that. My arguments against logicality as a basis for rationality are largely *a priori* rather than empirical. However, only by realizing that logicality does not equal rationality can we avoid the common belief that bias reasearch does conflict with belief in rationality. This insight has implications also for the construction of theories of reasoning. Any mechanism of deductive competence can account for little real-world reasoning.

ACKNOWLEDGEMENT

I would like to thank John Clibbens for a critical reading of an earlier draft of this chapter.

REFERENCES

Anderson, J.R. (1978) 'Arguments concerning representations for mental imagery', *Psychological Review* 85: 249–77.

Bar-Hillel, M. (1979) 'The role of sample size in sample evaluation', *Organisational Behavior and Human Performance* 24: 245–57.

Baron, J. (1985) *Rationality and Intelligence*, Cambridge: Cambridge University Press.

Barston, J.L. (1986) 'An investigation into belief biases in reasoning', unpublished PhD thesis, University of Plymouth, Plymouth, UK.

Braine, M.D.S. and O'Brien, D.P. (1991) 'A theory of If: a lexical entry, reasoning program, and pragmatic principles', *Psychological Review* 98: 182–203.

Chapman, L.J. (1967) 'Illusory correlation in observational report', *Journal of Verbal Learning and Verbal Behaviour* 73: 193–204.

Chapman, L.J. and Chapman, J. (1971) 'Test results are not what you think they are', *Psychology Today* November, pp. 18–22, 106–10.

Cheng, P.W. and Holyoak, K.J. (1985) 'Pragmatic reasoning schemas', *Cognitive Psychology* 17: 391–416.

Christensen-Szalanski, J.J.J. and Beach, L.R. (1984) 'The citation bias: fad and fashion in the judgement and decision literature', *American Psychologist* 39: 75–8.

Cohen, L.J. (1981) 'Can human irrationality be experimentally demonstrated?' *Behavioural and Brain Sciences* 4: 317–70.

—— (1982) 'Are people programmed to commit fallacies? Further thought about the interpretation of data on judgement', *Journal for the Theory of Social Behaviour* 12: 251–47.

Cosmides, L. (1989) 'The logic of social exchange: has natural selection shaped how humans reason? Studies with the Wason selection task', *Cognition* 31: 187–276.

Einhorn, H.J. (1980) 'Learning from experience and suboptimal rules in decision making', in T.S. Wallsten (ed.) *Cognitive Processes in Choice and Decision Behaviour*, Hillsdale, NJ: Erlbaum.

Ellis, M.C. (1991) 'Linguistic and semantic factors in conditional reasoning', unpublished PhD thesis, University of Plymouth, Plymouth, UK.

Evans, J. St B.T. (1977) 'Linguistic factors in reasoning', *Quarterly Journal of Experimental Psychology* 29: 297–306.

—— (1982) *The Psychology of Deductive Reasoning*, London: Routledge & Kegan Paul.

—— (1984) 'Heuristic and analytic processes in reasoning', *British Journal of Psychology* 75: 451–68.

—— (1989) *Bias in Human Reasoning: Causes and Consequences*, Brighton: Erlbaum.

—— (1992) 'Bias in thinking and judgement', in M.T. Keane and K.J. Gilhooly (eds) *Advances in the Psychology of Thinking*, vol. 1, Hassocks, Sussex: Harvester-Wheatsheaf.

Evans, J. St B.T. and Bradshaw, H. (1986) 'Estimating sample size requirements in research design: a study of intuitive statistical judgement', *Current Psychological Research and Reviews* 5: 10–19.

Evans, J. St B.T., Barston, J.L., and Pollard, P. (1983) 'On the conflict between logic and belief in syllogistic reasoning', *Memory and Cognition* 11: 295–306.

Fong, G.T., Krantz, D.H., and Nisbett, R.E. (1986) 'The effects of statistical training on thinking about everyday problems', *Cognitive Psychology* 18: 253–92.

Funder, D.C. (1987) 'Errors and mistakes: evaluating the accuracy of social judgements', *Psychological Bulletin* 101: 75–90.

Henle, M. (1962) 'On the relation between logic and thinking', *Psychological Review* 69: 366–78.

Holland, J.H., Holyoak, K.J., Nisbett, R.E., and Thagard, P.R. (1986) *Induction: Processes of Inference, Learning and Discovery*, Cambridge, MA: MIT Press.

Inhelder, B. and Piaget, J. (1958) *The Growth of Logical Thinking*, New York: Basic Books.

John, R.S., von Winterfeldt, D., and Edwards, W. (1983) 'The quality of user acceptance of multiattribute utility analysis performed by computer and analyst', in P. Humphreys, O. Svenson, and A. Vari (eds) *Analysing and Aiding Decision Processes*, Berlin: Springer-Verlag.

Johnson-Laird, P.N. (1983) *Mental Models*, Cambridge: Cambridge University Press.

Johnson-Laird, P.N. and Byrne, R. (1991) *Deduction*, Hove and London: Erlbaum.

Kahneman, D. and Tversky, A. (1979) 'Prospect theory: an analysis of decision under risk', *Econometrica* 47: 263–91.

Kahneman, D., Slovic, P., and Tversky, A. (1982) *Judgement under Uncertainty: Heuristics and Biases*, Cambridge: Cambridge University Press.

Klayman, J. and Ha, Y-W. (1987) 'Confirmation, disconfirmation and information in hypothesis testing', *Psychological Review* 94: 211–28.

Lichtenstein, S., Fischhoff, B., and Phillips, L.D. (1982) 'Calibration of probabilities: the state of the art to 1980', in D. Kahneman, P. Slovic, and A. Tversky (eds) *Judgement Under Uncertainty: Heuristics Biases*, Cambridge: Cambridge University Press.

Lopes, L.L. (1991) 'The rhetoric of irrationality', *Theory and Psychology* 1: 65–82.

Markovits, H. (1988) 'Conditional reasoning, representation, empirical evidence on a concrete task', *Quarterly Journal of Experimental Psychology* 40A: 483–95.

Newell, A. and Simon, H.A. (1972) *Human Problem Solving*, Englewood Cliffs, NJ: Prentice-Hall.

Nisbett, R.E., Krantz, D.H., Jepson, D.H., and Kunda, Z. (1983) 'The use of statistical heuristics in everyday inductive reasoning', *Psychological Review* 90: 339–63.

Oaksford, M. and Chater, N. (1992) 'Bounded rationality in taking risks and drawing inferences', *Theory and Psychology* 2: 225–30.

Overton, W.F. (ed.) (1990) *Reasoning, Necessity and Logic: Developmental Perspectives*, Hillsdale, NJ: Erlbaum.

Peterson, C.R. and Beach, L.R. (1967) 'Man as an intuitive statistician', *Psychological Bulletin* 68: 29–46.

Pollard, P. (1982) 'Human reasoning: some possible effects of availability', *Cognition* 12: 65–96.

Pollard, P. and Evans, J. St B.T. (1980) 'The influence of logic on conditional reasoning performance', *Quarterly Journal of Experimental Psychology* 32: 605–24.

Popper, K.R. (1959) *The Logic of Scientific Discovery*, London: Hutchinson.

—— (1962) *Conjectures and Refutations*, London: Hutchinson.

Rips, L.J. (1983) 'Cognitive processes in propositional reasoning', *Psychological Review* 90: 38–71.

Rumain, B., Connell, J., and Braine, M.D.S. (1983) 'Conversational comprehension processes are responsible for reasoning fallacies in children as well as adults', *Developmental Pscyhology* 19: 471–81.

Rumelhart, D., Smolensky, P., McClelland, J.L., and Hinton, G.E. (1986) 'Schemata and sequential thought processes in PDP models', in J.M. McClelland and D. Rumelhart (eds) *Parallel Distributed Processing: Explorations in Microstructure of Cognition*, Cambridge, MA: MIT Press.

Slovic, P., Fischhoff, B., and Lichtenstein, S. (1977) 'Behavioral decision theory', *Annual Review of Psychology* 228: 1–39.

Smedslund, J. (1970) 'On the circular relation between logic and understanding', *Scandinavian Journal of Psychology* 11: 217–19.

—— (1990) 'A critique of Tversky and Kahneman's distinction between fallacy and misunderstanding', *Scandinavian Journal of Psychology* 31: 110–20.

Sperber, D. and Wilson, D. (1986) *Relevance*, Oxford: Blackwell.

Tversky, A. and Kahneman, D. (1974) 'Judgement under uncertainty: heuristics and biases', *Science* 185: 1124–31.

—— (1983) 'Extensional vs intuitive reasoning: the conjunction fallacy in probability judgment', *Psychological Review* 90: 293–315.

von Neumann, J. and Morgenstern, O. (1947) *Theory of Games and Economic Behavior*, Princeton, NJ: Princeton University Press.

von Winterfeldt, D. and Edwards, W. (1986) *Decision Analysis and Behavioural Research*, Cambridge, Cambridge University Press.

Wason, P.C. (1960) 'On the failure to eliminate hypotheses in a conceptual task', *Quarterly Journal of Experimental Psychology* 12: 129–40.

—— (1966) 'Reasoning', in B.M. Foss (ed.) *New Horizons in Psychology*, vol. 1, Harmondsworth: Penguin.

Wason, P.C. and Johnson-Laird, P.N. (1972) *Psychology of Reasoning: Structure and Content*, London: Batsford.

Wildman, T.M. and Fletcher, H.J. (1977) 'Developmental increases and decreases in solutions of conditional syllogism problems', *Developmental Psychology* 13: 630–6.

Chapter 2

Reasoning theories and bounded rationality

M. Oaksford and N. Chater

INTRODUCTION

In this chapter we will argue that considerations of bounded rationality may fundamentally alter our present conception of the adequacy of psychological theories of reasoning. Since its inception cognitive science has been concerned with the limitations on the cognitive system which inhere in virtue of the organization of human memory and the need to act rapidly in real time (Simon, 1969; Kahneman *et al.*, 1982). Simon (quoted in Baars, 1986: 363–4), for example, says that: 'cognitive limitations have been a central theme in almost all of the theorizing I've done. . . . They are . . . very important limitations on human rationality, particularly if the rationality has to be exercised in a face-to-face real-time context'. Cognitive limitations mean that people may be incapable of living up to normative but computationally expensive accounts of their inferential behaviour,[1] i.e. human rationality is *bounded*.

The two most important limitative findings of cognitive science both affect human memory. The constraints imposed by people's limited short-term memory capacity have been mapped out in some detail (Miller, 1956; Baddeley, 1986) and have been appealed to in order to explain certain biases in reasoning experiments (Evans, 1983a; Johnson-Laird, 1983). Perhaps a less-well-known limitative finding applies to retrieval from long-term memory.

In artificial intelligence this limitation has been labelled the *frame problem* (McCarthy and Hayes, 1969; see Pylyshyn, 1987 for overviews). This term tends to be used generically to describe a cluster of related problems, which as Glymour observes, are all of the following form: 'Given an enormous amount of stuff, and some task to be done using some of the stuff, what is the *relevant stuff* for the task?' (Glymour, 1987: 65). Some variant of the frame problem may arise for any task requiring the deployment of prior world knowledge. In this chapter we will trace out the consequences of the frame problem for theories of reasoning. We will argue that a bounded-rationality assumption may have to be made in deductive-reasoning research, just as in research into risky decision making (Kahneman *et al.*, 1982).

We begin by outlining the range of contemporary theoretical approaches to reasoning based on the taxonomy provided by Evans (1991) and suggest that bounded rationality provides an additional criterion of theory preference. We then introduce an important and implicit assumption which motivates interest in these theories. This we have called the *generalization assumption* (Oaksford and Chater, 1992). It states that theories of reasoning developed to account for explicit inference in laboratory reasoning tasks should generalize to provide accounts of other inferential processes. We will also offer a general characterization of these inferential processes. We then outline more precisely how the limitations of the cognitive system may militate against certain process accounts by briefly introducing *computational complexity theory*. We will then show how complexity issues have raised problems for theories of perception and risky decision making and for theories of knowledge representation in artificial intelligence (AI). We then argue that contemporary reasoning theories are all likely to fall foul of the same problems. We therefore conclude that these theories are unlikely to be psychologically real.

An important corollary to this argument is that because our reasoning abilities are bounded, empirically observed deviations from optimal rationality need raise few questions over our rationality in practice. The interesting questions are how rational the system needs to be to qualify as a cognitive system (Cherniak, 1986), and what kind of mechanism needs to be postulated to implement it (see, for example, Levesque, 1988). To end on a positive note, therefore, we will suggest that, following Rumelhart *et al.* (1986) and Rumelhart (1989), recent advances in neural computation may suggest mechanisms which more adequately address the issues we raise in this chapter. We will also suggest some ways in which reasoning research may develop profitably in the future to identify the kind of rational mechanism (Fodor, 1987) people actually are.

THEORIES OF REASONING

Evans (1991) offers a four-way classification of reasoning theories and a three-way characterization of the questions they must try to answer. The questions which need to be addressed are: the competence question – the fact that human subjects often successfully solve deductive-reasoning problems; the bias question – the fact that subjects also make many systematic errors; the content-and-context question – the fact that the content and context of a problem can radically alter subjects' responses. Evans (1991) argues that the four theories of reasoning tend to concentrate upon one question or the other, but none provide a fully integrated account of all three. The first two theories address the competence question.

The *mental-logic approach* argues for the existence of formal inference rules in the cognitive system (Inhelder and Piaget, 1958; Henle, 1962; Braine, 1978; Johnson-Laird, 1975; Osherson, 1975; Rips, 1983). These rules, for example, modus ponens, i.e. 'given if p, then q and p you can infer q', rely on the syntactic form of the sentences encoding the premises. Thus, whatever sentences are substituted for p and q the same inferences apply. *Mental-models theory* suggests that the semantic content of the sentences encoding a hypothesis is directly represented in the cognitive system (Johnson-Laird, 1983; Johnson-Laird and Byrne, 1991). It is these contents which are subsequently manipulated in reasoning. Hence the actual meaning of p and q may be important to the reasoning process.

Two further theories are directed at explaining content affects and the errors and biases which infect people's normal reasoning performance. *Pragmatic-reasoning schema theory* proposes inference rules which are specific to particular domains to account for content effects. Cheng and Holyoak (1985), for example, invoke a permission schema to account for the facilitatory effects of thematic content. In these tasks contentful rules about permission relations were employed, for example, 'If you are drinking alcohol, you must be over 18 years of age'. Last, the *heuristic approach* proposes that a variety of systematic errors and biases in human reasoning may be explained by the cognitive system employing a variety of short-cut processing strategies (Evans, 1983a, 1984, 1989).

Evans (1991) was concerned to get reasoning theorists to agree some common ground rules concerning the adequacy of their theories. He does so by providing criteria of theory preference – completeness, coherence, falsifiability and parsimony – by which to judge reasoning theories and seems to view mental models as scoring most highly on these criteria. We will argue that along with these general criteria – common to all scientific domains – limitations on long-term memory retrieval may also provide a valuable criterion by which to assess reasoning theories.

Cognitive limitations have been appealed to in order to account for the biases which occur in people's reasoning. For example, limitations on short-term memory capacity have been appealed to in order to motivate the heuristic approach (Evans, 1983b, 1989) and to explain error profiles in syllogistic reasoning (Johnson-Laird, 1983). Given the prominence of the frame problem in AI, why has it not also been taken as a potential source of constraint on theories of reasoning? We believe there are two reasons. First, no analysis has been provided of these process theories which might indicate that they are profligate with computational resources. Second, when accounting for laboratory tasks the demands of a generalizable theory of inference can be ignored. We now suggest that contemporary reasoning theories are intended to generalize appropriately to other inferential modes.

THE GENERALIZATION ASSUMPTION

Why has the psychology of deductive reasoning been so prominent within cognitive psychology/science? The main reason appears to be the assumption that the principles of human inference discovered in the empirical investigation of explicit inference will generalize to provide accounts of most inferential processes. We call this the *generalization assumption*. The generalization assumption is, for example, implicit in the sub-title to Johnson-Laird's (1983) book *Mental Models: Towards a Cognitive Science of Language, Inference and Consciousness*. Little overt human activity involves deductive inference. Therefore, without the generalization assumption the study of deductive reasoning would warrant little more interest than, say, the psychology of playing Monopoly.

Within artificial-intelligence knowledge representation a similar generalization assumption encountered the problem of *scaling up*. Quite often programs which worked well in *toy domains*, i.e. small well-behaved databases rather like the abstract domains employed in laboratory reasoning tasks, failed when scaled up to deal with larger more realistic databases. This was because the inference regimes in these AI programs were generally computationally intractable but this was only apparent when they were scaled up to deal with more complex, real-world inferential problems. While a prominent issue in AI research (for example, Levesque, 1985, 1988; McDermott, 1986), scaling up has not been an issue in the psychology of reasoning.

Defeasible inference

What is the nature of the inferential processes to which we expect a generalizable theory of inference to generalize? As we have suggested, little overt human activity may involve deduction. However, these overt activities may be supported by implicit inferential processes which are deductive in nature. According to modern cognitivist accounts activities such as text comprehension, classification, categorization, and perception all rely on inferential processes. The inferences which are required in these areas all share a common characteristic: they are *defeasible*. That is, putative conclusions can be *defeated* by subsequent information.

For example, text comprehension relies on implicit inferences from prior world knowledge to elaborate the information given in the text (Bransford and Johnson, 1972, 1973; Bransford *et al.*, 1972; Bransford and McCarrell, 1975; Clark, 1977; Minsky, 1975; Stenning and Oaksford, 1989). These inferences can be defeated by subsequent sentences that contradict earlier conclusions. Theories of concepts designed to capture the family resemblance or prototype structure of human categorization implicitly recognize the defeasibility of semantic knowledge. So, although not all birds can fly, the prototypical bird is represented as flying, the majority of exemplar birds fly, the probability that a bird flies is high, etc., depending on the theory that one considers (Rosch, 1973, 1975; Medin and Schaffer, 1978; Nosofsky, 1986). Constructivist theories of perception take much of perceptual processing to involve inference to the best explanation about the state of the environment, given perceptual evidence. The possibility of perceptual illusion and error provides evidence for the defeasibility of such inference (Gregory, 1977; Fodor and Pylyshyn, 1981; MacArthur, 1982). Later on we will also see that defeasibility is observed in reasoning experiments (Byrne, 1989; Cummins *et al.*, 1991) and that the ability to account for these phenomena has been appealed to as arguing in favour of a particular theory of reasoning (Johnson-Laird and Byrne, 1991).

At least *prima facie*, the defeasibility of the inferential modes observed in these cognitive domains rules out a deductive approach. It has often been argued that the single most defining characteristic of a deductive system is that a valid inference *cannot* be defeated by subsequent information (e.g. Curry, 1956). That is, deductive validity is *monotonic*. However, many non-standard but equally *logical* accounts of connectives result in *non-monotonic* systems, for example, the Lewis–Stalnaker (Stalnaker, 1968; Lewis, 1973) semantics for the counterfactual conditional provides such a system (Glymour and Thomason, 1984). Hence, just because the inferences to be characterized are defeasible does not of itself exclude a formal, logical approach.

We now introduce a precise analysis of how a particular process theory may transcend the limitations of the cognitive system. This will involve a discussion of computational complexity theory (see, for example, Garey and Johnson, 1979; Horowitz and Sahni, 1978) which provides a characterization of the resources a computational process consumes.

BOUNDED RATIONALITY AND COMPUTATIONAL COMPLEXITY THEORY

How do we know whether or not a process theory transcends the limitations on the cognitive system? For short-term memory capacity, an answer can usually be provided at an intuitive level. Without 'chunking' if a particular process model requires more than 7 ± 2 items to be stored, then short-term memory capacity will be exceeded. However, more implicit cognitive processes, proceeding outside of conscious awareness, are not usually considered to be bounded by short-term memory capacity. How can it be estimated whether a process postulated at this level transcends the abilities of the cognitive system? On the assumption that cognitive processes are computational processes computational complexity theory provides an answer.

Some computational processes are more complex than others requiring more computational resources in terms of memory capacity and operations performed. There are two approaches to computational complexity: *a priori* analysis and *a posteriori* analysis (Garey and Johnson, 1979; Horowitz and Sahni, 1978). *A posteriori* analysis involves the observation of the run-time performance of an actual implementation of an algorithm, as the size of the input, n, is systematically varied. Such empirical observations can generate approximate values for best-, worst- and typical-case run-times. A more theoretically rigorous approach is to attempt to derive an expression which captures the rate at which the algorithm consumes computational resources, as a function of the size of n. The crucial aspect of this function is what is known in complexity theory as its *order of magnitude*, which reflects the rate at which resource demands increase with n. For present purposes, the relevant resource is the number of times the basic computational operations of the algorithm must be invoked. Orders of magnitude are expressed using the 'O' notation:

$$O(1) < O(\log n) < O(n) < O(n\log n) < O(n^2) < O(n^3) \ldots < O(n^i)$$
$$\ldots < O(2^n) \ldots$$

For example, $O(1)$ indicates that the number of times the basic operations are executed does not exceed some constant regardless of the length of the input. $O(n^2) < O(n^3) \ldots < O(n^i)$ indicate that the number of times the basic operations are executed is some polynomial function of the input length, such algorithms are *polynomial-time computable* (strictly speaking this class includes all algorithms of order lower than some polynomial function, such as $O(\log n)$, and $O(n\log n)$).

Within complexity theory an important distinction is drawn between polynomial-time computable algorithms ($O(n^i)$ for some n), and algorithms which require *exponential time* (for example, $O(2^n)$ or worse). As n increases, exponential-time algorithms consume vastly greater resources than polynomial-time algorithms. This distinction is usually taken to mark the difference between tractable algorithms (polynomial time) and intractable (exponential time) algorithms. Applying these distinctions to problems, a problem is said to be polynomial-time computable if it can be solved by a polynomial-time algorithm. If all algorithms which solve the problem are exponential time, then the problem itself is labelled 'exponential-time computable'.

An important class of problems whose status is unclear relative to this distinction is the class of *NP-complete problems*. 'NP' stands for *non-deterministic polynomial-time* algorithms. Problems which only possess polynomial-time algorithms that are non-deterministic are said to be 'in NP'. NP-complete problems form a subclass of *NP-hard* problems. A problem is NP-hard if satisfiability reduces to it (Cook, 1971).[2] A problem is NP-complete if it is NP-hard *and* is in NP. There are problems which are NP-hard but are not in NP. For example, the halting problem is undecidable, hence there is no algorithm (of any complexity) which can solve it. However, satisfiability reduces to the halting problem which thus provides an instance of a problem that is NP-hard but not NP-complete. The class of NP-complete problems includes such classic families of problems as the travelling-salesman problems – the prototypical example of which is the task of determining the shortest round-trip that a salesman can take in visiting a number of cities. It is not known whether any NP-complete problem is polynomial-time computable, but it is known that if any NP-complete problem is polynomial-time computable, then they all are (Cook, 1971). All known deterministic algorithms for NP-complete problems are exponential-time, and it is widely believed that no polynomial-time algorithms exist. In practice, the discovery that a problem is NP-complete is taken to rule out the possibility of a real-time tractable implementation. In practical terms this may mean that for some n an algorithm which is NP-complete may not provide an answer in our lifetimes if at all.

Examples

Issues of computational complexity have arisen quite frequently in the history of cognitive psychology and artificial intelligence, perhaps most notably in vision research and risky decision making. Early work on bottom-up object recognition of blocks worlds resulted in the notorious combinatorial explosion (see McArthur (1982) for a review, and Tsotsos (1990) for a more recent discussion of complexity issues in vision research). In research into risky decision making, it was realized very early that complexity issues were relevant. Bayesian inference makes exponentially increasing demands on computational resources even for problems involving very moderate amounts of information. A salutary example is provided by the discussion of an application of Bayesian inference to medical-diagnosis problems involving multiple symptoms in Charniak and McDermott's (1985) introduction to artificial intelligence. Diagnoses involving just two symptoms, together with some reasonable assumptions concerning the numbers of diseases and symptoms a physician may know about, require upwards of 10^9 numbers to be stored in memory. Since typical diagnoses may work on upwards of 30 symptoms, even if every *connection* in the human brain were encoding a digit, its capacity would none the less be exceeded. Such complexity considerations render it highly unlikely that human decision makers are generally employing Bayesian decision theory in their risky decision making. Such results were primarily responsible for the emergence of the heuristics-and-biases approach in the psychology of human decision making (Tversky and Kahneman, 1974).

For our present purposes, the most telling example where complexity issues have suggested the infeasibility of an approach is in artificial-intelligence knowledge representation (McDermott, 1986). Most AI programs require knowledge to be represented and accessed. Knowledge is represented in logical form and accessing it treated as a logical inference. A problem AI researchers encountered was that world knowledge is invariably *defeasible*. The standard example is 'All birds can fly'. From this rule and the knowledge that 'Tweety is a bird' you may infer that 'Tweety can fly'. However, this rule is defeasible. If you subsequently learn that 'Tweety is an ostrich', then the conclusion that 'Tweety can fly' is defeated. Note that strictly speaking that ostriches can't fly is a *counterexample* to the original generalization. That is, the generalization is false, and hence no valid conclusions can be drawn from it. This may suggest that only exceptionless generalizations should form the contents of world knowledge. However, as we have already indicated, at least at the level of people's common-sense classification of the world, such exceptionless generalizations would not appear to be available to characterize their everyday world knowledge.

The standard approach (e.g. Reiter, 1980, 1985) has been to argue that a closed world assumption should be made. That is, inferences are drawn based on what is in the knowledge base *now*. Informally, when it is learnt that 'Tweety is a bird', as long as a counterexample can not be generated from the current contents of the database, i.e. 'Tweety can not fly' cannot be established, then it is reasonable to infer that 'Tweety can fly'. This means that every time a conclusion is drawn from a default rule the whole of the database must be exhaustively searched to ensure no counterexample is available. This is equivalent to checking the consistency of the database. But consistency checking reduces to the satisfiability problem and is therefore NP-complete. In consequence *an NP-complete problem has to be solved every time a default rule is invoked*. Since in the human case the database may consist of the whole of world knowledge, this logical account looks unpromising.

Of course this is a variant of the frame problem. It would be a great advantage if, rather than exhaustively searching the whole of world knowledge, only some *relevant* subset needed to be checked. The problem is then how to achieve this in a non-arbitrary way. As we will see below, two reasoning theories – pragmatic reasoning schema theory and the heuristic approach – potentially address this problem. However, we will argue that they provide inadequate responses to the problem of intractability.

Summary

Let us sum up the argument so far. We have suggested that considerations of bounded rationality may serve to provide criteria by which to judge current theories of reasoning. The reason why such considerations have not been taken into account is a failure to address the generalization issue. That is, theories of laboratory tasks must be able to generalize to more realistic inferential contexts. This is analogous to the problem of 'scaling up' in AI knowledge representation: many inference theories are suitable only to 'toy', or alternatively, 'un-ecologically' valid, domains. The majority of real human inference is defeasible or non-monotonic. However, standard approaches to defeasible inference would appear to be computationally intractable because of their reliance on exhaustive searches for counterexamples. In the following section, we will discuss the four theories of reasoning introduced above in the light of these considerations. As we said above, we will argue that all these theories of reasoning either make unreasonable demands on cognitive resources or provide inadequate responses to the problem of cognitive limitations.

THEORIES OF REASONING AND BOUNDED RATIONALITY

We will deal with the four theories of reasoning in the order they were introduced: mental logics, mental models, pragmatic reasoning schemas, and the heuristic approach.

Mental logics

The contemporary mental-logic view explains explicit reasoning perform-ance by appeal to various natural deduction systems (Gentzen, 1934) with (Braine, 1978), or without (Rips, 1983) some specific assumptions concerning the processes which animate the inference rules.[3] From the perspective of computational complexity, mental-logic accounts appear particularly unpromising. Even for standard monotonic logics, the general problem of deciding whether a given finite set of premises logically implies a particular conclusion is NP-complete (Cook, 1971).[4] Moreover, the *a priori* complexity results discussed above were derived from logical attempts to account for default reasoning in AI knowledge representation. In consequence, it seems unlikely that the mental-logic approach is going to satisfy the generalization assumption. There would appear to be only two possible lines of retreat to avoid the conclusion that most inferential performance is beyond the scope of the mental-logic approach.

First, despite *a priori* arguments that most human reasoning is defeasible, people may employ a standard logic in much everyday reasoning. However, over the last 30 years or so it has been the failure to observe reasoning performance that accords well with standard, monotonic logic which has led to questions over human rationality. When as little as 4 per cent of subjects' behaviour accords with standard logic in tasks where it is appropriate, it seems odd to generalize such an account to situations where it is not. Nevertheless, it must be conceded that this is an empirical issue. People *may* treat everyday defeasible claims as exceptionless generalizations. This possibility is, however, sufficiently remote for us to consider it no further.

Second, the generality of mental logics may be restricted to explicit reasoning and it may be denied that they are intended to cover implicit inferential processes involved in common-sense reasoning. Intractability is therefore not an issue because of the small premise sets involved. This proposal of course explicitly denies that mental logics can satisfy the generalization assumption. It, moreover, may not save the mental-logic account from intractability problems. Above we suggested that it is highly unlikely that standard monotonic inference is generalized to everyday defeasible inference. We now argue that the converse is far more plausible, i.e. that explicit reasoning may be influenced by defeasible inferential processes. If this is the case then explanations of human inferential behaviour, even on explicit reasoning tasks, will have to address the tractability problems we have raised.

The proposal that explicit reasoning may be influenced by defeasible inferential processes derives from recent empirical work on conditional reasoning. It would appear that even in laboratory tasks conditional sentences may be interpreted as default rules (Oaksford *et al.*, 1990). Byrne (1989) and Cummins *et al.* (1991) have shown that background information derived from stored world knowledge can affect inferential performance (see also Markovits, 1984, 1985). Specifically they have shown that the inferences which are permitted by a conditional statement are influenced by *additional antecedents*. For example:

1 If the key is turned the car starts.
  (a) Additional antecedent: the points are welded.

(1) could be used to predict that the car will start if the key is turned. This is an inference by modus ponens. However, this inference can be *defeated* when information about an additional antecedent (a) is explicitly provided (Byrne, 1989). Moreover, confidence in this inference is reduced for rules which possess many alternative antecedents even when this information is left implicit (Cummins *et al.*, 1991). In these studies additional antecedents were also found to affect inferences by modus tollens. If the car does not start, it could be inferred that the key was not turned, unless, of course, the points were welded. Modus tollens is *defeated* when information about an alternative antecedent is explicitly provided (Byrne, 1989) and confidence in it is reduced for rules which possess many alternative antecedents even when this information is left implicit (Cummins *et al.*, 1991).

The rules employed in these laboratory tasks are being treated as default rules. Other evidence indicates that even abstract rules may be treated in this way. In conditional inference tasks (Taplin, 1971; Taplin and Staudenmayer, 1973) and Wason's (1966) selection-task subjects typically refrain from either drawing inferences that accord with modus tollens or adopting the strategy of falsification that is sanctioned by modus tollens. This can be at least partially explained if it were a general default assumption that all rules are default rules. If this were the case, then modus tollens may be suppressed because the rules are treated as defeasible, just as in Byrne (1989) and Cummins *et al.* (1991).[5]

In sum, it seems likely that conditionals employed in explicit reasoning tasks are treated as default rules. Restricting the applicability of mental-logic approaches to explicit reasoning does not, therefore, avoid the problems of computational intractability.

The influence of default rules on people's reasoning would appear to have been dismissed by mental logicians as interfering pragmatic or performance factors (Rumain *et al.*, 1983; Braine *et al.*, 1984). This is in marked contrast to the reaction of logicians and AI researchers. These researchers have almost uniformly abandoned restrictions on what is deducible to the monotonic case and have been exploring non-monotonic logics to capture just the phenomenon their mental counterparts dismiss (see, for example, the collection edited by Ginsberg, 1987). The intuition behind this reaction seems to be that unless logical methods can be applied to these cases then most interesting inferences may be beyond the scope of logical inquiry. Logical enquiry may proceed divorced from the require-ment to provide computationally tractable inference regimes. Most AI applications and the cognitive science of human reasoning cannot, however, avoid these problems.

In conclusion, providing a viable theory of human inference must resolve the issue of intractability. Unfortunately a solution does not appear to be forthcoming from within the formal, logical approach. This is not incompatible with continued logical enquiry into systems which can handle default reasoning. Further, the possibility can not be dismissed that some formal notation may be devised which allows for more tractable implementations. However, the lack of practical success in devising a tractable logic for default inference suggests that this may be what Lakatos (1970) referred to as a degenerative research programme (Oaksford and Chater, 1991). In consequence, it seems unlikely that the mental-logic approach will satisfy the generalization assumption.

Mental models

The apparent failure of logical accounts to generalize appropriately to everyday common-sense inference appears to add further weight to the mental modeller's claim that 'there is no mental logic'. On the mental-models view, the syntactic formalisms adopted by the mental logician should be abandoned in favour of semantic methods of proof (e.g. Johnson-Laird, 1983; Johnson-Laird and Byrne, 1991). Such methods do not possess formal, syntactic rules of inference like modus ponens or modus tollens. Rather, the semantic contents of premises are directly manipulated in order to assess whether they validly imply a conclusion.

In this section we will introduce two interpretations of mental models. One we refer to as 'logical mental models', the other as 'memory-based mental models'.

Logical mental models

In recent accounts of mental models the claim that 'there is no mental logic' has been tempered. For example, 'the [mental] model theory is in no way incompatible with logic: it merely gives up the formal approach (rules of inference) for a semantic approach (search for counterexamples)' (Johnson-Laird and Byrne, 1991: 212). So the dispute is not about *whether* there is a mental logic, but about *how* it is implemented. On this interpretation *logical* mental models may be seen as an attempt to provide the notation, to which we alluded above, that will allow a tractable implementation of logic.

Mental models contrast with some semantic approaches to searching for counterexamples but share similarities with others. Truth tables and semantic tableaux (e.g. Hodges, 1975), which are unquestionably logical,[6] contrast with mental models because they are defined over standard propositional representations. In this respect mental models are more related to graphical proof methods such as Euler circles and Venn diagrams. In these semantic-proof procedures the operations which correspond to the steps of a sound logical derivation are defined over graphical representations of the domains of the quantifiers.

As Evans (1991) observes, both the mental-logic approach and mental models are attempting to account for human deductive competence. In assessing the mental-models approach, it would be helpful, therefore, if answers could be found to the same *metatheoretical* questions concerning computational tractability that we asked of the mental-logic approach. Certainly on the *logical* mental-models interpretation, answers to these questions should be possible. However, none as yet would appear to be available. This makes it difficult to assess mental models by the same standards we have applied to mental logics. This is a general problem. While mental models are supposed to do the same job as a mental logic, there are no metatheoretical proofs that this is the case. None the less, in the absence of the appropriate proofs, we can speculate about how the answers to these questions may turn out.

The first tractability question we looked at with mental logics was the standard case of monotonic inference where we found that the general problem of deciding validity was NP-complete. While this is generally the case, the situation is even worse with standard 'semantic approache[es]'. At this point we must head off a possible confusion. The semantic methods we mentioned above – truth tables and semantic tableaux – are formal *proof* methods (Hintikka, 1985). In contrast, the intention behind the 'semantic approach' of mental models is to use *model theory* as a basis for inference. As Hintikka (1985) observes, model theory *per se* provides no inferential mechanisms. However, the models could be exhaustively checked. For example, the sentence 'Gordon is in his room' (indexed to a particular space-time location, say *now*) will be true if and only if Gordon is in his room now, i.e. Gordon actually being in his room now provides *a* model for this sentence. Of course, this is a contingent claim and therefore there are many models in which it is false. Nevertheless you could check this sentence is true by looking at the arrangement of objects about which the claim is made. Could you check the validity of a putative logical truth in a similar way? Logical validity is defined relative to *all* models, which are potentially infinite in number. Moreover, many of them will be infinite in size. Attempting to prove the logical validity of a statement in this way would be impossible, at least for the finite minds of human beings. In sum, basing a psychological theory of inference on model theory looks even less promising than using formal syntactic methods.

Mental-models theorists are well aware of this problem (Johnson-Laird, 1983) and argue explicitly that mental models may provide a way in which model theory may be developed in to a tractable proof procedure. Mental models only deal with small sets of objects which represent *arbitrary exemplars* of the domains described in the premises. This is analogous to Bishop Berkeley's claim that reasoning regarding, say triangles, proceeds with an arbitrary exemplar of a triangle, rather than the, in his view, obscure Lockean notion of an abstract general idea. Providing no assumptions are introduced which depend on the properties of this particular triangle, for example, that it is scalene rather than equilateral, then general conclusions concerning *all* triangles may be arrived at.

The introduction of arbitrary exemplars highlights the lack of an appropriate metatheory for mental models. There is no exposition of the rules which guarantees that no illegitimate assumptions are introduced in a proof. This does not mean that any particular derivation using mental models has made such assumptions. None the less, guaranteeing the validity of an argument depends on ensuring that in a particular derivation one *could* not make such assumptions. Hence explicit procedures to prevent this happening need to be provided. In their absence there is no guarantee (i.e. no proof) that the procedures for manipulating mental models preserve validity. That is, it is not known whether, relative to the standard interpretation of predicate logic, mental models provides a *sound* logical system.[7]

While soundness is unresolved, there are strong reasons to suppose that mental models theory is not *complete* with respect to standard logic, i.e. while all inferences licensed by mental models may be licensed by standard logic (soundness) the converse is not the case. Other *graphical* methods are restricted in their *expressiveness* due to physical limitations on the notation. Venn diagrams, for example, can only be used to represent arguments employing four or less *monadic* predicates, i.e. predicates of only one variable (Quine, 1959).[8] They therefore only capture a small subset of logic. While mental models have been used to represent relations, i.e. predicates of more than one variable, there is no reason to suppose that mental models will not be subject to analogous limitations. If so, then mental models will not provide a general implementation of logic.[9]

The employment of arbitrary exemplars is central to providing a tractable model-based proof procedure. However, there are no complexity results for the algorithms which manipulate mental models. Such demonstrations may be felt unnecessary, if, as with the mental-logic approach, mental-models theory were restricted to the explicit inferences involved in laboratory tasks. However, mental-models theory has been generalized to other inferential modes, including implicit inference in text comprehension (Johnson-Laird, 1983). As we mentioned above, these inferences are defeasible (see p. 34), as are most everyday inferences people make.[10] Further, in many laboratory reasoning tasks, conditional sentences would appear to be interpreted as default rules (see above). So in order to provide a general theory of inference, mental models must account for defeasibility.

Proposals for incorporating default reasoning into mental models (Johnson-Laird and Byrne, 1991) rely on incorporating default assumption into the initial mental model of a set of premises. These assumptions will be recruited from prior world knowledge and may be undone in the process of changing mental models. The problem of consistency checking can be avoided because no search for counterexamples to these default assumptions need be initiated. This proposal does not resolve the problem of default inference. A generalizable theory of reasoning must address the problem of *which* default assumption(s) to incorporate in an initial representation. For example, suppose you are told 'Tweety is a bird', you may incorporate the default assumption that 'Tweety can fly' in your mental model because most birds can fly. However, it would be perverse to incorporate this assumption if you also knew that 'Tweety is an ostrich'. To rule out perverse or *irrelevant* default assumptions requires checking the whole of world knowledge to ensure that any default assumption is consistent with what you already know (or some relevant subset of what you already know). This will involve an exhaustive search over the whole of world knowledge for a counterexample to a default assumption.

It could be argued that the problem of searching for counterexamples for default assumptions is part of the theory of memory retrieval which mental models, as a theory of inference, is not obliged to provide. Three arguments seem to vitiate this suggestion. First, as we have seen, in AI at least, these memory-retrieval processes are treated as *inferential* processes and therefore need to be explained by a theory of inference. Second, the memory-retrieval processes involve the search for counterexamples. This indicates that *in its own terms* they are exactly the kind of inferential processes for which mental-models theory should provide an account. Third, such an argument could only succeed if mental-models theory itself didn't already rely heavily on such processes to explain the results of reasoning tasks.

In recent accounts (e.g. Johnson-Laird and Byrne, 1991) the explanation of various phenomena depend on the way in which an initial mental model of the premises is 'fleshed-out'. Fleshing-out, for example, determines: (i) whether a disjunction is interpreted as exclusive or inclusive, or (Johnson-Laird and Byrne, 1991: 45) (ii) whether a conditional is interpreted as material implication or equivalence (Johnson-Laird and Byrne, 1991: 48–50), which in turn determines whether inferences by modus tollens will be performed; (iii) whether non-standard interpretations of the conditional are adopted (Johnson-Laird and Byrne, 1991: 67), including content effects whereby the relation between antecedent and consequent affects the interpretation (Johnson-Laird and Byrne, 1991: 72–3); (iv) confirmation bias in Wason's selection task (Johnson-Laird and Byrne, 1991; 80) and (v) the search for counterexamples in syllogistic reasoning (Johnson-Laird and Byrne, 1991: 119). Fleshing out depends on accessing world knowledge. Moreover, the explanatory burden placed on fleshing out demands that mental-models theory accounts for the processes involved. In consequence it is reasonable to expect mental-models theory to provide an account of how relevant defaults are also retrieved from world knowledge. Since this issue is not addressed it seems unlikely that logical mental models can satisfy the generalization assumption.

However, the processes of fleshing out may suggest another interpretation of mental models which we briefly present before closing this section.

Memory-based mental models

The explanatory burden placed on fleshing out suggests that the memory-retrieval processes involved may be primarily responsible for mental-model construction and manipulation. The representations that appear in, for example, Johnson-Laird and Byrne (1991) may be better regarded as the *products* of processes in which those representations are not explicitly involved. In other words they are the 'appearance(s) before the footlights of consciousness' (James, 1950/1890) of processes which are not defined over those representations themselves. This contrasts with logical mental models where the processes that transform one model into another *are* defined over the representations that appear on the pages of, for example, Johnson-Laird and Byrne (1991).

Memory-based mental models appear to accord with an earlier thread in mental models theory:

> Like most everyday problems that call for reasoning, the explicit premises leave most of the relevant information unstated. Indeed, *the real business of reasoning in these cases is to determine the relevant factors and possibilities*, and it therefore depends on knowledge of the specific domain. Hence the construction of putative counterexamples calls for an active exercise of memory and interpretation rather than formal derivation of one expression from others.
>
> (Johnson-Laird, 1986: 45, our emphasis)

On a memory-based mental-models position the 'active exercise of memory and interpretation' would represent the heart of all inferential processes. Moreover, existing accounts of mental models could be interpreted as specifying the intended outputs of these processes given certain inputs. In this respect mental-models theory could therefore be expected to provide a valuable source of constraint on a future memory-based theory of reasoning. We will return to this interpretation of mental models later on.

Summary

Recent accounts of mental-models theory appear to favour an interpretation in terms of a graphical semantic-proof procedure. On this interpretation, mental models provides an alternative notation for implementing logic in the mind. This invites a variety of *metatheoretic* questions which need to be answered to assess the adequacy of *logical* mental models as a general, tractable, implementation of logic. Unfortunately, answers to these questions are unavailable. Further, existing proposals for handling default inference are inadequate. Taken together these considerations argue for a Scots verdict of 'not proven' on logical mental models. However, the processes of fleshing out indicate that memory-based mental models, while less articulated, may act as a valuable source of constraint on a memory-based theory of inference.

Pragmatic-reasoning schema theory

Pragmatic-reasoning schema theory emphasizes the role of domain-specific knowledge in reasoning tasks (Cheng and Holyoak, 1985; Cosmides, 1989). Cheng and Holyoak (1985) suggested that people possess *pragmatic reasoning schemas*, which embody rules specific to various domains such as permissions, causation, and so on. Permission schema are invoked in explaining the results from some thematic versions of Wason's selection task where the rule determines whether or not some action may be taken. Cheng and Holyoak (1985) argue that the rules embodied in a permission schema match the inferences licensed by standard logic, thus explaining the facilitatory effect of these materials. Similarly, Cosmides (1989) appeals to domain-specific knowledge of 'social contracts' to explain the same data (but see Cheng and Holyoak, 1989, for a critique). While Cosmides' work on social contracts is important, it is only the postulation of data structures specific to particular domains which will concern us.

We have frequently remarked that if the domains over which the search for counterexamples takes place were suitably constrained, then exhaustive searches may be feasible. However, there are two reasons for suspecting that schema-theoretic or domain-specific approaches in general will not prove adequate.

First, default reasoning is about how beliefs are appropriately updated in response to new information (Harman, 1986). Within philosophy the processes involved have typically been discussed under the heading of confirmation theory (Fodor, 1983). In arguing that confirmation, and hence default reasoning, is subject to the frame problem, Fodor observes that confirmation is characteristically *isotropic*:

> By saying that confirmation is isotropic, I mean that the facts relevant to the confirmation of a scientific hypothesis may be drawn from anywhere in the field of previously established empirical (or, of course, demonstrative) truths. Crudely: everything that the scientist knows is, in principle, relevant to determining what else he ought to believe.
>
> (Fodor, 1983: 105)

Domain specificity can assist with intractability only if isotropy is abandoned. If default reasoning is isotropic, then placing rigorous boundaries on relevant information would be a move in exactly the wrong direction. A knowledge organization which excluded the possibility of isotropy would be hopelessly inflexible. Although cross-referencing schemata is a possibility, as Fodor (1983: 117) points out: 'an issue in the logic of confirmation . . . [becomes] . . . an issue in the theory of executive control (a change which there is, by the way, no reason to assume is for the better)'.

A second reason to suspect that domain-specific approaches are inadequate concerns the lack of any general principles concerning how an appropriate compartmentalization of knowledge is to be achieved. Such general principles are required since otherwise how knowledge is organized into discrete compartments from the flux of information that an organism receives in interacting with its environment remains opaque (Oaksford

and Chater, 1991). While it may be legitimate to appeal to compartmentalization, once appealed to, an account of how it is achieved must be
supplied. Pragmatic-reasoning schema theory does not explicitly address
this issue. In consequence it is unlikely that this theory can satisfy the
generalization assumption.

Heuristic approaches

The heuristic approach (Evans, 1983b, 1984, 1989) is that most concerned
with the issue of cognitive limitations (Evans, 1983a). In computer science
the use of heuristics may render a computationally intractable problem
manageable. Tractable, approximate solutions may be found for many
problem instances by employing the generally intractable algorithm with
a heuristic (Horowitz and Sahni, 1978). Accuracy is traded for speed. In
this section we will observe that the current heuristic approach does not
address the intractability problems we have raised: the heuristics proposed
are more often motivated by appeal to *pragmatic* rather than *processing*
factors. We will suggest, however, that with some minor reinterpretation,
one heuristic proposed by Evans (1983b) may address the intractability
issue. None the less, we will conclude that supplementing generally
intractable algorithms with heuristics is unlikely to provide a general
solution to the problem of intractability.

The *not*-heuristic (Evans, 1983b, 1984, 1989) is motivated by Wason's
(1965) proposal that negations are typically used to deny presuppositions.
For example, 'I did *not* go for a walk' denies the presupposition that you
went for a walk. The topic of this sentence – what the sentence is about –
is walking and not any of the things I could have done while not walking.
On the basis of this example it was proposed that the language understanding mechanism embodies a *not*-heuristic (Evans, 1983b). This heuristic
treats information about, for example, what you did while *not* walking as
irrelevant. Attention is therefore focused only on the named values. More
recently, this heuristic has been regarded as a manifestation of a general
bias towards positive information, i.e. information about what something
is rather than what it is not (Evans, 1989; see also Oaksford and Stenning,
1992).

Such a general preference for positive information may be better
motivated by processing rather than pragmatic considerations. A general
positivity bias may be one aspect of providing a tractable knowledge base
(Oaksford and Chater, forthcoming). The frame problem was first noticed
in reasoning about change. In a dynamic representation, the consequences
of something changing has to include all the things that did *not* change.
For example, along with the information that 'If your coffee cup is knocked
over your carpet gets wet', all the information about what did not happen
when your coffee cup is knocked over needed to be encoded. For example,

that the window does not open, the lights do not switch off and so on. There is a potentially infinite list of things which do not happen as a consequence of knocking your coffee cup to the floor, each of which would have to be explicitly represented. However, the *negation-as-failure* procedure obviates the need to represent all this information (Hogger, 1984).[11] If, from the current contents of the database, it cannot be proved that the window opens, then it is assumed that the window does not open. The upshot is that in a logic program *no* negative information is stored (Hogger, 1984). This represents a prime case of positivity bias in the service of tractability.

So at least one aspect of the current heuristic approach could address the tractability issues we have discussed. However, as Evans (1991) says, the heuristic approach is *not* an approach to human reasoning in its own right. It needs to be married to a particular theory of competence. Such an approach is unlikely to prove adequate, however. The problem is that:

> The use of heuristics in an existing algorithm may enable it to quickly solve a large instance of a problem provided the heuristic 'works' on that instance. . . . A heuristic, however, does not 'work' equally effectively on all problem instances. Exponential time algorithms, even coupled with heuristics will still show exponential behaviour on some sets of inputs.
>
> (Horowitz and Sahni, 1978)

There has been no attempt to articulate the sets of heuristics which would be needed to provide generally tractable inference regimes either within the heuristic approach or in AI knowledge representation. Hence, Evans (1991) may well be right that one way to proceed is to marry the heuristic approach to one or other of the theories which explicitly address the competence issue. However, it seems doubtful that an appropriate set of heuristics will be forthcoming to supplement these theories (Oaksford and Chater, 1991).

Default reasoning in particular presents new problems for the heuristic approach. Existing accounts of default reasoning fail to arrive at intuitively acceptable conclusions (McDermott, 1986). Quite often the only conclusion available is of the form p ∨ not-p, i.e. a logical truth (Oaksford and Chater, 1991). This is particularly uninformative. It has been suggested that one way to resolve this problem is by appeal to various heuristics. These heuristics may also assist with tractability by cutting down the number of possibilities which need to be considered. The disjunction above is all that can often be concluded because each default rule may lead to a different possible conclusion. Logically, the only conclusion that can be drawn therefore is their disjunction. However, if one default rule can be given preference, then all these possibilities need not be computed (see Oaksford and Chater, 1991).[12] Again, however, it is not at all clear that any of the heuristics proposed resolve this issue appropriately for all instances of a problem (Loui, 1987). In sum, it seems unlikely that an appropriate set of heuristics will be forthcoming to solve the problem of computational intractability. In consequence, the heuristic approach is unlikely to satisfy the generalization assumption.

Summary

In this section we have surveyed existing theories of reasoning with respect to their ability to generalize appropriately to everyday common-sense reasoning. The mental-logic approach was perhaps the least promising in this respect. This is largely because it is sufficiently well articulated for the relevant metatheoretic results to be available. This was in contrast to the logical mental-models approach. Although there is a possibility that arbitrary exemplars may provide for a tractable model-based inference regime, the absence of the relevant metatheoretic results means that it is impossible to decide one way or the other. However, when it comes to default reasoning the mental-models approach is demonstrably in-adequate: the real problem is avoided. The possibility remains that memory-based mental models may none the less be explained as emergent properties of a theory of memory retrieval (this possibility is discussed further below). The two theories perhaps most suited to addressing the tractability issue – pragmatic-reasoning schema theory and the heuristic approach – were equally unpromising. Without an account of how compartmentalization is achieved, schema theoretic approaches *presuppose* a solution, they do not provide one. It moreover seems unlikely that an appropriate set of heuristics can be specified to resolve the intractability problem.

DISCUSSION

There are two broad areas which require further discussion in the light of the above arguments. Both concern the issue of rationality. First, we will discuss philosophical implications for human rationality. Second, we will discuss the implications for psychological theories concerned to build rational mechanisms (Fodor, 1987).

Rationality

In this section we will discuss two issues, the implications of reasoning data for human rationality, and the possible charge that abandoning rule-based theories leads to relativism.

The intractability results we have reported indicate that a bounded-rationality assumption should be made. This has the consequence that the empirically observed deviations from normative theories could not bring human rationality into question. The complexity results we have discussed indicate that people *could not* generally be using the normative strategy. It is only possible to condemn people as irrational for not using a particular strategy if they *could* use it. To think otherwise, would be like condemning us because we can not breathe under water even though we do not possess gills. It could be argued, however, that for laboratory tasks involving just a few premises complexity issues are not a concern. We have partly replied to this response above where we observed that if just one rule is interpreted as a default rule, a feasible real-time inference is doubtful. It also seems highly unlikely that people have been endowed with all the logical machinery spontaneously to solve just those tasks small enough not to tax their limited resources. If nothing else this is because the empirical data appear to indicate that they just happen not to use that machinery! It seems far more parsimonious to suggest that the strategy which is used in everyday reasoning contexts is generalized to laboratory tasks.

It would be irrational to demand that people employ strategies which they are incapable of using. However, one attractive feature of rule-based theories is that they come with their own warrant of rationality, as it were. Brown argues that '[on] our classical conception of rationality . . . the rationality of any conclusion is determined by whether it conforms to the appropriate rules' (Brown, 1988: 17). If rule-based theories are abandoned, there may be no guarantee that the strategies which replace them are rational: since they will not be rule-based, they will not carry their own warrant of rationality. This, moreover, may be seen as the first step on the slippery slope towards *relativism*, i.e. the view that there are no universal principles of rationality.

Johnson-Laird and Byrne (1991) consider the same problem and conclude that rather than conformity to rules, the search for counter-examples provides a universal principle of rationality. However, this provides neither a necessary nor a sufficient condition for rational judge-ment. It is not necessary because it is not a principle universally adhered to in scientific practice which provides our paradigm case of rational activity (Brown, 1988). Within periods of normal science (Kuhn, 1962) scientists explicitly refuse to allow core theoretical principles to be subject to refutation. The search for counterexamples is also not a sufficient criterion for rational judgement. Continuing to search for counterexamples indefinitely is not rational when trying to reach a decision in real time.

However, the idea that the search for counterexamples provides a universal criterion of rationality need not be wholly abandoned. It will, however, need to be supplemented by a theory of *judgement*: 'Judgement is the ability to evaluate a situation, assess evidence, and come to a reasonable decision without following rules' (Brown, 1988: 137). It is a matter of judgement, for example, when and if counterexamples are allowed to falsify a core theoretical principle, or when the search for counterexamples has been sufficiently exhaustive. Quite frequently we appeal to experts, who have a wealth of experience and knowledge in order to make these judgements. A good example is the peer review system. There is no algorithm for determining whether an experimenter has made sufficient attempts to dismiss alternative explanations of a hypothesis. In consequence, it is left to a researcher's peers to decide whether she/he has adequately dealt with the *relevant* possibilities. A further example is provided by the legal concept of *precedent*. In certain cases a defence lawyer will seek to find a case in which the facts are as similar as possible and where a not-guilty verdict was returned. Equally, the prosecution may seek a similar case where a guilty verdict was returned. Both defence and prosecution are searching for counterexamples to each other's arguments that on the basis of the evidence the defendant should (or should not) be convicted. Judgement enters in to the decision process, in two ways. First, the judge of the present case must decide whether the cases are similar in the *relevant* respects. Second, the whole concept of precedent relies on allowing previous judgements to influence subsequent judgements.

In sum, the claim that we could not employ rule-based theories could lead to relativism. The search for counterexamples *per se* is an inadequate response to this charge. The examples we adduced indicate that the search for counterexamples must be supplemented by a theory of judgement before anything like a universal principle is available.

Rational mechanisms

Rule-based systems operating over formal symbolic representations have the advantage that they possess a transparent semantics which allows us to see how mental representations can be causally efficacious in virtue of their meaning (Fodor, 1987). If we abandon rule-based theories, do we also abandon the ability to provide causal, mechanistic explanations of the way representational mental states mediate behaviour? Part of an answer to this question has already been provided. If the concept of what it is to be rational changes, then the form that a theory of rational mechanism must take may also change. We now consider what kinds of mechanism may be consistent with our developing conception of rationality. We will first draw on an analogy with Kahneman and Tversky's work on risky decision making, and then propose that connectionist systems may provide alternative rational mechanisms.

In response to similar complexity results for Bayesian inference, Tversky and Kahneman (1974) proposed a qualitatively different theory to explain risky decison making in which the normative theory was not retained in any form. The problem of deriving probability estimates was radically reconceived largely in terms of the processes of memory retrieval. Their *heuristic* approach can be contrasted with the heuristic approach in theories of reasoning. As we mentioned above, within reasoning theory, heuristics are regarded as supplements to a theory of competence (Evans, 1991). However, in Kahneman and Tversky's approach various memory-based heuristics are regarded as wholesale replacements for the competence theory. We suggest that confronted with similar intractability problems reasoning theorists should adopt the same response.

What could represent an analogous reconceptualization of reasoning mechanisms? Levesque (1988) has suggested that connectionism may represent one strategy in the attempt to develop plausible cognitive mechanisms for inference. Rumelhart *et al.* (1986) and Rumelhart (1989) have also suggested that a predictive neural network may form the basis of people's reasoning abilities. What kind of reconceptualization of reasoning does this involve?

Inference is the dynamics of cognition. In classical approaches (Fodor and Pylyshyn, 1988; Chater and Oaksford, 1990) inference takes static symbolic representations and turns them to useful work, predicting the environment, explaining an experiment, drawing up a plan of action and so on. Formal inference over language-like representations has seemed the only way in which meaning and mechanism could combine (Fodor, 1987). Connectionism may offer a very different picture of how to achieve the marriage between mechanism and meaning. Logic provides a dynamics for representations of a particular type: atomic symbolic representations usually map one to one onto our common-sense classification of the world. Connectionism postulates distributed representations of a very different kind in which stable patterns of features represent items in that classification. The dynamics of the system, moreover, is defined at the featural level and owes more to statistical mechanics than to logic. Nevertheless it may be that these representations and the dynamics which transforms one such representation into another can form the basis of a theory of inference.

Let us consider the problem at a higher level of abstraction. Inference leads us from one interpreted mental state to another. The heart of the problem is how to get mental states to systematically track states of the world or, in other words, how to get the dynamics of cognition to 'hook up' to the dynamics of the world (Churchland and Churchland, 1983). We see no reason, *a priori*, why connectionist systems cannot also perform this function.

While there are serious problems for a connectionist theory of inference, there may also be advantages. It may be compatible, for example, with the second interpretation of mental models we offered above (Rumelhart, 1989). Given a set of inputs a network settles on an interpretation which least violates the constraints embodied in its weighted connections between units. These weighted connections embody the network's knowledge of a domain. One way of characterizing such a relaxation search, is that prior to input clamping all the knowledge that is embodied in the network is potentially relevant to interpreting the input. However, as the net relaxes into an interpretation only those items most relevant will remain on. The stable state arrived at can be regarded as the initial 'mental model' of the input. This model may embody default assumptions. For example, in the 'on-line' schema model (Rumelhart *et al.*, 1986), a constraint satisfaction network embodied information about prototypical rooms. If the bath unit was clamped on then units like toilet, toothbrush, and so on would come on as default values. In the search for counterexamples, intermediate mental models may be generated by selectively clamping off units and allowing the net to settle into a new stable state (Rumelhart, 1989).

Further, this mode of operation seems to capture something of what it means to make a *judgement*. As we said above, determining whether relevant counterexamples have been exhausted is a matter of judgement based upon what you know. In a simple connectionist system all that it knows (all its synaptic weights) contribute to determining what is relevant to interpreting current inputs. The example of precedent also indicates that counterexamples to *novel* situations may be sought by reference to *similar* situations. The partial pattern-matching capabilities of networks make them good candidates for implementing the processes responsible.[13]

The burden of complexity may also be located in the right place. Within connectionist systems learning is the computationally expensive process. Once learnt, however, an inference over the representations embodied in the network is effortless. In contrast, in classical systems inference is computationally expensive while learning is an issue rarely addressed. This may seem like just trading one complexity problem for another. However, the connectionist system at least mirrors the difficulty people actually appear to encounter with learning and inference.

There are serious problems, however. Current network dynamics are insufficiently articulated to provide an account of the productivity of language and thinking (Fodor and Pylyshyn, 1988). In particular, thinking is not a purely predictive process which is triggered by external events. Indeed in thinking people appear able to 'un-hook' the dynamics of cognition from the dynamics of the world, enabling them to step out of real time. This will require networks to have their own intrinsic dynamics to allow thoughts to chain together in the absence of provoking stimuli. While posing a serious problem there is, none the less, a great deal of work going on in this area (Chater, 1989; Elman, 1988; Jordan, 1986; Rohwer, 1990). We see no reason to be pessimistic about its outcome and the consequent prospects for a connectionist theory of inference.

CONCLUSIONS

We have argued that an adequate theory of reasoning must be able to 'scale up' to deal with everyday defeasible inferences in real time. We observed that no contemporary theory of reasoning provided a tractable account of everyday inference and that in consequence none of these theories were likely to be psychologically real. Concentration on limited laboratory tasks would appear to have led to the development of theories of dubious ecological validity. Further, it would appear more likely that people 'scale down' their everyday strategies to deal with laboratory tasks and that this is the source of the systematic biases observed in human reasoning. While these arguments do not bring human rationality into question, they do demand a reconceptualization of appropriate mechanisms for inference. We suggested that connectionist systems may be appropriate which appeared consistent with memory-based mental models and the requirements of a theory of judgement.

In conclusion, empirical research into human reasoning may need to be more ecologically valid. The boundaries of *real inference* need to be mapped out: how do people deal with defeasible knowledge, how do they make relevance judgements, and how does background information (Byrne, 1989; Cummins *et al.*, 1991) interact with reasoning processes? Answers to these questions could be pursued on two fronts. First the complexification of the laboratory situation. Most reasoning tasks are still pencil-and-paper exercises (although, see Mynatt *et al.*, 1977, for example). In contrast the computer game may offer the prospect of engaging subjects in novel dynamic environments over which the experimenter has control. In such environments, context-sensitive rules, varying difficulties of obtaining information, and differing utilities for correct inference can be arranged and their consequences for behaviour mapped out. Second, more direct analyses of real inferential settings such as the court room and science itself need to be conducted (e.g. Tukey, 1986; Tweney, 1985). Explaining the inferential processes that obtain in such real-world settings must be the ultimate goal of a psychological theory of reasoning.

ACKNOWLEDGEMENTS

We gratefully acknowledge the support of the Economic and Social Research Council, U.K., Contract No. R000231282, in conducting the research which led to this paper.

NOTES

1 It is important to be clear about whose inferential behaviour reasoning theorists are attempting to explain. Throughout this chapter it is assumed to be

the spontaneous, unassisted, inferential performance of logically untutored subjects. By 'spontaneous and unassisted' we mean that the subjects are not allowed to use aids such as pencil, paper or computer to make calculations nor are they able to consult with friends or experts. By 'logically untutored' we mean that subjects should have no explicit formal logical training. In other words reasoning theorists are attempting to explain the reasoning abilities which people possess solely in virtue of genetic endowment and general education.

2 The satisfiability problem is to determine whether a formula is true for some assignment of truth values to the variables. 'Reduces' is a technical term of complexity theory (see Horowitz and Sahni, 1978: 511).

3 Natural deduction systems contain no axioms and all inferences are drawn by the application of various inference-rule schemata, e.g. p OR q, not-p $\models$ q (where '$\models$' can be informally glossed as 'therefore').

4 This applies equally well to semantic-proof procedures, such as truth tables and semantic tableaux, as to syntactic procedures such as axioms or natural deduction systems.

5 This would appear to predict that inferences by modus ponens should also be suppressed in these tasks, which is not the case. We examine this issue in more detail elsewhere (Oaksford and Chater, forthcoming).

6 We should also note that under standard interpretations, the search for counterexamples does not distinguish syntactic from semantic approaches. All proof procedures are regarded as 'abortive counter-model constructions' (Beth, 1955; Hintikka, 1955; see also Hintikka, 1985).

7 There are logical systems which eliminate quantifiers, for example, *combinatory logic* (see Curry's and Feys' (1958) and Fine's (1985) theory of arbitrary objects. Perhaps a translation between these systems and mental models may provide the desired results.

8 This is simply due to the inability to draw more than four overlapping two-dimensional shapes such that all possible relationships between them are represented.

9 This is far less important than *soundness*. However, if mental-models theory is to avoid the charge of *ad hoc* extension to deal with new phenomena, then some account of *expressiveness* must be provided. Otherwise there can be little confidence that the notation is sufficiently well understood to perform the functions demanded of it.

10 At the beginning of Johnson-Laird and Byrne (1991) the example of a classic piece of default reasoning by Sherlock Holmes is provided which eloquently illustrates this point.

11 The cost is that logical negation is not fully implemented in such a database.

12 These possibilities are known as different *extensions* of a default theory. A default theory is simply a collection of axioms, including at least one default rule, which describes the behaviour of a particular domain.

13 It also suggests that sensible reasoning in novel domains does not demand an abstract inferential competence sensitive to the logical form of arguments. Just as with precedent, old judgements are brought to bear on new problems.

REFERENCES

Baars, B.J. (1986) *The Cognitive Revolution in Psychology*, New York: Guilford Press.

Baddeley, A.D. (1986) *Working Memory*, Oxford: Clarendon Press.

Beth, E.W. (1955) 'Semantic entailment and formal derivability', *Mededelingen van de Koninklijke Nederlande Akadamie van Wetenschappen, Afd. Letterkunde* 18: 309–42.

Braine, M.D.S. (1978) 'On the relationship between the natural logic of reasoning and standard logic', *Psychological Review* 85: 1–21.

Braine, M.D.S., Reiser, B.J., and Rumain, B. (1984) 'Some empirical justification for a theory of natural propositional logic', *The Psychology of Learning and Motivation*, vol. 18, New York: Academic Press.

Bransford, J.D. and Johnson, M. (1972) 'Contextual prerequisites for understanding: some investigations of comprehension and recall', *Journal of Verbal Learning and Verbal Behaviour* 11: 717–26.

—— (1973) 'Considerations of some problems of comprehension', in W.G. Chase (ed.) *Visual Information Processing*, New York: Academic Press, pp. 389–92.

Bransford, J.D. and McCarrell, N.S. (1975) 'A sketch of a cognitive approach to comprehension: some thoughts on what it means to comprehend', in W.B. Weimer and D.S. Palermo (eds) *Cognition and Symbolic Processes*, Hillsdale, NJ: Erlbaum, pp. 189–229.

Bransford, J.D., Barclay, J.R., and Franks, J.J. (1972) 'Sentence memory: a constructive versus interpretive approach', *Cognitive Psychology* 3: 193–209.

Brown, H.I. (1988) *Rationality*, London: Routledge.

Byrne, R.M.J. (1989) 'Suppressing valid inferences with conditionals', *Cognition* 31: 1–21.

Charniak, E. and McDermott, D. (1985) *An Introduction to Artificial Intelligence*, Reading, MA: Addison-Wesley.

Chater, N. (1989) *Learning to Respond to Structure in Time*, Research Initiative in Pattern Recognition Technical Report, Malvern: RSRE September.

Chater, N. and Oaksford, M. (1990) 'Autonomy, implementation and cognitive architecture: a reply to Fodor and Pylyshyn', *Cognition* 34: 93–107.

Cheng, P.W. and Holyoak, K.J. (1985) 'Pragmatic reasoning schemas', *Cognitive Psychology* 17: 391–416.

—— (1989) 'On the natural selection of reasoning theories', *Cognition* 33: 285–313.

Cherniak, C. (1986) *Minimal Rationality*, Cambridge, MA: MIT Press.

Churchland, P.M. and Churchland, P.S. (1983) 'Stalking the wild epistemic engine', *Nous* 17: 5–18.

Clark, H.H. (1977) 'Bridging' in P.N. Johnson-Laird and P.C. Wason (eds) *Thinking: Readings in Cognitive Science*, Cambridge: Cambridge University Press, pp. 411–20.

Cook, S. (1971) 'The complexity of theorem proving procedures', in *The Third Annual Symposium on the Theory of Computing*, New York, pp. 151–8.

Cosmides, L. (1989) 'The logic of social exchange: has natural selection shaped how humans reason? Studies with the Wason selection task', *Cognition* 31: 187–276.

Cummins, D.D., Lubart, T., Alksnis, O., and Rist, R. (1991) 'Conditional reasoning and causation', *Memory & Cognition* 19: 274–82.

Curry, H.B. (1956) *An Introduction to Mathematical Logic*, Amsterdam: Van Nostrand.

Curry, H.B. and Feys, R. (eds) (1958) *Combinatory Logic*, Amsterdam: North-Holland.

Elman, J.L. (1988) *Finding Structure in Time*, CRL Technical Report 8801, San Diego: Centre for Research in Language, University of California.

Evans, J. St B.T. (ed.) (1983a) 'Selective processes in reasoning', *Thinking and Reasoning: Psychological Approaches*, London: Routledge & Kegan Paul.

—— (1983b) 'Linguistic determinants of bias in conditional reasoning', *Quarterly Journal of Experimental Psychology* 35A: 635–44.

—— (1984) 'Heuristic and analytic processes in reasoning', *British Journal of Psychology* 75: 451–68.

—— (1989) *Bias in Human Reasoning: Causes and Consequences,* London: Erlbaum.

—— (1991) 'Theories of human reasoning: the fragmented state of the art', *Theory & Psychology* 1: 83–105.

Fine, K. (1985) *Reasoning with Arbitrary Objects,* Oxford: Basil Blackwell.

Fodor, J.A. (1983) *Modularity of Mind,* Cambridge MA: MIT Press.

—— (1987) *Psychosemantics: The Problem of Meaning in the Philosophy of Mind,* Cambridge, MA: MIT Press.

Fodor, J.A. and Pylyshyn, Z.W. (1981) 'How direct is visual perception? Some reflections on Gibson's "Ecological Approach"', *Cognition* 9: 139–96.

—— (1988) 'Connectionism and cognitive architecture: a critical analysis', *Cognition* 28: 3–71.

Garey, M.R. and Johnson, D.S. (1979) *Computers and Intractability: A Guide to the Theory of NP-Completeness,* San Francisco: W.H. Freeman.

Gentzen, G. (1934) 'Untersuchungen über das logishce Schliessen', *Mathematische Zeitschrifft* 39: 176–210.

Ginsberg, M.L. (ed.) (1987) *Readings in Nonmonotonic Reasoning,* Los Altos, CA: Morgan Kaufman.

Glymour, C. (1987) 'Android epistemology and the frame problem: comments on Dennett's "Cognitive Wheels"', in Z.W. Pylyshyn (ed.) *The Robot's Dilemma: The Frame Problem in Artificial Intelligence,* Norwood, NJ: Ablex, pp. 65–76.

Glymour, C. and Thomason, R.H. (1984) 'Default reasoning and the logic of theory perturbation', unpublished manuscript, History and Philosophy of Science Department, University of Pittsburgh.

Gregory, R.L. (1977) *Eye and Brain,* 3rd edn, London: Weidenfeld & Nicolson.

Harman, G. (1986) *Change in View,* Cambridge, MA: MIT Press.

Henle, M. (1962) 'On the relation between logic and thinking', *Psychological Review* 69: 366–78.

Hintikka, J. (1955) 'Form and content in quantification theory', *Acta Philosophica Fennica* 8: 11–55.

—— (1985) 'Mental models, semantical games, and varieties of intelligence', unpublished manuscript, University of Florida.

Hodges, W. (1975) *Logic,* Harmondsworth: Penguin.

Hogger, C.J. (1984) *An Introduction to Logic Programming,* London: Academic Press.

Horowitz, E. and Sahni, S. (1978) *Fundamentals of Computer Algorithms,* Rockville, Maryland: Computer Science Press.

Inhelder, B. and Piaget, J. (1958) *The Growth of Logical Reasoning,* New York: Basic Books.

James, W. (1950) *The Principles of Psychology,* vol. 1, New York: Dover (originally published in 1890).

Johnson-Laird, P.N. (1975) 'Models of deduction', in R.J. Falmagne (ed.) *Reasoning: Representation and Process,* Hillsdale, NJ: Erlbaum.

—— (1983) *Mental Models: Towards a Cognitive Science of Language, Inference and Consciousness,* Cambridge: Cambridge University Press.

—— (1986) 'Reasoning without logic', in T. Myers, K. Brown, and B. McGonigle (eds) *Reasoning and Discourse Processes,* London: Academic Press, pp. 13–50.

Johnson-Laird, P.N. and Byrne, R.M.J. (1991) *Deduction,* Hillsdale, NJ: Erlbaum.

Jordan, M.I. (1986) *Serial Order: A Parallel Distributed Approach,* Institute for Cognitive Science Report 8604, San Diego: University of California.

Kahneman, D., Slovic, P., and Tversky, A. (eds) (1982) *Judgement Under Uncertainty: Heuristics and Biases*, Cambridge: Cambridge University Press.

Kuhn, T.S. (1962) *The Structure of Scientific Revolutions*, Chicago: University of Chicago Press.

Lakatos, I. (1970) 'Falsification and the methodology of scientific research programmes', in I. Lakatos and A. Musgrave (eds) *Criticism and the Growth of Knowledge*, Cambridge: Cambridge University Press, pp. 91–196.

Levesque, H.J. (1985) 'A fundamental tradeoff in knowledge representation and reasoning', in R.J. Brachman and H.J.Levesque (eds) *Readings in Knowledge Representation*, Los Altos, CA: Morgan Kaufman.

—— (1988) 'Logic and the complexity of reasoning', *Journal of Philosophical Logic* 17: 355–89.

Lewis, D. (1973) *Counterfactuals*, Oxford: Oxford University Press.

Loui, R.P. (1987) 'Response to Hanks and McDermott: temporal evolution of beliefs and beliefs about temporal evolution', *Cognitive Science* 11: 283–97.

McArthur, D.J. (1982) 'Computer vision and perceptual psychology', *Psychological Bulletin* 92: 283–309.

McCarthy, J.M. and Hayes, P. (1969) 'Some philosophical problems from the standpoint of artificial intelligence', in B. Meltzer and D. Michie (eds) *Machine Intelligence* 4, New York: Elsevier.

McDermott, D. (1986) *A Critique of Pure Reason*, Technical Report, Department of Computer Science, Yale University, June, 1986.

Markovits, H. (1984) 'Awareness of the "possible" as a mediator of formal thinking in conditional reasoning problems', *British Journal of Psychology* 75: 367–76.

—— (1985) 'Incorrect conditional reasoning among adults: competence or performance', *British Journal of Psychology* 76: 241–7.

Medin, D.L. and Schaffer, M.M. (1978) 'Context theory of classification learning', *Psychological Review* 85: 201–38.

Miller, G.A. (1956) 'The magical number 7±2: some limits on our capacity for processing information', *Psychological Review* 63: 81–97.

Minsky, M. (1975) 'Frame-system theory', in R. Schank and B.L. Nash-Webber (eds) *Theoretical Issues in Natural Language Processing*, Cambridge, MA, 10–13 June 1975.

Mynatt, C.R., Doherty, M.E., and Tweney, R.D. (1977) 'Confirmation bias in a simulated research environment: an experimental study of scientific inference', *Quarterly Journal of Experimental Psychology* 29: 85–95.

Nosofsky, R.M. (1986) 'Attention, similarity and the identification-categorisation relationship', *Journal of Experimental Psychology: General* 115: 39–57.

Oaksford, M. and Chater, N. (1991) 'Against logicist cognitive science', *Mind & Language* 6: 1–38.

—— (1992) 'Bounded rationality in taking risks and drawing inferences', *Theory & Psychology* 2: 225–30.

—— (forthcoming) *Cognition and Inquiry*, London: Academic Press.

Oaksford, M. and Stenning, K. (1992) 'Reasoning with conditionals containing negated constituents', *Journal of Experimental Psychology: Learning, Memory & Cognition* 18: 834–54.

Oaksford, M., Chater, N., and Stenning, K. (1990) 'Connectionism, classical cognitive science and experimental psychology', *AI & Society* 4: 73–90. Also in A. Clark and R. Lutz (eds) (1992) *Connectionism in Context*, Berlin: Springer-Verlag, pp. 57–74.

Osherson, D. (1975) 'Logic and models of logical thinking', in R.J. Falmagne (ed.) *Reasoning: Representation and Process*, Hillsdale, NJ: Erlbaum.

Pylyshyn, Z.W. (ed.) (1987) *The Robot's Dilemma: The Frame Problem in Artificial Intelligence*, Norwood, NJ: Ablex.

Quine, W.O. (1959) *Methods of Logic*, New York: Holt, Rinehart, & Winston.

Reiter, R. (1980) 'A logic for default reasoning', *Artificial Intelligence* 13: 81–132.

—— (1985) 'On reasoning by default', in R. Brachman and H. Levesque (eds) *Readings in Knowledge Representation*, Los Altos, CA: Morgan Kaufman (originally published in 1978).

Rips, L.J. (1983) 'Cognitive processes in propositional reasoning', *Psychological Review*, 90: 38–71.

Rohwer, R. (1990) 'The "Moving Targets" training algorithm', in L.B.Almeida and C.J. Wellekens (eds) *Lecture Notes in Computer Science 412: Neural Networks*, Berlin: Springer-Verlag, pp. 100–9.

Rosch, E. (1973) 'On the internal structure of perceptual and semantic categories', in T. Moore (ed.) *Cognitive Development and the Acquisition of Language*, New York: Academic Press.

—— (1975) 'Cognitive representation of semantic categories', *Journal of Experimental Psychology: General* 104: 192–233.

Rumain, B., Connell, J., and Braine, M.D.S. (1983) 'Conversational comprehension processes are responsible for reasoning fallacies in children as well as adults. IF is not the biconditional', *Developmental Psychology* 19: 471–81.

Rumelhart, D.E. (1989) 'Toward a microstructural account of human reasoning', in S. Vosnaidou and A. Ortony (eds) *Similarity and Analogical Reasoning*, Cambridge: Cambridge University Press, Ch. 10, pp. 298–312.

Rumelhart, D.E., Smolensky, P., McClelland, J.L., and Hinton, G.E. (1986) 'Schemata and sequential thought processes in PDP models', in J.L. McClelland and D.E. Rumelhart (eds) *Parallel Distributed Processing: Explorations in the Microstructure of Cognition, vol 2: Psychological and Biological processes*, Cambridge, MA: MIT Press, Ch. 14, pp. 7–57.

Simon, H.A. (1969) *The Sciences of the Artificial*, Cambridge, MA: MIT Press.

Stalnaker, R. (1968) 'A theory of conditionals', in N. Rescher (ed.) *Studies in Logical Theory*, Oxford: Oxford University Press.

Stenning, K. and Oaksford, M. (1989) *Choosing Computational Architectures for Text Processing*, Technical Report No. EUCCS/RP-28, Edinburgh: Centre for Cognitive Science, University of Edinburgh, April, 1989.

Taplin, J.E. (1971) 'Reasoning with conditional sentences', *Journal of Verbal Learning and Verbal Behaviour* 10: 219–25.

Taplin, J.E. and Staudenmayer, H. (1973) 'Interpretation of abstract conditional sentences in deductive reasoning', *Journal of Verbal Learning and Verbal Behaviour* 12: 530–42.

Tsotsos, J.K. (1990) 'Analyzing vision at the complexity level', *Behavioral & Brain Sciences* 13: 423–69.

Tversky, A. and Kahneman, D. (1974) 'Judgement under uncertainty: heuristics and biases', *Science* 185: 1124–31.

Tukey, D.D. (1986) 'A philosophical and empirical analysis of subjects' modes of inquiry in Wason's 2–4–6 task', *Quarterly Journal of Experimental Psychology* 38A: 5–33.

Tweney, R.D. (1985) 'Faraday's discovery of induction: a cognitive approach', in D. Gooding and F. James (eds) *Faraday Rediscovered*, London: Macmillan, pp. 159–209.

Wason, P.C. (1965) 'The contexts of plausible denial', *Journal of Verbal Learning and Verbal Behavior* 4: 7–11.

—— (1966) 'Reasoning', in B. Foss (ed.) *New Horizons in Psychology*, Harmondsworth: Penguin.

Chapter 3

Rationality and reality

R.J. Stevenson

The concept of rationality assumes that people can engage in abstract deductive arguments and derive valid conclusions from a set of premises, as the following examples show:

All authors are human,
All humans are mortal,
Therefore, all authors are mortal.

If there is a seminar,
then I'll stay at work till six.
There is a seminar.
Therefore, I stay at work till six.

Inferences are said to be valid as a consequence of their form and irrespective of their content. The examples above conform to the formal rules of the syllogism (the first example) and propositional reasoning (the second example). In the case of the syllogism, the inference depends on the following form:

All A are B.
All B are C.
Therefore, all A are B.

In the case of the propositional example, the inference (known as modus ponens) depends on a form of the following kind:

If p then q.
p.
Therefore, q.

Since content is irrelevant, the following conclusions are also valid:

All socialists are idealists.
All idealists are rational.
Therefore, all socialists are rational.

If the moon is made of cheese,
then it will soon be eaten.
The moon is made of cheese.
Therefore, the moon will soon be eaten.

In these cases, no matter how much the truth of the premises and the resulting conclusions might be disputed, the inferences are logically impeccable. What this means is that if people are to be rational, then they must be able to reason on the basis of the form of the argument alone, without regard to the content of the propositions. The problem is that people do not seem to be very good at this: they frequently diverge from the dictates of logic in ways that suggest that they are seduced by the content rather than the form of the argument. This seems to be due to two things. First, people are loathe to accept a valid conclusion if the conclusion is undesirable, as in this example adapted from Lefford (1946):

War times are prosperous times.
Prosperity is highly desirable.
Therefore, wars are much to be desired.

Second, people are loathe to accept a valid conclusion if the conclusion is unbelievable (at the time of evaluating it), as in this example from Oakhill *et al.* (1989):

Some of the communists are golfers.
All of the golfers are capitalists.
Therefore, some of the communists are capitalists.

These and other kinds of 'errors' in reasoning have led some to conclude that people are irrational (e.g. Morgan and Morton, 1944; Chapman and Chapman, 1959). Others have maintained that people are rational and that the problem lies somewhere else, in the way that the problem is interpreted (e.g. Braine, 1978; Fillenbaum, 1978; Henle, 1962). Still others have suggested that there is a grain of rationality in the way that people reason but that this is offset by a variety of observable errors and biases (e.g. Evans, 1989; Kahneman *et al.*, 1982). The currently popular move seems to be a development of these latter two views: people have been attempting to provide a model of human reasoning that accounts for both logical and non-logical behaviour (e.g. Cheng and Holyoak, 1985; Cosmides, 1989; Johnson-Laird and Byrne, 1991).

There is, though, a problem with all of these views. This is that rationality is deemed to be the peak of intellectual achievements. Any departure from rationality – in the sense of purely logical thinking – is seen as error, or bias, more generally as somehow wrong. These 'errors' may be taken as evidence for irrationality, as problems to be explained away, or as masking truly intelligent behaviour. What I wish to argue is that many of these 'errors', in particular the ones arising from the content rather than the form of the problem, indicate an aspect of our thinking which is intimately bound up with rationality and which, just as much as rationality, is the hallmark of human thinking. I refer to induction and learning.

I would like to discuss the relationship between deduction and induction by reference to other debates in psychology – the debate between feature similarity and causal theories in concept formation, and the debate about the possibility of distinguishing between semantics and pragmatics in language comprehension.

Theorizing about concept formation has traditionally focused on the importance of feature similarity. An instance is a member of a category if the features which define the instance and the features which define the concept are above a critical level of similarity. Similarly, objects in the world come to be grouped together to form a new concept when they are deemed to have certain features in common. Despite other differences in theoretical perspectives, this view of concepts has pervaded much of the thinking on the topic (e.g. Hull, 1920; Bruner *et al.*, 1956; Clark, 1973; Smith and Medin, 1981; Rosch, 1973; Smith *et al.*, 1988). A standard objection to this view has been to query the idea that feature similarity can be apparent in the absence of prior knowledge of the concept itself (e.g. Bolton, 1972; Macnamara, 1982; Nelson, 1974). Recently, this objection has been fleshed out into an alternative view of the nature of concepts (e.g. Medin, 1989; Murphy and Medin, 1985; Murphy, 1988, 1990). The alternative states that conceptual behaviour is knowledge-based and that knowledge in the form of causal understanding underlies most acts of categorization. That is, categorization is based on inferences derived from our general knowledge of the world. This debate between feature similarity views and knowledge-based views can be seen to be analogous to the rationality debate in reasoning. The feature similarity view assumes that information about categories can be gleaned from information about the objects themselves; it depends upon induction. The knowledge-based view assumes that categorization requires the use of inferences based on what is already known or acquired about the relevant domain. Prior knowledge provides the premises for inferences that are deductive.

The role of features in a theory-based account of concepts remains ambiguous. Some people claim that when there is no underlying knowledge of the relevant kind, as in the case of novices, for example, then people will classify things on the basis of perceptual similarity (e.g. Carey, 1985; Keil, 1989). Others hold a view that is rooted in the notion of 'psychological essentialism'. People act as if things have essences or underlying natures that make them the things that they are. This is part of the intension of a concept. But the aspect of intension that enables us to pick out instances of the concept may consist of a prototype or set of exemplars, together with a similarity metric for determining the similarity between instances in the world and the prototype or exemplar (e.g. Medin, 1989).

Medin gives the example of the belief, or theory, in our culture that membership of the concepts male and female is genetically determined. Yet, when we pick someone out as male or female we rely on characteristics such as hair length, height, facial hair, and clothing that represent a mixture of secondary sexual characteristics and cultural conventions. Although these characteristics are not as reliable as genetic evidence, they are far from arbitrary. Not only do they have statistical validity, they are also tied to our biological and cultural conceptions of male and female. This view of concepts suggests that during categorization people can and do indulge in both inductive and deductive thinking. Let me illustrate my point with an experimental example.

Langer and Abelson (1974) showed a film of a diagnostic interview to a group of psychoanalysts and a group of behaviour therapists. Half the members in each group were told that the woman being interviewed was a student who had asked for psychotherapy. The other half were told that the student had volunteered for a psychological research project. All the subjects were asked to judge whether or not the student was neurotic. The two subgroups of psychoanalysts gave different results depending on what they had been told: they were more likely to rate the student as neurotic if they were told that she had sought psychotherapy than if they were told that she was a volunteer in an experiment. By contrast, the two subgroups of behaviour therapists did not show this difference in ratings of neuroticism: they gave the same rating of neuroticism no matter what they were told.

Langer and Abelson argued that the psychoanalysts were 'biased' by what they had been told about the student and that the behaviour therapists were unbiased. However, Davis (1979) has argued that these results suggest that the psychoanalysts were sensitive to the prior probabilities, whereas the behaviour therapists were not. In terms of the present debate, the psychoanalysts seem to have assumed certain facts and the neuroticism of the student followed from those facts. The behaviour therapists were probably doing something very similar, but with a different theory. The main difference between the two groups seems to be that the psychoanalysts placed most weight on theory, while the behaviour therapists placed most weight on the appearance of the student. I suspect that in a real situation both kinds of therapists would make more measured decisions. Yet both strategies have their merits. In a world where there is an imperfect fit between theory and data, between category and instance, a reliance on one or the other strategy may well be dominant in a given situation. The problem is that conclusions derived from theory may be inappropriate for any given instance, in this case the student. It is necessary both to modify theory in the light of new information, an inductive process, and to be able to make and test predictions about new situations, which is a deductive process.

The example highlights the nature of much of our everyday reasoning: valid conclusions may not be true of the world we inhabit and so they need to be checked against reality. To take an example from Johnson-Laird and Byrne (1991), from the premises:

Alicia has a bacterial infection.
If a patient has a bacterial infection, then the preferred treatment for the patient is penicillin.

one can validly infer:

Therefore, the preferred treatment for Alicia is penicillin.

But if Alicia is allergic to penicillin then this inference, though logically impeccable, is clearly inappropriate and so should be withdrawn. Logic must be tempered by the constraints of reality.

The major argument that I wish to make is that human intelligence, as opposed to pure rationality, depends upon the ability to tailor the demands of logic to the needs of the real world. The argument has two parts. First, people are inherently rational. We cannot help deriving valid inferences from premises that are already known or acquired. I present an argument below to support this view. Second, in order to make our way in the practical world, we cannot avoid discarding many of these inferences, in favour of others that are inductive in nature. The result of this is that deduction and induction are inextricably linked and cannot be separated in any simple way. I will illustrate this point by referring to the second debate that I mentioned above: that concerning semantics and pragmatics in language comprehension and by discussing the competence/performance distinction. After that I will turn to cognitive development. If human intelligence is characterized as the integration of inductive and deductive processes, then cognitive development must be seen from this perspective. I will also consider 'pure' deduction, as it is used by logicians and mathematicians, for example, and by psychologists who wish to study it. If human intelligence is characterized by the integration of induction and deduction, what is it that enables people to detach themselves from the world and deduce conclusions in a content-free manner? Finally, I will examine the implications of my views for some current ideas about reasoning.

THE PRIMACY OF DEDUCTIVE THINKING

It is rare for people to base their thinking on appearances alone without the use of premises from which to derive a conclusion. Much of the work on acquiring expertise supports this contention. Even in novices, once some causal knowledge is acquired, the use of this knowledge to form premises in an argument is hard to prevent. This is evident in the studies by Lesgold and his colleagues (e.g. Lesgold, 1988; Lesgold *et al.*, 1988) on expert and novice radiographers. The expertise of radiologists lies mainly in their ability to perceive complicated patterns in very noisy displays, so their need to acquire information about the real world cannot be in doubt. They must diagnose on the basis of what they see. Yet the work of Lesgold and his colleagues suggests that even the novices prefer to use prior knowledge to infer a conclusion about a patient.

Lesgold *et al.* presented X-ray pictures to experts and novices. The experts were senior hospital staff who had had at least ten years' post-residency experience and in general had dealt with in the region of 500,000 X-ray pictures each. The novices had completed their medical training and an internship in a hospital and generally had had experience of perhaps 10,000 X-ray pictures. (It might be better to call them *intermediate experts*.) Lesgold *et al.* investigated a number of aspects of the way that the radiographers reached a diagnosis. I wish to describe their ability to incorporate new evidence from laboratory tests into diagnoses that had already been made.

One of the films that was presented to the radiographers showed the chest of a healthy person who had the lobe of a lung removed 20 years previously. This resulted in the heart appearing to be wider than usual, since it had shifted round when it occupied some of the resulting space. Many novices and some of the experts mistook that appearance for an enlarged heart, which is a sign of congestive heart failure, a severe condition. These radiologists were therefore told that the patient had been found to be healthy in a recent physical examination and had undergone surgery a number of years before. They were then told to re-examine the X-ray. However, this new information failed to alter the diagnoses of the novices: they still insisted that the patient was close to death. In other words, the novices' initial conclusions, derived from prior knowledge, were not modified by subsequent information about the actual state of the patient. The novices failed to withdraw their inferences. It seems that they could not help making deductions, but that they failed to tailor them to the state of the world.

The experts, on the other hand, quickly solved the case when presented with the new evidence. They were able, in other words, to modify their inferences in the light of new information about the world. This brings me to the second part of my argument: that the constraints of reality force us to discard many of our deductive inferences in favour of inductive ones.

THE IMPORTANCE OF INDUCTION

I have already made it clear that intelligent behaviour *requires* the ability to withdraw valid inferences, and to use inductive inferences. Consider the case of language comprehension. In the following example the pronoun 'she' is linguistically ambiguous:

> Jane was late for her appointment with Sue, and she hurried to get a taxi.

Linguistic rules (syntactic and semantic) can only state that, in this sentence, neither Jane nor Sue can be ruled out as potential antecedents of the pronoun. The pronoun is in a separate clause from the one containing the two potential antecedents. This means that on syntactic grounds both potential antecedents are available. Similarly, a semantic analysis of the sentence will not help either. For example, suppose that a discourse model of the event described in the first clause has been constructed and that the second clause is being integrated into the discourse model. Then, it does not matter whether the pronoun in the second clause is interpreted as Jane or as Sue. Either interpretation would be true in the discourse model constructed so far. In other words, both interpretations follow validly from the premise specified by the first clause.

However, there is a sense in which the sentence is not truly ambiguous. This is because we can make inferences based on general knowledge about the likely consequences of someone being late for an appointment to infer that 'she', in fact, refers to Jane. Of course, we could interpret the pronoun as referring to Sue, although the resulting interpretation would describe a much less likely event. Yet, the text could continue in a way that cancelled the most likely interpretation and showed that the unlikely one or indeed some other interpretation was intended. So the notion of cancellability, the need to withdraw an inference, is crucial for comprehension. Typically though, the kinds of inferences needed to resolve a pronoun, as in the example above, are thought of as inductive inferences: they are not deductively closed, since many different inferences are possible.

The use of inferences derived from conceptual knowledge is also prevalent in texts. If I read 'Rover is a dog', then I can validly infer that Rover has four legs:

> Dogs have four legs.
> Rover is a dog.
> Therefore, Rover has four legs.

However, the inference is cancellable, just as the one required for pronoun identification was. In the case of Rover, he might have been run over and lost all or some of his legs. Indeed, most textual inferences are based on either arbitrary assumptions, as in the pronoun example, or default assumptions, as in the Rover example, although the two kinds of inference have been treated rather differently. While the pronoun cases are typically thought of as due to pragmatic, that is inductive, inferences, class-inclusion cases, based on conceptual knowledge, have been dealt with by non-monotonic logics, logics which allow a deductive conclusion to be cancelled. It may be that they are all best thought of as inductive inferences rather than deductive ones that are cancellable. However, I will not debate that issue here, except to note that the distinction between induction and deduction is not clear cut, and that the problem of distinguishing between the two arises when the premises have to be supplied by the reader (or categorizer) and so are not explicitly stated.

This brief discussion of textual inferences brings me to the debate concerning the distinction between semantics and pragmatics. In general, logic is equated with semantics while induction is equated with pragmatics. It is instructive, therefore, to examine the semantics/pragmatics distinction in more detail.

In his account of conversation and communication, Grice (1975) made a clear distinction between semantics and pragmatics. He distinguished between what is said: the intended sense and reference of a sentence, and what is tacitly implicated. He argued that what is said, the literal or linguistic meaning, is largely determined by linguistic rule – by semantics – while what is conversationally implicated, what speech act or non-linguistic meaning was intended, is largely determined by conversational maxims – by pragmatics. Semantics, therefore, is concerned with those aspects of meaning that contribute to the truth conditions of sentences and with specifying the entailments of sentences. The truth conditions determine the set of situations of which the sentence could be a correct description. The specification of entailments follows from the truth conditions: a sentence A entails a sentence B if the truth of B follows logically from the truth of A. For example:

John killed Mary.

entails:

Mary died.

By contrast, what is conversationally implicated is not logically entailed by what is said. For example, in an appropriate context, the utterance:

It's hot in here.

may conversationally implicate that the speaker is making a request to have the window opened, but it clearly does not entail it. Implicatures, therefore, are inductive rather than deductive. This distinction, then, mirrors the distinction between deduction and induction in work on thinking, and is prevalent in much current thinking about meaning (e.g.

Gazdar, 1979). Yet not everyone agrees that the distinction is so clear cut. Logic (or entailments) alone will never be sufficient to guarantee successful communication; inductive implicatures are also necessary. Again, this is similar to the ideas expressed above concerning intelligence: deductive inferences alone will not guarantee intelligent behaviour; inductive inferences based on a knowledge of the world are also needed to withdraw or cancel valid but inappropriate conclusions.

However, the work on pragmatics goes further than saying that inductions (implicatures) invariably accompany deductions (entailments). Many people argue that inductions also contribute to the truth conditions of a sentence. For instance, Sperber and Wilson (1986) argue that the distinction between saying and implicating is not as clear cut as Grice suggested and that the hearer uses Gricean implicatures to work out intended literal meanings as well as to determine the non-literal meanings of figurative expressions. Sperber and Wilson point out that there are two aspects to the literal or linguistic meaning of a sentence. One is the truth conditions of a sentence that specify the circumstances in which it would be true. This yields a range of possible situations of which the sentence would be a true description. However, knowing the total set of situations that could be described by a sentence does not allow successful communication. For that, the second aspect of the linguistic meaning is required. This is the determination of the particular situation that the speaker intended to refer to. Sperber and Wilson argue that this second aspect is grasped through the use of implicatures, that is, it is determined pragmatically rather than semantically. This view is also espoused by Clark and his colleagues in discussions of the role of mutual knowledge in conversations (e.g. Clark and Marshall, 1981), and by Johnson-Laird (1983; Johnson-Laird and Byrne, 1991) in his use of a mental model to represent a unique interpretation of a sentence out of all interpretations of it that are possible.

Since many of our deductions are based on linguistic input, the pervasive use of inductive implicatures supports the proposal made above that intelligence depends on the use of induction in conjunction with deduction. However, this work can also be seen to support my first claim that deduction is primary. When discussing successful communication, or any joint activity, most people agree that it would not be possible without the assumption that the participants are rational (e.g. Clark and Marshall, 1981; Grice, 1975). This assumption of rationality is necessary to ensure that each participant makes the appropriate set of assumptions about the other's intentions. What then of rationality as the hallmark of human endeavours? It is one contribution to that hallmark certainly, but it is not the only contribution. There is the contribution of induction, too, of being sensitive to the constraints of reality. Nor are deduction and induction clearly dissociable in practical reasoning, which brings me to a discussion of the competence/performance distinction.

COMPETENCE AND PERFORMANCE

Chomsky was the first to make an explicit distinction between competence and performance when he distinguished between tacit knowledge of the abstract rules of a language (competence) and how language is used by people in communication (performance). However, even though such a distinction may be possible in the abstract, the discussion of communication above suggests that it may not be possible in practice, at least as far as semantics and pragmatics are concerned. The two are closely intertwined. Applying the distinction to logic raises similar issues.

Some people have proposed that there is a 'mental logic' but that it reflects competence not performance (e.g. Flavell and Wohlwill, 1969; Henle, 1962; Macnamara, 1986). According to this view, errors in reasoning are due to performance factors, such as those involved in interpreting the problem, and do not undermine a competence theory of logic. When the competence/performance distinction is used in discussions of deduction, it raises the question of how deductive ability is investigated. To return to the example of language, the study of linguistic competence makes use of linguistic intuitions concerning grammaticality to discern the nature of people's knowledge of language. Linguistic theory, then, accounts for the knowledge people have that enables them to have such intuitions. By contrast, the study of performance considers the ease of remembering or comprehending sentences, that is, it considers language use. Psychological theory thus accounts for the processes and representations that people use when using language. However, these two different approaches are beginning to converge in theories of linguistic processing that attempt to show how linguistic knowledge might interact with non-linguistic knowledge in performance.

Thus, if we want to take seriously the distinction between competence and performance in deduction, then it might help to think about the distinction in the same way as has been done in work on language. That is, if we want to find out about peoples' knowledge of deduction, we need to find out which arguments they regard as valid and which they regard as invalid. This is the deductive equivalent of linguistic intuitions. Psychological studies of reasoning that measure the time taken to evaluate a conclusion in relation to its premises will indicate the nature of the psychological processes that contribute to human reasoning, but they will have little to say about our underlying knowledge of deductive logic. Inferring competence from reasoning performance is equivalent to taking the utterances of young children and using them to infer children's underlying linguistic competence and as I have argued elsewhere (e.g. Stevenson, 1988, 1991) such inferences are not warranted. Not surprisingly, therefore, psychological studies of reasoning converge on the view that logical knowledge contributes to performance (e.g. Evans, 1982).

However, just as linguistic processing never reflects a pure use of linguistic knowledge, so logical thinking never reflects a pure use of logical knowledge. Inductive inferences are very pervasive.

If deductive and inductive processes are so closely linked in performance, how can we account for their development? In other words, how can we account for the use of logic that is heavily overlaid by induction? It is to this developmental issue that I will now turn.

DEVELOPMENTAL ISSUES

Piaget assumed that cognitive development resulted in deductive thinking that is untrammelled by the constraints of the world. For Piaget, development involved children gradually overcoming various mental barriers to systematic logical thinking. One of these barriers seemed to be that, prior to the formal operational stage, children are tied to the concrete world and so are unable to indulge in abstract thought. Piaget viewed thinking as the use of internalized operations, so it was the development of these operations that he sought to explain (e.g. Piaget, 1962).

Thus, at the concrete operational stage, children are able to carry out the internal operations of inversion and reciprocity, but only on concrete objects. Children at this stage can grasp the concept of class inclusion, through the use of inversion, and solve class-inclusion problems when presented with real objects. This is the precursor of syllogistic inference. They can also solve seriation problems, through the use of reciprocity, when presented with actual objects, such as sticks, to sort into a serial order. This is the precursor of transitive inference. However, according to Piaget, the ability to use these operations is severely limited because they can only be used on concrete objects. Thus, the negation operation can be used in situations that involve class inclusion and the reciprocity operation can be used in those situations that involve seriation. But at this stage children cannot act independently of the outside world. They cannot detach these internal actions from objects in the world. In terms of Piaget's notion of maintaining an equilibrium between accommodation and assimilation, it is as if the children are indulging in too much assimilation: new experiences – new situations in the world – are acted upon by pre-existing structures – the internal actions of negation and reciprocity.

This lack of equilibrium between accommodation and assimilation is, according to Piaget, what forces the children into the next and final stage of development, the formal operational stage. At this stage of development, children are able to detach themselves from the environment and carry out internal operations on symbolic representations. This means that they can now combine the operations of inversion and reciprocity, which was not possible before. They are capable of reasoning about hypotheses and propositions and not only about objects in the world.

According to Piaget, they can therefore make propositional inferences, which require the combination of inversion and reciprocity, as well as abstract syllogistic and transitive inferences.

Of course, Piaget said much more than this, and there is much that can be said about all of his pronouncements, but I wish to focus on his views of the relationship between logic and the world. These views seem to suggest that Piaget saw the development of logic as being intimately connected with the world. He claimed that it was through interaction with the world that logical thinking is constructed. Yet he also claimed that at the final stage of development logic was divorced from the world.

How, then, do these views fit with the discussions above of the relationship between logic and reality, between deduction and induction? On the face of it, not very well. For Piaget, the peak of cognitive development was the attainment of abstract logical thought. This contrasts with my claims above, that in normal everyday reasoning logic is inextricably tied to reality. Indeed, I suggested that to pursue logic at the expense of reality would result in counterproductive behaviour. Yet, it may be that this contrast with Piaget's views is more apparent than real. This is because Piaget's own tests of formal operational thought were not divorced from the world. Instead, they were tests of hypothesis testing, that is, they were clear examples of the way that logic and reality are combined.

To illustrate this, I will discuss one of the tasks that Piaget conducted to test his views of formal operational thought: the pendulum problem. In this task, a child was given all the necessary experimental materials and asked to find out what causes variations in the frequency of oscillation of a pendulum. Piaget argued that children in the formal operational stage are able to think about this problem as if it were a problem in propositional logic. That is, when children investigate whether or not a particular factor, such as the weight of the suspended object, affects the frequency of oscillation they act as if they were reasoning with propositions of the form:

if p then q.

It is as if the child has formulated a rule such as:

If the weight is changed,
then the frequency of oscillation changes.

and then tests whether or not this rule is true. Piaget described four mental operations which he claimed children use when evaluating this rule (see, for example, Piaget and Inhelder, 1969). However, the point I wish to make is that Piaget did not in fact test whether the children could engage in abstract thought. What he did test was the children's ability to form a hypothesis about the world and their ability to test whether the hypothesis was true or false. Children at the formal operational stage of development were very good at these kinds of tasks. But their ability to engage in abstract thought was never tested.

Indeed, when an abstract version of Piaget's tasks is given to adults, performance turns out to be very poor. This was observed by Wason when he put Piaget's views to the test in his selection task (e.g. Wason, 1968), which is a very close analogue of the kind of task that Piaget gave to children when investigating the achievements of the formal operational stage of development. Wason presented his subjects with four cards, two showing letters (e.g. E, K) and two showing numbers, (e.g. 4, 7). The subjects were told that each card had a number on one side and a letter on the other. The task was to turn over the minimum number of cards that they thought were necessary to find out whether the following rule was true or false:

If a card has a vowel on one side,
then it has an even number on the other.

which is formally equivalent to:

if p then q.

Subjects should select the card with E on it to check, by modus ponens, that it has an even number on the back; and they should select the card with 7 on it to check, by modus tollens, that it does not have a vowel on the back. These selections would parallel the performance of Piaget's formal operational children when they were testing their hypotheses about the pendulum. However, what Wason found was that very few people got the right answer. Instead, the preferred solution was to select the card with E on it and the card with 4 on it. Choosing the card with 4 on it is equivalent to choosing q in the rule 'if p then q', and to check that 'p' is present. That is, it is equivalent to committing the fallacy of affirming the consequent. Wason concluded therefore that contrary to the predictions of Piaget's theory, adults do not seem to use the rules of logic when evaluating a rule. In particular, they fail to use modus tollens since they fail to select the 'not q' card in the selection task.

The picture that emerges, therefore, is that the young adolescents in Piaget's experiments showed a clear ability to formulate and test hypotheses about the world, but intelligent adults in Wason's experiments showed very little ability to test hypotheses in an abstract task. This suggests, contrary to Piaget, that the endpoint of development is the integration of logic with the constraints of reality, not its dissociation from reality. The ability to separate logic from thinking about everyday situations seems to be very difficult.

Subsequent work on Wason's selection task has, of course, supported the idea that reasoning is facilitated when the task is concrete and familiar (e.g. Griggs and Cox, 1982; Johnson-Laird *et al.*, 1972; Wason and

Shapiro, 1971), although the precise nature of the facilitating effect has been hard to pin down. It appears, though, that by making the task more familiar to the subjects, it has been changed from Wason's original one involving propositional logic to one involving deontic logic (Manktelow and Over, 1990a).

As Manktelow and Over (1990a, 1990b, 1991) point out, the original Wason task was a clear example of an exercise in propositional logic. The subject's task was to determine whether or not the conditional rule was a true description of the state of affairs depicted by the cards. However, many of the tasks using familiar materials involve concepts of obligation, such as the following postal regulation used by Johnson-Laird *et al.* (1972):

> If a letter is sealed,
> then it has a 5d stamp on it.

Manktelow and Over argue that the logic of obligations does not conform to the standard propositional logic. It conforms instead to *deontic logic*, which is specifically concerned with permissions and obligations. An interesting feature about deontic logic is that it is not possible to determine whether or not such a rule is true or false simply by inspecting the state of affairs in the environment. Whether or not a rule of permission, such as 'If you tidy your room then you may go to the cinema', is true or false depends not just on the state of the world but on the goals and intentions of the speaker and the listener. So subjects in the tasks using familiar materials are not simply trying to see whether the rule is true or false. Rather they are trying to see whether or not people have violated the rule, and this is very different from Wason's original task.

Manktelow and Over go on to discuss the semantics of simple deontic statements, such as 'You ought to wear rubber gloves'; that is, how we might try to determine their truth or falsity. They suggest that a key part of the evaluation involves an assessment of the relative utilities of doing or not doing the action. That is, it involves an analysis of the costs and benefits associated with the alternative courses of action. To take their example, suppose you are working in a hospital and want to know whether it is true that you ought to wear rubber gloves. To reach a decision you are likely to imagine a situation in which you wear the gloves and compare it to one in which you do not. While the costs of wearing or not wearing the gloves may differ little from each other, it may be clear that wearing them may have much higher benefits than would not wearing them: the former action would protect you from a serious disease but the latter would not. This would mean that the former action had a much higher utility than the latter, so you could conclude that it was true that you ought to wear the gloves. When the deontic statement is a *conditional* one (one having an 'if-then' form), then the context is set by the information in the antecedent; for example: 'If you work in a hospital you ought to wear rubber gloves'.

What this discussion highlights is that evaluating a deontic statement is not simply an exercise in pure deduction; it requires in addition the use of pragmatic, that is inductive, inferences about the intentions of the speaker, the context of the utterance, and the relative utilities of following or not following the injunction. In other words, it is a good example of the way that deduction and induction are interlinked. Moreover, the example emerges in an everyday situation where people are good at hypothesis testing, despite the complexity of the judgements that have to be made. The ability to evaluate deontic statements, therefore, stands in stark contrast to people's lack of ability to evaluate statements from propositional logic – at least in abstract tasks.

Where does this leave Piaget's theory of cognitive development? First of all, his view that cognitive *development* is intimately tied up with interacting with, that is learning about, the world is consistent with the ideas presented here. In order to use logic intelligently so that inappropriate and unrealistic conclusions can be cancelled it is obviously necessary to learn about the world and to discover the real world constraints on logical inferences. Piaget's ideas about interacting with the environment seem ideal for that purpose. What this suggests though is that the interaction with the environment does not allow the construction of abstract logic, as supposed by Piaget. What it does allow is the acquisition of knowledge about the world. The problem for development is less likely to be how children learn to think, but how they learn about the world, that is, what they learn to think about.

All the work suggesting that young children can solve Piagetian tasks earlier than predicted by Piaget's theory is consistent with this view (e.g. Brown, 1990; Donaldson, 1978; Mills and Funnell, 1983). In all of these cases, the early ability is observed in situations with which the child is familiar, that is, in situations where the child has learned what the constraints of reality might be. These observations are also compatible with an alternative view of cognitive development to Piaget's, one that sees the change from child to adult as the same as the change from novice to expert (e.g. Chi, 1978; Keil, 1989).

If we view infants as universal novices and cognitive development as the acquisition of expertise, what are the implications for development? There seem to be two, both of which are apparent in the literature on cognitive development, particularly from the various adherents to the information-processing view of development. The first implication is that during development, routine procedures become automatized and so free up working memory for new learning (e.g. Chi, 1978). The second is that development results in the acquisition of more and more knowledge about the world and its integration into existing knowledge structures. This enables memory to be enhanced through 'chunking', and new concepts to be formed through the reorganization of existing knowledge in the light of new knowledge.

It is this second aspect of development that I am primarily concerned with in this chapter, although both knowledge acquisition and the automatization of skills are necessary components of development. It seems, though, that if human rationality is to be exploited to its full potential, it needs to be enriched by an understanding of the world and of the culture that we inhabit. This, I suggest, is one of the major achievements of development.

The notion of the integration of deductive and inductive processes can also be used to reassess and reinterpet Piaget's emphasis on the developmental importance of maintaining an equilibrium between accommodation on the one hand and assimilation on the other. For Piaget, this was a biological analogy. As far as the arguments presented here are concerned, it can be seen as a balance between induction (or data) on the one hand and deduction (or theory) on the other. Sticking to a set of deductive principles and premises regardless of the environment is to err in the direction of assimilation. It is to try to make the world fit the dictates of logic. Abandoning premises based on prior knowledge and sticking only to what can be observed in the world is to err in the direction of accommodation. It is to try to make logic fit the vagaries of the world.

Of course, just as Piaget argued, these two extremes are unlikely – all adaptation is a combination of the two. Nevertheless, there are likely to be times when one predominates over the other. Intermediate novices, for example, seem to go through a period when they adhere quite rigidly to prior knowledge and ignore new information, as was discussed above in the case of the radiologists. The experts however seem to have acquired an understanding which allows them to be more flexible in their use of pre-established routines and categories and which enables them to recognize and deal with novel problems. A similar progression to expertise has also been suggested in the literature on medical diagnosis (e.g. Patel and Groen, 1986) and clinical diagnosis by psychologists (e.g. Murphy and Wright, 1984). It is possible that the weight of new evidence conflicting with a current point of view is what forces developmental change: there is a reorganization of the knowledge underlying the domain – a push towards an equilibrium, as Piaget suggested. However, the literature on expertise also suggests that such shifts in understanding underlie all learning, not just learning in childhood.

THE ABILITY TO THINK ABSTRACTLY

The idea that development is geared towards an integration of deductive and inductive processes runs counter to the view that pure deduction is the peak of human achievement. This latter view certainly seemed to be held by Piaget in his claims for formal operational thinking. The notion that integration is the key factor suggests on the other hand that the ability to detach oneself from the world and think abstractly is an unnatural activity. Indeed, in the terminology of Piaget himself, it is to err in the direction of assimilation. I do not wish to hold such a counterintuitive view of human rationality. Instead, I suggest that the ability to think in the abstract is a higher-order skill that requires the ability to make explicit the implicit processes of deduction that are routinely used in everyday reasoning. Once explicit, they can then be used in situations that require such abstract ability, in mathematical thinking, for example, and the development of new logics, and in the study of the reasoning process itself. However, unless a situation requires that general inferential processes be abstracted from their use in specific domains, such abstract thought may well be unnecessary and, indeed, in everyday reasoning may even be counterproductive.

SOME IMPLICATIONS FOR THEORIES OF DEDUCTION

I will now consider some implications of the arguments presented here for theories of deduction. In essence I have been arguing that a basic human skill is the ability to integrate logic and reality: to make deductive inferences that can be modified rapidly by information about the world that is obtained through induction, and to make inductive inferences that can act as premises to derive a deductively valid conclusion. This ability can be seen in concept formation and categorization, in the use of expertise, and in language comprehension. In short, they characterize people's ability to act in the world, and to make sense of the world, the people in it, and what they say. They are efficient and (probably) implicit. To go beyond these abilities to an ability to think in the abstract requires that these implicit processes be made explicit, a requirement that the evidence on reasoning suggests is not achieved very easily. How, then, does this fit with other views of reasoning?

I will consider two aspects of work on reasoning that seem relevant to this argument. One is the proposal that reasoning involves two types of processes – heuristic and analytic (Evans, 1984, 1989). The other is the proposal that deduction and non-monotonic reasoning can be combined in the use of mental models (Johnson-Laird and Byrne, 1991).

Evans (1989) has proposed a distinction that is compatible with the views presented here. He suggests that heuristic processes are implicit processes. They are pre-conscious in that they determine what we attend to. They primarily involve recognition processes that are responsible for the rapid retrieval of information from long-term-memory (see, for example, Ericsson and Simon, 1980). According to Evans, these processes are responsible for the errors in original versions of the Wason selection task. He also seems to suggest that they are due to the pragmatic inferences used in language comprehension, that is, they seem to correspond to the inductive processes discussed in this chapter. By contrast, analytic processes are of two kinds. First, there are implicit analytic processes. These are the processes by which logical deductive inferences are drawn and they correspond to what Ericsson and Simon call *automatic* processes, except that they may never have been explicit. These implicit analytic processes seem to correspond to the deductive processes discussed in this chapter. Second, there are explicit analytic processes. These are evident when subjects are asked to *explain* and justify the inferences they have made in Wason's selection task. It seems that this instruction forces subjects to analyse the logical relationships explicitly, but they fail to do this in the absence of instructions. Indeed, they fail to do so when they are actively engaged in the selection task. These explicit analytic processes seem to correspond to the abstract logical processes discussed in this chapter, the ones that require implicit processes to be made explicit before they can be used in the abstract. Taken together, therefore, the views presented here support the ideas of Evans.

Johnson-Laird and Byrne (1991) have suggested that conclusions are cancelled in non-monotonic reasoning in very much the same way as valid conclusions are reached. They argue that the process depends on the use of mental models. According to the theory of mental models the reasoner constructs an internal model of the situation described by the premises, tries to formulate a potential conclusion from that model, and then tests the validity of the conclusion by considering whether there are alternative models of the premises which are compatible with this or with another conclusion. The construction of the initial model depends on both deductive and inductive inferences, since it is the product of language comprehension. Specifically, the construction of a model requires that a unique interpretation be given to the sentence out of all the possible interpretations that could be true of the sentence. Since, as discussed above, this depends on pragmatic, inductive processes, the model could turn out to be the wrong one and so have to be changed.

The procedures that manipulate mental models allow both validity to be established and models constructed from inappropriate inferences to be changed. For this to be possible, the model treats each assertion as a potential conclusion and tests for its validity. If the assertion is true in the current model, then a search is made for an alternative model that would make it false. If none is found, then the conclusion is valid. If the assertion turns out to be false then a search is made for an alternative model that would make the assertion true. Thus inferences based on default values, such as the inference that a particular dog has four legs, are overruled if they turn out to be false according to later assertions in the discourse.

These ideas are also compatible with those in this chapter. They also suggest that cancelling an unwarranted or unrealistic inference and deriving a valid inference are equally difficult, since both tasks depend on the ability to evaluate an assertion in the current mental model of the discourse. Work on reasoning suggests that there are many occasions when deriving a valid inference is very difficult (e.g. Johnson-Laird and Bara, 1984), and that this is largely due to constraints of working memory: when more than one model is true of the premises, capacity may be exceeded. It remains to be shown that this is also the case when unwarranted assumptions have to be cancelled.

CONCLUSIONS

In this chapter, I have ranged rather widely over a number of issues rather than stuck fastidiously to one. I have drawn on work on concepts, work in problem solving and studies of expertise, work on language comprehension, and work on cognitive development. But the main point that I wished to make has, I hope, emerged in all the issues raised; namely, that logic alone is not a guarantee of successful thinking about the world or of the ability to act appropriately in the world. For such success, logic must be tempered by the constraints of reality and valid conclusions cancelled when they turn out to be unrealistic. It turns out that this kind of thinking, based on both deduction and induction, is what people seem to be particularly good at and may well lie behind the content errors observed in laboratory tests of deduction. What people do not seem to be very good at is the ability to dissociate logic from beliefs about the world and derive logical conclusions from abstract premises. But it would be strange if people were good at the latter and poor at the former. Rationality divorced from reality seems strange indeed, unless it is in the service of an abstract problem.

REFERENCES

Bolton, N. (1972) *The Psychology of Thinking*, London: Methuen.

Braine, M.D.S. (1978) 'On the relation between the natural logic of reasoning and standard logic', *Psychological Review* 85: 1–21.

Brown, A.L. (1990) 'Domain-specific principles affect learning and transfer in children', *Cognitive Science* 14: 107–33.

Bruner, J.S., Goodnow, J.J., and Austin, G.A. (1956) *A Study of Thinking*, New York: Wiley.

Carey, S. (1985) *Conceptual Change in Childhood*, Cambridge, MA: MIT Press.

Chapman, L.J. and Chapman, J.P. (1959) 'Atmosphere effect reexamined', *Journal of Experimental Psychology* 58: 220–6.

Cheng, P.W. and Holyoak, K.J. (1985) 'Pragmatic reasoning schemas', *Cognitive Psychology* 17: 391–416.

Chi, M.T.H. (1978) 'Knowledge structures and memory development', in *Children's Thinking: What Develops?*, Hillsdale, NJ: Erlbaum.

Clark, E.V. (1973) 'Whats in a word? On the child's acquisition of semantics in his first language', in T.E. Moore (ed.) *Cognitive Development and the Acquisition of Language*, New York: Academic Press.

Clark, H.H. and Marshall, C.R. (1981) 'Definite reference and mutual knowledge', in A. Joshi, B. Webber, and I. Sag (eds) *Elements of Discourse Understanding*, Cambridge: Cambridge University Press.

Cosmides, L. (1989) 'The logic of social exchange: has natural selection shaped how humans reason?' *Cognition* 31: 187–276.

Davis, D.A. (1979) 'What's in a name? A Baysian rethinking of attributional biases in clinical judgement', *Journal of Consulting and Clinical Psychology* 47: 1109–14.

Donaldson, M. (1978) *Children's Minds*, London: Fontana.

Ericsson, K.A. and Simon, H.A. (1980) 'Verbal reports as data', *Psychological Review* 87: 215–51.

Evans, J. St B.T. (1982) *The Psychology of Deductive Reasoning* London: Routledge & Kegan Paul.

—— (1984) 'Heuristic and analytic processes in reasoning', *British Journal of Psychology* 75: 457–68.

—— (1989) *Bias in Human Reasoning: Causes and Consequences*, Hove and London: Erlbaum.

Fillenbaum, S. (1978) 'How to do some things with IF', in J.W. Cotton and R.L. Klatzky (eds) *Semantic Factors in Cognition*, Hillsdale, NJ: Erlbaum.

Flavell, J.H. and Wohlwill, J.F. (1969) 'Formal and functional aspects of cognitive development' in D. Elkind and J.H. Flavell (eds) *Studies in Cognitive Development*, New York: Oxford University Press, pp. 67–120.

Gazdar, G. (1979) *Pragmatics: Implicature, Presupposition and Logical Form*, New York, San Francisco, London: Academic Press.

Grice, H.P. (1975) 'Logic and conversation', in P. Cole and J. Morgan (eds) *Syntax and Semantics, vol. 3: Speech Acts*, New York: Seminar Press.

Griggs, R.A. and Cox, J.R. (1982) 'The elusive thematic-materials effects in Wason's selection task', *British Journal of Psychology* 73: 407–20.

Henle, M. (1962) 'On the relation between logic and thinking', *Psychological Review* 69: 366–78.

Hull, C.L. (1920) 'Quantitative aspects of the evolution of concepts', *Psychological Monographs* 28 (whole no. 123).

Johnson-Laird, P.N. (1983) *Mental Models*, Cambridge, MA: Harvard University Press.

Johnson-Laird, P.N. and Bara, B.G. (1984) 'Syllogistic inference', *Cognition* 16: 1–61.

Johnson-Laird, P.N. and Byrne, R.M.J. (1991) *Deduction*, Hove and London and Hillsdale NJ: Erlbaum.

Johnson-Laird, P.N., Legrenzi, P., and Legrenzi, M.S. (1972) 'Reasoning and a sense of reality', *British Journal of Psychology* 63: 395–400.

Kahneman, D., Slovic, P., and Tversky, A. (eds) (1982) Judgement under uncertainty: Heuristics and Biases, Cambridge: Cambridge University Press.

Keil, F.C. (1989) *Concepts, Kinds, and Cognitive Development*, Cambridge, MA: MIT Press.

Langer, E.J. and Abelson, R.P. (1974) 'A patient by any other name . . . : Clinician group differences in labelling bias', *Journal of Consulting and Clinical Psychology* 42: 4–9.

Lefford, A. (1946) 'The influence of emotional subject matter on logical reasoning', *Journal of General Psychology* 34: 127–51.

Lesgold, A.M. (1988) 'Problem solving', in R.J. Sternberg and E.E. Smith (eds) *The Psychology of Human Thought*, Cambridge and New York: Cambridge University Press.

Lesgold, A., Rubinson, H., Feltovich, P., Glaser, R., Klopfer, D., and Wang, Y.

(1988) 'Expertise in a complex skill: diagnosing X-ray pictures', in M.T.H. Chi, R. Glaser, and M.J. Farr (eds) *The Nature of Expertise*, Hillsdale, NJ, Hove, and London: Erlbaum.

Macnamara, J. (1982) *Names for Things: A Study in Human Learning*, Cambridge, MA and London: MIT Press.

—— (1986) *A Border Dispute: The Place of Logic in Psychology*, Bradford Books; Cambridge, MA: MIT Press.

Manktelow, K.I. and Over, D.E. (1990a) 'Deontic thought and the selection task', in K.J. Gilhooly, M.T.G. Keane, R.H. Logie, and G. Erdos (eds) *Lines of Thinking: Reflections on the Psychology of Thought*, vol. 1, Chichester: Wiley.

—— (1990b) *Inference and Understanding. A Philosophical Perspective*, London: Routledge.

—— (1991) 'Social roles and utilities in reasoning with deontic conditionals', *Cognition* 39: 85–105.

Medin, D.L. (1989) 'Concepts and conceptual structure', *American Psychologist* 4: 1469–81.

Mills, M. and Funnell, E. (1983) 'Experience and cognitive processing', in S. Meadows (ed.) *Developing Thinking*, London and New York: Methuen.

Morgan, J.J.B. and Morton, J.T. (1944) 'The distortion of syllogistic reasoning produced by personal convictions', *Journal of Social Psychology* 20: 39–59.

Murphy, G.L. (1988) 'Comprehending complex concepts', *Cognitive Science* 12: 529–62.

—— (1990) 'Noun phrase interpretation and conceptual combination', *Journal of Memory and Language* 29: 259–88.

Murphy, G.L. and Medin, D.L. (1985) 'The role of theories in conceptual coherence', *Psychological Review* 92: 289–316.

Murphy, G.L. and Wright, J.C. (1984) 'Changes in conceptual structure with expertise: differences between real world experts and novices'. *Journal of Experimental Psychology: Learning, Memory, and Cognition* 10: 144–55.

Nelson, K. (1974) 'Concept, word and sentence: interrelations in acquisition and development', *Psychological Review* 4: 13–30.

Oakhill, J., Johnson-Laird, P.N., and Garnham, A. (1989) 'Believability and syllogistic reasoning', *Cognition* 31: 117–40.

Patel, V.L. and Groen, G.J. (1986) 'Knowledge based solution strategies in medical reasoning', *Cognitive Science* 10: 91–116.

Piaget, J. (1962) 'The stages of the intellectual development of the child', *Bulletin of the Meninger Clinic* 26: 120–8.

Piaget, J. and Inhelder, B. (1969) 'Intellectual operations and their development', in P. Fraisse and J. Piaget (eds) *Experimental Psychology: Its Scope and Method*, London: Routledge & Kegan Paul.

Rosch, E. (1973) 'On the internal structure of perceptual and semantic categories', in T.E. Moore (ed.) *Cognitive Development and the Acquisition of Language*, New York: Academic Press.

Smith, E.E. and Medin, D.L. (1981) *Categories and Concepts*, Cambridge, MA: Harvard University Press.

Smith, E.E., Osherson, D.A., Rips, L.J., and Keane, M. (1988) 'Combining prototypes: a selective modification model', *Cognitive Science* 12: 485–527.

Sperber, D. and Wilson, D. (1986) *Relevance: Communication and Cognition*, Oxford: Blackwell.

Stevenson, R.J. (1988) *Models of Language Development*, Milton Keynes: Open University Press.

—— (1991) 'Maturation and learning: linguistic knowledge and performance', in

J. Weissenborn, H. Goodluck, and T. Roeper (eds) *Theoretical Studies in Language Acquisition*, Hillsdale, NJ: Erlbaum.

Wason, P.C. (1968) 'Reasoning about a rule', *Quarterly Journal of Experimental Psychology*, 20: 273–81.

Wason, P.C. and Shapiro, D. (1971) 'Natural and contrived experience in a reasoning problem', *Quarterly Journal of Experimental Psychology* 23: 63–71.

Chapter 4

Human rationality

N.E. Wetherick

Since the time of Aristotle, rationality has been regarded as the defining characteristic of the human species – man is 'the rational animal'. Aristotle's views on the subject may be found in his *De Anima* (On the Soul). For him, the 'soul' ('psyche' was his word) was essentially what distinguished living matter from dead. It made no more sense to think of soul and body as separate than to think of the form impressed on wax by a seal as separate from the wax. Plants possess a nutritive soul since they live and reproduce and die. Animals possess a sensitive soul since they have all that plants have and, in addition, sensation and (in all but the lowest species) locomotion. Minimally, animals possess the sense of touch (since touch is intimately involved in nutrition and reproduction) but higher animals have also vision, hearing, etc. Only the human, among animal species, possesses a capacity to calculate and to think, a rational soul.

Aristotle's views were in due course incorporated into Christian dogma, since his 'rational soul' (distinguishing man from the lower animals) could conveniently be equated with the humanity impressed on man by God on the fortieth day after conception or whenever. Christian dogma maintained Aristotle's view of the soul till the time of Descartes when all parties agreed to treat soul and body as separate, the former being the province of theology and the latter of natural science. Rationality was, however, still the mark of the human species. Everyone knew that human beings needed to be taught logic and that they made mistakes even after they had been taught. The important thing was that they could be taught and could recognize that their errors of logic were errors when it was pointed out to them.

It has always been accepted that rationality relies on propositions – statements about what is or ought to be the case – but, strictly, it is not irrational to believe a (possibly false) proposition unless logically it is incompatible with some other proposition that one also believes. Many years ago I knew a young man who deduced the principle of universal chastity from two premises: that every man is entitled to marry a virgin and that there are only about the same number of women as men in the world. From the point of view of rationality the argument is impeccable and the second premise is true. The young man might be regarded as irrational for having held the first premise, but to convince him of that it would have been necessary to convince him that the premise was incompatible with some other belief that he held even more strongly. I tried and failed, I sometimes wonder what became of him. One may be personally committed to the truth of a doubtful proposition (as he was) without being strictly irrational.

Disagreement on serious matters usually reduces to commitment to the truth of incompatible propositions. G.K. Chesterton was strongly opposed to abortion. In arguments on the subject he would frequently propose a test case. Consider a pregnancy in which both mother and father are affected by poverty, alcoholism, moral degradation, low mentality, etc. (naming several characteristics sometimes thought to justify abortion on social grounds). Would you recommend abortion in such a case? Usually Chesterton's interlocutor agreed that he would. Chesterton's triumphant response was: 'Then you would have murdered Beethoven!' For Chesterton, there was not the slightest doubt that a one-in-ten million chance that a child might grow up to be another Beethoven outweighed a one-in-ten (or fewer) chance that he would grow up to be a burden to himself and the community. Chesterton's belief was not irrational. Moral philosophers have laboured for two thousand years to find rational, knock-down arguments proving that some propositions of this kind are true and others false, but it cannot be done. At this level we all have to exercise our human prerogative by making a personal commitment to the truth of this or that proposition.

I shall not be concerned in this chapter with the word 'irrational' used as a term of abuse to describe opinions with which one strongly disagrees. In the last thirty or forty years experimental work in psychology has been directed to showing that human beings are irrational because they fail to give the answers to experimental problems that rationality is supposed to demand. I shall first of all try to show that human beings are inherently rational animals (despite the fact that subhuman animals are not inherently rational). I shall then try to account for the human being's propensity for 'error' in experimental situations, which I take to arise partly from the structure of the human intellect but more from the unrepresentativeness of the problems that subjects are asked to solve, which has frequently persuaded experimenters to draw conclusions about human rationality that are not warranted by the evidence. First of all, we must go back to Aristotle to see how the argument was presented originally.

ARISTOTLE'S VIEW OF RATIONALITY

The rationality of man consisted, in Aristotle's view, in man's ability to think about the world and his place in it in terms of scientific or other propositions and to recognize the fact that pairs of propositions having a term in common sometimes allow a conclusion to be drawn in the form of another proposition that follows logically from them as premises (see his *Prior Analytics*). He recognized four types of 'simple' proposition: type A (universal affirmative) – 'all s is p' (where s stands for subject and p for predicate); type I (particular affirmative) – 'some s is p'; type E (universal negative) – 'no s is p'; and type O (particular negative) – 'some s is not p'. 'Some' here means 'at least one, possibly all'; that is not the only sense in which the word 'some' is used but the other senses can be conveyed exactly using combinations of the four simple types. (Aristotle recognized that not all propositions are 'simple'. He regarded complex propositions as conjunctions of simple propositions but this is only part of the truth. Theories of quantification did not, however, appear until two thousand years after his death.) Aristotle's simple propositions require what is now called first-order predicate logic, which permits quantification over individuals ('all s's are . . .'; 'some s's are . . .'). Higher-order logics permit quantification over sets of individuals or over sets of sets. They are the stuff of modern pure mathematics and beyond the scope of this chapter but they continue to employ the same logical constants as Aristotle, i.e. 'some' ($\exists\ x$, 'there exists an x . . .'), 'all' ($\forall\ x$, 'for all x . . .') and 'not'.

If two simple propositions have a term in common (called the middle term, or m) then a valid syllogistic conclusion may follow. There are as we have seen four types of proposition (A, I, E, and O) and, consequently, sixteen possible pairings. The letters s and p now stand for the subject and predicate of a putative conclusion and m for the middle term (which will not appear in the conclusion). The m term may appear in the premises in four different positions (called the figures ('f') of the syllogism); as subject of both premises (f.3), as predicate of both (f.2), or as subject of one and predicate of the other (f.1 or f.4). Each premise links the m term with either s or p, as either subject or predicate of the premise. There are 64 possible pairs of premises and from each pair a valid conclusion may or may not follow.

Standard syllogistic logic (i.e. Aristotle's system as refined by the medieval logicians) recognizes 19 pairs of premises as having valid conclusions. It is taken for granted that all parties to a discourse will know what the topic of the discourse is and, consequently, what term will be the subject of any conclusion drawn; so only conclusions of the form s . . . p are recognized. In fact many pairs of premises permit two conclusions, one s . . . p and one p . . . s. The eight pairs of premises allowing an O conclusion of the form s . . . p, allow no p . . . s conclusion but there are another eight pairs that allow an O conclusion of the form p . . . s but no s . . . p conclusion. These last eight pairs are not counted as having a valid conclusion in standard logic because they have no s . . . p conclusion. In this chapter, however, we shall allow these pairs, making 27 valid syllogisms in all and shall assume the existence of members of the classes designated by the terms s, p, and m. It did not occur to Aristotle or to the medieval logicians that anyone would ever be faced with a pair of premises out of context and be asked what conclusion(s) could be drawn from them. They knew that in some cases two conclusions might be drawn but would have seen no point in the exercise. Syllogistic logic represented for them the structure of human knowledge. All teaching and all learning was done in syllogistic form. Logic was the first thing one learned at university and was subsequently taken for granted (as calculus is now taken for granted in the physical sciences). So highly regarded was it that when Dean Colet refounded St Paul's School in 1509, he specifically forbade the teaching of logic on the grounds that it was far too powerful an instrument to be put into the hands of schoolboys!

It is not difficult to see that some of the possible pairings of premise types will not yield valid conclusions. Two premises that are both negative will not; each premise will assert a form of separation between the classes designated by its terms (e.g. 'no s is m') but the m term will not establish either the presence or the absence of a relationship between the s and p terms and no valid conclusion will follow. This rules out EE, EO, OE, and OO pairings. Two particular premises will not yield a valid conclusion because 'some' has a minimal sense of 'at least one' and though there is no way of knowing how many members there are of the class designated by the m term, there are likely to be at least two. This rules out II, IO, OI, and OO pairings (OO for the second time). Nine pairings remain, 36 syllogisms of which 27 have valid conclusions.

Notice that OI and IO, OE, and EO, are listed separately here. It is conventional to present the premise containing the predicate of the conclusion (the major premise) first and the premise containing the subject (the minor premise) second, since in a textbook example there may be no way except by convention of indicating which of the non-middle terms is to be taken as subject of the conclusion. (Suppose that the premises are type A and type I; 'all m is p' and 'some s is m' (AI) have the valid conclusion 'some s is p' (I) but 'some m is p' and 'all s is m' (IA) have no valid conclusion.) A convention is clearly necessary, the opposite convention would have done as well (i.e. presenting the premise containing the subject first) but the one adopted here is the one usually adopted by logicians.

Of the 36 pairings still under consideration, 27 yield valid conclusions and may be seen intuitively to do so, though in some cases grasping the implication demands a considerable mental effort and perhaps the help of a teacher. What of the other nine? Neither Aristotle nor the medieval logicians could offer any reason why the valid syllogisms were valid and the rest not. Aristotle was content (by analogy with geometry) to derive the validity of his valid syllogisms from that of two basic syllogisms whose validity he regarded as self-evident, AAA and EAE – both in the first syllogistic figure. Very few people have any difficulty in seeing that the conclusion follows in these two cases. If 'all m is p' and 'all s is m' then 'all s is p' (AAA) and if 'no m is p' and 'all s is m' then 'no s is p' (EAE). I have suggested elsewhere (Wetherick, 1989) that the 'self-evidence' of the validity of these two syllogisms springs from the fact that they derive directly from the basic paradigms of approach and avoidance learning. The medieval logicians were not familiar with Greek geometry and the idea of a deductive system derived from postulates was foreign to them. They concentrated on finding rules of thumb that would permit valid syllogisms to be recognized as such because they did not contravene any of the rules. The rules were essentially teaching devices for use by students who had not learned to intuit the validity/invalidity of syllogisms. (That practice can make the perception of validity/invalidity intuitive is not in doubt. Dominican monks preserved until recently the tradition of disputation – debate conducted entirely in syllogisms – and may do so still. Some disputations were broadcast in the 1950s.) The rules of thumb specify that (1) if there is a negative premise then the valid conclusion, if any, will be negative; and (2) that if there is a particular premise then the valid conclusion, if any, will be particular. These rules always hold but more important was the idea of 'distribution of terms'. The medieval logicians asserted that a term in a proposition was distributed if it referred to every member of the designated class. Thus if 'all m is p', m is distributed but p is undistributed because there may be p's that are not m and these are not referred to in the proposition. If 'some m is p', both m and p are undistributed because there may be p's that are not m and m's that are not p. If 'no m is p', both terms are distributed as the proposition refers to all the m's and to all the p's. If 'some m is not p', the theory asserts that m is undistributed (because there may be some m's that are p) but that p is distributed. Most people find it difficult to see why we must here be referring to all the p's and end by accepting the fact for the sake of symmetry. Two further rules of thumb were derived from the theory of distribution. Rule 3 asserts that any pair of premises yielding a valid conclusion distributes the m term in at least one premise (possibly in both) and Rule 4, that no term can be distributed in a valid conclusion unless it was distributed in one of the premises. Rule 3 holds for all the intuitively valid syllogisms, they distribute the m term in at least one premise (five of them do so in both). The rule appears reasonable, if 'all p is m' and 'all s is m', no conclusion follows. We know that we are not referring to all the m's, so the set of m's that are p and the set of m's that are s may or may not overlap. This rule eliminates seven of the nine invalid premise pairs on the ground that neither premise distributes the middle term. However, two pairs (AOOf.2 and OAOf.3) which have valid conclusions, meet the criterion only by virtue of having an O premise that distributes m as the predicate term.

The reasonableness of rule 4 is not so obvious but all 27 intuitively valid syllogisms pass (eight of them were not of course recognized as valid in classical logic). There remain two premise pairs that fail this test though they passed all the others, AO-f.1 and OA-f.4. They have no valid conclusion but the rules of thumb eliminate them only because a valid conclusion would have to be of type O (particular negative) as one of the premises is particular (rule 2) and one negative (rule 1). But an O conclusion would distribute either the subject or the predicate term, neither of which is distributed in the premises.

ALTERNATIVES TO CLASSICAL THEORY

The four rules of thumb do in fact eliminate all and only the invalid premise pairs but not without a whiff of *adhoccery*. They have to be recognized as a superb intellectual achievement but they do not amount to an explanation of why the valid syllogisms are valid and the rest not. We intuit or can learn to intuit which syllogisms have valid conclusions. Sometimes this is difficult, though in the studies I have conducted there have always been one or two otherwise unremarkable individuals who experienced no difficulty. The intuition of validity feels like a psychological act though often it is unaccompanied by any introspectible mental content (see Wetherick, 1991a) and it was taken for granted till the middle of the nineteenth century that logic was in some sense part of psychology: John Stuart Mill, for example, held that it was 'a part or branch of psychology'. Such a belief is not inherently unreasonable. It is not difficult to imagine a real law-governed world like ours that does not contain any rational being capable of coming to understand it. Such a world would in a sense contain natural laws but it would not contain propositions and, since logic relies on propositions, it would not contain logic. However, in 1847 George Boole began the process of mathematizing logic (which had up to his time been considered a completed science, incapable of further development) and mathematicians have always been Platonists at heart, believing that as yet undiscovered mathematical truths somehow nevertheless exist – as America existed before any European discovered it!

In 1884, Frege (1884/1950) wrote that 'a proposition may be thought and again it may be true, never confuse these two things'. The divorce between the truth/falsity of a proposition and thinking the proposition was completed and the decree nisi issued by Husserl (1900/1970) in the first volume of his *Logical Investigations*. He condemned psychologism on the grounds that if logical laws were in any sense based on psychological laws (as psychologism proposed) they ought to be vague and approximate, to be based on induction and therefore probable not certain, and the existence of psychic events like representation and judgement ought to be deducible from them. None of these things was true; the laws of logic concerned necessary relations, independent of facts whether psychological or other. It thus became possible to ask the question 'Is man rational?' It had always been recognized that man's reason might in some cases be overridden by his baser passions but this was regarded simply as a consequence of the fact that he was a rational *animal*. Now it could be asked whether man was rational in principle, since logic was now thought to derive its validity from abstract postulate sets enjoying a Platonic existence independent of the human mind. Husserl's argument appeared at a time when there was already an overwhelming desire among logicians to accept it or some argument like it and the demise of psychologism is always dated from its publication. His work on logic is rarely cited in any other connection and when the second volume of *Logical Investigations* appeared (1901/1970) he was accused of having reverted to psychologism. In his last work on logic, the *Formal and Transcendental Logic* (1929/ 1969), he made it clear that, thirty years before, he had been concerned with 'a psychologism with a quite particular sense' (p. 152) . . . 'namely the psychologizing of the irreal significational formations that are the theme of logic'. 'No one [he says] would designate as the province of natural science the psychic processes of experiencing Nature and thinking about it, rather than Nature itself' but that is what had happened to logic and what he had attacked as 'psychologism'. It could not be denied, in his view, that logic had a transcendental as well as a formal aspect. 'Transcendental' here refers to the roots of logic in the cognizing process, which were in Husserl's view as significant as the 'irreal significational formations' of formal logic. Only the latter were, however, of interest to British and American logicians because their concern was with the mathematical development of logic, not with its foundations. Husserl was interested in founding the sciences (including logic and mathematics) in the human cognizing capacity because he could conceive of no other foundation for them. For that reason his work ought to be of special interest to psychologists interested in cognition but few of them have taken the trouble to read it and it must be admitted that the task is not easy – but only because, unlike philosophers writing in English, he was never prepared to sacrifice faithfulness to the complexity of the phenomena for the sake of clarity of exposition!

To found logic in the human cognizing capacity is an objective that ought to appeal to cognitive psychologists but in fact most of them have accepted the logicians' verdict that logic's validity is extra-human and devote themselves to speculations that the human organism may have evolved so as to embody all or part of logic because doing so favoured individual survival or breeding chances. Or even that the parallel (such as it is) between human behavioural processes and logic is purely contingent. Their arguments will be considered later in this chapter, meanwhile I wish to show how Husserl's objective may in fact be achieved. First, I shall consider the special case of syllogistic logic and then the general case of modern formal logic. For the general case I shall rely on George Spencer Brown's remarkable book, *Laws of Form* (1969), which was hailed as a work of genius when it first appeared (by Bertrand Russell and Stafford Beer among others) but has sunk almost without trace and is now out of print.

My argument in the special case of syllogistic logic depends on the account I have given of the inductive process of formulating propositions of Aristotle's four types (Wetherick, 1989; 1991b). I maintain that perception furnishes human and other organisms with information about objects and events in their immediate environment and that this information is registered in the organism's nervous system by the establishment of neural 'instance-nodes' (corresponding to the perception of a particular object or event at a particular time) which are connected (separately for each attribute) to every other instance-node that possesses that attribute. 'Attributes' are represented by circuits connecting every instance-node that possesses the attribute. 'Objects' and 'events' in the generic sense are represented by the overlap of sets of attribute circuits that define the object or event. The assertion of an affirmative proposition is grounded in awareness that there are nodes on the circuits corresponding to the set of attributes defining 's' that are also on the circuits of the set of attributes defining 'p'. The assertion of a negative proposition is grounded in awareness that there are s's that are not p. These are of course particular propositions. In order to assert a universal proposition it is necessary to add a warranty that the organism has never experienced an s that was not p (for a universal affirmative proposition) or has never experienced an s that was p (for a universal negative proposition) and this the human organism is uniquely in a position to do, being able to search his episodic memory for instance-nodes of the relevant kind and be aware that he has not found any. The four types of proposition may be characterized as follows:

Instance-nodes . . .		Exist	Do not exist	May exist	Irrel.
Type A	'All s is p'	sp	s–p	–sp	–s–p
Type E	'No s is p'	s–p	sp	–sp	–s–p
Type I	'Some s is p'	sp	–	–sp,s–p	–s–p
Type O	'Some s is not p'	s–p	–	–sp,sp	–s–p

A bar in front of (or above) the letter is a negation sign; –s means 'not s', –p means 'not p'. It may be seen in every case that –s–p's are irrelevant and that –sp's may or may not exist. An A proposition asserts that sp's do exist (at least for the purposes of argument) and that s–p's do not. An E proposition asserts the opposite. An I proposition asserts that sp's exist and that s–p's may exist. An O proposition asserts the opposite.

Instance-nodes of s and p may be represented by sets of points in a plane surface (which is not to imply anything about their actual, physical location in the brain) and the sets may then be represented by Euler circles. It may be shown that there are only five possible relationships between a pair of Euler circles: s and p may coincide; s may be wholly inside p; p may be wholly inside s; s and p may partially overlap; and s and p may be completely separate. These five relationships do not however map directly onto the four types of proposition with which we are concerned. The first two Euler relationships are consistent with the truth of an A proposition and the last three with the truth of its contradictory O proposition. The first four Euler relationships are consistent with the truth of an I proposition and the last one with the truth of its contradictory E proposition. Direct spatial representation of the four types of proposition may however be achieved by a modification of the Euler circles shown in Figure 4.1. Type A propositions are here represented by a continuous circle s inside a dotted circle p; the dotted circle indicates that although there are

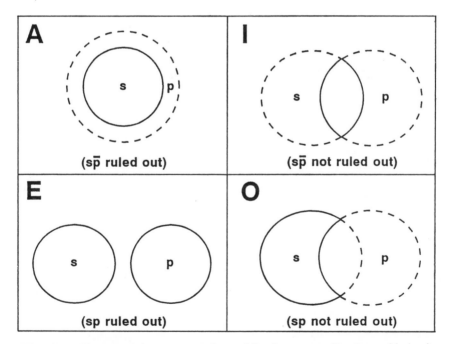

Figure 4.1 Diagrammatic representations of the four proposition types (derived from the Euler circles)

A and A

⊢r   mAp, sAm : sAp (f.1)
r⊣   pAm, mAs : slp (f.4)

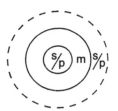

mAp, mAs : slp (f.3)

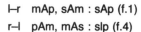

A and O

⊢r   pAm, sOm : sOp (f.2)
r⊣   pOm, sAm : pOs (f.2)

⊢r   mOp, mAs : sOp (f.3)
r⊣   mAp, mOs : pOs (f.3)

⊢r   mAp, sOm : NVC (f.1)
r⊣   pOm, mAs : NVC (f.4)

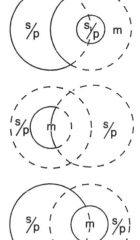

Figure 4.2 Diagrammatic representations of the twenty-seven valid syllogisms plus two exceptional invalid syllogisms
Note: The diagrams are obtained by superimposing pairs of proposition diagrams (see Figure 4.1).

A and I

⊢r { mAp, sIm : sIp (f.1)
     mAp, mIs : sIp (f.3)

r⊣ { mIp, mAs : sIp (f.3)
     pIm, mAs : sIp (f.4)

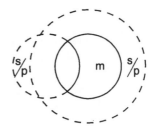

A and E

⊢r { mEp, mAs : sOp (f.3)
     pEm, mAs : sOp (f.4)

r⊣ { mAp, sEm : pOs (f.1)
     mAp, mEs : pOs (f.3)

⊢r { mEp, sAm : sEp (f.1)
     pEm, sAm : sEp (f.2)

r⊣ { pAm, sEm : sEp (f.2)
     pAm, mEs : sEp (f.4)

Figure 4.2 (cont.)

I and E

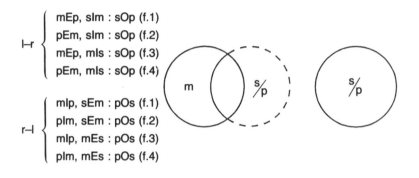

⊢r	mEp, slm : sOp (f.1) pEm, slm : sOp (f.2) mEp, mls : sOp (f.3) pEm, mls : sOp (f.4)
r⊣	mIp, sEm : pOs (f.1) pIm, sEm : pOs (f.2) mIp, mEs : pOs (f.3) pIm, mEs : pOs (f.4)

Figure 4.2 (cont.)

p's that are s (inside the continuous circle), there may or may not be p's that are not s. If there are none, the dotted circle collapses onto the continuous one, thus the diagram corresponds to the first two Euler relationships as required. Type E is represented by two separate continuous circles, s and p, corresponding directly to the fifth Euler relationship. Type I is represented by two overlapping dotted circles, s and p, where the lens shape defining the area of overlap (i.e. sp) has been made continuous; if there are no s–p's the dotted circle s collapses onto the lens, if there are no –sp's the dotted circle p does likewise, if there are neither s–p's nor –sp's both dotted circles collapse, if there are both, the representation stands as drawn. Thus the diagram corresponds to the first four Euler relationships as required. Type O is represented by two overlapping dotted circles, s and p, where the lune shape defining the area of s's that are not p (i.e. s–p) has been made continuous. If the lens-shaped overlap is empty (i.e. if there are no sp's) the dotted segment of circle s collapses onto the lune, corresponding to the fifth Euler relationship. If there are no –sp's, the dotted segment of the p circle does likewise, corresponding to the third Euler relationship. If there are both sp's and –sp's then the diagram stands as drawn, corresponding to the fourth relationship as required. The next step in my argument will be to represent syllogisms by superimposed pairs of proposition diagrams but before proceeding it may be noted that Adams (1984) treated each of the five

Euler relationships separately, in each figure of the syllogism, making one hundred premise pair comparisons in all. Her results are consistent with the argument presented here.

THE REPRESENTATION OF SYLLOGISMS

In Figure 4.1 the diagrams indicate by means of continuous lines that the points enclosed correspond to all the instance-nodes of a certain kind. In type A to all the s nodes (which are in fact all p); in type E to all the s nodes (which are in fact all –p); in type I to all the sp nodes (though not necessarily to all the s nodes or to all the p nodes); and in type O to all the s–p nodes (though not necessarily to all the s nodes or to all the –p nodes). Figure 4.2 shows how syllogisms may be represented by super-imposing two proposition diagrams, it turns out that only eight such diagrams are required to represent all 27 valid syllogisms. In fact, nine diagrams will be presented, the ninth being included to show exactly how the premise pairs represented (AO-f.1 and OA-f.4) come to have no valid conclusion (NVC) even though they conform to all the rules except one (the one requiring that a term must have been distributed in a premise if it is distributed in the conclusion). Similar diagrams can be drawn for the invalid syllogisms but they show nothing except that the syllogisms are invalid. Each diagram represents a relationship between three terms, a middle term (m) and two end terms (both indicated as s/p) and can be read either left to right (l–r) or right to left (r–l). If the left-hand s/p is read as s then the right-hand s/p must be read as p and vice versa. Consider the first diagram presented for 'A and A'; read from left to right this represents the simultaneous assertion of two A premises in f.1, yielding a valid A conclusion. We have, from the second premise, 'all s is m' (sAm), the m circle would be drawn dotted if we were considering only the one proposition but the first premise gives us 'all m is p' (mAp) so we know that, in this argument, we are considering all the m's and the m circle may therefore be drawn continuous, leaving only the p circle dotted. But if the m circle is ignored, what is left is the standard propositional representation of 'all s is p' (sAp). The simultaneous assertion of the premises asserts the conclusion. Read from right to left, the diagram shows that from the second premise we have mAs, with m a continuous circle and s dotted, and from the first premise, pAm, where the dotted m circle may be superimposed on the continuous m circle already in place. It follows that some at least of the s's must be m and therefore p. Once again the simultaneous assertion of the premises asserts the conclusion but the fact is not so obvious because attention must be switched from the end term that was subject of its premise to the end term that was predicate of its premise (which is the general problem in syllogistic figure 4). In data collected from 36 subjects by Wetherick and Gilhooly (1990), 25 drew the correct conclusion in AAAf.1 and 14 in AAIf.4.

The second diagram presented for 'A and A' represents only one syllogism, AAIf.3. The m term appears as subject of both premises, referring to all the m's in both. So we have one continuous circle for m and dotted circles for s and p. In the worst case (where both s and p collapse on m) there will nevertheless be some s's that are p. In syllogistic figure 3 both end terms appear as predicate of their premise, so neither is favoured and the task is somewhat easier. Twenty subjects drew the correct conclusion. (No diagram is presented for AA–f.2 since here the m term is undistributed, i.e. it appears as predicate of both premises and would have to be represented as a dotted line. Both s and p would certainly be inside the dotted line but nothing can be said about the relationship between them, so no conclusion follows.)

Three diagrams are presented for 'A and O'. The first two correspond to pairs of syllogisms with valid conclusions and the third to a pair of exceptional invalid syllogisms. The two remaining premise pairs involving A and O have no valid conclusion because the m term is undistributed, as was the case with AA-f.2 just now considered. The first diagram represents AOOf.2 and OAOf.2. each of which has a valid O conclusion. Reading from left to right we have sOm by the second premise and pAm by the first. All the p's are inside the m circle and some at least of the s's are outside it, so some s's are not p. The m circle is dotted not continuous but we do not need to know that we are referring to all the m's – somewhere there is an m boundary and we know that all the p's are inside it and some of the s's outside it, that is sufficient. Classical theory granted honorary distributed status to m here. Reading from right to left we have a similar state of affairs. All the s's are inside the m circle and some at least of the p's outside it, so some p's are not s. The converse conclusion cannot validly be asserted in either case because the continuous circle representing p or s may fall wholly inside that part of m that is also inside the s or p boundary (i.e. the lens).

The second diagram represents OAOf.3 and AOOf.3 both of which have valid O conclusions. Reading from left to right we have mAs and mOp. All the m's are s and some of them are not p, so those s's that are m will include some that are not p. The dotted segment of the p circle may collapse onto the continuous lune, so nothing follows about p. Reading from right to left it follows by the same argument that some p's are not s. (Notice that we cannot here make the right-hand side of the lens continuous since that would imply that there are sp's (i.e. that some s's are p) and the premises do not assert this. It would also make the diagram identical to that for 'A and I'.)

In the first and second 'A and O' diagrams simultaneous assertion of the premises asserts the conclusion. Eighteen subjects drew the correct conclusion in AOOf.2 and 21 in OAOf.3. An erroneous I conclusion was sometimes drawn to syllogisms like these, though the error rarely occurs in the other types of syllogism that yield an O conclusion.

The third diagram shows why AO-f.1 and OA-f.4 have no valid conclusion. There are certainly s's (or p's) that are not m but all the m's are p (or s) and the boundary of p (or s) is marked with a dotted line. Though it is here drawn through the area corresponding to s's (or p's) that are not m it could include all of them or none of them; we do not know so no conclusion follows.

Only one diagram is required for 'A and I' since this represents all four syllogisms with valid I conclusions and the remaining four have no valid conclusion because the middle term is undistributed. AIIf.1 and AIIf.3 are identical; they both have the premise mAp and sIm and mIs are equivalent (since if some s's are m, some m's are certainly s). Reading from left to right, some s's are m because the lens-shaped segment of m is surrounded by a continuous line, but all m's are p. So the s's that are m must also be p. The simultaneous assertion of the premises asserts the conclusion. IAIf.3 and IAIf.4 are also identical by the same argument and correspond with the diagram read from right to left. Thirty-two subjects drew the correct conclusion in AIIf.1, 31 in AIIf.3, 30 in IAIf.3 and 24 in IAIf.4. Syllogistic figure 4 is, as usual, more difficult than the other figures.

Two diagrams are presented for 'A and E'. The first represents four syllogisms having valid O conclusions and the second, four having valid E conclusions. In the first diagram, reading from left to right we have two identical syllogisms, EAOf.3 and EAOf.4; both have the premise mAs, one has pEm and the other mEp but these are equivalent (since if no p's are m it follows immediately that no m's are p). All the m's are s but no m's are p, so those s's that are m are not p. Reading from right to left we have two more identical syllogisms, AEOf.1 and AEOf.3, which yield a valid pOs conclusion. Eight subjects drew the correct conclusion in EAOf.3 and 8 in EAOf.4.

The second diagram read from left to right gives us two identical syllogisms, EAEf.1 and EAEf.2. All the s's are m but no m's are p; since we know that we are referring to all the m's, the boundary may be drawn as a continuous line and it follows that no s's are p. Reading from right to left we have AEEf.2 and AEEf.4 which are also identical. All the p's are m but no s's are m, so no s's are p. Twenty-nine subjects drew the correct conclusion in AEEf.2, 20 in AEEf.4, 34 in EAEf.1 and 30 in EAEf.2. Syllogistic figure 4 is, as usual, more difficult than the rest.

Only one diagram is required for the eight syllogisms involving 'I and E'. Since both premises are symmetrical (in the sense that both have a converse of the same propositional form) they are in effect all identical. Reading from left to right we see that some s's are m but that no p's are m, so some s's (those that are m) are not p. This argument covers all four

EIO syllogisms. Reading from right to left we see that no s's are m but that some p's are m, so some p's (those that are m) are not s. This covers all four IEO syllogisms. Twenty-three subjects drew the correct conclusion in EIOf.1 and 20 in EIOf.2.

It follows from my argument that, in a sense, there are only eight valid syllogisms though between them they can take on twenty-seven different propositional forms. (Eight would still be required, even if the eight syllogisms with valid pOs conclusions were rejected.) No calculation, model building or comparison with external standards is required. If an individual entertains two propositions simultaneously, then in all and only those cases where a valid conclusion follows from them as premises, the pattern of neural activity corresponding to the conclusion will have been set up as an immediate consequence of setting up the patterns corresponding to the premises. Any pair of premises may be regarded as a postulate set comparable to the postulate set for, say, Euclidean geometry. Having accepted the postulate set, what follows cannot be denied without self-contradiction though, as in geometry, the fact may not be immediately apparent. (Some immediate responses may be like that of the philosopher Thomas Hobbes on his first encounter with geometry – 'By God, this is impossible!')

Any term may serve as subject of a proposition, so the fact that all the diagrams may be read either from right to left or from left to right need cause no concern and the fact that five of the 19 syllogisms generally accepted as valid make use of this facility is a further argument in favour of admitting the eight pOs syllogisms that are frequently rejected, all of which do so. Syllogistic figure 4 always presents special difficulty because a term that appeared as predicate of its premise has to be selected as subject of the conclusion drawn. But it must be remembered that the difficulty is mainly apparent in the psychological laboratory, where the experimental subject is often faced with a pair of premises out of context and given no indication what the subject term of the conclusion should be. Subjects usually assume that since only one non-middle term appears as subject of its premise that must be it, which leads them to treat syllogistic figures 1 and 4 as identical.

In a real argument every participant knows what the argument is about and, consequently, what term is likely to be the subject of the conclusion drawn. Consider the following argument such as might be overheard in any saloon bar. Two men are discussing the merits of politicians. One of them is reluctant to allow that politicians have any merits, at last the other says:

'Well, you must admit that politicians are quick-witted.'
'I don't mind admitting that. All politicians are liars and liars need to be quick-witted!'

The last remark is a disguised syllogism (AAAf.1) with 'all politicians are quick-witted' as its conclusion. Notice that the premises could have been stated in either order and that the speaker could have concluded from the same premises that 'some quick-witted people are politicians' (AAIf.4). If he had, his companion would have been startled because the argument was about politicians and a conclusion about politicians was to be expected. Moreover, the alternative conclusion would not have made the speaker's point.

Consider now another saloon bar argument – this time an Irish saloon bar. The village priest is supping his Guinness and complaining that only priests know what it is like to be hard up (i.e. 'all hard-up men are priests'):

> His companion replies:
> 'Bedad Father, 'tis nonsense you are talking. No priests are married and all married men are hard-up, so there are plenty of hard-up men who aren't priests!'

This remark is also a disguised syllogism (EAOf.4). No valid conclusion follows about priests but the context inclines the hearer to expect a rebuttal of 'all hard-up men are priests' in the form of an O proposition 'some hard-up men are not priests' and that is what he gets.

The second argument is no more difficult to follow than the first although the syllogistic form is often said to be one of the most difficult *in abstracto*, whereas the form of the first is one of the easiest. This would not have come as a surprise to Aristotle, or to the medieval logicians, or to some modern logicians and psychologists (e.g. Henle, 1962; Cohen, 1981) who hold that thinking naturally follows logical courses. But it becomes necessary to explain how and why subjects make so many errors in experimental tests of syllogistic reasoning.

LANGUAGE AND REASONING

Most fluent speakers of a language are quite unable to give an account of the structure of the language they speak and until the last thirty years or so no-one at all knew how to give an account of the general features of language structure that underlie all languages. Logic may appropriately be regarded as a description of the structure of thinking and that structure has been made explicit and developed in its own right by mathematical logicians but it is understood by everyman only in the same sense that he understands the structure of his language (as evidenced by speaking it correctly). So far, no-one has developed a psychological test of understanding of the technical concepts of linguistics but if someone did, and found that ordinary people do not do very well on the test, and concluded that they did not understand their language, that would more or less parallel what has happened in logic. The subject faced with an experimental syllogism wants to do what he thinks the experimenter requires (or he/she would not have agreed to take part in the experiment) and wants to avoid looking foolish in the eyes of the experimenter and/or the other subjects. There may be more than one way of achieving these objectives. It can be shown that many subjects use a matching strategy that does not really involve logic at all. If a subject concludes that 'some s is p' from the premises 'all m is p' and 'some s is m', he is marked right. However, if he goes on to draw the same conclusion from 'some m is p' and 'all s is m' he is wrong and we may reasonably suspect that his earlier, apparently correct conclusion may not have been obtained by logic! In eleven of the 19 valid syllogisms (or fourteen of the 27) the correct conclusion may be obtained by constructing a proposition, using the non-middle terms of the premises, which is of the same logical form as the more conservative premise (i.e. the premise making the less general claim). A subject using this matching strategy could draw an A conclusion from two A premises but from an A combined with an I, E, or O premise he would conclude I, E, or O, not A. In the remaining eight (or thirteen) valid syllogisms the correct conclusion is not of the same logical form as either of the premises and the matching strategy fails. Subjects genuinely trying to use logic will have more success on the latter type of syllogism but the performance of matchers and logicians will look alike on the former. The fact that a proportion of subjects are matching can be shown by including in the test series syllogisms like AAf.2, II, EE, OO, which are particularly attractive to matchers. The number of times a matching response (A, I, E, or O; always wrong) is chosen to these premise pairs is a crude measure of the susceptibility of the subject to matching and may be correlated with his success on the remaining syllogisms in the series. Significant correlations of around $r = -0.4$ or -0.5 have been obtained from several data sets. A stronger indication may be obtained from data comparing subjects' capacity to draw conclusions from premises and their capacity to construct premises yielding given conclusions. The latter task must employ the same mental processes as are employed by the logician solving syllogisms but the matcher does not use these processes. Two groups were selected, consisting of subjects who had done well on syllogisms to which the correct conclusion could be obtained by matching (the groups scored 89 per cent and 83 per cent correct, respectively; the remaining subjects scored only 59 per cent). The first group (89 per cent correct) had also done well on syllogisms where matching gives the wrong conclusion (70 per cent correct as against 33 per cent; the remaining subjects scored 28 per cent). The scores of the first group (logicians, $n = 16$) correlated $r = +0.72$ with their premise construction scores but those of the second group (matchers, $n = 25$) correlated only $r = +0.10$. The scores of the remaining subjects ($n = 30$) correlated $r = +0.50$, indicating that they were trying to do logic but doing it badly. They would have appeared to do better if they had resorted to matching but the appearance would have been deceptive. Notice that the remaining group and the matching group did not differ significantly on syllogisms to which matching gives a wrong answer (28 per cent correct as against 33 per cent), their poorer performance on syllogisms to which matching gives the right answer (59 per cent correct as against 83 per cent) simply reflects the use of matching – a non-logical strategy – by the matching group. If as appears to be the case most subject samples in this type of experiment include both logicians and matchers, then it is illegitimate to place any weight at all on the number of correct conclusions drawn irrespective of syllogism type, still less to construct theories of the syllogism-solving process on the basis of such scores.

The foregoing discussion implies that two levels of analysis are employed in cognition. The idea is not new but has received its most recent formulation in Derek Bickerton's book *Language and Species* (1990). Bickerton calls the two levels the primary and secondary representation systems (PRS and SRS). We share the PRS with subhuman organisms but are unique possessors of an SRS. The resemblance to Pavlov's first and second signalling systems (the first operating on conditioned-response principles, the second 'definitely not') is close but goes unremarked. Bickerton is interested mainly in language and deploys a great deal of evidence suggesting that while the PRS is capable of regulating all the kinds of behaviour we have in common with animals (including learning) and even of elementary language use in the naming of objects and events, it cannot get beyond pidgin in language ability because it cannot structure the names it uses and give meaning to their sequence or grammatical form. He argues convincingly that ape language only reaches the PRS level, as does the language of children under two and as did, conceivably, the language of protohuman species before the appearance of *Homo sapiens*. Pidgin arises in circumstances where masters and servants (sometimes slaves) have to communicate with each other though both already have a fully structured language of their own. It functions effectively only in the presence of the objects/events referred to. But the children of pidgin speakers develop a fully structured creole language adequate for most purposes. The structure of the creole may not, however, resemble that of either original language. Possession of an SRS thus allows the use, understanding and even the construction from scratch of a genuine language, since the structural principles required are innately given in the SRS.

Bickerton (1990) does not consider logic but logic is clearly language-dependent since it is concerned with relations between propositions. The theory of premise construction propounded earlier in this paper concerns activity in Bickerton's PRS, where information input by the experience of the organism is summarized over time so as to permit more effective forms of response. But an organism possessing only a PRS can formulate no genuinely universal premises. It can be highly probable that an s is p and the PRS organism will then respond to s as if it were p. If it turns out on a particular occasion that s is not p, the probability of responding to s as if it were p on the next occasion that it appears will be slightly reduced. An organism possessing an SRS can however (amongst many other things) search his episodic memory for examples of s that were not p and, if he does not find any, can assert that 'all s's are p'. Doing so brings many advantages in its train; it permits the development of logical and mathematical systems that depend on universal propositions. (Space does not permit the consideration here of modal logics but these do not, in any case, yield much that is of direct use to the individual organism.) The organism that has only PRS has some kind of threshold mechanism that determines when sufficient instances of sp have been encountered to justify responding to s as if it were p (see Wetherick, 1991b). In effect such an organism elevates its proto-universal to the status of a universal proposition at the moment of its decision to act as if this example of s is p, since otherwise the decision could not be justified. But the proto-universals available to a PRS organism have no continuing existence.

In an SRS organism, genuine universal propositions can be formulated derived from the organism's own experience as recorded in the PRS; or information input verbally can be entered into the PRS and processed as if it were the organism's own. But such information can also be retained at the SRS (language) level and processed at that level only. The latter possibility may be clarified by an example from my own experience. When I am told that a man is 6 feet tall and weighs 12 stones, I feel intuitively that I know how tall and heavy he is. If, however, I am told that he is 1.83 metres tall and weighs 76.3 kilos I have no such intuitive feeling – I have first to translate the figures into their non-metric equivalents. (Wide use of the metric system came too late for me!) Input of a metric measure is, for me, an SRS event that forms no immediate links with the PRS that would enable me to intuit its significance. Most of us, in our everyday lives, use and understand logic in its PRS form and those I have termed 'logicians' do so in the experimental situation as well. But our only experimental access to other human beings is via the SRS and, if an individual subject responds at the SRS (verbal) level only, there is no direct way in which we can tell that he/she has done so. One category of such individuals I have termed 'matchers'. They may not consciously choose to respond in this way, they may so far as they are aware be doing exactly what is required of them. If they are given feedback their responses will frequently be judged correct and no-one in such a situation expects to be correct all the time. Other categories of SRS responder include individuals who report what they know to be true (e.g. 'all dogs have four legs', where the valid conclusion is 'all dogs have five legs') or what they wish were true (e.g. 'some church-goers are honest' where the valid conclusion is 'some church-goers are not honest'). These individuals have, in Henle's (1962) terms, 'failed to accept the logical task'. Their behaviour cannot be judged irrational if they see the task as one in which they are expected to bring to bear their lifetime's knowledge and experience.

CURRENT THEORIES OF REASONING

Galotti (1989) reviews contemporary approaches to the study of formal and everyday reasoning. She distinguishes three approaches which she calls the componential approach, the rules/heuristics approach and the mental-models/search approach, but draws attention to the fact that there has been 'very little explicit discussion regarding the nature of reasoning'. The componential approach is mainly associated with the work of Sternberg, though it derives from Guilford's 'structure of intellect' model. The approach clearly has little in common with the one adopted in this paper and there is no need to repeat Galotti's criticisms. The rules/heuristics approach is associated with the work of Braine, Rips, and others. It takes for granted that the rules, etc. are somehow external to the organism and has been extensively criticized by the principal proponent of the third (mental-models) approach (Johnson-Laird in e.g., 1983; Johnson-Laird and Bara, 1984; Johnson-Laird and Byrne, 1991). Johnson-Laird has the advantage that rule theory has been expressed with some precision, so it is not difficult either to derive consequences from it or to show that some of the consequences are not supported by the experimental evidence. Johnson-Laird's own theory asserts that the individual makes composite mental models of the states of affairs implied by the premises of a syllogism and then determines whether any one conclusion is compatible with all the models that need to be made. He asserts that these activities take place in the working memory (Baddeley, 1986) but that the mental models may or may not be in consciousness. Presumably the various mental activities – constructing a model, deciding how many additional models it may be necessary to construct, generating a putative conclusion, deciding whether it is compatible with the model or not and so forth are under the control of the central executive (although Johnson-Laird usually refers only to the 'manipulator' of the models). Certainly, several kinds of mental operation need to be performed but these are not explained in the theory, which is concerned solely with the models constructed and is supported by experimental evidence showing only that if more than one model is needed, then the syllogism is more difficult to solve. The proposed solution procedure has a degree of face validity. Models may indeed be constructed in consciousness of sets of individuals that are a or b or c. (As before, a bar in front of the letter is a negation sign.) If it is desired to represent, say, 'all b's are c' there will be in the model, bc's and –bc's but no b–c's. If it was further desired to represent 'some a's are b' there would be ab's and –ab's and a–b's. But since there are no b–c's in the model, it will then appear that the a's that are b must also be c, i.e. 'some a's are c'. Only the presence of a–b's in the model shows that it is not the case that 'all a's are c' and if they are inadvertently omitted or overlooked then a false conclusion may be drawn. This is the procedure that would be required for AIIf.1, one of the easiest syllogisms, requiring only one mental model. The most difficult syllogisms require three, implying awareness that two or three models but not more may sometimes need to be constructed, and ability to maintain an accurate running count of putative conclusions, remembering which of them have been tried and seen to be consistent with one or more of the models. If, at the end of this process, more than one conclusion (or none) remains uneliminated then the syllogism has no valid conclusion. All these mental operations are described as if they are performed in consciousness but it is not clear what happens if one or more of the models is not in consciousness. Description of Johnson-Laird's procedure is sufficient to suggest that, in the more difficult cases, it would make impossible demands on the working memory. Moreover, individuals do not usually report mental contents of the kind required (Wetherick, 1991a). The fact is however that some individuals can solve all types of syllogism without difficulty and almost everybody can solve the easier types. The empirical support relied upon by Johnson-Laird comes from experiments showing that fewer individuals solve the syllogisms that require more than one mental model and while this is true, such a result supports any theory that makes that prediction, for whatever reason. Earlier in this paper I showed that a proportion of subjects in any experiment are likely to be matchers not logicians, a matcher constructs a conclusion of the same logical form as the more conservative premise. In Johnson-Laird and Byrne (1991), the ten valid syllogisms said to require only one model are ten to which matching gives the correct conclusion (two type A, four type I and four type E). The thirteen said to require three models are those to which matching gives a wrong conclusion (correct conclusions; one type I and twelve type O). The four said to require two models (which are therefore of intermediate difficulty) are the valid OAO and AOO syllogisms, which benefit to some extent from matching. Subjects who are matching will therefore obtain precisely the pattern of results that Johnson-Laird regards as support for his theory. Moreover, it cannot always be decided unequivocally how many models are required to represent a given pair of premises. AAIf.3 was said to require two models in 1983, one in 1984 and three in 1991!

THE GENERAL CASE – 'LAWS OF FORM'

Logicians and mathematicians have succeeded in developing numerous abstract logical systems from agreed postulate sets. How is this possible?

George Spencer Brown provides an answer to this question in his *Laws of Form* (1969). He develops a deductive system from very simple postulates; defining only two operations – 'distinction' and 'indication'.

> A distinction is drawn by arranging a boundary with separate sides so that a point on one side cannot reach the other without crossing the boundary. For example, in a plane space a circle draws a distinction.

and

> Once a distinction is drawn, the spaces, states or contents on each side of the boundary, being distinct, can be indicated.

> (Spencer Brown, 1969: 1)

Thus, when an organism identifies a state of affairs (or its absence) as being of interest or importance, either by its behaviour or verbally, it has satisfied the postulates of Spencer Brown's system. When it links different states of affairs in its experience, so that one may be treated as predictor of another, then the logic that determines what new links may validly be deduced from links already established (e.g. the syllogistic logic considered earlier) derives its validity from the same source as the behaviour itself – behaviour and logic are co-extensive.

Spencer Brown introduced a new formalism which he justified by using it to solve problems that are difficult to solve by existing methods. He went on to prove as theorems the postulates of Sheffer's (1913) single-functor logic. The importance of this step is that 'proof of Sheffer's postulates will serve to prove all postulates in every description of Boolean algebra' (p. 107). Every other postulate set may be regarded as a set of theorems in Spencer Brown's logic. It may be justifiable in many cases to rely on such a set rather than trace the argument back to Spencer Brown's own postulates but they all ultimately derive their validity from the fact that this could be done, in principle. It follows that Gödel's theorem (that no logical system rich enough to include arithmetic can be proved consistent, and that if it could it would certainly be incomplete) is an 'occasion for celebration' not a 'reason for despair, as some investigators have taken it to be' (p. 96). There are infinitely many possible distinctions to be made and indicated but a given finite subset of these will yield only a finite number of logical interrelations between its members. If Gödel's theorem were false, the implication would be that there was an upper limit to the number of possible distinctions. The scope of human knowledge is however (*pace* Russell) without limit – which is, in Spencer Brown's view (and mine), 'an occasion for celebration'.

THE EVIDENCE AGAINST HUMAN RATIONALITY

My argument in this chapter has been directed to showing that human beings are in fact rational animals and that their rationality is implicit in their evolved animality – not a superimposed (and supernatural) addition to it. The capacity of the human organism to stand back from his perceptual input and consider what might be the case in the future or what has been the case in the past as well as what is the case now, gives us most of our specifically human capabilities. Probably the most important of these for rationality is the capacity to search our episodic memory for individual cases of s that are –p (or p) that would, if found, preclude us from asserting a universal proposition (positive or negative as the case may be) and allow only 's is p (or –p) with high probability'. Without universal propositions, logic and mathematics cannot get off the ground but such propositions can never be known to be true of the real world. We can only commit ourselves to their truth on the basis of our (direct or indirect) experience – and we cannot legitimately do that unless we can recall no counterinstances.

There remain to be considered certain experimental tasks, performance on which has been taken to show that human subjects are irrational. The best known of these is Wason's four-card problem but I will consider first his earlier 2-4-6 problem. Wason posed this problem in the following terms:

> I have a rule in mind that generates triplets of numbers like 2-4-6. I want you to discover the rule by proposing further triplets and I will tell you whether or not each triplet conforms to my rule. When you are certain you know what my rule is, tell me.

(Wason, 1960)

Wason's rule was 'any three numbers in ascending order' and he interpreted the results he obtained as evidence that his subjects did not attempt to eliminate their hypotheses, limiting themselves to the generation of instances that conformed to the hypotheses. I pointed out (Wetherick, 1962, 1970) that this interpretation is illegitimate, since it is impossible to know whether a subject is trying to confirm or eliminate a hypothesis, unless one knows what hypothesis he/she has in mind. Furthermore, the task is misleading in so far as 2-4-6 conforms to many less general rules than 'three numbers in ascending order'. If a subject selects a hypothesis like 'three successive even numbers' any number of triplets conforming to this rule will also conform to the experimenter's rule. If he/she decides to try a negative test, a triplet like 6-4-2 may be offered which will be negative by both rules and so will not eliminate the hypothesis. Hypothesis evaluation in real life rarely has to cope with a situation in which there are numerous (false) hypotheses that generate any number of instances that are positive or negative according to the true hypothesis. Usually a real-life investigation begins with a hypothesis derived from a batch of instances whose positive or negative status is already known, which serve to rule out in advance hypotheses that are too narrow in scope to explain the phenomenon. The 2-4-6 task is simply not representative enough to justify conclusions about human rationality.

Wason (1966) introduced another task, which inspired (and continues to inspire) hundreds of experimental studies. I shall argue that this, too, is unrepresentative and tells us no more about human rationality than the 2-4-6 task. (Unless it be admitted that what Wason and his successors judged to be the wrong response is in fact correct; in which case the studies furnish strong experimental support for the view that man is rational!) In the four-card task, the subject is given four cards and told that, for example, each card has either E or K on one side and either 4 or 7 on the other. The cards are laid out in a row so that only one side can be seen – E, K, 4, and 7. There is a rule stipulating that any card with a vowel on one side must have an odd number on the other. The question is which cards should the subject turn over in order to see whether the rule is being observed? In this task virtually every subject turns over the E and almost no-one ever turns over the 4, but according to Wason the correct answer is 'E and 4'. The E will falsify the rule if it has not got an odd number (i.e. 7) on the back; the 4 will do so if it has got a vowel (i.e. E) on the back. Any subject who does not choose 'E and 4' (very few do) is condemned as irrational!

When this task appeared (in the 1960s) the philosophy journals of the time were full of papers on the 'paradox of confirmation'. Take an empirical law like 'all ravens are black'. This law is logically equivalent to 'all non-black things are non-ravens'. But observation of a black raven is universally held to confirm the law, so why is observation of, say, a red book (i.e. a non-black non-raven) not also held to confirm it? Problems in philosophy are never solved to everyone's satisfaction but the most widely accepted explanation seemed to be that to do so would imply that it would be rational to test the law by searching out non-black things to see whether they were ravens. Admittedly, if a non-black thing is found that is a raven, the law stands refuted. But there are so many non-black things in the world that to adopt this procedure would in fact be impractical. The law should, rationally, be tested by searching out ravens to see whether they are black. It did not occur to philosophers to condemn as irrational anyone who did not agree that observation of a red book confirms the law 'all ravens are black' but psychologists have no compunction in doing so. Any choice but 'E and 4' is condemned even though a subject interpreting the task as a laboratory model of the real-world task (which is what most of them do) would, rationally, avoid choosing 4 (which is equivalent to choosing a 'non-black thing') and might well choose 7 – which could confirm the rule though admittedly it could not refute it.

Subjects do not always agree immediately that 'all non-black things are non-ravens' is logically equivalent to 'all ravens are black'; nor that 'cards with an even number on one side have a consonant on the other' is logically equivalent to 'cards with a non-consonant on one side have a non-even number on the other' but they do immediately agree that 'under-eighteens must not drink alcohol' is equivalent to 'alcohol drinkers must be over eighteen'. They also assume that 'if you do not tidy your room you may not go out to play' follows immediately from 'if you tidy your room you may go out to play' and that 'anyone purchasing jewellery worth more than £1000 will receive, as a free gift, a gold chain worth £100' means that anyone not purchasing the jewellery will not get the free gift. The assumptions illustrated in these examples are commonplace in ordinary language and they have the effect of inducing subjects to make what appear to experimenters to be 'rational' choices. But the appearance is misleading. Subjects do choose 'alcohol drinkers and under-eighteens' (the equivalent of 'E and 4') but they are in fact choosing the equivalent of E (in the first task considered) for both the rule presented ('alcohol drinkers must be over eighteen') and its immediate equivalent ('under-eighteens must not drink alcohol').

The position is complicated in the last two examples by the fact that they involve equivalences not implications. 'Tidying the room' and 'going out to play' on the one hand and 'not tidying the room' and 'not going out to play' on the other, both satisfy the rule and, in the jewellery example, it is equally important that the £1000 purchaser gets the free gift and that the non-£1000 purchaser does not. In these problems the rational choice is 'all four cards' and intelligent subjects often choose all four.

ACKNOWLEDGEMENTS

Earlier drafts of this chapter were read by my colleagues, Professor E.A. Salzen and Dr W.P. Brown. This version has benefited greatly from their comments and criticisms.

REFERENCES

Adams, M.J. (1984) 'Aristotle's logic', in G.H. Bower (ed.) *The Psychology of Learning and Motivation*, vol. 18, Orlando: Academic Press.
Aristotle (1964) *Prior and Posterior Analytics*, trans. J. Warrington, London: Everyman's Library.
—— (1986) *De Anima* (On the Soul), trans. H. Lawson Tancred, London: Penguin.
Baddeley, A. (1986) *Working Memory*, Cambridge: Cambridge University Press.
Bickerton, D. (1990) *Language and Species*, Chicago and London: Chicago University Press.
Boole, G. (1847/1948) *The Mathematical Analysis of Logic*, Oxford: Blackwell.
Cohen, L.J. (1981) 'Can human irrationality be experimentally demonstrated?' *Behavioral and Brain Sciences* 4: 317–70.
Frege, G. (1884/1950) *The Foundations of Arithmetic*, trans. J.L. Austin, Oxford: Blackwell.

Galotti, K.M. (1989) 'Approaches to studying formal and everyday reasoning', *Psychological Bulletin* 105: 331–51.

Henle, M. (1962) 'On the relation between logic and thinking', *Psychological Review* 69: 366–78.

Husserl, E. (1900–1901/1970) *Logical Investigations* (two vols), trans. J.N. Findlay, London: Routledge.

—— (1929/1969) *Formal and Transcendental Logic*, trans. D. Cairns, The Hague: Martinus Nijhoff.

Johnson-Laird, P.N. (1983) *Mental Models*, Cambridge: Cambridge University Press.

Johnson-Laird, P.N. and Bara, B.G. (1984) 'Syllogistic inference', *Cognition* 16: 1–64.

Johnson-Laird, P.N. and Byrne, R.M.J. (1991) *Deduction*, Hove and London: Erlbaum.

Sheffer, H.M. (1913) *Transactions of the American Mathematical Society* 14: 481–8.

Spencer Brown, G. (1969) *Laws of Form*, London: Allen & Unwin.

Wason, P.C. (1960) 'On the failure to eliminate hypotheses in a conceptual task', *Quarterly Journal of Experimental Psychology* 12: 129–40.

—— (1966) 'Reasoning', in B.M. Foss (ed.) *New Horizons in Psychology*, London: Penguin.

Wetherick, N.E. (1962) 'Eliminative and enumerative behaviour in a conceptual task', *Quarterly Journal of Experimental Psychology* 14: 246–9.

—— (1970) 'On the representativeness of some experiments in cognition', *Bulletin of the British Psychological Society* 23: 213–14.

—— (1989) 'Psychology and syllogistic reasoning', *Philosophical Psychology* 2: 111–24.

—— (1991a) 'What goes on in the mind when we solve syllogisms?' in R.H. Logie and M. Denis (eds) *Mental Images in Human Cognition*, Amsterdam: North Holland.

—— (1991b) 'Logic in the evolution of mind', *Newsletter of the BPS History and Philosophy of Psychology Section* 12: 24–35.

Wetherick, N.E. and Gilhooly, K.J. (1990) 'Syllogistic reasoning: effects of premise order', in K.J. Gilhooly, M.T. Keane, R.H. Logie, and G. Erdos (eds) *Lines of Thinking*, vol. 1, Chichester: Wiley.

Chapter 5

Mental logic and human irrationality

We can put a man on the moon, so why can't we solve those logical-reasoning problems?

D.P. O'Brien

Are people rational or are they irrational? Before starting to write this paper I posed this question to an undergraduate class in cognitive psychology. No shortage of evidence was offered for either alternative. On the one hand, it was pointed out that people do many things that most of us would judge to be irrational: we fail to wear seatbelts while knowing that this decreases our safety; we smoke cigarettes while knowing that this may lead to a frightful disease; we spend the weekend drinking at parties while knowing that an exam is being given on Monday; we continue to use our credit cards while knowing that we are unable to repay the debts already accumulated. On the other hand, people do many things that reflect a rational nature: we plan for the future, anticipating the effects of our actions; we have created mathematics, formal logic, complex engineering and computing systems, high-technology, science, and philosophy. Ironically, our apparently most rational accomplishments can lead to the most irrational results, for example, modern physics has provided for the development of weapons that threaten to bring about our extinction. For me, the tenor of the discussion was captured when one student posed the popular rhetorical protasis: 'If we can put a man on the moon', and another student provided the apodosis, 'why can't we solve the THOG problem or the selection task?'

The consensus of my class was that as humans we have it in our nature to be both rational and irrational, a conclusion with which I expect the other authors in this volume to agree. Differences among us are apt to concern which aspects of human nature we propose are rational and which ones we propose are irrational. Evans (this volume, Chapter 1), for example, proposes that people possess a kind of rationality that enables us to make decisions so as to maximize the prospects of benefit to ourselves, but we do not possess a rationality of inherently logical thought processes. I disagree. People may be motivated to seek benefits for themselves and their families, clans, tribes, nations, and so forth, but my undergraduate students provided many examples of the ways in which people are not adept at maximizing such benefits. Further, I will argue, people's thought processes are, in many ways, profoundly logical. I also believe that the empirical evidence *per se* does not settle the issue: in the practical realm we successfully do some things that appear to be in our self-interest and some that appear to be irrational, and in the realm of laboratory logical-reasoning tasks we do some things that appear to be logical and some that appear to be irrational.

The classical Greek view of human nature included a rationality that allows for logical reasoning. My colleagues and I have argued elsewhere (Noveck *et al.*, 1991) that we have no adequate reason to abandon this view, and that this rationality includes a mental logic that accounts for our basic logical intuitions. In recent years the claim that human reasoning includes a mental logic has met considerable resistance, and the death of mental logic is proclaimed with some regularity (e.g. Cheng and Holyoak, 1985; Cosmides, 1989; Johnson-Laird, 1983; Johnson-Laird and Byrne, 1991; Legrenzi and Legrenzi, 1991). To paraphrase Mark Twain, news of this death is premature; theories of mental logic are alive and well, though often misunderstood. Indeed, I believe that most criticisms of the mental-logic approach stem from a misunderstanding of what it is.

The first section of this paper describes the mental-logic approach. Theories of mental logic are not monolithic, and what counts as evidence against a particular theory does not necessarily count as evidence against all mental-logic theories. I first discuss the mental-logic approach generally, noting that a mental logic consists of propositional activities, then focus on the three-part theory proposed by Braine (1990, in press), Braine and O'Brien (1991), Lea *et al.* (1990), Noveck *et al.* (1991), and O'Brien (1991). The second section addresses some principal criticisms of mental logic. In particular, I argue that (a) failure to solve complex reasoning problems does not count as evidence against mental logic; and (b) we should not interpret evidence of the effects of content on logical reasoning as counting against mental logic. The third section addresses why I do not find the competing non-logical theories compelling, and focuses on the content-bound theories proposed by Cosmides (1989) and Cheng and Holyoak (1985) and the mental-models theory proposed by Johnson-Laird and his associates (e.g. Johnson-Laird, 1983; Johnson-Laird and Byrne, 1991). Finally, I address irrationality from the perspective of the mental-logic approach.

THE MENTAL-LOGIC APPROACH

An adequate theory of human logical reasoning needs to account for both logically correct and erroneous judgements. We thus are faced with an apparent dilemma. On the one hand, we can assume that the human reasoning repertory includes a mental logic, in which case we have an explanation for those valid logical judgements that people make, but we still require an explanation for reasoning errors. On the other hand, we can assume that there is no mental logic, which provides an explanation for errors in reasoning, but leaves the valid judgements unexplained. The proposal that there is no mental logic, though, is based on a misunderstanding of the nature of logic, and adoption of the first horn of this apparent dilemma – that there is a mental logic – is the rational choice.

Kant (1781/1966) proposed that human understanding is made possible in part by a mental logic, and that in the two thousand years since Aristotle nothing had been added to this logic and nothing altered, so logic could be considered completed and perfect. As Macnamara (1986) noted, this view of logic reflects a Platonic heritage, and encourages the view of a mental logic as the manipulation of symbolic forms. This logic of forms is the sort of logic, I believe, that is being decried by opponents of the mental-logic approach. Since Frege at the end of the nineteenth century, however, logic has undergone a revolution, and logicians have come to view logic as propositional and intentional (Kneale and Kneale, 1962).

Propositions take truth values, that is, a proposition is either true or false. Note that sentences *per se* are not propositions. The sentence 'I am travelling with an American passport' is neither true nor false, but is true when asserted by myself outside America and false if asserted by Margaret Thatcher. Were logic concerned with sentences, it would be concerned merely with the manipulation of symbolic forms. However, the assumptions and conclusions of logical arguments are propositions.[1]

Logical reasoning consists of propositional activities. Propositions are proposed, supposed, assumed, considered, claimed, believed, disbelieved, doubted, asserted, denied, inferred, and so forth. All of these propositional activities concern judgements about truth and falsity, for example, to believe x is to believe that x is true, to doubt x is to doubt that x is true, to deny x is to claim that x is false. Such propositional activities concern intentional states of affairs. When I assert that 'Napoleon was in Egypt', I refer to a historical person and his relation to a country, not to a symbolic idea in my mind that I can manipulate. This intentionality does not presuppose any claim to realism – it would be no less propositional were Napoleon merely the figment of historical imagination. Note that I also could assert that 'Ahab was obsessed with a white whale', which we also would judge true even though its intentional state of affairs is fictional. The reason that the sentence 'I am travelling with an American passport' is neither true nor false until its utterer and circumstances are known is that sentences *per se*, unlike propositions, do not concern intentional states of affairs.

Because propositional activities refer to intentional states of affairs, they coexist with pragmatic activities, having to do with the practical consequences of propositions for their referred states of affairs (James, 1978/1885; Peirce, 1958/1931). These pragmatic activities include setting goals and understanding goals set by others. The logical processes that infer propositions and make inferences from them cohabit easily with other processes that are pragmatic and rely on knowledge of intentional states of affairs.

Propositions can be atomic or compound, i.e. atomic propositions can be negated, or joined in conjunction, disjunction, conditionality, and so forth. For example, the sentence 'If I am travelling with an American passport, then I must be an American citizen' supposes the proposition described above, and joins it with a conclusion drawn from that supposition together with other assumed propositional information. We need an account of how we reason to and from such compound propositions, that is, how we form and use them.

Forming a compound proposition requires an inference – one does not observe a disjunction or a conditional. Such connections are inferred, as both Hume and Kant noted in their different ways, in the understanding. It would be both a cruel hoax and evolutionarily disadvantageous for nature to provide us with propositional representations if our ways of connecting them and reasoning with them failed to preserve their propositional status. Because propositions are profoundly truth functional, their inference procedures ought to be truth preserving, that is, given a set of propositions assumed true, further propositions drawn from them by logical procedures also would be true. Logicians refer to this property as logical soundness, and a set of inference procedures is sound if, and only if, given a set of true propositions, the inference procedures will provide true conclusions only.

Soundness is distinct from validity; an argument is valid unless there is a possible assignment of truth values such that its premises taken conjunctively are true while its conclusion is false. Thus, in standard logic any argument with necessarily false premises is valid. This property is not part of our ordinary logical intuitions, with which we proceed from propositions assumed true. (See Braine and O'Brien, 1991, for a discussion of deliberately counterfactual suppositions.) Indeed, it is not uncommon for people to reject an argument because they do not accept its premises. Thus, ordinary reasoning proceeds not from premises, but from assumptions, that is, from premises that are assumed true (see Leblanc and Wisdom, 1976; Braine et al., 1984; Braine and O'Brien, 1991; Noveck et al., 1991; Politzer and Braine, 1991). Unlike the standard logic of textbooks, people draw no conclusions from contradictory premises – such premise sets cannot qualify as assumptions. No-one ordinarily would assume a contradictory set of premises, but would see such as absurd.

To summarize, logical reasoning is profoundly propositional, and propositional activities, such as asserting, denying, believing, doubting, and so forth, require intentional states of affairs; logical inference procedures cohabit with pragmatic inference procedures that concern the practical consequences of propositions for intentional states of affairs. A mental logic is not, therefore, a matter of mere symbol manipulation, but is about making propositional inferences, and ordinary reasoning applies sound inference procedures to propositions assumed true to infer propositions that inherit that truth.

Inference-schema models

Piaget (e.g. Inhelder and Piaget, 1958, 1964) proposed that the structure of concrete-operational thought corresponds to a logic of classes, and formal-operational thought is equivalent to the 16 truth-functional operators of normal-disjunctive form processed by the mathematical INRC group. This proposal, however, has been criticized on logical grounds (e.g. Braine and Rumain, 1983; Ennis, 1975; O'Brien, 1987; Parsons, 1959), and in recent years a consensus has developed among mental-logic adherents that reasoning proceeds through the application of sound inference schemas (e.g. Braine, 1990, in press; Braine and O'Brien, 1991; Braine *et al.*, 1984; Johnson-Laird, 1975; Macnamara, 1986; O'Brien, 1987, 1991; Osherson, 1975; Rips, 1983; Sperber and Wilson, 1986). Inference schemas are procedures that specify which propositions can be derived from assumed propositions of a particular form, and sound inference schemas assure that propositions derived from true assumptions inherit that truth. Thus far, psychological models proposing inference schemas have been developed only for sentential connectives and have not yet addressed the role of quantifiers. People make many sentential inferences that are sanctioned by standard systems of sentential logic, but routinely fail to make others. The primary task of a psychological inference-schema model is to describe those inferences that are made regularly and routinely. A secondary task is to describe those logical inferences that people make only sometimes.

Following Gentzen (1964/1935) logicians have described two sorts of inference schemas: those used to introduce a propositional connective in a line of reasoning, for example, a schema for conditional proof to introduce propositions of the form *if p then q*, and those used to eliminate a propositional connective in a line of reasoning, for example, a schema for disjunction elimination (*p or q, not-p*; therefore *q*), modus ponens (*if p then q, p*; therefore *q*). Note that inference schemas address the forms of propositions, but this syntactic nature of the inference procedure does not diminish the propositional nature of either the atomic or compound propositions that are inferred. Sound inference procedures insure that the drawn inferences will be truth preserving, that is, that only true propositions will be drawn from true assumptions.

The several varied inference-schema models that have been proposed do not make identical claims about the role of the schemas. For example,

Macnamara (1986) proposes that inference schemas are used as logical checking devices, checking the soundness of inferences made by other, non-logical, devices. Sperber and Wilson (1986) propose that only elimination schemas are used. The models proposed by Rips (1983), Osherson (1975), Johnson-Laird (1975), Braine *et al.* (1984), and Braine and O'Brien (1991) all use both introduction and elimination schemas to make inferences in lines of reasoning. Differences exist among these theories, however, concerning the particular schemas that are proposed. For example, the Braine *et al.* (1984) model does not include the disjunction-introduction schema, that draws propositions of the form *p or q* from *p*, although the models of Rips (1983) and Johnson-Laird (1975) do include such a schema.

The approach that I advocate proposes a three-part model (hereafter referred to as 'The Model'), which includes (a) a set of inference schemas; (b) a reasoning program that implements the schemas in a line of reasoning; and (c) a set of independently motivated pragmatic principles that influence interpretation of surface–structure propositions and can suggest or inhibit certain inferences and reasoning strategies (see Braine and O'Brien, 1991; Braine, 1990; O'Brien, 1991; Lea *et al.*, 1990; Noveck *et al.*, 1991). The description of The Model in the next few pages is intended to describe the present state of work – both what has been accomplished and what has yet to be done.

The inference schemas and the reasoning program

The inference schemas of The Model have been presented in detail elsewhere (Braine *et al.*, 1984; Lea *et al.*, 1990) so I do not do so here. The Model includes both introduction and elimination schemas, with a set of core schemas and some feeder schemas, both of which are implemented through a direct-reasoning routine, and a set of complex schemas that require co-ordination through an indirect-reasoning routine. The core schemas describe a set of inferences that people make routinely and without apparent effort, and includes a disjunction-elimination schema like the one described above, modus ponens, a disjunctive extension of modus ponens (*p or q, if p then r, if q then r*; therefore *r*), and some incompatibility schemas that are used in making *false* judgements, among others. The feeder set includes a conjunction-introduction schema (*p, q*; therefore p and q), a conjunction-elimination schema (*p and q*; therefore *p* [or *q*]), and a distributivity schema (*p and* [*q or r*] ↔ [*p and q*] *or* [*p and r*]).

The Model holds that the core schemas are applied automatically through a direct-reasoning routine whenever the appropriate propositions are considered together, for example, when both *p or q* and *not-p* are jointly considered, *q* will be inferred automatically. The feeder schemas, however, are not applied unless their propositional output feeds into a subsequent inference (see also Johnson-Laird, 1975, on 'auxilliary schemas'), in which case they are applied automatically by the direct-reasoning routine. Lea *et al.* (1990) presented two reasons for this differentiation of the feeder schemas from the core schemas. One is theoretical: the feeder schemas can lead to infinite loops, for example, from *p and q* to *p*, to *p and (p and q)*, and so forth. People exhibit no tendency to make such inference strings. The second reason to designate these as feeder schemas is empirical; when subjects are asked to write down every inference they can from a set of assumptions, subjects usually omit the output of the feeder schemas while writing down the output of the core schemas, even when the output of feeder schemas is required to make the core-schema inferences.

The complex schemas require use of an indirect-reasoning routine. For example, in order to falsify a proposition *p*, one can suppose *p* and seek to find a contradiction under this supposition. When this indirect-reasoning strategy does lead to a contradiction, a negation-introduction schema allows assertion of *not-p*. Unlike the core and feeder schemas, which are applied effortlessly and routinely, the complex schemas are in nowise claimed to be universally available, and their application depends on the effortful use of an indirect-reasoning routine.

Acquisition of the indirect-reasoning routine requires some tuition or reflection, and its use may be either encouraged or discouraged by knowledge of the referred intentional state of affairs. The direct-reasoning routine, however, is considered basic to logical reasoning. The Model thus predicts that problems requiring sophisticated reasoning strategies will not be solved readily by most people, whereas problems that can be solved through the direct-reasoning routine will be solved most of the time.

Differences exist among the inference-schema models concerning the nature of the reasoning program. Rips (1983) proposed a model in which the line of reasoning proceeds towards a goal, either a conclusion to be evaluated or a lemma required to evaluate a conclusion. Hence, if subjects are presented a set of assumptions with no conclusion to judge, the model generally would draw no inferences. However, several investigations have reported a wide variety of problems without any conclusions to be evaluated on which subjects have demonstrated no difficulty in drawing logically appropriate inferences (e.g. Lea *et al.*, 1990; O'Brien and Lee, 1992).

As described above, The Model proposes that both the core and feeder inference schemas are applied automatically both in processing discourse and in reasoning. This claim of automaticity is problematic, though, when one considers that the inferences of the feeder schemas are drawn only when they provide the input for drawing further inferences. This seems to indicate that people look ahead to see what inferences are needed before they make these inferences – hardly what one expects of an automatic process.

An additional, empirical reason to think that people look forward when drawing inferences is found in comparison of problems with and without conclusions to be judged. Consider the following two problems that I gave to some undergraduates recently (about toy animals and fruits in a box). The first problem presents assumptions of the form *p or q, if p then r*, and *if q then r*. This problem presents no conclusion to be evaluated, but requires subjects to write down everything that can be inferred. Most subjects write down only *r*. which follows directly through one of the core inference schemas. On the second problem subjects are given the same set of assumptions, but are asked to evaluate as a conclusion *If not-p then r*. On this problem subjects usually write down first q, and then r, before judging the conclusion as true – a line of reasoning that follows from The Model's schema for conditional proof. Clearly, were subjects not looking forward to consider the conclusion, the line of reasoning on the second problem should be the same as on the first problem. At least some of the time, people seem to look forward when they are applying the basic schemas of The Model.

As yet, the reasoning program of The Model does not capture adequately when subjects look ahead and when they do not, but then, neither does the reasoning program proposed by Rips (1983), with its focus on goal-attaining inferences. Relative to the schemas, little empirical work has been done on the reasoning program, but the need for further investigation of how the inference schemas are implemented becomes apparent *a fortiori* with the realization that lack of sophistication in using the reasoning program is a principal source of reasoning errors. Clearly, future developments in describing a reasoning program must include some forward-looking as well as some automatic processes.

Several possible solutions could be suggested. One possibility is that the feeder schemas are applied automatically, but are under processing constraints and subject to a response filter. The processing constraint might limit each feeder schema to a single application for a set of assumptions, and as a function of a filter its output would not be noticed unless it feeds a subsequent inference. A second possibility is that the reasoning program always looks ahead to seek potential goals – either logical or pragmatic. When a clear goal is discovered, reasoning proceeds towards that goal; when no goal is presented, the core schemas are applied automatically.

As the investigation proceeds, the description of the reasoning routines, as well as of the schemas, will rely on empirical investigation. The basic part of The Model is intended to describe real-time processes, and these should be open to real-time measurement. Brooke Lea, as part of a doctoral dissertation with Martin Braine, is investigating the core and feeder schemas, both in logical-reasoning problems and in text comprehension, measuring reaction times to investigate when subjects make these inferences, and I believe that this sort of investigation, among others, is needed to address the matter.

Pragmatic principles

That propositions are not identical to their surface-structure expressions is well known among memory and text-comprehension researchers (e.g. Bransford and Franks, 1971; Bransford *et al.*, 1972). Likewise, the logical connectives in a mental logic are not identical to the natural-language particles used to express them, although the two should be in close correspondence, so that certain words in a natural language would provide regular ways of expressing certain sorts of propositional connectives, such as the English-language words 'and' for conjunction, 'or' for disjunction, 'not' for negation, and 'if' for conditionality.

Natural-language logic particles have meanings that allow people to solve problems and draw inferences. Suppose we are given a problem providing assumptions of the form *if p or q then r* and *p*; we would conclude *r*. Given instead *if p and q then r* and *p*, we would conclude that nothing follows. The two problems differ only in the use of 'or' in one problem and 'and' in the other, so the difference in responses must be based only on the meanings of these words. Braine and O'Brien (1991) proposed that the basic meaning of a logic particle – its lexical entry – is provided by its basic inference schemas. For example, the basic meaning of 'if' is provided by modus ponens and a schema for conditional proof.

The basic meaning of a logic particle, given by the basic schemas, can be extended by *invited inferences*. Geis and Zwicky (1971) provide an example of an invited inference that derives *if not-p then not-q* from *if p then q*. Another example of an invited inference for 'if' is found in the pragmatic-reasoning schemas of Cheng and Holyoak (1985), who claim that modus-tollens inferences are provided by conditionals that express permissions and obligations.

Invited inferences can be encouraged or discouraged by knowledge of the intentional state of affairs to which the proposition is referred. For example, the Geis and Zwicky invited inference is encouraged by promissory content, for example, 'If you mow the lawn, I'll give you five dollars' invites the listener to infer that 'If I don't mow the lawn, I'll not receive the five dollars'. O'Brien *et al.* (1986) found that the Geis and Zwicky inference is more likely on problems within a mechanical domain than within a biological domain, where knowledge of spontaneous remissions discourages the invited inference. Staudenmayer (1975) has reported that this inference is encouraged when the problems express a causal connection.

Such invited inferences, as supplements to the basic inferences, extend rather than restrict the available inferences. Unlike the basic inferences, invited inferences may or may not be sound. Invited inferences can lead to appropriate responses, as with the pragmatic-reasoning schemas of Cheng and Holyoak (1985), or to logically inappropriate responses, such as those that follow from the invited inference of Geis and Zwicky (1971) and lead to the fallacies of the conditional syllogisms.

An invited inference that is not logically sound, however, is not necessarily irrational. The inference that one will not receive the five dollars if the lawn is not mowed is not sanctioned by logic, but is sanctioned by knowledge of the intentional state. Invited inferences are inherently pragmatic because they concern the practical consequences of the considered proposition for its referred intentional state of affairs.

Knowledge of an intentional state of affairs also can suggest alternatives or suppositions to be considered. For example, a mechanic faced with a motor that fails to start might draw on intentional knowledge and infer that the problem is either in the electrical system or the fuel system. If testing the electrical system reveals no problem, the mechanic would conclude that the problem must be with the fuel system. Logical inference schemas and pragmatic sorts of inference-making processes cohabit easily within a single line of reasoning, with the output of one sort of process feeding into the inferences made by the other. Generally, it seems unlikely that an inference is marked for its source – whether the inference stems from a logical inference schema or from intentional knowledge. Although the source of the inference is of interest to a cognitive investigator, there is no reason to think it is important to the mind engaged in the line of reasoning.

Some evidence for The Model

Direct evidence

Several studies have provided direct tests of The Model's claim that the core and feeder schemas together with the direct-reasoning routine are readily available. On one type of problem subjects were provided propositions that refer to letters written on an imaginary blackboard, for example, 'On the blackboard there is either a T or an X'. On another type of problem the propositions refer to boxes containing toy animals and fruits, for example, 'In this box there is either a lion or an elephant'. Note that these blackboard and box problems present materials that allow subjects to refer the propositions to an intentional state of affairs, although not to one that would provide the necessary inferences for solution on a basis other than the meanings of the logic particles.

The problems in Braine et al. (1984) presented assumptions together with conclusions to be evaluated, and The Model predicted successfully which problems were solved correctly, response times on simple problems and subjects' judgements about relative problem difficulty. Lea *et al.* (1990), Fisch (1991), and O'Brien and Lee (1992) presented one set of problems with conclusions to be evaluated on which subjects were asked to write down every intermediate inference they drew on the way to evaluating the conclusion, and another set of problems that presented assumptions without any conclusions, on which subjects were asked to write down everything they could infer from the assumptions. On both sorts of problems, The Model predicted successfully which inferences subjects wrote down, and the order in which they were written down. Subjects almost always wrote down the output of the core schemas in the order predicted by the model, but they almost never wrote down the output of the feeder schemas, even though the output of the core schemas often depended on the previous output of the feeder schemas. A few subjects, perhaps responding to the instructions to write down *everything*, wrote down the output of the feeder schemas, and when they did, this output was in the order predicted by The Model.

The inferences that The Model predicts should be made effortlessly and routinely were made routinely and with little apparent effort. These findings are not limited to American undergraduate students. Fisch (1991) found that 9- and 10-year-olds make the basic Model inferences as easily as do adults, and O'Brien and Lee (1992) found the same results when American college students were presented problems in English and Hong Kong college students were presented the same problems in Chinese. Although there may be other inferences also made routinely, those included in The Model appear secure. (One possible exception is the distributivity schema described above. Some subjects solve some of these problems successfully using another line of reasoning.)

In an investigation of The Model's predicted inferences in text comprehension, Lea *et al.* (1990) and Fisch (1991) presented story vignettes of four or five sentences each, and required subjects to judge whether or not a final sentence makes sense in the context of the story. These judgements required integration of logical information in reading the stories – corresponding to the introduction and elimination inferences of the core and feeder schemas of The Model. The stories were isomorphic in logical form to a parallel set of box and blackboard problems, on which subjects made the inferences predicted by The Model. Almost all subjects made the appropriate judgements on the story vignettes, demonstrating that they must have made the basic logical inferences described by The Model. Following this, on each story subjects were asked to judge each of three different sorts of statements. One was a paraphrase of information in the story, one was the output of a core inference of The Model, and a third was the output of a valid inference of standard logic, but was not predicted by The Model. Subjects were asked whether the information in each of the test sentences was presented in the story or had to be inferred from other information in the story. Whereas the non-Model logical inferences were judged as requiring an inference, both the paraphrase items and the items predicted by the core schemas of The Model were judged as having been presented in the story. Fisch (1991) found that subjects, including 9- and 10-year-olds, judged Model-predicted core items as having been presented in the stories even when these inferences were not required to comprehend the story. Thus, the inferences predicted by The Model are made in text comprehension so effortlessly that neither school children nor adults were aware that they made the inferences.

In sum, people seem to behave in the ways that The Model predicts both on logical-reasoning problems and in text comprehension. The Model successfully predicts which problems subjects solve, the relative perceived difficulty of the solved problems, response times on simple problems, and the order in which inferences are written down. I know of no competing model that has had this sort of empirical success.

Indirect evidence

The basic schemas should be available across languages and cultures. All natural languages should have regular ways of expressing conjunction, disjunction, conditionality, and negation, coresponding to such English language words as 'and', 'or', 'if', and 'not'. These words should enter early in language acquisition, and the early usage should be like that of adults. Although no exhaustive search has been made of which I am aware, all of those languages that have been surveyed do have such expressions. Across the half-dozen languages surveyed, 'and' and 'not' appear in speech in the second year, and 'or' and 'if' appear in the third year (Bates, 1974; Bloom *et al.*, 1980; Bowerman, 1986; Kuczaj and Daly, 1979; Lust and Mervis, 1980; Pea, 1980; Reilly, 1986). These studies show that early use of these particles is like that of adults, these particles are applied across a wide variety of situations and content from the beginning of their use, and the particles are used in ways that are consistent with the basic schemas of The Model.

A REPLY TO SOME ARGUMENTS AGAINST MENTAL LOGIC

No shortage of reasons have been put forth to deny the existence of a mental logic, and those discussed here are not intended to be exhaustive, but rather to be instructive. One argument against mental logic stems from the failure of most people to solve a variety of laboratory logical-reasoning tasks. Most notable are the algebraic-content versions (that is, about arbitrary letters, numbers, shapes, colours, etc.) of Wason's selection task and the THOG task, a failure that has been interpreted as an impeachment of mental logic, particularly when compared to successful solution on some meaningful-content versions (e.g. Johnson-Laird *et al.*, 1972; Griggs and Cox, 1982; Cheng and Holyoak, 1985; Cosmides, 1989).

On Wason's selection task (Wason, 1968) subjects are presented four cards showing, for example, A, D, 4, and 7, respectively. They are told that each card has a letter on one side and a number on the other, and presented with a conditional rule for the four cards, such as: 'If a card has a vowel, then it also has an even number.' Finally, they are told that the rule may be true, but could be false, and are asked to select those cards, and only those cards, one would need to turn over for inspection to test the truth status of the rule. Typically, few people are able to select correctly only the cards showing A and 7 (see Evans, 1982, for a review).

Cheng and Holyoak (1985) noted that in some studies up to 20 per cent of subjects can fail to select the card showing A, which they interpret as evidence against the ubiquitous availability of modus ponens. However, consider the line of reasoning that is required to select this card. To solve the problem one begins by supposing that the rule is true. The card showing an A provides a satisfying instance of a vowel, and taken together with the supposition of the rule, by modus ponens it follows that the other side of the card must show an even number. At this point there is still no reason to turn over the card; this realization requires the reasoner now to consider the possibility of there being instead an odd number, in which case the supposition that the rule is true could be falsified by reductio ad absurdum, because there might be an odd number where there has to be an even number. Note, then, that selection of the card showing an A goes well beyond making a modus-ponens inference. Indeed, it exceeds the basic skills of The Model. The other potentially falsifying card, showing the number 7, requires an even more complex line of reasoning, with an additional reductio embedded under the original supposition of the rule.

With the exception of Piaget (see Beth and Piaget, 1966: 181 which seems to indicate that the selection task should be solvable), none of the theories of mental logic predicts that such problems will be solved, and the basic parts of The Model, including the core and feeder schemas together with the direct-reasoning routine, are nowhere near being sufficient to solve such problems. Thus, failure to solve these complex problems does not count as evidence against The Model.

The literature now includes an algebraic-content version of the selection task that many subjects solve (Griggs, 1989). This problem presents four cards drawn from two decks of ordinary playing cards, one deck with red backs and the other with blue backs. The rule states that: 'If a card has a value greater than 6, then it must have a blue back.' Perhaps subjects perform better on this task version because they can anticipate more easily what might be on the other side of the card. Whatever the reason, these correct responses are difficult to explain unless one assumes some logical reasoning.

Another complex logical reasoning problem that few people are able to solve is the THOG task (Wason and Brooks, 1979), and its solution also requires a reasoning strategy that goes well beyond the basic parts of The Model. Recently, several versions of the THOG task have been reported that many people solve (O'Brien *et al.*, 1990; Girotto and Legrenzi, 1989). None of these task versions seem solvable by non-logical means, and the finding that some algebraic-content versions of the selection and THOG tasks can be solved indicates that many adults have developed considerable logical-reasoning skills that go well beyond the core and feeder schemas and the direct-reasoning program of The Model.

I discuss the claim that some realistic-content versions of the selection task have led to successful solution later in this paper. For now I limit my comments to how we should interpret the effects of content on reasoning. Cheng and Holyoak (1989: 286) state that 'content effects cannot be explained by theories based solely on formal rules', and I agree. Likewise, theories based entirely on content-bound processes cannot explain success on algebraic-content problems, such as the box and blackboard problems discussed above. This is why I advocate the three-part theory. A finding of a content effect presents no problem for The Model, for it does not claim exclusivity for the logical inference schemas. The reason that some algebraic-content problems are more difficult than their realistic-content isomorphs is that the algebraic-content versions are intentionally impoverished – they do not readily evoke an understandable state of affairs and are disconnected from the ordinary concerns of propositional activities.

Not all errors on laboratory logical-reasoning tasks are made on complex problems. For example, on the same problem sets on which subjects (both adults and children) routinely make modus-ponens inferences, they also often commit the denial-of-the-antecedent fallacy. For example, Rumain *et al.* (1983) reported that given the assumptions: 'If there is a dog in the box, then there is an apple' and 'There is a dog in the box', people almost always conclude that 'There is an apple', an inference that follows straightforwardly by modus ponens. When given the same first assumption, but with 'There is not a dog in the box' as a second premise, many people erroneously accept 'There is not an apple'. This fallacy disappears, however, when (a) the asymmetry of the conditional is made explicit, for example: 'If there is a dog in the box then there is an apple, but if there is not a dog, there may or may not be an apple'; and (b) when an additional conditional assumption is provided, for example, 'If there is a lion in the box, there is an apple' (see also Markovits, 1984, 1985). Inference-schema theorists, such as Rumain and colleagues, have interpreted the finding that such fallacies can be suppressed as indicating that the fallacies are invited rather than basic inferences.

Recently, Byrne (1989) has claimed that a similar procedure can suppress valid modus-ponens inferences. This claim, if correct, would be a serious challenge to The Model, which includes modus ponens as a core inference. Consider, however, Byrne's evidence. Subjects were told to assume, for example: 'If Mary has an essay to write then she will study late in the library', and 'She has an essay to write'. Most subjects concluded that she will study late in the library. Given the same two assumptions together with the additional premise: 'If the library stays open then she will study late in the library', however, many subjects did not conclude that she will study late in the library. Thus, concludes Byrne, valid modus-ponens inferences can be suppressed in the same way as the fallacious ones, and although modus ponens is a valid inference of logic, the mind includes no such rule.

From the perspective of mental logic, the finding that subjects fail to assert on the expanded premise set that Mary will study late in the library is not surprising. The additional premise, together with knowledge about libraries, suggests that the library might close earlier than Mary would like, and the first premise might, then, not be true. Thus, the expanded premise set does not serve as a set of assumptions, as the first conditional is open to doubt. The Model predicts a 'can't tell' response in such cases, which is what subjects often conclude.

Politzer and Braine (1991) have made a similar argument to which Byrne (1991) has replied. According to Byrne, the Politzer and Braine argument proceeds as follows. The subject begins with the two conditional premises:

1 If Mary has an essay to write then she will study late in the library.
2 If the library stays open, then she will stay late in the library.

Based on a conversion of (2), the subject next asserts:

3 If she studies late in the library, then the library necessarily stays open.

By transitivity, propositions (1) and (3) lead to:

4 If she has an essay to write, then necessarily the library stays open.

On the basis of world knowledge, the subject asserts:

5 It is false that if she has an essay to write, then the library necessarily stays open.

This leads to:

6 It is false that if she has an essay to write, then she stays late in the library.

This supports the inference:

7 She has an essay to write and does not stay late in the library.

And from conjunction elimination:

8 She does not stay late in the library.

So, says Byrne, according to Politzer and Braine, subjects should conclude that Mary does not stay late in the library. However, the data reported in Byrne (1989) do not support this prediction, and instead, most subjects conclude that

9 She may or may not stay late in the library.

The problem with Byrne's reply to Politzer and Braine is that it mis-represents their argument. First, Politzer and Braine do not claim that the inference in (3) is based on a conversion of (2). Rather, they claim, it comes from knowing that libraries do not always stay open late, and that one can study late in a library only if that library remains open. More importantly, Politzer and Braine do not claim that subjects make the inference in (6); they argue simply that (1) and (3) together lead to the false inference in (4), so that one cannot consider (1) and (3) true together. Thus, premise (1), on which the modus-ponens inference is based, is open to doubt. Finally, because Politzer and Braine do not assert (6), they do not commit themselves to the line of reasoning in (7)–(8). Whereas Byrne claims that Politzer and Braine predict the conclusion in (8), Politzer and Braine state specifically that the rational interpretation of the two conditional premises is:

10 If she has an essay to write and if the library is open, then she will study late in the library,

And the rational conclusion is 'She may or may not study late in the library', which is (9), and, as Byrne tells us, this is what most subjects conclude. My reading of the situation is that the suppression of modus ponens reported by Byrne (1989), in all of her examples, is based on premise sets that subjects find open to doubt. For such premise sets, the mental-logic approach predicts exactly the sort of responses that Byrne is reporting.

An additional empirical argument against mental logic concerns the demonstrated effects of a variety of non-logical heuristics, most notably the use of matching (e.g. Evans, 1982; Evans and Lynch, 1973). The matching hypothesis holds that many responses on a variety of logical-reasoning tasks are merely matches to the values named in the task's rule, for example, selecting the cards showing a vowel and an even number in the original selection task. Some empirical evidence has been reported that supports the claim, particularly the manipulation of negatives with the selection task. However, the matching hypothesis has not yet been worked out in sufficient detail so that its predictions are always apparent. Although there is agreement concerning the matching-hypothesis predictions for the selection task, this is not so for the THOG task. The problem presents four designs: A black triangle, a white triangle, a black circle, and a white circle. Subjects are told that the experimenter has written down one of the shapes and one of the colours, and that any design is a THOG if, and only if, it has either the shape or the colour written down, but not both. Told that the black triangle is a THOG, subjects are asked to classify each of the remaining designs as: (a) definitely a THOG; (b) insufficient information to decide; or (c) definitely not a THOG. Responses predominantly fall into two erroneous response patterns: Pattern A in which the white triangle and the black circle are judged as possible THOGs and the white circle is judged as definitely not a THOG, and Pattern B in which the white triangle and the black circle are judged THOGs and the white circle is judged as definitely not a THOG. Evans (1982) has used the matching hypothesis to account for Pattern A, whereas Griggs and Newstead (1983) and Girotto and Legrenzi (1989) claim that the matching hypothesis predicts Pattern B. To date, then, the matching hypothesis has not been described in sufficient detail to know what its predictions are. Griggs and Newstead, and Girotto and Legrenzi, take a strong view of matching, and assume that subjects are matching without using any logical resources. Evans, though, describes a situation in which subjects use both the matching heuristic and some logical processes.

Evans and I are in agreement on an essential point – human reasoning consists both of logical and non-logical processes. We differ, though, in emphasis. In Evans's view, problems are first processed by non-logical heuristics, which are sufficiently primitive that our fairly weak logical resources are rarely of much use. Indeed, Evans sees such little use for a mental logic that he has not described what he thinks it includes. From the perspective of mental logic, I see people using logic frequently, both in ordinary tasks and in laboratory-reasoning tasks. When mental logic can be applied straightforwardly, it will be. When the reasoner has available the strategic skills required to solve a complex problem, and grasps the problem's requirements, mental logic will allow solution. Otherwise, the problem solver has no other recourse but to non-logical heuristics or to pragmatic inferences.

Finally, I consider the conceptual question raised by Johnson-Laird (1983): which logic do we propose is the appropriate model for a mental logic? After all, infinitely many possible logic systems for quantifiers and modal operators could be constructed. Part of the answer is intuitive. I assume a two-valued logic of truth and falsity rather than a three-valued logic. Esoteric logical systems are just that: esoteric. As to which schemas for a two-valued logic should be included, I think this an empirical question – those that are easily expressible across languages, that people make readily, and that appear early in language acquisition, should be included. Unlike some theories, the inference-schema models make a wide variety of specific empirical predictions that can be tested and compared, and the appropriate specific features will emerge from experimental investigations motivated by the existing models.

COMPETING NON-LOGICAL THEORIES HAVE THEIR OWN PROBLEMS

This section is not meant to provide an exhaustive review of the competing non-logical theories. First, I address the content-bound theories proposed by Cosmides (1989) and by Cheng and Holyoak (1985), then the mental-models approach of Johnson-Laird (1983) and Johnson-Laird and Byrne (1991).

Content-bound theories

Cheng and Holyoak (1985, 1989), Cheng *et al.* (1986), and Holland *et al.* (1986) have proposed that people reason typically not using logical-inference schemas, but using inductively learned rules defined in terms of classes of goals, such as taking desirable actions or predicting future events. Thus far, their theory has described only two rules – one for permission and one for obligation. The permission rule holds that: 'If the action is to be taken, then the prerequisite must be fulfilled.'

Cosmides also has argued that people rarely reason 'according to the canons of logic' (Cosmides, 1989: 191), and proposed that because 99 per cent of human bioevolutionary history has consisted of hunter/gatherer activities, our biological endowment includes special abilities to reason about social contracts and their associated costs and benefits. These social contracts have a conditional form: 'If one takes a benefit then one must pay the cost.' Social-contract rules appear to be a subset of permission/ obligation rules (paying a cost is a special case of fulfilling a prerequisite, and taking a benefit is a special case of taking an action). Thus, supporting evidence for the social-contract theory would also be supporting evidence for the pragmatic-schemas theory. Cosmides would need to show that only problems presenting social-contract rules are solved, and the larger class of other permission/obligation problems are not. This does not seem to be the case. Pollard (1990), Cheng and Holyoak (1989), and Manktelow and Over (1990) have shown that subjects are not influenced by the degree of costs or benefits, and that subjects can solve some permission task versions that have neither perceivable costs nor benefits.

The empirical evidence both for the social-contract and for the pragmatic-reasoning-schemas theories thus far has been limited to performance on some quasi selection-task versions, such as the 'Drinking-age Problem' introduced by Griggs and Cox (1982). The subject is told to imagine being a policeman enforcing the rule that: 'If a person is drinking alcohol, that person must be at least 21 years old.' Four cards are presented, each with a person's age on one side, and their beverage on the other. Subjects are instructed to turn over those cards, and only those cards, that might lead to the discovery of a rule violator. Most people are able to select the logically appropriate cards (the card showing someone who is underage and the card showing an alcoholic beverage).

Note that the realistic-content versions of the selection task that have led to solution, such as the Drinking-age Problem, are structurally distinct from the selection task. On the pragmatic-schemas problems, the rule is assumed true and can be used directly to draw a conclusion. This is not a trivial difference, for the original selection task is a metalogical rather than a logical-reasoning problem. After all, the title of Wason's seminal paper (Wason, 1968) was 'Reasoning about a rule', not 'Reasoning from a rule'. On these quasi-selection tasks, the need to turn over the card corresponding to A in the original task follows straightforwardly by modus ponens. The problem is inherently easier.

The most impressive evidence for the pragmatic-reasoning-schemas theory has been Cheng and Holyoak's (1985) abstract-permission problem. On this problem subjects are told to imagine that they are working in a company enforcing the rule: 'If a person takes Action A, then that person must first fulfil Prerequisite P.' The four cards show: 'Has taken Action A, has not taken Action A', 'has fulfilled Prerequisite P', and 'has not fulfilled Prerequisite P'. This problem differs from the original selection task in three crucial ways. First, it requires a search for a rule violator rather than a test of the rule's truth status. Second, it presents what Jackson and Griggs (1990) refer to as 'a checking context', that is, subjects are asked to assume the role of a rule enforcer. Third, the cards present explicit rather than implicit negatives – 'has not taken Action A', rather than the card showing D. Jackson and Griggs found that when any of these three task features are changed to parallel the original task, subjects fail to solve the abstract-permission problem. Recently, in work with Ira Noveck and with two undergraduate students at Baruch College, I have found non-pragmatic algebraic versions that include these three crucial features and that many people are able to solve. It may be that solution of the abstract-permission problem has nothing to do with the permissionary nature of the rules, but stems from these other extraneous task features.

I agree with Cosmides that our reasoning skills are the result of our bio-evolutionary history, but this history has provided us with some basic logical intuitions that make propositional language and reasoning possible. I see no *a priori* reason that evolution should provide domain-specific processes but not general processes. Species with overly specified behavioural traits are at an evolutionary disadvantage when their environmental situation changes. A set of content-free inference procedures would be of evolutionary benefit, providing a basis for logic particles that allow communication in a wide variety of situations. To the extent that people have some content-bound inference procedures, they coexist with a set of more general logical inference procedures.

Mental models

Johnson-Laird (1983, 1986) and Johnson-Laird and Byrne (1991) have proposed that when people process discourse, they construct internal representations, called mental models. Inferences are drawn from models by describing information explicitly represented in them. Reasoning consists of searching for alternative models that could falsify a tentative conclusion. Whereas the mental-logic approach does not claim exclusivity, the mental-models approach claims that it can account for all reasoning, and that people never use inference schemas of the sort in The Model.

Johnson-Laird and his colleagues have not provided a clear description of what a mental model is. Mental models can be images, but clearly are intended to go beyond images. As was discussed earlier, images are not propositional, and unlike propositions, mental models do not include variables. The elements of a mental model always refer to specific instances. This absence of variables in mental models leads to a representational confusion.

Early versions of the theory represented the universally quantified: 'all p are q' as:

11 p = q
   p = q
      (q)

where each line in the model represents an individual case. The parenthetical term in line 3 represents an optional instance of q without p. The problem with the representation in this model is that it fails to capture the universality of 'all p are q'. How does one know that other possible instances that could be added to the model fit this pattern? Johnson-Laird and Byrne (1991) seem to have recognized this problem, and now propose the following model instead:

12 [p] q
   [p] q
      . . .

where the square-bracket notation is an exhaustivity tag. The third line is an ellipsis that functions as a reminder that there might be other model interpretations that have not been considered, but the exhaustivity of p in lines 1 and 2 means that any 'fleshing out' of the ellipsis cannot include a p. A fully explicit model can be fleshed out as follows:

13 [p]   [q]
   [p]   [q]
   [~p]   [q]
   [~p]   [~q],

which includes a 'propositional-like tag representing negation' (Johnson-Laird and Byrne, 1991: 44). So, mental-model representations are not propositional, but contain propositional-like tags; they do not contain variables, but can attach individual cases with an exhaustivity tag to constrain all other possible cases.[2]

This attempt at solving the problem of variables has not been successful. Suppose we ask someone to judge the truth or falsity of: 'All natural numbers that end in zero are divisible by five.' What would the representation of [p] in (13) become? It could not be [a natural number that ends in zero], because this expresses a variable, and the elements in a mental model must refer to individual cases. So suppose [p] in line 1 is represented as [20] and in line 2 as [5970], in other words, we choose some positive exemplars randomly. The representation of [q] in lines 1, 2, and 3 presumably would be [divisible by five]. How, then, does one know that *all* natural numbers ending in zero are divisible by five? To know that 5970 is divisible by five requires more than reading the model – it requires a computation (unless, of course, the proposition is more primitive than the model). A rigorous proof that all such numbers have this property requires a complex line of propositional reasoning that refers to variables.

The propositional-like tag for negation also strikes me as problematic; representation of negative instances has been a well-known difficulty since the concept-attainment work of Bruner *et al.* (1956). My intuition is that negations are represented propositionally, and the propositional activities associated with them are consistent with the inference schemas for 'not'.

In sum, there are many sorts of propositions that are difficult, if not impossible, to represent with a mental model. Thus, there is a clear need for some representational and inference processes other than those provided by mental models. I make no claim that people never use mental models – only that inferences from mental models would cohabit with inferences from other sources, including those of a mental logic. I do not think, though, that Johnson-Laird and his associates have provided an adequate account of what such mental models would be, and their introduction of propositional-like tags suggests that part of a mental-models theory should be a propositional mental logic.[3]

IRRATIONALITY AND THE MODEL

Both the content-bound theories of Cosmides (1989) and Cheng and Holyoak (1985) and the mental-models theory of Johnson-Laird and his colleagues, have framed the debate in terms of an exclusive disjunction: People use only social-contract rules or only the canons of logic; they use only pragmatic-reasoning schemas or only content-free formal rules; they use only mental models or only formal rules. Thus, when these theorists find support for their accounts, they conclude that people do not use logical-inference schemas. Such arguments against theories that rely only on formal content-free inference rules are straw-man arguments. Mental-logic theorists have never claimed exclusivity. Even Piaget thought that formal-operational skills are constrained by real-world knowledge. The mental-logic approach does not claim that all of human reasoning is described by some content-free formal rules. To the contrary, a mental logic is what makes reasoning propositional, and propositions refer to intentional states of affairs. Thus, the inference schemas of a mental logic cohabit easily with pragmatic reasoning processes having to do with the practical consequences of propositions for their referred states of affairs. Evidence for some effects of extralogical processes is not inconsistent with the claims of the mental-logic approach.

That people make errors on some reasoning tasks is not a sufficient reason to proclaim the absence of any mental logic. Given the explanatory value of a mental logic, particularly a model that has generated a variety of empirical support, the obituaries are hasty and ill-advised. Just as the grammatically untutored might be surprised to learn that they had been using nouns and verbs all of their lives, the non-logical theorists will be surprised to discover that they have been using a mental logic all along.

A mental logic provides the basis for rational judgements, but does not ensure them. Mental logic provides the experience of deductive certainty that often accompanies a logical inference, and leads people to seek consistency among the propositions they assume. Even rationalization is rational in its intent, which is to maintain a consistent set of propositions. When people are irrational, it is not because they lack a mental logic, but because the demands of the situation exceed their logic skills, because inferences from non-logical sources are made, or because they are reasoning from irrational assumptions.

Consistent failure of someone to accept such basic inferences as modus ponens, disjunction elimination, and cancellation of a double negative would make that person irrational. Without such inferences, a person could not maintain the soundness of a line of thought. Accepting a modus ponens inference, however, is not enough to make one rational; many deluded residents of mental hospitals make such inferences routinely. When one applies sound inference procedures to an irrational set of assumptions, one is apt to draw irrational conclusions.

Reasoning can be done skilfully or clumsily, and, as with any skill, practice, coaching, and a joy for the activity can improve the level of skill.

A mental logic provides the basis for sound logical reasoning, but does not guarantee skilled play.

ACKNOWLEDGEMENT

The author expresses appreciation to Martin Braine for several years of discussion, debate, and argument. He is, of course, responsible for nothing written here.

NOTES

1 Images are not propositional; although an image might be an accurate or an inaccurate representation, it can be neither true nor false. Propositions that refer to images, though, are true or false. Probabilistic propositions, however, take truth values (the claim that 'there is an 80 per cent probability of showers next Tuesday' is either true or false; it is not 80 per cent true and 20 per cent false.)
2 The model in (13) is identical to the fully 'fleshed out' representation for the simple conditional ('if p then q'), except for the redundancy of lines 1 and 2. Thus, the representation of 'if p then q' is equivalent to (13) without line 1. However, Johnson-Laird and Byrne tell us that the representation of 'if p then q' contains three models instead of one model in the representation for 'all p are q'. At the least this seems notationally weak. How does the mind holding (13) know that it is universal solely because of the redundancy of lines 1 and 2, and how does the mind holding the fully 'fleshed out' counterpart for 'if p then q' know that it contains three models, whereas (13) contains only one?
3 Additional criticisms of the theory of mental models are provided by Braine (in press), Braine and O'Brien (1991), Ford (1985), and Rips (1986).

REFERENCES

Bates, E. (1974) 'The acquisition of conditionals by Italian children', *Proceedings of the 10th Regional Meeting of the Chicago Linguistic Society*, Chicago: Chicago Linguistic Society.

Beth, E. and Piaget, J. (1966) *Mathematical Epistimology and Psychology*, Dordrecht: Reidel.

Bloom, L., Lahey, M., Hood, L., Lifter, K., and Feiss, K. (1980) 'Complex sentences: acquisition of syntactic connectives and the semantic relations they encode', *Journal of Child Language* 7: 235–61.

Bowerman, M. (1986) 'First steps in acquiring conditionals', in E. Traugott, A. ter Meulen, J.S. Reilly, and C.A. Ferguson (eds) *On Conditionals*, Cambridge: Cambridge University Press.

Braine, M.D.S. (1990) 'The "natural logic" approach to reasoning', in W.F. Overton (ed.) *Reasoning, Necessity, and Logic: Developmental Perspectives*, Hillsdale, NJ: Erlbaum.

—— (in press) 'Mental logic and how to discover it', in J. Macnamara and G.E. Reyes (eds) *The Logical Foundations of Cognition*, Oxford: Oxford University Press.

Braine, M.D.S. and O'Brien, D.P. (1991) 'A theory of *if*: a lexical entry, reasoning program, and pragmatic principles', *Psychological Review* 98: 182–203.

Braine, M.D.S. and Rumain, B. (1983) 'Logical reasoning', in J.H. Flavell and

E. Markman (eds) *Handbook of Child Psychology. vol. 3. Cognitive Development*, New York: Wiley, pp. 263–339.

Braine, M.D.S., Reiser, B.J., and Rumain, B. (1984) 'Some empirical justification for a theory of natural propositional logic', in G. Bower (ed.) *The Psychology of Learning and Motivation: Advances in Research and Theory*, vol. 18, New York: Academic Press.

Bransford, J.D. and Franks, J.J. (1971) 'The abstraction of linguistic ideas', *Cognitive Psychology* 2: 331–50.

Bransford, J.D., Barclay, J.R., and Franks, J.J. (1972) 'Sentence memory: a constructive versus interpretive approach', *Cognitive Psychology* 3: 193–209.

Bruner, J.S., Goodnow, J.J., and Austin, G.D. (1956) *A Study of Thinking*, New York: Wiley.

Byrne, R.M. (1989) 'Suppressing valid inferences with conditionals', *Cognition* 31: 61–83.

—— (1991) 'Can valid inferences be suppressed?' *Cognition* 39: 71–8.

Cheng, P.W. and Holyoak, K.J. (1985) 'Pragmatic reasoning schemas', *Cognitive Psychology* 17: 391–416.

—— (1989) 'On the natural selection of reasoning theories', *Cognition* 33: 285–313.

Cheng, P.W., Holyoak, K.J., Nisbett, R.E., and Oliver, L.M. (1986) 'Pragmatic versus syntactic approaches to training deductive reasoning', *Cognitive Psychology* 18: 293–328.

Cosmides, L. (1989) 'The logic of social exchange: has natural selection shaped how humans reason? Studies with the Wason selection task', *Cognition* 31: 187–276.

Ennis, R.H. (1975) 'Children's ability to handle Piaget's propositional logic', *Review of Educational Research* 45: 1–41.

Evans, J.St B.T. (1982) *The Psychology of Deductive Reasoning*, Boston: Routledge & Kegan Paul.

Evans, J.St B.T. and Lynch, J.S. (1973) 'Matching bias in the selection task', *British Journal of Psychology* 64: 391–7.

Fisch, S.M. (1991) 'Mental logic in children's reasoning and text comprehension', unpublished doctoral thesis, New York University.

Ford, M. (1985) 'Review of Johnson-Laird, P.N.', *Mental Models: Towards a Cognitive Science of Language, Inference, and Consciousness*, Cambridge, MA, Harvard University Press, 1983; *Language* 61: 897–903.

Geis, M. and Zwicky, A.M. (1971) 'On invited inferences', *Linguistic Inquiry* 2: 561–6.

Gentzen, G. (1964/1935) 'Investigations into logical deduction', *American Philosophical Quarterly* 1: 288–306.

Girotto, V. and Legrenzi, P. (1989) 'Mental representation and hypothetico-deductive reasoning: the case of the THOG problem', *Psychological Research* 51: 129–35.

Griggs, R.A. (1989) 'To "see" or not to "see": that is the selection task', *Quarterly Journal of Experimental Psychology* 41A: 517–29.

Griggs, R.A. and Cox, J.R. (1982) 'The elusive thematic-materials effect in Wason's selection task', *British Journal of Psychology* 73: 407–20.

Griggs, R.A. and Newstead, S.E. (1983) 'The source of intuitive errors in Wason's THOG problem', *British Journal of Psychology* 74: 451–9.

Holland, J.H., Holyoak, K.J., Nisbett, R.E., and Thagard, P. (1986) *Induction*, Cambridge, MA: MIT Press.

Inhelder, B. and Piaget, J. (1958) *The Growth of Logical Thinking from Childhood to Adolescence*, New York: Basic Books.

—— (1964) *The Early Growth of Logic in the Child*, London: Routledge & Kegan Paul.

Jackson, S.L. and Griggs, R.A. (1990) 'The elusive pragmatic reasoning schemas effect', *Quarterly Journal of Experimental Psychology* 42A: 353–73.

James, W. (1978/1885) *Pragmatics and the Meaning of Truth*, Cambridge, MA: Harvard University Press.

Johnson-Laird, P.N. (1975) 'Models of deduction', in R. Falmagne (ed.) *Reasoning: Representation and Process*, Hillsdale, NJ: Erlbaum.

—— (1983) *Mental Models: Towards a Cognitive Science of Language, Inference, and Consciousness*, Cambridge: Cambridge University Press.

—— (1986) 'Reasoning without logic', in T. Myers, K. Brown, and G.M. McGonigle (eds) *Reasoning and Discourse Processes*, London: Academic Press.

Johnson-Laird, P.N. and Byrne, R.M. (1991) *Deduction*, Hove: Erlbaum.

Johnson-Laird, P.N., Legrenzi, P., and Legrenzi, M.S. (1972) 'Reasoning and a sense of reality', *British Journal of Psychology* 63: 395–400.

Kant, I. (1781/1966) *Critique of Pure Reason*, Garden City, NY: Anchor Books.

Kneale, W.G. and Kneale, M. (1962) *The Development of Logic*, Oxford: Clarendon Press.

Kuczaj, S.A. and Daly, M.J. (1979) 'The development of hypothetical reference in the speech of young children', *Journal of Child Language* 6: 563–79.

Lea, R.B., O'Brien, D.P., Fisch, S.M., Noveck, I.A., and Braine, M.D.S. (1990) 'Predicting propositional logic inferences in text comprehension', *Journal of Memory and Language* 29: 361–87.

Leblanc, H. and Wisdom, W. (1976) *Deductive Logic*, Boston, MA: Allyn & Bacon.

Legrenzi, P. and Legrenzi, M.S. (1991) 'Reasoning and social psychology: from a mental logic to a perspective approach', *Intellectica* 11: 53–80.

Lust, B. and Mervis, C.A. (1980) 'Development of coordination in the natural speech of young children', *Journal of Child Language* 7: 279–304.

Macnamara, J. (1986) *A Border Dispute: The Place of Logic in Psychology*, Cambridge, MA: MIT Press.

Manktelow, K.I. and Over, D.E. (1990) 'Deontic thought and the selection task', in K.J. Gilhooly, M. Keane, R, Logie, and G. Erdos (eds) *Lines of Thought: Reflections on the Psychology of Thinking*, Chichester: Wiley.

Markovits, H. (1984) 'Awareness of the "possible" as a mediator of formal thinking conditional reasoning problems', *British Journal of Psychology* 75: 367–76.

—— (1985) 'Incorrect conditional reasoning among adults: competence or performance?' *British Journal of Psychology* 76: 241–7.

Noveck, I.A., Lea, R.B., Davidson, G.M., and O'Brien, D.P. (1991) 'Human reasoning is both logical and pragmatic', *Intellectica* 11: 81–109.

O'Brien, D.P. (1987) 'The development of conditional reasoning: an iffy proposition', in H. Reese (ed.) *Advances in Child Behavior and Development*, vol. 18, New York Academic Press, pp. 66–91.

—— (1991) 'Conditional reasoning development', in R. Dulbecco (ed.) *Encyclopedia of Human Biology*, San Diego, CA: Academic Press.

O'Brien, D.P. and Lee, H-W. (1992) 'A cross-linguistic investigation of a model of mental logic: the same inferences are made in English and Chinese', unpublished manuscript.

O'Brien, D.P., Costa, G., and Overton, W.F. (1986) 'Evaluation of causal and conditional hypotheses', *Quarterly Journal of Experimental Psychology* 38A: 493–512.

O'Brien, D.P., Noveck, I.A., Davidson, G.M., Fisch, S.M., Lea, R.B., and

Freitag, J. (1990) 'Sources of difficulty in deductive reasoning: the THOG task', *Quarterly Journal of Experimental Psychology* 42A: 329–51.

Osherson, D. (1975) *Logical Abilities in Children. vol. 3. Reasoning in Adolescence: Deductive Inference*, Hillsdale, NJ: Erlbaum.

Parsons, C. (1959) 'Inhelder and Piaget's "The growth of logical thinking", II. A logician's viewpoint', *British Journal of Psychology* 51: 75–84.

Pea, R.D. (1980) 'Development of negation in early child language', in D.R. Olson (ed.) *The Social Foundation of Language and Thought: Essays in Honor of Jerome Bruner*, New York: W.W. Norton.

Peirce, C.S. (1958/1931) *Collected Papers of Charles Sanders Peirce*, Cambridge, MA: Harvard University Press.

Politzer, G. and Braine, M.D.S. (1991) 'Responses to inconsistent premisses cannot count as suppression of valid inferences', *Cognition* 38: 103–8.

Pollard, P. (1990) 'Natural selection for the selection task: limits to social exchange theory', *Cognition* 36: 195–204.

Reilly, J.S. (1986) 'The acquisition of temporals and conditionals', in E. Traugott, A. ter Meulen, J.S. Reilly, and C.A. Ferguson (eds) *On Conditionals*, Cambridge: Cambridge University Press.

Rips, L.J. (1983) 'Cognitive processes in propositional reasoning', *Psychological Review* 90: 38–71.

—— (1986) 'Mental muddles', in M. Brand and R.M. Harnisch (eds) *Problems in the Representation of Knowledge and Belief*, Tucson, AZ: University of Arizona Press.

Rumain, B., Connell, J., and Braine, M.D.S. (1983) 'Conversational comprehension processes are responsible for reasoning fallacies in children as well as adults: *If* is not the biconditional', *Developmental Psychology* 19: 471–81.

Sperber, D. and Wilson, D. (1986) *Relevance: Communication and Cognition*, Cambridge, MA: Harvard University Press.

Staudenmayer, H. (1975) 'Understanding conditional reasoning with meaningful propositions', in R. Falmagne (ed.) *Reasoning: Representation and Process*, Hillsdale, NJ: Erlbaum.

Wason, P.C. (1968) 'Reasoning about a rule', *Quarterly Journal of Experimental Psychology* 20: 273–81.

Wason, P.C. and Brooks, P.G. (1979) 'THOG: The anatomy of a problem', *Psychological Research* 41: 79–90.

Chapter 6

Rational reasoning and human implementations of logic

K. Stenning and M. Oaksford

INTRODUCTION

Recent psychological debate about the role of logic in human reasoning orientates itself to logical calculi, either by proposing them as mechanisms of reasoning (e.g. Braine, 1978) or by rejecting any role for them and proposing to supplant them with purportedly non-formal mechanisms (e.g. Johnson-Laird, 1983; Johnson-Laird and Byrne, 1991).

Logics are themselves just consequence relations – inert mappings from sets of premises onto valid conclusions. For a logic to play a role in a computational process of reasoning, it must be implemented in some process. Or, from another perspective, any process whose inputs and outputs can be systematically interpreted as the premises and conclusions of a logic, implements that logic. The debate about the role of logic in human reasoning has failed to distinguish between logics and their implementations. The concept of implementation remains implicit in tacit assumptions about particular implementations of, say, natural deduction systems. These assumptions do not generalize.

Issues of implementation have probably been dismissed by cognitive psychologists because they have supposed, with authors such as Fodor and Pylyshyn (1988), that implementations of systems of knowledge are irrelevant to the characterization of knowledge, and that cognitive science is about characterization of knowledge. In contrast, logicians and computer scientists have become increasingly interested in issues of implementability because of complexity results derived since the 1960s (e.g. Cook's theorem (Cook, 1971)) which show just how little of general reasoning systems are implementable within plausible resources. These results have made it clear that one can study implementation at a degree of abstraction well above the hardware concerns which the term tends to bring to mind. It is ironic that psychology, which is the discipline most obviously concerned with characterizing the implementation of cognitive processes, should have paid so little attention to the distinction between logic and implementation.

This distinction between logic and implementation indicates a division of cognitive issues. Broadly there are two cognitive questions which arise about the relation between a logic and reasoning performance. The first is whether the reasoner is engaging, *inter alia*, in deductive reasoning for which the logic adequately captures the patterns of validity. The second is how the reasoner's processes implement the logic. It is only when we have answers to both these questions that a particular reasoning performance can be judged rational or irrational.

Many of the central requirements of a psychological theory of reasoning must be addressed at the implementational level, albeit at a suitable level of abstraction. What representations does the reasoner employ in drawing inferences? What resource limitations (both of time and 'space') does the reasoner exhibit? Under what circumstances does the subject make errors and of what kind? Even questions which seem to be abstract with regard to implementation may not be able to avoid addressing this level. An example is the question, when does the reasoner resort to a process of reasoning (rather than some other process)? Metaknowledge of the resource limitations of one's mental processes plays a crucial role in rational decisions about whether to engage them. It is evident from even our current understanding of computational complexity that many of the processes of reasoning which psychologists have regarded as constitutive of rationality are so far beyond our computational resources that it would be quite irrational to engage them on any but the most trivial problems.

Our knowledge of the relationship betwen logics and their implementations comes from two sources. First, extremely abstract results from mathematical studies. In the early part of this century, mathematicians actually adopted a program proposed by Hilbert (1925) of reducing mathematics to calculation, or providing algorithms for the decision of all mathematical problems. Gödel, Turing, and Church founded our knowledge of relations between logic and implementation in the 1930s by showing that there are algorithms for some logics but not for others. In particular, there are no algorithms for some very basic areas of mathematics such as number theory. If there is no algorithm, there is no implementation though there may be implementations of systems usefully considered as fragments. Considerably later, under the impetus of the developing technology of computing, 'complexity theory' came about from the realization of the enormous gap between the in-principle existence of algorithms for deciding logical issues and the practical computability in time and memory space. The subject was founded on the proof that although propositional calculus is easily shown to be decidable, it is not possible to decide whether in general some trivially simple formulae are satisfiable in time/space less than necessary for exhaustive search (Cooke, 1971). This discovery has in turn focused attention on what can be achieved by reasonable resources, where resources are defined in terms of how bad problems get as a function of increasing 'size'.

Although these complexity results are much closer to bearing on practical problems than the early decidability-in-principle results, it is still controversial whether they are misleading about human computation. Psychologists quite often cannot specify the 'size' of problems that human beings can solve in the metrics the theories require, and the analyses are, in their nature, worst-case analyses. It is often hard to tell whether the problems facing humans in their environments are actually drawn from a simpler subset of the domain as defined in the problem's formulation. Nevertheless, some of these general results are clearly relevant to the debates between psychologists about the role of logic in human reasoning.

Our second source of knowledge about implementability comes from more empirical attempts to design computers and programs which solve problems. Much of practical computer science consists of the development of efficient algorithms for solving problems, and the design of architectures suitable for their execution. Until fairly recently, psychological simulation has chiefly exploited the off-the-shelf products of computer science and AI modelling human mental processes. Connectionism might reasonably be seen as a current flowing in the opposite direction in that it was inspired by philosophers, biologists, and psychologists as a style of computational device based on associationistic psychology which has recently been taken up by computer scientists as potentially usable for their practical concerns. Knowledge gained from the empirical approach is less structured but much richer – it is knowledge of ways of performing practical tasks in reasonable time and available space, and also knowledge of what is hard to achieve within these limits. This fine-grained knowledge leads to rough generalizations about what is good for what even if only by 'natural' selection – the survival of designs. So connectionist architectures are good for fuzzy constraint satisfaction but not so good at capturing recursion.

These two sources of knowledge are gradually beginning to converge. Formal analysis is looking at much more tractable fragments of logics and computational practice is leading to generalizations that plausibly may be related to formal findings. Yet much remains to be done in bridging the gap. A central topic in building this bridge, one which will occupy us here, is the implementation of variables. Patterns of quantifier/variable binding play the major role in determining the course-grain complexity of logics (Church, 1936; Kowalski, 1979; Levesque, 1988). Current connectionism, the movement in cognitive science which has been most concerned with implementational issues, is much taken up with proposals for implementing variable binding, precisely because this is difficult for these architectures (e.g. Shastri and Ajjanagadde, 1989; Lange and Dyer, 1989; Touretsky and Hinton, 1988; Stenning and Levy, 1988). Here we explore the reasons why variables are the central topic in theories of implementation, and what implications there are for what we know of human reasoning.

As two illustrative areas we take 'reflexive reasoning' and categorical syllogisms, chosen for their contrasting human performances. In the first, Shastri and Ajjanagadde (1989) studied a fragment of reasoning they call *reflexive* which can be executed in linear time over very large databases. They propose a connectionist implementation which illustrates how the implementation of variable binding determines the characteristics of reasoning performance. In the second area, we show that syllogisms have some distinctive logical properties which are especially relevant to implementation. It is well-known that syllogisms are a fragment of monadic predicate calculus (MPC), itself a decidable fragment of the undecidable polyadic first-order predicate calculus, but less attention has been paid to the nature of syllogisms as a fragment of MPC. We will then discuss the implications of these logical facts for human implementations of syllogistic reasoning. We show how the logical limitations of the syllogism allow implementation in a particular type of working memory. Thus both areas illustrate that theories of implementation can explain why people exhibit their distinctive profiles of ability in two disparate tasks.

But before setting out on this specific illustration of the approach, we first begin with a more general introduction of the relation between logics and implementations. It is important that biological information-processing systems in general are configured to perform a type of task that contrasts with the most usual implementations of logic. We draw a distinction between these two different sorts of task, the testing of truth-in-a-model and the proving of theorems. These two functions clarify the distinction between common-sense reasoning and deductive reasoning which exhibit such different characteristics in human performance. These two functions also present different problems for implementation. Having made this distinction we turn to an introduction of theorem-proving implementations: these are where most of the existing body of knowledge about implementation has come from. Our strategy is to show that even in this area where there is such a direct relation between logical system and implementation, implementing a logic in a process introduces non-logical decisions.

We begin by illustrating some issues with the example of Prolog, the best-known system of implemented logic. This involves a discussion of the way various heuristic and procedural decisions must be made in order to achieve an implementation. Given the well-documented resource limitations on human reasoners, similar decisions must have been made in the evolution of the deductive capacities of humans. Focus on implementation directs attention to the computational architecture in which these capacities are implemented. This introduction to implementation concludes with a section on the role of variables in determining complexity which leads into the discussion of our two example areas.

Finally, by way of conclusion, we argue that abandoning the guiding role of the distinction between logics and implementations for talk of 'non-formal mechanisms' cuts psychology off from half of cognitive science just when that half has begun to return results on complexity of reasoning in sufficient detail to apply to psychologists' concerns.

TESTING TRUTH-IN-A-MODEL AS OPPOSED TO PROVING THEOREMS

We begin by sketching a crude way of putting one sort of logical implementation into correspondence with a hypothetical simplified organism. Primitive biological computation is quite naturally thought of as the testing of the truth value of preselected propositions in a model which is specified by data arriving through the senses. The propositions are preselected for their value in determining courses of action. The 'Here comes a tiger' proposition's truth value is of evident continuing concern and plays its role in determining action. Stripe detectors, eye detectors, optical flow detectors continually monitor the environment and provide the premises from which the value of this proposition are inferred by computing functions of their simultaneous values. The sensory inputs at any given time provide a current interpretation of a language fragment and the outputs are inferences of truths in this model. Evolution has wired the functions which relate the values of the inputs to the values of the outputs. For the moment we will assume that it has done its job perfectly for the range of combinations of environmental parameters which our organism's senses monitor.

Such an idealized and primitive beast may be thought of as something like a Pitts-McCulloch network which implements some fragment of propositional calculus. The sensory inputs correspond to atomic propositions; their states to truth values of these propositions; the beast's wiring to the network; and the output propositions correspond to some pre-motor neurons' states. Let us suppose, for the moment, that evolution has efficiently picked non-redundant sensors in such a manner that every possible combination of inputs can be reached by some possible state of the environment (this of course would correspond to a very poor design for a beast since this type of efficiency is the last that evolution would seek out).

Let us call our beast PM.[1] PM is an implementation of a fragment of propositional calculus. While it is a particularly easy fragment to implement in an efficient network mechanism, it is a peculiarly limited fragment in terms of its logical generality. First, its inputs are values of propositions, not values of propositional variables. The physical nature of the sensory detectors and the environment determine the corresponding propositions. If we want to think of the inputs instead as variables p, q, . . ., then we would need to be able to causally connect them to other environments which would endow them with other semantics. Second, the output propositions are fixed by the functions that evolution has chosen to wire into the beast. We may expect examples like 'Here comes a tiger' but not examples like 'Here comes a tiger or here doesn't come a tiger' – theorems (and their negations) are the last concern of evolution. Conclusions that are true in all environmental states or none can safely be left out of beasts.

Yet PM implements a fragment of propositional calculus. Every part of its network corresponds to a part of a formula, and a setting of its inputs followed by the resultant values of its outputs corresponds to a deduction. So its logic gates correspond to logical connectives. What is it that characterizes the difference between this deduction and the theorem proving which we typically regard as the paradigm case of deduction? After all, standing back from PM, we can interpret each setting of inputs and its effect on outputs as corresponding to the employment of a theorem. The outputs will not be theorems, but the inputs are premises and the outputs are conclusions which jointly constitute theorems. Under this interpretation, beasts specialize in theorems but ones which do not have null-premise lists on the left of their turnstiles. They need to know what is true in all possible models *of certain types* (characterized by their sensors' current settings) as a basis for action. However, the deduction theorem which defines the relation betweeen turnstile and implication within well-behaved logics, guarantees that even this limitation on PM as theorem-prover is rather slight. For every theorem with no assumptions can be derived from one with assumptions, by trivial substitutions.

But even under this interpretation, PM is a severely limited theorem prover. The spirit of theorem proving is the free selection of target theorems and the provision of processes which can operate on all such targets to decide theoremhood. This is the sense in which propositional calculus is decidable and the origin of algorithms such as truth tabling which exemplify this property. These are what we are inclined to think of as the essence of logic, but as long as we are concerned with what can be implemented in limited time and space, we must remember that both PM-style networks, and conventional rewriting systems, are severely limited by the complexity of the computations involved. The comparison is further complicated by the fact that the 'theorem finding' in PM's case is done either during the evolution of the wiring or by learning. A network which is subject to an algorithmic adjustment of its connections strengths so that it comes to compute say a boolean function from its inputs to its outputs represents a space of possible formulae at the inception of this process, and a theorem which has been found by learning at the end.

So what we find is that biological systems are most obviously assimilated to logic as deployed in computing truth-in-a-model rather than to theorem proving. Computing truth-in-a-model can be construed formally as theorem proving of a restricted kind but that should not camouflage the stark contrast between systems set up to track the truth values of pre-identified propositions under varying input assumptions, and systems set up to seek a proof or disproof of an arbitrary input sentence.

How do these deployments of logic relate to observations of beasts more sophisticated than PM, such as human beings? Human beings are, from an early age, capable of sophisticated common-sense reasoning in the sense that they detect environmental regularities and infer courses of action based on them (roughly, Piaget's sensory-motor and concrete operations). Even in this sense they are much more sophisticated than PM. They are capable of functioning in a wider range of environments. But they are still, in general, extremely poor at performing paradigmatically 'logical' tasks. They cannot distinguish easily between what is or isn't true *in all possible models* of some set of propositions. They are, at least to some extent, at the mercy of their beliefs about one particular model, namely the one they think is currently actual. And this is hardly surprising on the view of biological implementations of logic which we have developed so far.

The result is that psychologists are confronted by subjects who para-doxically are capable of immensely sophisticated contextualized reasoning, but are pathetically incapable of what is formally identical reasoning when these problems are set in the style of a symbol-shuffling calculus. Psychologists are also faced by mathematical approaches to reasoning which have spawned fancy technology for performing inferences about what is true in all models of relatively arbitrary collections of premises. So it is perhaps not surprising that psychologists have found it hard to find the relevance of logic to their interests. It is easy to forget that such technology so far has no ability to tell whether any of these propositions are true in the current model, or any other model (unless, of course, they are true in all models or in none).

There is of course, a long road from PM to the human condition, even the sensory-motor stage of the human condition. And the notion of a propositional calculus beast like PM is in fact fairly fanciful as a model of the most primitive biological system. Even the simplest beasts have the capacity for predicting the environment to some degree – they are not cine-cameras which respond to a simultaneous frame at a time. They should be seen as having ontologies which introduce the notion of individuals with enduring properties which may or may not be known. Ontologies are data-reduction exercises, but with the individuals that they posit they introduce generality which brings with it the potential for computational complexity in the general case, and problems of implementation. We return later to the part that variables play in determining the complexity of implementations.

But before we do that, we should note that human beings do get beyond the sensory-motor stage and do develop at least rudimentary abilities to perform formal operations about all possible models of sets of premises. However imperfectly they may perform these formal operations, it is our judgement that there is a qualitative difference between human performance in this area and that of their nearest rivals. This raises the issue of what architectural change underlies this evolutionary new ability. We contrast two different sorts of explanations of how human beings have come to have at least rudimentary abilities to emulate our paradigmatic theorem prover.

At least two quite contrasting pictures of the evolution of human cognitive abilities are suggested by our sketch of two ends to which implementations of logic may be put. Perhaps the dominant picture is one that suggests that our albeit limited capacity for solving decontextualized logic problems is evidence that human beings, through language, have developed string-shuffling architectures akin to those which logic has inspired engineers to design. These are the architectures which are capable of theorem proving in the general style, albeit limited by resource considerations. On this picture our 'highest' cognitive abilities are implementations of general logics.

A quite different picture arises if we take a biological perspective and ask how evolution might have set about implementing more generalized reasoning starting with a PM-like organism designed for computing truth-in-a-model. How can such a beast turn propositions into propositional variables and explore combinations of inputs other than those which the current environment chooses to set? Some decoupling of beast from environment is required, or at least decoupling of the network component with which we are concerned. Alternatively, the ability to manipulate the environment (or perhaps its own transducers) would allow disengagement of the inputs from the tyranny of the environment. But still, manipulating the actual environment into all its possible states (relevant to the interpretation of some set of premises) is a strenuous method of reasoning.

Even this effort would not turn propositions into propositional variables. For that it is necessary to perceive analogies between different sets of inputs and their effects on the same set of outputs. If there is a correspondence between a set of inputs in one sensory domain and a set in another, then the outputs of a network wired for computing a certain function of the first set of inputs can be interpreted as the conclusions from the analogous sets of inputs suitably transposed. A capacity for recognizing analogies does not immediately turn propositions into propositional variables, but it is a step in the direction of generalizing the sort of computation which our truth-in-a-model machine performs – a step in the direction of theorem proving.

The innovation of analogy also has a more indirect effect in this direction. It makes the strategy of manipulating the environment in order to manipulate one's sensors more efficient. External systems of representation are analogies. Perhaps number systems are the most obvious example, but diagrams and written language are equally analogies for other things. External representations reduce the energy required for manipulating actual environments into other possible states.

In summary, our two functions which implementations of logic serve give rise to two different approaches to the question of how human reasoning abilities are implemented. The contrasting human performances in our example areas of detailed implementation (reflexive and syllogistic reasoning) illustrate the importance of our distinction between computing truth-in-a-model and theorem proving. Reflexive reasoning is extremely fluent but tied strictly to reasoning over logical relations between pre-interpreted concepts. Syllogistic reasoning is far from fluent and is error prone but represents the kernel of theorem proving over uninterpreted symbols. The implementations of both fragments illustrate the centrality of the issue of how variables are implemented.

But first, as a general introduction to implementation, we now turn to the issues that arise when theorem provers are implemented on conventional computers. Our psychological interest will eventually centre on less expressive logics but it is still useful to start with the most familiar of the relation between logic and implementation.

ENGINEERING ARCHITECTURES AND DEDUCTIVE RELATIONS

In this section we first look at how a straightforward deterministic implementation of logic makes such large demands on available memory as to prevent the construction of a practical theorem prover. We will then show how various heuristic *control* decisions have been incorporated into Prolog in order to circumvent an exponential explosion of resource requirements thereby providing a practical theorem prover. We will then argue that further information may be required to delimit the search space created by a deduction. This information need not be based on general heuristic assumptions but may be more principally based on various *metrical* properties of the information contained in a database. Certain parameters, e.g. *confirmation strengths* (Sperber and Wilson, 1986), may be assigned to rules which further delimit their chance of specifying a path to explore in a current derivation. However, we will argue that such supplements to a standard theorem prover yield resource limitations of their own. We will suggest that connectionist systems attempt to avoid these problems via *inductive* processes which evolve (i) incorporating more and different forms of metrical information; and (ii) specifying the bulk of the heuristic pruning of the search space over these metrical properties (which also less than coincidentally permit learning in these systems).

Logic programming and Prolog

What happens if we try to implement a logic[2] as an algorithm for computing conclusions from premises? What does such an implementation require? First, and most innocuously, it needs a memory for its axioms or rules of inference. Since logics are usually parsimonious in this regard,[3] this creates few problems. The implementation, however, will also require a memory for the intermediate products of its derivations. The derivation creates a branching search space, all of which must be stored since backtracking may be required. Memory for the search tree must be total, since no prior step can be excised if the derivation is to guarantee conclusions. Variable bindings assigned at each step in the derivation must also be retained at the appropriate point of assignment further increasing the memory load. In sum, logical calculi are voracious consumers of memory resources. Moreover the number of distinct operations required, which provides the metric of complexity,[4] shows an exponential order of growth as a function of the length of the input. This appetite looks particularly ill-matched to the human computational architecture. Humans appear to be good at holding very large numbers of complex general rules, often highly context-sensitive ones, but they are bad at retaining the products of a particular episode of calculation (Newell and Simon, 1972; Oaksford *et al.*, 1990).

Direct implementations of logical systems were attempted in the 1960s in the form of general problem solvers.[5] A problem situation was encoded in non-logical axioms and the to-be-solved problem or goal was encoded as a theorem which was proved from those axioms (plus the logical axioms). The non-logical axioms represent the knowledge base over which the logic operates in order to solve the problem. This was usually achieved using the resolution method (Robinson, 1965). However, these theorem provers were generally intractable. That is, they led to a combinatorial explosion in the computational resources required to run them. This led many researchers to abandon the view that logic could provide a theory of reasoning by intelligent agents (e.g. Newell, reported in Moore, 1982).

More recently there has been a resurgence of interest in logic as a formalism for knowledge representation in AI. This has come about by the exploitation of various *heuristic control* processes embodied in Prolog which effectively delimit the growth of the branching search space. Prolog only employs *query-time* backward-chaining through the implicative statements in the knowledge base. That is, inferences are only drawn when a query is made, and then only to ensure that the goal could be reached from the statements in the database. For example, take the following database: 1.A → B; 2. A → D; 3. C → A; 4. C. If I make the query A?, then Prolog will backward-chain, i.e. it will only match the input A to the consequents of rules. Thus it would match rule 3. setting up the proof of C as a subgoal.

Since C is already in the database, the query would be anwered in the affirmative.

Earlier theorem provers also employed *assert-time* forward-chaining which was identified as primarily responsible for the combinatorial explosion in resource requirements. In forward-chaining when the query A is made, antecedents of rules are also matched. Thus the database would now have to record that B and D have been derived. Moreover, this also occurs at assert time, so if I asserted A, i.e. added A to the database, then all possible inferences would be drawn. So, in this case B and D would be added to the database. However, inferring B and D is not relevant to proving C. Restricting the theorem prover to backward-chaining effectively reduces the number of assumptions introduced in a derivation and guarantees that all inferences will be relevant to the problem at hand (Hogger, 1984).

Prolog's rule interpreter goes through responding procedure calls in the order in which they appear in the text of a program. Hence appropriate textual ordering can also improve efficiency. However, this is only if an exhaustive search for all solutions is not required. Since such an exhaustive search is not normally required, once an intermediate result has been obtained, the remainder of a branch can be excised and garbage collected, by the use of the *cut* operator. Cut is effectively a domain-specific heuristic, since where or whether it is employed is determined by the particular problem at hand. Loop checkers, which excise a branch when some large but arbitrary depth is reached, can circumvent infinite left recursions.[6] The cut operator and the use of loop checkers mean that Prolog *cannot* guarantee to find a solution since both may excise the branch along which the solution lies before it is reached. The control problem in Prolog is not which inference rule to apply since there is only one: resolution. Resolution provides a sound and complete logic with respect to the database language. Prolog's control regime simply fails to exploit the completeness of its resolution theorem prover.

One may have thought that decidability results for logical systems would provide the best guide to the tractability of implementations of these systems. However, *a priori* decidability results provide only a negative guide as to the practical computational tractability of a logical system. The undecidability of first-order logic at least shows that any practical implementation has to be based on heuristic principles. However, decidability is not a strong positive guide to the practical tractability of logical systems. Even for decidable propositional logic, heuristic control processes are required in order to provide practical implementations, or theorem provers, which exploit the specification of deductive relations in proof theory. We will argue below that Johnson-Laird's theory of mental models provides a novel logical notation. This observation shifts the burden of explanation for subjects' syllogistic reasoning performance on to the heuristics specified to manipulate that notation, just as in any implementation of a logical system.

Even with these implementational considerations in place, Prolog is notoriously slow. It has, moreover, failed to provide the logic programming framework which in the early 1980s was supposed to underpin fifth-generation computers. In particular applications, inferences need to be drawn more rapidly than allowed by these standard implementational considerations. Inferencing in sentence processing is an example. Computers can outstrip human performance at numerical calculation by many orders of magnitude. However, we are still many years away from devising a parser which can assign meanings to uttered sentences in anything like the time scale of normal human comprehension. One problem is that in Prolog, as we have seen, *all* responding procedure calls are checked in the order they appear in the text of the programme. It would be far more parsimonious if the most likely procedure calls were checked first.

Relevance Theory Sperber and Wilson, 1986) adopts such a solution in attempting to account for the almost instantaneous updating of beliefs which occurs in sentence comprehension. They suggest that the inferential processes underlying sentence comprehension must exploit only the *accessible* information. Sperber and Wilson (1986) therefore outline what we will term a *hybrid* inferential regime consisting of a restricted deductive mechanism and a non-logical component which is responsible for updating the *confirmation strengths* which attach to propositions stored in memory. The restricted logical component, which contains no introduction rules, is motivated primarily by issues of tractability but also represents a substantive claim about the nature of people's inferential processes in language comprehension. Sperber and Wilson (1986) are careful to emphasize that they *do not* intend their notion of confirmation strength to be conflated with the assignment of subjective probabilities to propositions which are explicitly manipulated in judging the relative strengths of those propositions. 'Confirmation strength' is to be understood as a purely processing notion determined by a proposition's prior history of being accessed from memory.

However confirmation strengths are to be understood, their role is clear. They provide a metric by which to judge the relevance of a responding procedure call to the current derivation. So of the responding procedure calls those with the highest confirmation strengths will be checked first. This provides a measure of the utility of a particular rule to reaching goals and thus could practically improve efficiency. We can think of confirmation strengths as numbers which are incremented every time the rule participates in a successful derivation. Then, of the responding procedure calls, instead of textual ordering selecting the first path to follow, the highest-valued responding procedure call would take precedence. These numbers are obviously related to the probability that a procedure call will lead to a successful derivation.[7]

We may also desire these numbers to participate in other functions which could be performed by the database. For example, we may want the database to retrieve *plausible* explanations in abductive inference. However, as Charniak and McDermott (1985) observe, combining these numbers using standard Bayesian techniques, as required in, for example, medical diagnosis to deal with multiple disease problems, results in the familiar combinatorial explosion. Thus, to achieve all of the functions the operations over the knowledge base need to compute, may require abandoning the employment of *algorithmic* optimization procedures. None the less the assignment of numbers indicating prior utilities to achieving goals, is directly analogous to the use of similar metrics by connectionist systems.

Standard implementations of logic would appear to require heuristic processes to provide practical implementations. Moreover, to provide tractable accounts of inference in specific domains, such as sentence comprehension, metrical properties of information must be manipulated and updated. Such updating of parameters is normally called *learning*. Perhaps the most important aspect of this discussion of how logic may be implemented is that logic, as we emphasized in the introduction, does not dictate how a proof or derivation should proceed. It says nothing about which rules to apply when, nor what are the most likely ways in which a solution could be achieved. Crucially, as the discussion of Sperber and Wilson indicates, such decisions are largely based on experience. A further crucial point about real implementations of logic, is that decisions about which rules apply are *not* content-free. All practical implementations of logic use the resolution method in which *there is only one inference rule*. Thus we know that at every stage the same inference rule applies. How an inference proceeds (its locus of control), however, is defined over the *non-logical* axioms. Matching queries or subgoals depends on content, i.e., which particular predicates occur in the antecedents and consequents of implicative statements.[8] It is these non-logical statements to which confirmation strengths attach, further guiding a derivation. It is only experience with the contents of the predicate symbols which could allow the confirmation strengths to be appropriately updated.

For the purposes of this chapter, it is useful to distinguish two different classes of problem that arise in implementing logics to perform reasoning tasks. The problems we are concerned with here are problems of implementing heuristics which guide the search for proof within systems which are still sets of absolute constraints. The heuristics may involve decisions based on metrical properties and probabilistic constraints but they control processes which correspond to the application of rules. The second class of problem are ones in which the reasoning is inherently about soft constraints. Much of human reasoning is probably of this latter type, or at least contains component processes which are of this latter type. One might extend the sort of approach we advocate here to this class of problem by considering such processes as limited implementations of mathematical systems. Indeed some of the same implementational issues arise in doing so. In concentrating here on the first class of problem we seek a simplification so that we can focus on variable binding, which is one of the most general implementation issues, and one that arises in tackling either sort of reasoning.

Implementing logics in the service of reasoning involves much more than logic. In fact the focus becomes the non-logical control process and their interactions with representations in memory. One reaction to this fact is to conclude that logic therefore has nothing to offer in the study of reasoning and so seek for 'non-logical' theories. The problem with this invalid conclusion is that the non-logical heuristic processes which guide deduction can only be adequately specified relative to some logical framework. Logic provides only the barest of frameworks, but one which it is unwise to abandon. We now turn to the pivotal role of variables in understanding implementations, before working through our two example areas.

VARIABLES AND IMPLEMENTATIONAL COMPLEXITY

To approach questions about how human beings implement logics we need to look at the full range of expressiveness of logical systems and to examine human deductive abilities of different sorts. A general account is certainly beyond our grasp at this point and yet there are enough examples to give some signposts. We will focus on the role of different sorts of variable in determining, on the one hand, the logical power of deductive systems, and on the other their implementability.

We first review how the introduction of different sorts of variable into logical systems increases their expressiveness and thereby decreases their computational tractability. Turning to implementation, we then examine the reasons variables present particular issues of implementation. These issues are solved by symbol manipulation architectures in well-known ways with consequences which have just been discussed in connection with Prolog. Recently, there has been a series of proposals as to how variables may be implemented in connectionist architectures. Variable binding presents particular difficulties in these architectures and the methods by which these problems are solved must have far-reaching consequences for the reasoning abilities of systems based on them. In the next section we take up two of these proposals in more detail and look at how they may be the basis for two different human deductive abilities which show very different functional characteristics.

How are variables related to logical expressiveness and computational tractability? There is a dimension of logical expressiveness from propositional calculus to monadic predicate calculus (MPC) to first-order polyadic predicate calculus (FPPC) to second-order calculi. This dimension is syntactically characterized by the introduction of more and more types of variables. It begins with only propositional variables, and adds individual and finally predicate variables. In terms of tractability, this dimension takes us from the most tractable system to the least. Propositional calculus is decidable – there is an algorithm which will determine for any arbitrary formula whether that formula is a theorem or not. At the other extreme, second-order calculi are not even complete – they can express formulae which should be theorems (they are, semantically speaking, consequences) but which do not have derivations within the system. In between these two extremes are a whole series of graded tractabilities – FPPC, for example, is not decidable but is complete. Roughly, it is possible to prove on general grounds that every formula which should be a theorem is a theorem, but there is no algorithm for finding out which formulae are theorems.

We can get some grasp of this dimension and the role that variables play in determining its nature by looking at expressivity in terms of the number of models expressible as a function of the size of various categories of vocabulary in the different systems. In propositional calculus, the only variables are propositional variables – the p's and q's. The number of interpretations (possible assignments of truth values to propositional variables, or rows in the truth table) is 2^{PROP} where PROP is the number of propositional variables. In other words, the only accessible features of the domain of reasoning are combinations of truth values of propositional variables, and there is this number of such combinations (assignments to one variable are independent of assignments to all the others).

Monadic predicate calculus analyses propositions into subjects and predicates, and has variables ranging over individuals which are then bound by quantifiers. Thus, the system has access to individuals and their coinstantiation of properties. In MPC, individuals can only be logically distinct in so far as they have different combinations of properties. So with MPC, there are 2^{PRED} possible types of individual (where PRED is the number of predicates) and therefore $2^{2^{PRED}}$ models which are collections of these types. Since combinations of properties are all that is accessible, it makes no logical difference how many individuals there are of the same type in a model.

First-order polyadic predicate calculus introduces relations between individuals as well as properties of them: 2-ary relations such as 'greater than' or 'is identical to'; 3-ary relations such as 'between'; and so on. It can therefore distinguish between models by the *identity* of individuals of various types there are in the model. It is this step which takes us from the decidable to the undecidable, and the basic reason is very simple. The number of possible models is now a function of the number of individuals in the domain instead of the number of symbols in the language, and there may be infinitely many individuals.

With FPPC, PRED predicates of 'arity' N+1 can be reduced to PRED (IND) predicates of arity N, (where IND) is the number of individuals in the domain, by freezing one argument. So the 2-ary relation 'x is greater than y' can be reduced to a series of monadic predicates 'x is greater than a', 'x is greater than b', . . . where a, b, . . . are names of particular individuals. So if the maximum arity of a predicate is POLY we can reduce FPPC to MPC with $IND^{(POLY-1)}$ predicates. Substituting this term into the formula for number of models for MPC we get $2^{2^{IND^{POLY-1}}}$. Notice that the number of individuals in the domain only enters into the formula with the transition from MPC to FPPC.

It remains to introduce predicate variables to get second-order logic. Predicates stand for properties which are partitionings of the domain of individuals into those within and those outwith the predicate's extension. So, for a domain of IND individuals, there are 2^{IND} partitionings and therefore 2^{IND} properties over which predicate variables range. The resulting complexities of second-order logic fortunately will not concern us here.

With the introduction of each type of variable there is a sharp increase in the expressive power of a given-sized vocabulary. To give a simple example, a proposition, expressed by 'Vx(Fx)' in MPC would require a conjunction 'Fa & Fb & . . .' without quantifiers. This representational efficiency brings with it logical transparency. The form of the more expressive representations allows the logic to capture more inferences but it also makes the problem of discovering these inferential relations more computationally intractable. We understand the formula 'Vx(Fx)' in terms of substitutions into the variable of example individuals. The significance of the formula changes with each substitution instance – where we are in a cycle of substitutions of all possible individuals. It is this contextual dependency which poses implementational difficulties. Whereas a truth value of a fixed proposition might be represented by say a voltage at a point in a circuit, variables require the passing of more complex messages about the identity of the substitution instance represented at that point in time.

When symbol manipulation architectures pass messages corresponding to tokens of symbols it is easy to see how this solves this particular implementational problem. Symbols, and more particularly, strings of symbols of indefinite length, are complex messages, and when representations of them reside in registers, they are complex states of parts of machines. At least at first pass, machines whose components communicate only in terms of simple scalar quantities would not seem to be able to enjoy the representational benefits of variables. However, this is only at first pass. There are well-known schemes for encoding complex formulae as single numbers – perhaps Gödel numbering is the original and best-known scheme. Of course, a system which functioned by passing scalar quantities to be interpreted as Gödel numbers would have to maintain great precision in order to encode long formulae and would have formidable decoding work to do in order to make inferences based on the structure of formulae encoded. But the existence of such theoretical examples has recently brought forth a number of more practical suggestions in the same spirit about how variables can be encoded in connectionist systems, some cited above.

Of what interest is it to us here whether variables are implemented in symbolist or connectionist architectures? If the implementation schemes have no consequences for the complexity of reasoning, over and above the impact that the variables implemented have on computational complexity, then the answer must be 'none'. But if the implementation schemes have differential consequences for the complexity of different sorts of reasoning, then we may ask how these complexity profiles accord with different types of reasoning performance which human beings display. If we can make the case that particular implementation schemes explain functional characteristics of human reasoners, then we have examples of psychological explanation of reasoning performance through the relation between logics and their implementations.

It is an obvious corollary of this approach that there is unlikely to be one implementation of one logic at the back of all human deductive-reasoning performance. Just the very intractability of logics and the variety of uses for which they might be implemented is enough to give the lie to such notions. We illustrate the approach by taking two examples where human beings exhibit extremely divergent functional capacities and where quite different implementations have been proposed to explain these observations. We doubt that the fine detail of the implementations is correct, but nevertheless we believe these two examples are powerful argument for exploring the relation between logic and human reasoning through the concept of implementation.

REFLEXIVE REASONING IN TEXT COMPREHENSION

Our first example is Shastri and Ajjanagadde's (1989) proposals for implementing what they call 'reflexive reasoning'. This is the sort of reasoning which is most explicitly exhibited in tasks such as story understanding. In their example, in understanding the story of Red Ridinghood, we rapidly access inferences about the nature of wolves, little girls, grandmothers, and wood-cutters, and of their likely intentions towards each other. We must do this on-line for we cannot otherwise retrieve the necessary references for pronouns or choices of lexical meaning, for example. This sort of reasoning is characterized by the fact that it involves accessing knowledge about words chosen unpredictably from an extremely large vocabulary. The 'database' of concepts and rules relating them is large and contains many relational concepts.

We have just seen that this performance cannot be due to the complete implementation of FPPC – that is the *perpetuum mobile* of logic programming. Shastri's strategy is to identify a fragment of FPPC which can be found an implementation which can explain performance. His implementation for variable binding is central to the theory. He proposes

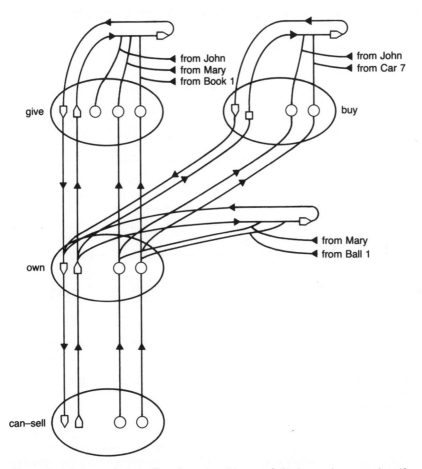

Figure 6.1 A network encoding the rules: $\forall x, y, z$ [*give*(*x, y, z*) $\Rightarrow$ *own*(*y, z*)], $\forall x, y$ [*buy*(*x, y*) $\Rightarrow$ *own* (*x, y*)], and $\forall x, y$ [*own*(*x, y*) $\Rightarrow$ *can-sell*(*x, y*)]; and the long-term facts: *give* (*John, Mary, Book*1), *buy* (*John, Car*7), and *own* (*Mary, Book*2). *Source*: Shastri and Ajjanagadde, 1989.
Note: The links between arguments are in the reverse direction because the rules are wired for 'backward reasoning'.

to cut down the explosive connectivity required for reasoning with polyadic relations between variables by using temporal relations to connect instantiations of variables.

The database of rules connecting concepts is implemented as a network of units each representing concepts. During reasoning these nodes cycle in their activation, and the relative *phase* of two units determines whether or not they are bound to the same or distinct variables – same phase sector, same variable. This means that units very far apart in a large network can be represented as bound to the same variable without direct connection. Units representing logically related concepts are stimulated to cycle in activation with the same phase as other units bound to the same variable,

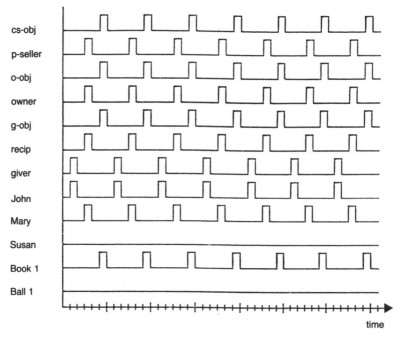

time

Figure 6.2 Pattern of activation representing the dynamic bindings (*giver = John, recipient = Mary, give-object = Book1, owner = Mary, own-object = Book1, potential-seller = Mary, can-sell-object = Book1*)
Source: Shastri and Ajjanagadde, 1989.
Note: These bindings constitute the facts: give (*John, Mary, Book1*), own (*Mary, Book1*), and *can-sell* (*Mary, Book1*). The bindings between *Mary* and the arguments *recipient, owner*, and *potential-seller* are represented by the in-phase firing of the appropriate nodes. The transient representation of an entity is simply a *phase* or time slice within an oscillatory pattern of activity. The number of *distinct* phases required to represent a set of dynamic bindings only equals the number of *distinct individuals* participating in the bindings and is independent of the *total number of bindings*. In this example, only three distinct phases are required to represent seven bindings.

and this pattern spreads through the database reflecting the drawing of inferences about the conceptual relations. The nodes of the network are sensitive to temporally extended boolean functions of their inputs (a node might, for example, only fire if one of its inputs is active at every phase of a cycle). The main outlines of the system are illustrated in Figures 6.1 and 6.2.

At first it seems that this implementational trick has few consequences for reasoning performance – it is equivalent to certain sorts of marker-passing architecture. However, with some reasonable assumptions about implementations, it has some profound implications for what the system can and cannot do. First, there are a group of limitations on the patterns of variables that may be bound. There are restrictions on the quantifier patterns and certain sorts of cyclicity are not implemented at all. There are also more subtle restrictions on repetition of variables. In forward reasoning, variables bound in the consequent must also be bound in the antecedent, and in backward reasoning, vice versa. There has to be a particular 'fix' for repetitions of variables within clauses. Secondly, there are limits on the number of distinct variables that may be involved in any episode of reasoning. This limitation stems directly from the assumption that any implementation will only be able to support a small number of discriminations between phases of activation cycle. Thirdly, there are restrictions on employing more than one binding to a concept node within one episode of reasoning. For example, one cannot have premises of the form 'give (Mary, John, Book1) & give (John, Mary, Car7)'.

Within these limitations it is possible to prove that the system can answer a query of its database in time linear with the length of the shortest proof. This is not just good, but optimal. It lives up to the promise of an implementation of reflexive reasoning – reasoning which occurs without strategic control. It is worth stressing that in purely logical terms it implements a very considerable fragment, even if nothing like the fragment Prolog implements.

How do the system's limitations compare with human performance? For us this must be a more important question than how large a logical fragment is implemented. If the fragment is too large to fit with what humans can do, then so much the worse for the implementation as an explanation of human reasoning. What is interesting about this implementation is that it appears to fit rather well with this particular human ability, and in fact 'predicts' some general features of human reasoning which are so 'obvious' that they are hardly mentioned in the literature.

While the system can reason over a very large database of rules in long-term memory, it can employ only rather few variables in any episode of reasoning. Furthermore, the system makes a clear distinction between a large long-term vocabulary of concepts which are fixed during an episode of reasoning, and the short-term information relevant to a query. Human beings exhibit the extreme facility of reflexive reasoning when reading text about concepts whose interrelations they understand – little girls and wolves. They do not reason easily with material which demands they entertain interpretations of concepts contrary to their general knowledge or ones which have to be established during an episode of reasoning. 'All women are men. No women are female. Therefore some men are not female' is a valid syllogism and even has a true conclusion, but it also defeats reflexive reasoning. Similarly, 'All the artists are beekeepers. None of the beekeepers are chemists. Therefore some of the beekeepers are not chemists' defeats reflexive reasoning because our long-term database has not encoded relations about these unspecified sets of hypothetical individuals, and encodes no logical relations between these three properties. People have great trouble eliminating enthymatic premises from reflexive reasoning. Indeed, coherent text depends on an enormous amount of inference from the suppressed premises of general knowledge. This sort of reasoning is more easily assimilated to the computation of truth-in-a-model than to theorem proving. Human beings also can only reason reflexively about small numbers of variables at a time.

Even some of the limitations on patterns of variable binding exhibited by Shastri's system appear to have echoes in human reasoning. Bach-Peters sentences which violate the cyclicity requirements have never seemed the easiest to understand.[9] All human languages have reflexives to mark identical variables occurring within clauses. Though there are fine details of reflexivization which do not immediately fit the Shastri system's behaviour, we know of no other explanation offered for the phenomenon at all. These details might well reward further investigation.

In summary, Shastri and Ajjanagadde's system performs deductive reasoning over a fragment of FPPC with optimal speed. It is most suited to reasoning over large long-term databases of rules and facts so long as only small numbers of variables are employed in any given episode of reasoning. As such its behaviour accords rather well with the outlines of the sort of general-knowledge-based reasoning involved in human text comprehension, and there is a reasonable correspondence between the reasons the implementation behaves as it does, and the reasons for human performance being as it is. The system's limitation to working with a fixed interpretation built up by learning in long-term memory places it nearer the 'truth-in-a-model' style of computation than to theorem proving, but the inclusion of variable binding takes it well beyond the behaviour of PM. The fluency of this type of reasoning is a good biological reason for supposing that it is implemented by a primitive mechanism compared to our next example ability.

THE LOGIC OF SYLLOGISTIC REASONING

The logic of the syllogism and the tasks that psychologists have used to explore its human implementation make a good contrast to the domain of reflexive reasoning. Reflexive reasoning is a natural part of language understanding which we all attain. It is notoriously hard to implement adequately in a machine, not least because of the size of the database involved, and so it is an impressive human capacity. Syllogistic reasoning is a highly artificial domain which owes its very existence to the exigencies of intellectual history. It is only ever encountered explicitly by a rather small proportion of highly educated people. It is trivially easy to implement on the simplest of computers but nevertheless is in general done very poorly by all but a small proportion of this small proportion of the people who ever encounter it. Human-operating characteristics couldn't be more different in the two reasoning domains.

As far as logics are concerned, the syllogism is paradoxically a tiny fragment of the already small fragment that Shastri's system implements. In fact the syllogism is only a small fragment of MPC, itself a small fragment of Shastri's fragment of FPPC. So there must be something different about the nature of the task to which this logic is put that explains why human performance is so much poorer, and this in turn must explain why human implementations have this rather dismal level of success.

The relevant difference between reflexive and syllogistic reasoning is not hard to find. The one reasons over a database of facts and logical relations which are already established in long-term memory, and are not susceptible to reinterpretation during reasoning. If we suddenly inform our listener that Red Ridinghood is a wolf, and the wolf is the grandmother, and the wood-cutter is the litle girl, and 'kills' now means 'loves on Tuesday' we will observe very poor comprehension. The words of natural languages are not like the p's and q's of logical calculi and do not support interchangeability in our long-term memory. Syllogisms, on the other hand, require that we reason, whether with A's, B's and C's or with artists, beekeepers, and chemists, in ways which are valid for all possible assignments of these properties to domains. And the information that we are given about the range of models which we are to entertain is given to us during the episode of reasoning. This makes all the difference. Shastri and Ajjanagadde's system does not purport to explain how the database is initially configured, but it is clear that the system only works if it is.

The difference between these task demands makes the world of difference to the implementation of the relevant fragments of logic. Human working memory has a very severely limited capacity for holding bindings of properties to variables, and does this in very particular ways. Shastri's system is very limited in the number of distinct variables it can bind in an episode even though it enjoys the advantage that the logical relations between the predicates they are bound to have been set up in long-term memory by a whole history of learning. We believe that a different mechanism has to be employed when setting up arbitrary sets of bindings in working memory, and that it is this mechanism which fundamentally limits human calculation of syllogistic conclusions.

However, there are other pitfalls which also stem from the different tasks involved. Many naïve subjects do not fully understand the nature of the syllogistic task they are being asked to perform, and this misunderstanding stems from conflict between their habitual use of reflexive reasoning in expository language understanding and the demands of reasoning over all interpretations of a set of premises. But we are chiefly concerned here with explaining the performance of subjects who have understood the task – subjects who no longer make Gricean implicature interpretational errors, but who nevertheless find it a difficult computational task. The majority of the recent literature on syllogisms is also (if implicitly) about this group of subjects.

Before entering on the details of implementation of syllogistic reasoning we need to examine the nature of the logical fragment in more detail. It is clearly a fragment of MPC. But what is the principle behind the restriction of MPC? Or did Aristotle pick some highly arbitrary collection of arguments (not knowing anything about MPC as we do)? The key to these questions lies in a property of syllogisms which we will call *case identifiability*. Syllogisms are a case-identifiable fragment of MPC, and this is the key to understanding human syllogistic reasoning processes, even perhaps to understanding why syllogisms became a historically important fragment.

As we have seen, MPC models consist of sets of types of individuals defined by their possession of the properties of a fragment of a language. In syllogisms, there are just three predicates, A, B, and C, so there are eight 'maximal' types of individual – ABC's, AB's that are not C, AC's that are not B, and so on. As we saw above, in considering MPC in general, interpretations of MPC are constructed as collections of maximal types. So, for a three-predicate fragment there are just 2^8 such interpretations.

Now it turns out that syllogisms have the very restricted property that if a pair of premises establish a conclusion, they also identify a *maximal* type of individual which must be in any model of the premises. This is what we mean by case identifiability. For example, the syllogism 'All As are Bs. All Bs are Cs' establishes that there are individuals of the type ABC, and has the two valid conclusions 'Some As are Cs' and 'All As are Cs'. The syllogism 'Some As are Bs. Some Bs are Cs' identifies no maximal type that appears in all models of the premises, and has no valid conclusion.

To see that case identifiability is not generally a property of MPC, consider a disjunctive argument. 'If there's either something that's A or something that's B, and there's either something that's B or something that's C, and there's nothing that's B, then there's either something that's A or there's something that's C'. This is a valid MPC argument, but it does not establish that there must be any of the eight maximal types in models of the premises. In fact it establishes that there is one or more of three maximal types (either ACs that aren't B, As that aren't B or C, or Cs that aren't B or A) but not which. (There may of course be other types in addition.)

Case identifiability is a property in terms of which we can define other logical properties of the syllogism in a revealing way. The nature of conclusions which can be validly drawn is closely related to the maximal types established to exist. There are at most two maximal types established by any given syllogism (only one for positive syllogisms), and these maximal types are not only necessary for models of the premises but also sufficient – models consisting of them alone make the premises true. Or, put another way, these cases identified by premises are minimal models of them. Furthermore, the converse of the relation between having valid conclusions and establishing maximal types very nearly holds. With only a few interesting exceptions which we discuss below, syllogisms which do not have valid conclusions, do not establish any maximal types.

So syllogisms are tacitly inferences which involve the identification of cases. This fact underlies traditional graphical processes for teaching them to which we turn below. But it also underlines an important relation between syllogistic inference and what goes on in language comprehension, and this relation is important for understanding what subjects may assimilate the task to. As we saw above in considering Shastri's treatment of reflexive reasoning, text comprehension involves deductions. It also involves the construction of logical models of the text – inventories of types of individual defined in terms of their properties and relations. The fact that constructions of individuals are so central to this task is witnessed by the overriding need for anaphor resolution in texts. People simply cannot process texts which fail to provide the cross-referencing of identity and distinctness relations which allow this construction of individuals (see, for example, Stenning, 1978, 1986). People find logical models for texts, but they do not generally try to establish only models *which satisfy the text under every possible interpretation*. Discourse comprehension is a co-operative exercise in which the reader tries to construct the model which the speaker/author 'has in mind'.

Because syllogisms are a case-identifiable fragment of MPC, they allow subjects to carry over from text comprehension this general goal of constructing a single model. But there are two crucial divergences in the syllogistic task. The first is the general difference between exposition and deduction. In the former, there is a presumption that speaker and hearer co-operate to arrive at a single mutual model. Whereas deductive argument is best seen as a 'competitive' game in which the participants (perhaps the reasoner and God) try to find counterinterpretations of the premises in which the conclusion is false (see, for example, Hintikka, 1983). This is another way of putting our earlier point about deduction being about all possible interpretations – not just the most plausible current intent. This type of divergence is quite general to 'formal' tasks. It is what makes 'Gricean' interpretations of premises errors in these tasks. The second divergence is much more specific to the arbitrary way in which the syllogistic task is posed. Although the syllogistic fragment has the distinctive property of being case-identifying, the conventional task hides this fact. It allows subjects only to draw conclusions of the same form as the premises – 'Quantifier A are C' or 'Quantifier C are A' with the same quantifiers that can appear in premises. This obscures the fact that syllogistic reasoning is about identifying maximal types.

When subjects are given a different task which emphasizes the identification of cases and therefore maps more closely onto their customary discourse comprehension skills, they can actually make deductively valid inferences from syllogisms which Aristotle's formulation does not capture. As mentioned above, some few syllogisms which have no conventional conclusion do establish maximal types of individual. For example, 'No A are B. No B are C' establishes that there are Bs which are neither A nor C (remember that we, and the vast majority of the subjects in the relevant experiments, and Aristotle himself, conventionally assume the syllogism to be interpreted with a no-empty-sets axiom). One might conclude from this syllogism that 'Some non-As are non-Bs', if only Aristotle had provided such a quantifier.

Peter Yule (1991) has recently shown that when subjects are instructed to find maximal types of individual established by syllogistic premises they can do so very effectively, and often succeed in finding these 'missing conclusions'. In doing so they are demonstrating an ability to see through the arbitrariness of Aristotle's principle that no conclusion follows from two negative premises. Logically identifying established maximal types is a more complex task than the conventional one (it demands finding maximal conclusions rather than mere conclusions), but it appears to be psychologically easier. This is evidence that subjects do readily approach the syllogism task as a search for maximal types.

Before leaving the logic of the syllogism, we note some implications of our analysis for the logical nature of the *tasks* which have been used to study these processes. The traditional task of assessing the validity of a syllogism where both premises and conclusion were provided by the experimenter corresponds to a *proof-checking* task. But this task has largely given way to the task of producing a valid conclusion from a pair of premises presented alone. The latter task is more informative about the processes involved. However, it is worth pointing out that it does not correspond to theorem proving in any straightforward way – the subject is not provided with a target theorem. But neither is the task sensibly assimilated to unguided inference. Since there are four quantifiers and two orderings of the A and C terms, there are only eight conclusions possible for any pair of premises. The subjects' task is therefore a sort of multiple choice. In theorem-proving terms, instead of being given a single target theorem, and being asked to produce a derivation, the subject is implicitly given eight targets and asked to decide whether any of them can be derived.[10]

IMPLEMENTING SYLLOGISTIC REASONING

We now turn to questions about what impact the property of case identifiability has on the problem of implementing syllogistic reasoning, particularly in human working memory.

Case identifiability is important to implementation because it determines that a particularly simple class of algorithms can be applied to syllogism solution. It means that reasoning can pursue the strategy of representing all possible types consistent with the premises, and all types established by the premises in one representation. Since the presence or absence of one type does not interact with the presence or absence of any other type in determining consequences there is no need to explore disjunctions of models in searching for a conclusion from a pair of syllogistic premises. They permit the encapsulation of their logical properties in a single strategically chosen model. This places the syllogism between discourse comprehension and general logical deduction: reasoning can still proceed by constructing a single model of the premises but that model must be strategically chosen (rather than merely taking the one the text invites) and it must be strategically interpreted when drawing conclusions.

The carry-over of text comprehension habits into syllogistic reasoning is a phenomenon that would repay more detailed study. The most difficult syllogisms are ones in which the only valid conclusions are anti-figural (in Johnson-Laird's terminology). Anti-figural conclusions are ones which are anti-thematic from a discourse-processing perspective. We look at the syllogism from a production point of view, and ask ourselves what selection of premises we can make which would lead our hearer to a certain conclusion. It is an intriguing fact that when we take this perspective, there is no conclusion which can only be reached by anti-thematic premises. In other words, if we are being co-operative there is no reason to ever pose these difficult syllogisms. Having an analysis of the logic makes it possible to relate people's behaviour with syllogisms to their other behaviours on a range of dimensions.

All this logic still leaves a wide range of algorithms for performing syllogistic reasoning and an even wider range of implementations for them. These logical properties are related to certain traditional approaches to syllogistic reasoning. In a well-defined sense of 'graphical', syllogisms are graphical arguments (see Stenning and Oberlander, 1991 (in press)) and it is this property which Euler exploited in his diagrammatic method. Graphical methods are themselves implementations of fragments of logic in a computational mechanism. We will use a computationally well-specified method of using Euler circles to illustrate such an implementation, and then compare the graphical approach to some other algorithms that have been proposed. This comparison reveals that all of the proposals share a common representational requirement for holding sets of bindings of attributes into maximal types. We then relate this requirement to properties of human working memory which constrain solutions to the binding problem. Thus, we aim to show that properties of human working memory can explain not only how people reason syllogistically but also how the syllogism is a non-arbitrary fragment of MPC. Aristotle constructed a fragment which could encompass quantificational reasoning but allow representation in a single simultaneous set of attribute bindings.

In order to make these logical properties of the syllogism vivid we begin by describing an implementation of syllogistic reasoning in the medium of Euler circles (see Stenning and Oberlander (in press) and Stenning and Oberlander (1991) for more extensive treatments of this approach to graphical reasoning). Graphical methods exploit case identifiability in a

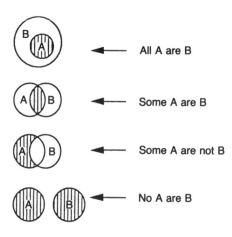

Figure 6.3 Characteristic Euler-circle representations of syllogistic premises
Note: Regions represent types of individual consistent with premises. Shaded regions represent types of individual established by the premises.

particularly transparent way. To define a system of reasoning with Euler circles we need to specify how syllogistic premises are represented, how they are combined and then how conclusions are read off (or denied to follow) from the resulting diagrams. What we have learned of the logic suggests that just one diagram should represent what is relevant to conclusions, and that we should focus on maximal types of individuals which are entailed by the premises. The very nature of the graphical

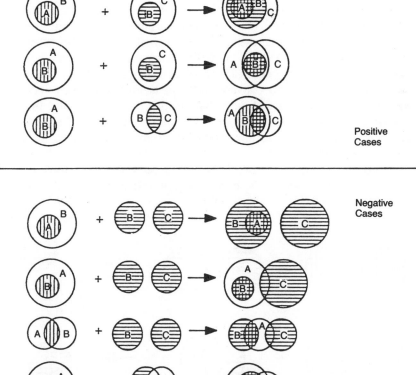

Positive Cases

Negative Cases

Figure 6.4 Registration diagrams with valid conclusions
Note: Premise + premise = registration diagram. Registration involves the superimposition of the 'b' circles of each premise.

medium means that all types represented will be maximal in any diagram which relates three circles representing the extensions of three predicates. Any region of a diagram is either inside or outside all three circles. But we need a notation for distinguishing types required in any model of the premises (necessary elements of minimal models) from types which are consistent with but not established by the premises. This is supplied by the convention of shading areas of diagrams which represent necessary types. It is additionally convenient to shade these areas horizontally in the diagram of one premise and vertically in the other so that when the two diagrams are 'registered', overlapping areas of shading appear as doubly shaded.[11]

Figure 6.3 shows the diagrams that result for each premise. There is a one-to-one correspondence of diagrams to premises. Note that positive and negative particular premises are only distinguished by their shading. Figures 6.4, 6,5, and 6.6 show the 21 different cases which result when registering premises in graphically distinct syllogisms: ones with valid conclusions; ones with no conventional conclusions but which establish maximal types; and ones with no valid conclusions, respectively. In each case the B circles of each premise have been superimposed and the A and C circles have been arranged with the maximum number of types consistent with the premises.

A relatively simple procedure now determines whether there is a valid conclusion, and if so which it is. If the syllogism is to establish a conclusion,

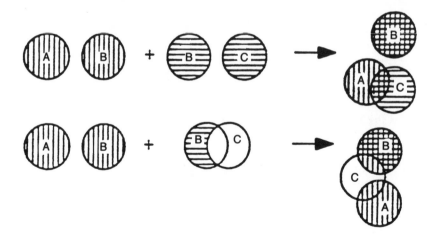

Figure 6.5 Registration diagrams with u-valid conclusions
Note: Premise + premise = registration diagram. These syllogisms warrant conclusions of the 'u'-form, i.e. 'Some not A are not C'.
N.B. The A and C circles can adopt any of the five Gergonne relations, but constraint lies in their mutual relation to B.

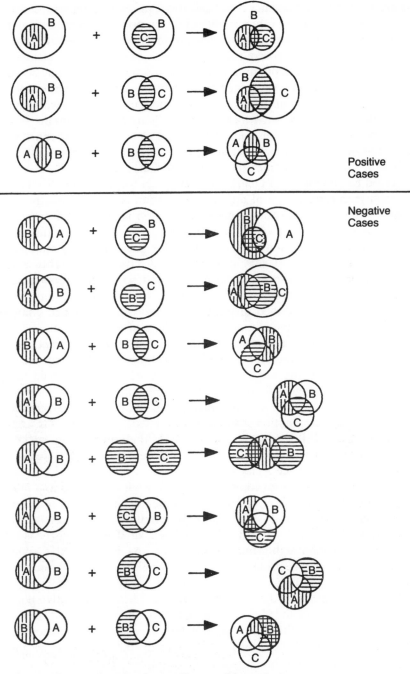

Figure 6.6 Registration diagrams with no valid conclusions
Note: Premise + premise = registration diagram.

it must establish a maximal type, and this can only be represented by a region shaded in one or other or both of the component premise diagrams. If there is such a shaded area which is not intersected by a circle from the other component diagram, then there is a maximal type established (namely the one corresponding to this non-intersected area) and so there is a valid conclusion. An existential conclusion can be drawn simply by stripping the B out from this type's description and prefacing with 'some'. So from the ABC type one concludes 'Some A are B', and from the AB~C type one concludes 'Some A are not C', and so on. Universal conclusions only follow if the non-intersected region is circular, and in this case, the label on the circle becomes the subject of the conclusion. The reader is referred to Stenning and Oberlander (in press) for more detail.

Each graphical feature of the implementation is related directly to the logic of the syllogism. For example, if a region is intersected by a circle from the other diagram when the two premises are registered, this means that different registration strategies (than the present one of establishing maximum types) would eliminate either of its two halves. This in turn means that neither subregion must exist and so neither represents an established maximal type.

What we have described, if rather sketchily, is a mechanical syllogism computer. This implementation of the logic is of particular interest here because it shows how a mechanism is tailored to a logical fragment. Circles on a plane force representation of maximal types. Syllogisms are case identifiable. It is the expressive *limitations* of the mechanism which dovetail with the logical limitations of the fragment to provide an efficient process which uses no more expressive power than it needs and therefore requires less computation to make inferences. Euler circles cannot implement full MPC reasoning and that is their processing *advantage* (Stenning and Oberlander (in press) has a more detailed discussion of the expressive power of the Euler notation).

How does this syllogism computer relate to what we know about human syllogistic reasoning? It is not here developed as an account of people's actual reasoning. Here it is merely a representation system and algorithm for its normative use. However, we do believe that it is the basis for developing novel insights into performance. As is usual, this style of representation can be used to develop a whole family of different but related implementations. The most obvious entry point for explaining different strategies and the production of errors lies in alternative policies for registering the A and C circles during premise combination. The doubly shaded areas are also intimately related to strategies for identifying necessary maximal types, but are intriguingly misleading or absent in exactly the syllogisms which prove most difficult. But here we are not concerned to develop detailed models of data. Here our concern is to look at this particular implementation and compare it with others that have been proposed for the syllogism. By doing this we can see that all the proposals in fact agree on the central features of human syllogistic reasoning. We can then relate these to implementation in human memory.

The obvious starting point for comparison is Erickson's (1974) model of syllogistic reasoning which actually employs Euler circles as its system of representation. Unfortunately Erickson did not incorporate the strategies of diagram choice that are implicit in the use of Euler circles in logic teaching, nor any equivalent of the shading notation into his model based on the circles. The result is that there is a many-to-many mapping of diagrams onto premises, shown in Figure 6.7, and an explosion of combinations. In the worst case there are four diagrams consistent with 'Some A are B' and so sixteen pairs of diagrams to combine for the syllogism 'Some A are B. Some B are C'. There are also several ways of combining each pair of diagrams. Erickson's response is to introduce random selection of diagrams into his model, a move that runs quite counter to the spirit of Euler's system and fails to exploit the case identifiability property of the syllogisms. More recently Guyote and Sternberg (1981) have proposed a Euler circle-based theory which preserves the same arbitrariness in the way that it prevents combinatorial explosion in graphical reasoning.

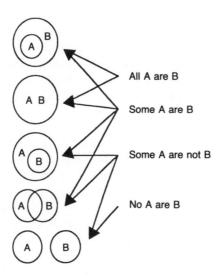

Figure 6.7 The five Gergonne relations between two circles mapped onto the four syllogistic premises
Note: Arrows point from a premise to each of the diagrams in which the premise is true.

Johnson-Laird has proposed the most elaborated theory of syllogistic reasoning in a series of papers (Johnson-Laird and Steedman, 1978, Johnson-Laird and Bara, 1984, Johnson-Laird, 1983). It was Erickson's idiosyncratic use of Euler circles which attracted Johnson-Laird's criticism that such graphical methods inevitably lead to combinatorial explosion and to claim that his own 'mental model' theory was quite distinct (Johnson-Laird, 1983). In fact, as we have shown elsewhere (Stenning and Oberlander, 1991), the mental-models family of theorem provers is a member of the same family as the graphical algorithm we have described here. Mental models' only difference is that there are no obvious constraints on the notation employed – nothing in the apparatus of letters, arcs, parentheses, etc. (basically the ingredients of semantic network notation) limits their expressive power. Euler circles, in contrast, are constrained by the geometry of circles on a plane to represent maximal types and, as we have argued, exploit exactly this constraint in capturing the central logical feature of syllogisms, their case identifiability.

So implementations can be studied at many levels of detail. At one level, two notations may be equivalent, whereas at another they have quite different properties. Conversely, two notations which appear quite distinct may actually turn out to be equivalent. For the psychologist, the crucial problem is to identify the level of description of implementation that can be related to what is known about human computational architecture, especially human memory, We can take either Euler circles or mental-models notations and ask what relation they bear to internal representations that subjects use to reason syllogistically. It may be that the differences between notations are crucial in understanding how human memory implements syllogisms. But our belief is that a much better departure point for investigations is what the notations have in common.

The property of case identifiability is vital to the way that human working memory implements the binding of attributes to ephemeral individuals – ones that are not established in long-term memory. Stenning et al. (1988) showed that the pattern of complex errors which result when subjects attempt to hold bindings of values to two individuals clearly indicates that the representation of binding is distributed. A subject who has just read a paragraph describing such a set of bindings has represented about twenty conjunctive existential facts which are then synthesized into a canonical description of the pair of individuals by a constraint satisfaction mechanism. Stenning and Levy (1988) demonstrated that a simple multi-layer perceptron can be trained by backpropagation on the logic of the twenty features, and then makes retrieval errors of a similar pattern to those of human subjects when noise is injected into the distributed database. This general architecture for working memory can explain several facts about the style of reasoning human beings adopt when faced by syllogisms, and why this working memory can be applied to these problems but not to ones in which there is no unique minimal model.

Constraint-satisfaction networks are radically parallel devices viewed at the level of the behaviour of their individual units operating settling, but viewed at the level of the whole network on an occasion of its interpretation, they are radically serial. One set of constraints is set as inputs and the network relaxes into a single solution to those constraints. If bindings are held as sets of feature values distributed over the input units, and read off in their canonical form from output units, only one set

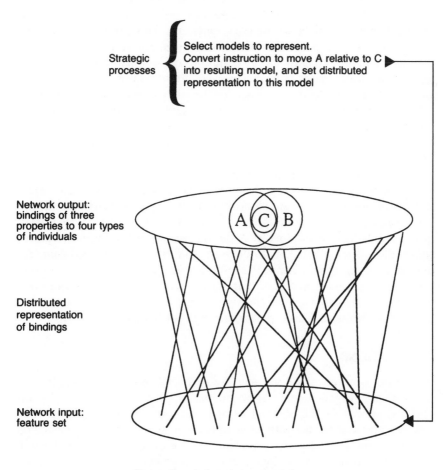

Connections to long-term associative

Figure 6.8 Schematic embedding of a distributed memory for bindings in a syllogism-solution system

of bindings can be held at one time. Furthermore, these networks settle into a total solution whether or not the information input is sufficient to uniquely determine a total solution. Representing partial solutions is not possible. Thus, if syllogisms required consideration of disjunctions of partial models, these disjunctions could only be represented by sequences of settlings; see Stenning and Oberlander (in press) for a discussion of how syllogism solution might be implemented in an architecture in which bindings are held by a constraint satisfaction network. Figure 6.8, taken from that discussion, gives an overall view of the architecture. There are several other sorts of memory which must be involved beyond the constraint-based memory for bindings.

For example, there is memory for the grammatical structure of the premises and memory used for formulating conclusions, strategic memory, and probably several other memory functions. This proposal is agnostic about the nature of these other memory systems. At the very general level of description offered here, it may either be considered as holding bindings representing Euler circles or mental models – there really is no difference (see Stenning and Oberlander (in press) for a more extensive discussion of the different implications of graphical representations at greater levels of detail).

In summary, our graphical implementation of syllogistic reasoning can be related quite directly to the case identifiability property of syllogisms. The nature of the limitations on binding arbitrary properties in human working memory explains why human beings should adopt a strategy of conglomerating all the information they have into a single representation and therefore pursuing an algorithm of the type exemplified in this graphical method or mental models, rather than one more closely related to natural deduction systems. It is the limitations of the logical fragment which allow these algorithms to be used. In this very limited domain, the implementation does permit the proving of theorems about arbitrary concepts which have not had their logical relations built into long-term memory. As befits an evolutionarily recently acquired ability to perform a rather 'unbiological' task, performance is not fluent and is errorful.

CONCLUSIONS

Psychology, and cognitive science, are about the resource constraints on performance which result from human implementations of abstract systems, as well as the abstract competences which they implement. In fact, we have argued that without studying both system and implementation and the intimate relation between them, little progress can be expected. Quite detailed study of the logical properties of curious fragments is both necessary and revealing. Interpretations of the behavioural data which result from studies of human performance can be informed by the *logical* properties of the fragments investigated.

The problem of insensitive applications of abstract systems to biological computation has recently been revealed in vision research. The overriding problem with Marr's topdown methodology for studying competences is that it is far from obvious how to draw a line around competences with enough reliability to be able to take seriously the detail of the formal description of competence as a guide to the study of implementation.

But we cannot avoid making some identification, however defeasibly we may treat it, of the competences we study. Psychologists have taken natural deduction proof theories of MPC or even FPPC as the obviously correct competence description of the reasoning which they wish to analyse. But in doing this they have missed the most important logical properties of the *fragment* which they have in fact studied. Once a logical description of this fragment is available it provides a framework for describing what is in common and what differs between alternative implementations. More recent work of Johnson-Laird and his co-workers (e.g. Johnson-Laird and Byrne, 1991) has extended his mental-models approach to relational arguments which are a fragment of FPPC. It will be interesting to see whether there is a similarly illuminating description of the logical nature of this fragment, but that is a project for another place.

By comparing *reflexive* reasoning over a fragment of FPPC in the service of text comprehension, with *considered* reasoning over a small fragment of MPC in the service of formal theorem proving, we have emphasized that we should not expect just one implementation of logic in human reasoning. All the empirical evidence of the radical differences in performance points in this direction. Once we are on the lookout for differences, the most striking implementation issue for human beings is what information resides in LTM and what has to be created during an episode of reasoning. We can see why this should be from our comparison of computing truth-in-a-model with theorem proving. In biological computation, the theorem proving is typically done by evolution and by learning. A long-term database can be crafted to our environment by such processes, but that does not allow access to indeterminate reinterpretations of it in deductive theorem proving. Human beings appear to be unique in having at least a limited ability to reason deductively over domains which are not represented in long-term memory, but their abilities are almost pathetically limited in this sphere unless they can find some analogy between the novel domain and some domain well-established in long-term memory. This weakness should not be allowed to obscure the fact that this limited innovation may well be the basis of much else that is at the root of human uniqueness. Syllogisms themselves are of little intrinsic interest, but the limited ability to perform arbitrary variable bindings in working memory which is revealed by this formal task perhaps has wider significance.

We hope that the distinction between the tasks of computing truth-in-a-model and theorem proving helps to clarify the relation between logic and biological computation. For views of rationality it is important to be clear about what task the subject has set itself. From our two example areas we can see that it would be a mistake to fault the reasoning involved in understanding texts because it is not deductively valid. It seeks to find the model the author has in mind, not the class of all models logically consistent with the text. It is a mistake to identify rationality with theorem proving, even if one includes all the non-logical mechanisms necessary to implement logic within one's notion of deduction. But there is an element to rationality which is related to this distinction through the degree of freedom to reason about general subject matters. If reasoning about truth-in-a-model were literally tied to reasoning about one model, it would be barely reasoning at all. Shastri's reflexive reasoning system is a nice example of something intermediate between being tied to a single model, and being able to reason about all possible models. It can reason about small numbers of novel instantiations of variables with respect to their combinations of large numbers of pre-interpreted properties. Before logicians discovered the intractability of general logics, it might have been tempting to identify rationality only with reasoning with respect to all possible models. Now that temptation must recede. Rationality, like intelligence, has to do with suitability to environment. The balance between the tyranny of extreme generality and tyranny of extreme particularity must lie somewhere in between the two.

Psychologists with whom we have discussed these views are often dismissive of the importance of getting the relation between logic and theories of reasoning and rationality right. They have done their experiments and they have their findings and they do not see why they need to understand that logicians' understanding of logic has changed radically in the last half century. They are at least dimly aware that once they enter into the territory of comparing different representations and processes involved in computation they enter a hall of a thousand mirrors in which nothing is quite what it seems. They may also be aware that logicians get around in this hall in so far as they do because they have some theorems which demonstrate for at least systems of some expressive power, what can and cannot be captured in syntactic descriptions of reasoning. But psychologists tend to react defensively when the logician tells them confidently that the experiments cannot discriminate whether people's reasoning is based on 'a formal logic' or on some 'non-logical' mechanism because mathematics shows that *nothing* can do that within some particular domain of study.

We think this reaction is unfortunate and has had some rather severe consequences for the psychology of reasoning. The most important of these consequences is that while psychologists have focused on issues about whether reasoning is logical or non-logical (issues of which the relevant parts were elegantly understood some years ago) they have been deflected from the really important psychological issue which is how reasoning is implemented in human memory.

In arguing that the main burden of explanation for reflexive reasoning and for human syllogistic reasoning performance lies at a 'lower' level than is conventionally assumed, our theory opens up the possibility of an extensive *rapprochement* of traditions of experimental psychology which have remained rather distinct. An enormous body of research on immediate memory has remained rather separate from an almost equally voluminous literature on reasoning, long-term memory and language processing. There have been a few notable attempts at bridging this gap (e.g. Anderson, 1983; Baddeley, 1986). They have tended either to be computationally explicit, but couched in the sort of rule-based architectures which make explaining resource limitations difficult, or they have limited themselves to showing experimentally that resource limitations in rote tasks do affect text processing but without computationally explicit models of the processes involved. Explicitly addressing the problem of implementing human reasoning in human memory should bring these literatures together and force them both to develop in interesting ways.

We hope we have made a case that this view of the relation between logic and implementation throws new light on some old psychological issues and refocuses attention in the psychology of reasoning. The view that we have taken of the relation between logic and implementation is nearly universal among contemporary logicians but contrasts strongly with an earlier view of logic which appears to be retained to this day by many psychologists studying reasoning. On this latter view, logic describes a *mechanism* which, if it were completely embodied, would constitute a competence for reasoning. The question then becomes whether some version of this mechanism can be found in the subject, however much obscured by other mechanisms which intervene between it and observed behaviour. This mechanistic view of logic is anachronistic.

We have shown how the modern view of a logic as an abstract consequence relation is further removed from mechanism than its older counterpart but nevertheless does constructively constrain classes of possible mechanism. This new flexibility is important to psychologists who want to use logic to guide their investigations. The newer view of logic is also less imperialistic. If a logic is an abstract consequence relation there is little chance of failing to see that there is more to rationality than logic. In particular, there are all those issues of what is in principle implementable and what is implementable biologically. The modern logician is hardly likely to inveigh against psychologism when it comes to theories of rationality.

As is common with thoroughly modern streamlined views which have dispensed with much metaphysics from their imperial baggage, this one may leave some commentators with a feeling of disappointment. If logics are just mathematical abstractions, and psychologists are just reverse engineers studying implementation in a way recognizable to a computer scientist, what has happened to all those dilemmas about whether man is really a rational animal? For example, how does a reasoner know that such and such a procedure of reasoning is justified – rational to employ in these and these circumstances? We might even confess to some disappointment ourselves here. It is notoriously unclear how to give an account of issues of phenomenological access to reasoning processes within the sort of computational framework we have been assuming. We do not accept the arguments that it is in principle impossible to do so, but we do not pretend to have a satisfying account.

But this is a circumscribed sort of disappointment. One of the great virtues of a clear and contemporary view of how logic relates to reasoning is that it reveals quite clearly that none of the opposing non-logical theories of reasoning cast one ray of light on these issues of phenomenology. They also describe mechanisms, in various degrees of detail, which on this score are only distinguished from our implementations of logical fragments by their claim to be so unrelated. Such an approach is analogous to a stance that says that one should do physics without mathematics. Logic may be nothing but mathematics, and mathematics is certainly not the *topic* of a theory of rationality, but logic and psychology had better be at least as closely intertwined as mathematics is with physics.

ACKNOWLEDGEMENT

The support of the ESRC for the Human Communication Research Centre is gratefully acknowledged.

NOTES

1 Any association with the political environment past, present or future is purely fortuitous.
2 A recursive specification of an infinite set of deductive relations.
3 Resolution theorem provers, for example, have but one rule of inference.
4 For a summary of issues in computational complexity see Garey and Johnson (1979).
5 For discussion, see Moore (1982).
6 See Hogger (1984) for details.
7 However, Sperber and Wilson (1986) explicitly eschew the identification of confirmation strengths with subjective probabilities.
8 Although the matching process only relies on the shape of the predicate symbols.
9 The pilot who shot at it saw the Mig which chased him.
10 There is ample evidence that subjects, not surprisingly, adopt the goal of finding the most informative rather than just any valid conclusion. For example, they tend to seek the universal positive response where it is valid, rather than resting content with the weaker existential conclusion.

11 Although this system of shading appears to be novel in the psychological literature on Euler circles, it is certainly not original. It figures in many teaching schemes that use logic diagrams, and has undoubtedly been invented many times. It does not appear to have been used explicitly by Euler.

REFERENCES

Anderson, J.R. (1983) *The Architecture of Cognition*, Cambridge, MA: Harvard University Press.

Baddeley, A. (1986) *Working Memory*, Oxford: Oxford University Press.

Braine, M.D.S. (1978) 'On the relationship between the natural logic of reasoning and standard logic', *Psychological Review* 85: 1–21.

Charniak, E. and McDermott, D. (1985) *An Introduction to Artificial Intelligence*, Reading, MA: Addison Wesley.

Church, A. (1936) 'A note on the Entscheidungs problem', *Journal of Symbolic Logic* 1: 40–1.

Cook, S.A. (1971) 'The complexity of theorem-proving procedures', *The Third Annual ACM Symposium on the Theory of Computing*, New York: Association for Computing Machinery, 1971, pp. 151–8.

Erickson, J.R. (1974) 'A set analysis theory of behaviour in formal syllogistic reasoning tasks', In R. Solso (ed.) *Loyola Symposium on Cognition*, vol. 2, Hillsdale, NJ: Erlbaum.

Fodor, J.A. and Pylyshyn, Z.W. (1988) 'Connectionism and cognitive architecture: a critical analysis', *Cognition* 28: 3–71.

Garey, M.R. and Johnson, D.S. (1979) *Computers and Intractability: A Guide to the Theory of NP-Completeness*, New York: Freeman.

Guyote, M.J. and Sternberg, R.J. (1981) 'A transitive chain theory of syllogistic reasoning', *Cognitive Psychology* 13: 461–525.

Hilbert, D. (1925) 'On the infinite', repr. and trans. in P. Bernacerraf and H. Putnam *The Philosophy of Mathematics*, Englewood Cliffs, NJ: Prentice-Hall, 1964.

Hintikka, J. (1983) *The Game of Language*, vol. 1, Dordrecht: Reidel.

Hogger, C.J. (1984) *Introduction to Logic Programming*, London: Academic Press.

Johnson-Laird, P.N. (1983) *Mental Models*, Cambridge: Cambridge University Press.

Johnson-Laird, P.N. and Bara, B.G. (1984) 'Syllogistic inference', *Cognition* 16: 1–61.

Johnson-Laird, P.N. and Byrne, R.M.J. (1991) *Deduction*, Hillsdale, NJ: Erlbaum.

Johnson-Laird, P.N. and Steedman, M.J. (1978) 'The psychology of syllogisms', *Cognitive Psychology* 10: 64–99.

Kowalski, R.A. (1979) *Logic for Problem Solving*, Amsterdam: North Holland.

Lange, T. and Dyer, M. (1989) *High-level Inferencing in a Connectionist Neural Network*, Technical Report No. UCLA-AI-89-12, Computer Science, Los Angeles: UCLA.

Levesque, H.J. (1988) 'Logic and the complexity of reasoning' *Journal of Philosophical Logic* 17: 355–89.

Moore, R.C. (1982) *The Role of Logic in Knowledge Representation and Commonsense Reasoning*, Technical Note No. 264, Menlo Park, CA: SRI International, June, 1982.

Newell, A. and Simon, H. (1972) *Human Problem Solving*, Englewood Cliffs, NJ: Prentice-Hall.

Oaksford, M.R., Chater, N.J., and Stenning, K. (1990) 'Connectionism, classical cognitive science and experimental psychology', *AI and Society* 4: 73–90 (special edition on connectionism in context).

Robinson, J.A. (1965) 'A machine-oriented logic based on the resolution principle', *Journal of the Association for Computing Machinery* 12: 23–41.

Shastri, L. and Ajjanagadde, V. (1989) *A Connectionist System for Rule Based Reasoning with Multi-place Predicates and Variables*, Technical Report No. MS-CIS-89-06, Philadelphia: Department of Computer and Information Science, School of Engineering and Applied Science, 1989.

Sperber, D. and Wilson, D. (1986) *Relevance: Communication and Cognition*, Oxford: Blackwell.

Stenning, K. (1978) 'Anaphora as an approach to pragmatics', In M. Halle, J. Bresnan, and G.A. Miller (eds) *Linguistic Theory and Psychological Reality*, Cambridge, MA: MIT Press.

—— (1986) 'On making models: a study of constructive memory', in T. Myers, K. Brown, and B. McGonigle (eds) *Reasoning and Discourse Processes*, London: Academic Press, ch. 7, pp. 165–85.

Stenning, K. and Levy, J. (1988) 'Knowledge rich solutions to the "Binding" problem: some human computational mechanisms', *Knowledge Based Systems* 1: 3, June.

Stenning, K. and Oberlander, J. (1991) *A Cognitive Theory of Graphical and Linguistic Reasoning: Logic and Implementation*, Research Paper no. 20, Edinburgh: Human Communication Research Centre, Edinburgh University, 1991.

—— (in press) 'Spatial containment and set membership: a case study of analogy at work', in J. Barnden and K. Holyoak (eds) *Analogical Connections*, Hillsdale, NJ: Erlbaum.

Stenning, K., Shepherd, M., and Levy, J. (1988) 'On the construction of representations for individuals from descriptions in text', *Language and Cognitive Processes* 2: 129–64.

Touretsky, D. and Hinton, G.E. (1988) 'A distributed connectionist production system', *Cognitive Science* 12(3): 422–66.

Yule, P. (1991) 'An experimental investigation of a new theory of syllogistic reasoning based on Euler', Masters thesis, Centre for Cognitive Science, University of Edinburgh.

Chapter 7

Models and deductive rationality

P.N. Johnson-Laird and R.M.J. Byrne

INTRODUCTION

Rationality means different things to different people. During its long history as a theoretical concept, it has referred to logical thought, to a prudent choice among alternative courses of action, to a wise allocation of resources, to a capacity to arrive at truth, and much else besides. We intend to address the question: are human beings rational? But, before we can do so, we need to choose a yardstick against which to measure performance. One strategy, which has been adopted by Anderson (1990), is to assume that rational behaviour is whatever is optimized to the structure of the environment. This strategy calls for the almost impossible task of characterizing the structure of the environment in a way that is independent of human conceptions, so that one can then specify what would count as optimal behaviour. Another strategy, which has been pursued by students of decision making, is to propose a set of *a priori* principles. The 'rational man' of classical economics and modern decision theory, however, is a singularly implausible psychological individual. The burden of recent investigations is that human beings make decisions not by choosing among alternatives according to their expected utilities – the *sine qua non* of such theories – but by constructing reasons for one choice as opposed to others (see Shafir, 1991; Tversky and Shafir, 1991). Rationality in still other domains, such as inductive and probabilistic inference, depends on technical knowledge. Anyone who had known the calculus of probabilities in Roman times, as Hacking (1975) has remarked, would soon have won all of Gaul. To conclude that Romans, and others unfamiliar with the calculus, are therefore irrational seems to miss the point.

The sense of rationality that is central to life is what enables individuals to cope with its everyday exigencies. They have certain beliefs and certain desires and needs: to attain these goals, they must infer from their beliefs what they have to do to attain them and then carry out those actions. Their beliefs need to be true more often than not, and so do the conclusions that they infer from them. We therefore assume that the two central precepts of rationality are: (i) to believe what is true (the precept of rational belief); and (ii) to infer what is true (the precept of rational thinking).

To believe what is true depends on the facts of the matter, and to determine the facts is sometimes easy, sometimes hard, and sometimes impossible: it is a question of obtaining evidence and evaluating it. The precept of rational belief therefore raises interesting psychological problems, but it brings us back to the difficulty of determining what counts as rational in the domain of inductive and probabilistic inference. The precept of rational thinking, however, allows us to examine the question of rationality in at least one unproblematic way. We can ask to what extent human beings are able to make *valid* deductions, that is, inferences which yield conclusions that must be true given that the beliefs on which they are based are true. A capacity to make valid deductions is indeed one measure of rationality, and, in comparison to others, it provides a yardstick that is easy to use.

There are three mutually exclusive and exhaustive views about our topic:

1 Human reasoning is impeccably rational.
2 Human reasoning is intrinsically irrational.
3 Human reasoning is sometimes rational, sometimes not.

Perhaps surprisingly, each view has its proponents, and the resulting conflicts have led to controversies, often pursued independently of one another, in philosophy, psychology, and anthropology. Our goal in this chapter is to resolve the controversy in psychology by proposing a new way in which to think of deductive competence – a way that is borne out by experimental observations, and then to use this result as a stepping stone to the resolution of the other controversies.

We begin by considering what inferences human reasoners actually draw. This sketch of deductive competence (in the first section of this chapter (pp. 179–80)) shows that they have a grasp of the precept of rational thinking – indeed, they transcend it by appreciating the need to draw valid conclusions that are useful rather than trivial. However, when we consider the mechanism by which the precept is put into practice (in the second section (pp. 180–91)), the evidence suggests that it is *not* equipped with logical rules of inference, which it sometimes uses correctly and sometimes misuses, misapplies, or forgets. This analogy with grammar, which has seduced so many theorists, is a fundamental mistake. The reasoning mechanism constructs a mental model of the premises, formulates a putative conclusion, and tests its validity by searching for alternative models of the premises in which it is false. The search is constrained by the meta-principle that the conclusion is valid only if there are no such models, but it is not governed by any systematic or comprehensive principles. Hence, human reasoners try to follow the rational precept but are logically fallible. We then use this theory to resolve the three main controversies about rationality. The first controversy concerns the alleged conceptual impossibility of showing that subjects in psychological experiments make errors in reasoning. We argue to the contrary (in the third section (pp.191–4)) that subjects are not impeccably rational. Because they lack systematic inferential principles (rules of inference), they make genuine mistakes in reasoning. The second controversy concerns the claim that without a training in logic deductions in some simple domains are beyond the rational competence of subjects. They therefore resort to intrinsically irrational strategies. We show (in the fourth section (pp. 194–204)) that this argument overlooks both the method that subjects use to reason and many of the empirical phenomena. What looks like an irrational choice of conclusion – on the grounds that it matches the superficial linguistic form of a premise – is merely a consequence of reasoning by searching for alternative models. Finally, we consider (in the fifth section (pp. 204–5)) the controversy over rationality in other cultures. Anthropologists have sometimes argued that members of certain cultures are unable to think rationally. This claim raises the deep question of how to frame an analysis of rationality that is independent of any particular culture. Perhaps, it is said, cultures that appear deviant to our eyes are rational according to their own lights, that is, the notion of rationality is relative to a culture. We argue that there is no need to swallow the unpalatable pill of relativism. No culture appears to reject the precept of rational thinking; all cultures are capable of logical error.

HUMAN DEDUCTIVE COMPETENCE

Human reasoners are able to make valid deductions, and they often *know* that they have made such a deduction. They exercise intelligence in ways that are conspicuously not part of formal logic. In logic, any set of premises supports infinitely many different valid conclusions, many of which are entirely trivial, such as a conjunction of a premise with itself some arbitrary number of times. Hence, a procedure based on logic alone could not isolate useful conclusions from trivial ones. Human reasoners, however, draw conclusions for themselves, and in so doing they abide by sensible constraints (Johnson-Laird, 1983). For instance, they do not normally throw semantic information away. Given a premise A, they never spontaneously draw a final conclusion of the form:

A or B, or both

even though such a deduction is valid. They are parsimonious. They never, for example, draw a conclusion that merely conjoins all the premises. They try to reach a simpler conclusion and one that is not explicitly stated in the premises. If no conclusion meets these constraints, then rather than draw some trivial, but valid, conclusion, they say, 'There's no valid conclusion' – a response that can never be sanctioned by logic alone. In short, we can refine the precept for rational thinking: to make a rational deduction is to maintain semantic information, to simplify, and to reach a new conclusion (Johnson-Laird and Byrne, 1991).

The human deductive mechanism is rapid, and seems to put as minimal a load as possible on the processing capacity of working memory. Because the heart of computational power is an ability to retain and to exploit the results of intermediate computations, a limited working memory is computationally weak and so performance rapidly degrades with increasingly complex problems. But a further sign of human intelligence is the invention and use of systems of notation, including writing, which can serve as a substitute for working memory. Writing enables human reasoners to cope with problems that demand more computational power. The meta-cognitive capacity to reflect on inferences and to develop notational systems, such as formal logic, to deal with them is a quintessential human competence. We will not pursue the development of formal logic as an intellectual discipline, but it does presuppose some existing deductive competence – some native ability to reason validly and an awareness of the fallibility of the inferential mechanism.

A further mark of intelligence is the use of general knowledge in everyday deductive inference. A reasoner's goal is to reach true, or at least plausible, conclusions rather than merely valid conclusions. Knowledge can assist this process by providing pertinent information and a means for assessing the truth of conclusions. You are likely to judge that a conclusion is true if it corresponds to the state of affairs in the world, or if it coheres with your other beliefs. Can beliefs directly affect the *process* of reasoning? The issue is highly controversial. If reasoning is based on formal rules, then it cannot be affected by beliefs which, by definition, are blind to the specific content of premises. But such effects are possible if reasoning is a semantic rather than a syntactic process (see Oakhill *et al.*, 1989). Our view of the deductive mechanism, to which we now turn, is that it is indeed semantic in its operation.

MENTAL MODELS AND THE DEDUCTIVE MECHANISM

Many people suppose that the only way to establish that an argument is valid is to derive a formal proof of it in a logical calculus. They are mistaken. Logicians distinguish such 'proof-theoretic' methods, which depend on formal rules of inference, from 'model-theoretic' methods, which depend on a semantic way to demonstrate validity. Perhaps because model theory is a more recent development than proof theory, students of human thinking have assumed almost without reflection that the deductive mechanism depends upon formal rules of inference like those of a logical calculus. These rules are not consciously accessible, but they are none the less supposed to underlie inferences. Piaget was an early and influential proponent of this doctrine (see, for example, Piaget, 1928; Inhelder and Piaget, 1958), but it continues to be popular (see, for example, Osherson, 1975; Rips, 1983; Braine, 1978; Braine *et al.*, 1984; Macnamara, 1986; Pollock, 1989). In our view, however, reasoning is not a formal or syntactic process but a matter of understanding meanings, and manipulating their mental representations, that is, *mental models* of the world. These models can be constructed by perception, by comprehending a verbal description, or by imagining a state of affairs. The precise details of these representations may not be germane to deduction: some individuals report forming visual images, but the subjective experience does not appear to be important, and images have at best a limited representational power. The function of a model is to make explicit those objects, properties, and relations in a situation that are relevant to potential actions, that is, to make them available to inference and decision making without the need for further processing. The structure of a model therefore corresponds to the structure of the situation, as humans conceive it, not to the linguistic structure of discourse. The nature of these structures will become clearer as we consider different sorts of deduction.

Deductive reasoning depends on three principal skills: the comprehension of some initial information, the generation of a putative conclusion, and the evaluation of the validity of the conclusion. We take the first step to be the normal process of comprehension, and the second step to be the normal process of verbal description – that is, the description of the content of a mental model in a parsimonious way. The critical step is thus the evaluation of validity. A valid conclusion, by definition, is one that must be true given that the initial information is true. In logic, such a test can be made using proof-theoretic methods that operate syntactically, using formal rules. But, in certain domains, tests can be made using model-theoretic methods that operate semantically. Psychological theories based on formal rules follow the spirit of the proof-theoretic method; the theory of mental models follows the spirit of the model-theoretic method. The mental-model theory has been described in detail elsewhere (see Johnson-Laird and Byrne, 1991). Here, we will merely sketch how it works for propositional and quantificational reasoning.

Propositional reasoning

Deductions that depend on propositional connectives, such as 'not', 'if', 'and', and 'or', underlie most reasoning and thus are common in everyday thought. The meanings of such connectives specify their contribution to the truth conditions of assertions. For example, an inclusive disjunction of two propositions:

Arthur loves Betty, or Betty loves Arthur, or both

is true if at least one of the two propositions is true, and is false only if they are both false. In logic, these truth conditions are often laid out in a truth table. Strictly speaking, however, it is a mistake to assign truth values to sentences in natural language: a speaker uses a sentence to assert a proposition, and it can assert many different propositions depending on who asserts it, for example, the sentence 'Arthur loves Betty' asserts different propositions depending on the particular Arthur and Betty to whom it refers. Hence, it is propositions, not sentences, that have truth values.

Much confusion has arisen over the idea of mental models because accounts differ from one theorist to another. Our previous studies have led to a theory based on the following simple principles:

1 Each entity is represented by a corresponding token in a mental model.
2 The properties of entities are represented by the properties of their tokens.
3 Relations among entities are represented by relations among their tokens.

Thus, a model of the assertion, 'The circle is on the right of the triangle' has the structure:

△ ○

A model may be experienced as an image, but many models contain elements that cannot be visualized, for example, the representation of negation. What matters is, not the subjective experience, but the structure of the model: entities are represented by tokens, their properties are represented by properties of the tokens, and the relations between them are represented by the relations between the tokens (Johnson-Laird, 1983).

According to the mental-model theory, reasoning is a semantic process resembling the manipulation of truth tables, but people with no training in logic are most unlikely to use truth tables: the number of rows in them increases exponentially with the number of elementary propositions contained in an argument, and fails to correlate with the difficulty of deductions (Osherson, 1974–6). The theory therefore postulates that reasoners use mental models, which are much less bulky than truth tables. Mental models differ from other proposed forms of representation, such as semantic networks (e.g. Quillian, 1968) and propositional representations of the sort used by formal rules (e.g. Braine et al., 1984). The difference is clear in the case of connectives such as disjunction. The disjunctive assertion:

There is a circle or there is a triangle

requires at least two alternative models, which we represent by the following diagram:

O

　　△

using the notational convention that each line in a diagram denotes a separate model of a different possible state of affairs. The first model is of a state of affairs in which there is a circle, and the second model is of a state of affairs in which there is a triangle. The further categorical assertion:

There isn't a circle

can be integrated with the existing models in only one way. The model of the state of affairs in which there is a circle must be eliminated because it is incompatible with this premise, and so the only remaining model is:

△

A procedure that scans models for conclusions not explicitly stated among the premises will yield the conclusion:

There is a triangle.

There are no models of the two premises in which this conclusion is false, and so it is valid. The conclusion is also parsimonious and new; it has been drawn without using a formal rule for disjunctive inference, and without even deciding whether the disjunction is inclusive (circle or triangle, *or both*) or exclusive (circle or triangle, *but not both*). The conclusion emerges solely from the construction and evaluation of models based on the meaning of the premises.

The initial representation of the disjunction:

There is a circle or there is a triangle

is consistent with an inclusive or an exclusive interpretation, but the models can be fleshed out to represent either sort of disjunction. The distinction depends on making explicit that all instances of a particular contingency, for example, those in which there is a circle, have been exhaustively represented in the set of models. In other words, reasoners may know that there could be other instances of a circle, or that they have represented all of them. Strictly speaking, exhaustion is a relative notion: one contingency is exhaustively represented in relation to another, but we will ignore this point for the moment. We will use square brackets as our notation for an exhaustive representation. Thus, the exclusive disjunction:

Either there is a circle or else there is a triangle, but not both

has the following models:

[O]
    [△]

which represent explicitly that all states containing circles, and all states containing triangles, have been represented exhaustively. An inclusive disjunction, such as:

There is a circle or there is a triangle, or both

calls for three distinct possibilities including the joint occurrence of a circle and a triangle:

[O]   [△]
[O]
      [△]

The initial models of a conditional, such as:

If there is a circle then there is a triangle

are as follows:

[O]   △
 .   .   .

where the first model represents the state of affairs in which there is a circle, which is exhaustively represented in relation to the triangle. The second model depicted by the three dots has no explicit content, but it allows for its subsequent specification, and this possibility rules out any simple conjunctive description of the models. Because the triangles have not been exhausted, the models can be fleshed out to represent either a weak conditional:

[O]   [△]
      [△]
 .   .   .

or a strong biconditional (i.e. 'If and only if there is a circle, there is a triangle'):

[O]   [△]
 .   .   .

Readers who are interested in computer programs for reasoning with such models should consult Johnson-Laird and Byrne (1991).

The essence of the model theory is that people construct models that make explicit as little information as possible; in this way, they minimize the processing load on working memory. Because a model retains all the semantic information in the premises, the main task is to draw a parsimonious conclusion which, if possible, expresses a proposition that is not stated explicitly by the premises. In order to test the validity of a conclusion, reasoners must search for alternative models of the premises that falsify it. If there are no such models, the conclusion is valid; if there is such a model, then the conclusion must be rejected – it is necessary to formulate a weaker conclusion, if possible, that accommodates it; if it is uncertain whether there is such a model, then the conclusion can be drawn only on a tentative or inductive basis. Simple deductions are those where the premises yield only one model; difficult deductions depend on more than one model. In such cases, different individuals draw different conclusions, and the same individuals often draw different conclusions if the premises are presented again after they have forgotten their previous conclusions. Erroneous conclusions almost always correspond to a proper subset of the possible models of the premises (see Johnson-Laird and Byrne, 1991). Reasoners therefore lack any comprehensive procedures for finding alternative models.

Syllogistic reasoning

The most powerful forms of deduction depend on quantifiers, such as 'all', 'some', and 'none'. When assertions contain only a single quantified predicate, they can form the premises of syllogisms, such as:

All the angels are blessed.
All the blessed are cherubim.
∴ All the angels are cherubim.

A syllogism has two premises and a conclusion in one of four 'moods' shown here:

All A are B   (a universal affirmative premise)
Some A are B   (a particular affirmative premise)
No A are B   (a universal negative premise)
Some A are not B   (a particular negative premise)

To support a valid conclusion the two premises must share a common term (the so-called 'middle' term), and hence the premises can have four different arrangements (or 'figures') of their terms:

| A – B | B – A | A – B | B – A |
| B – C | C – B | C – B | B – C |

The syllogism above is in the first of these figures (where A = angels, B = blessed, and C = cherubim). In general, a syllogism in the figure:

A – B
B – C

tends to elicit conclusions of the form:

A – C

This figural bias is probably a result of the order in which information is combined in working memory: conclusions are formulated in the same order in which the information is used to construct a model. Alternatively, the bias may reflect a pragmatic preference for making the subject of a premise into the subject of the conclusion (Wetherick and Gilhooly, 1990). This linguistic bias, however, fails to explain the progressive slowing of responses over the four figures shown above, or the increasing proportion of 'no valid conclusion' responses. The phenomena are accounted for by the working-memory hypothesis, which postulates both the reordering of information in a premise and the reordering of the premises themselves in order to bring the two ocurrences of the middle term into temporal contiguity (Johnson-Laird and Bara, 1984).

No theory of syllogistic reasoning based on formal rules of inference has so far been proposed by psychologists, probably because the lengths of formal derivations fail to account for differences in difficulty among valid syllogisms (see Johnson-Laird and Byrne, 1991: 116). Most theories have accordingly been based on models. Some theories have used Euler circles or strings of symbols equivalent to them (e.g. Guyote and Sternberg, 1981), but, as we shall see, these representations do not generalize to more complicated quantified assertions. The model theory, however, extends in a natural way to deductions based on quantifiers. The key, as always, is that reasoners must know the meanings of terms and use them to construct models of the situations described by premises. Indeed, there is nothing special about connectives and quantifiers: their meanings must be grasped along with the meanings of nouns, verbs, adjectives, and other parts of speech. Unlike semantic networks and propositional representations, the model theory postulates that an assertion about a finite set is represented by a finite set of mental tokens (Johnson-Laird, 1983). Hence, the interpretation of a premise of the form:

All the angels are blessed

yields a single model, which we represent with the following diagram:

[a]   b
[a]   b
 . . .

In this case, unlike the diagrams of models for connectives, each line represents a separate individual in the same model. There is an arbitrary number of angels (as denoted by the a's in the diagram), which are each represented as blessed (as denoted by the b's in the diagram). The representation of the angels is exhausted in relation to the blessed, as is indicated by the square brackets, and so any further angel that might be added to the model must also be represented as blessed. Because the blessed are not exhausted in relation to the angels, the converse does not apply: b's can be added to the model without accompanying a's. Connoisseurs of Scholastic logic will recognize that the notion of exhaustion is related to the traditional concept of a distributed term, but, as far as we can tell, the Scholastics never grasped the need to make the notion a relational one. The three dots in the model indicate the possible existence of other sorts of individual, who are not explicitly represented in this initial model. The model can be fleshed out, for example, in the following way:

```
[a]      [b]
[a]      [b]
[¬a]     [b]
[¬a]     [¬b]
```

where '¬' represents negation, so the final individual in the model is neither angelic nor blessed (for a defence of such annotations as '¬' in models, see Polk and Newell, 1988; Newell, 1990; and Ch. 6 of Johnson-Laird and Byrne, 1991).
The interpretation of a premise of the form:

Some of the A are B

yields the following sort of model:

```
a      b
a      b
.  .  .
```

in which neither set of individuals is exhaustively represented. The interpretation of a premise of the form:

None of the A is a B

yields the following sort of model:

```
[a]
[a]
        [b]
        [b]
.  .  .
```

in which both sets are exhausted in relation to each other. Finally, the interpretation of a premise of the form:

Some of the A are not B

yields the following sort of model:

```
a
a
a      [b]
        [b]
.  .  .
```

This initial model supports the converse assertion:

Some of the B are not A

which is a fallacious inference that is often made (see, for example, Wilkins, 1928). However, this conclusion is falsified by an alternative model of the premise:

a
a
a   [b]
a   [b]
 . . .

The number of tokens representing a set is arbitrary, though always small and plural.

The first premise of a syllogism is interpreted by an appropriate initial model. The information from the second premise is then added to this initial model. For example, given premises of the form:

None of the A is a B
All the C are B

the first premise yields the model:

[a]
[a]
    [b]
    [b]
 . . .

There is then no choice about how to add the information from the second premise to this model:

[a]
[a]
    [b   [c]]
    [b   [c]]
 . . .

in which the c's are exhausted in relation to the b's. This model supports the conclusion:

None of the A is a C

and no alternative model of the premises refutes this conclusion. The premises yield only one model, and such one-model problems, as the theory predicts, are easy.

In other cases, the inference is harder. For instance, given premises of the form:

All the B are A
All the B are C

the first premise yields the model:

```
[b]   a
[b]   a
 . . .
```

The second premise can be accommodated by switching round the order of the items in this model and then adding the new information:

```
a   [b]   c
a   [b]   c
     . . .
```

in which the b's are exhausted in relation to both the a's and the c's. This model supports the conclusion: All the A are C, and its converse, All the C are A. But the first conclusion is refuted by an alternative model of the premises:

```
a   [b]   c
a   [b]   c
a

     . . .
```

And the second conclusion is refuted by another model:

```
a   [b]   c
a   [b]   c
           c
     . . .
```

Each model is a possible situation described by the premises, and a valid conclusion must hold in all of them – unless it merely states a possibility. Reasoners who reach the correct valid conclusion:

Some of the A are C

or its converse, may have constructed all three of the models, or instead they may have constructed only two models of the premises:

```
a   [b]   c              a   [b]   c
a   [b]   c              a   [b]   c
     . . .               a

                                   c

                              . . .
```

At present, we have no way of discriminating between these alternatives (cf. Johnson-Laird and Bara, 1984, who described two distinct computer programs: one that never constructs more than two models for syllogisms, and one that constructs three models for certain syllogisms). The critical distinction is accordingly between one-model problems and multiple-model problems. The evidence on syllogistic inference has been published elsewhere (e.g. Johnson-Laird and Bara, 1984). It shows that for every single subject whom we have ever tested, one-model problems are considerably easier than multiple-model problems. The theory also accounts for the most common errors: as in the case of propositional reasoning, they are conclusions that correspond to some of the possible models of the premises – typically, just a single model.

The model theory extends naturally to multiply quantified assertions, such as:

'None of the Avon letters is in the same place as any of the Bury letters'

which cannot be represented by Euler circles or Venn diagrams (see Gardner, 1982). Granted a semantic analysis of spatial relations, for example:

x is in the same place as y = x is in a place that has the same spatial co-ordinates as those for y.

It is a straightforward matter to devise a program for spatial inference, which will put different items into the same cell of a spatial array in order to satisfy the relation, 'in the same place as'. Emergent properties of this meaning include the transitivity and symmetry of the relation. Hence, the model theory assumes that reasoners who are given the premise above construct a model of the state of affairs:

/ [a] [a] [a] / [b] [b] [b] /

where the barriers demarcate separate places, and there are arbitrary numbers of tokens of each sort (a's denote Avon letters, and b's denote Bury letters), which in this case are all exhausted (see Johnson-Laird *et al.*, 1989).

The evidence for models

In general, the bottleneck in inferential processing is the capacity of working memory, and so the model theory makes two principal predictions. First, it predicts that the greater the number of explicit models needed for an inference, the harder the inference will be. Second, it makes a prediction about the nature of erroneous conclusions: they should be conclusions that hold in only some models of the premises, because subjects will sometimes fail to construct all the possible models. These predictions have been corroborated experimentally for all the major domains of deduction (see, for example, Byrne, 1989; Johnson-Laird and

Byrne, 1991). It is difficult to see how a theory based on formal rules of inference could account for either phenomenon. Derivations using formal rules at no point yield erroneous conclusions, and the lengths of derivations do not correlate with the number of models. Indeed, where the two theories make conflicting predictions about difficulty, the evidence bears out the model theory (Byrne and Johnson-Laird, 1989; Johnson-Laird *et al.*, 1992).

We have outlined our view of deductive competence, and we have described a theory of performance – the model theory – that accounts for both competence in principle and for the errors in reasoning that occur in practice. We now turn to the controversies about rationality in order to use our theory to resolve them.

AGAINST IMPECCABLE RATIONALITY

The position that our empirical results have established is that human reasoners are neither wholly rational – they make mistakes in reasoning, nor wholly irrational – they can make valid deductions for the right reasons. This position flagrantly conflicts with the case of impeccable rationality, and so we will examine this case in more detail.

Thinking, in principle, might be based on processes that apply universally to any content and that are exercised wholly without error. Certain philosophers have allegedly held such views. It is said, for example, that Spinoza had such a metaphysical dread of illogicality that he deemed invalid inferences to be valid but based on other premises. This doctrine has been echoed more recently by Henle (1962). She argues that subjects forget or reinterpret the premises, or import additional knowledge, and so they argue validly but from different premises than those presented by experimenters. From this position, it is a short step to the view, which Henle espouses, that the underlying deductive competence of ordinary individuals untutored in logic cannot be at fault. The same argument has been made more recently by Hamill (1990) in a cross-cultural study of syllogisms. He remarks that the syllogism is a logical pattern that is found in every language and culture so far studied, and he posits that all people are born with an innate knowledge of logical structure. Of his own study of syllogistic reasoning with English, Ojibwa, Navajo, and Mande-kan speakers, he writes: 'My analysis of their responses shows that the consultants never drew an invalid conclusion.' He also writes: 'No person living in any given culture is any more or less prone to error than any person living in another culture.'

In fact, there are vast differences in syllogistic ability, at least among the English, American, and Italian subjects whom we have tested: some individuals make many more mistakes than others (see, for example, Johnson-Laird, 1983: 117). Whether there are differences between cultures is a question that probably cannot be answered. To pose the question one needs a standardized test that is independent of cultural background, and the only way to establish its fairness would seem to be to show that individuals from different cultures do equally well on it. Hamill's method of developing his materials ensured that they were matched to the particular culture under investigation. This admirable procedure, however, undermines his claims about the universal nature of syllogistic reasoning.

Claims such as Henle's and Hamill's are consistent with the stronger philosophical doctrine that no empirical results could ever cast doubt on the intrinsic rationality of human beings. The underlying competence of individuals could not be at fault, though errors in performance may occur. There are several bases for arguments of this sort, but Stich has scrutinized them all and shown that they are unconvincing (see Stich, 1990a; and, for the same case in epitome, Stich 1990b). One argument is that systematically irrational thought is a conceptual impossibility. Suppose, to paraphrase Quine's (1960: 58) celebrated example, you were to encounter a group of extraterrestrials who appear to accept blatant self-contradictions as true. You are likely to be sceptical about the accuracy of the translation of their utterances, but if it seems accurate, then you may cease to treat these individuals as having any meaningful beliefs, much as you do in particularly florid cases of schizophrenia. Some philosophers go further and argue that impeccable rationality is a prerequisite if an individual is to be said to hold any meaningful beliefs (Davidson, 1975; Dennett, 1978: 20).

The case against impeccable rationality is twofold – and here we follow the general tenor of Stich's argument. First, granted the finiteness of our lives and our mental resources, none of us can be perfectly rational, because we cannot draw all the infinite consequences of our beliefs (cf. Simon, 1957, 1982; Cherniak, 1986). Second, subjects make errors in reasoning – errors that they even acknowledge in some experiments. They draw invalid inferences that should not occur if their thinking is guided by valid formal rules of inference. Proponents of rationality make a heroic denial of this phenomenon. Thus, Henle declares: 'I have never found errors which could unambiguously be attributed to faulty reasoning. If they are found under clear conditions, I will be forced to a drastic revision of my view of the relation of logic to thinking' (Henle, 1978). She argues, as we remarked earlier, that subjects are arguing validly but from different premises than those provided by the experimenter. The errors that we have observed, however, suggest that this defence of universal reason is mistaken. The errors are predictable: they occur with multiple-model problems, they tend to be conclusions that hold only for a proper subset of the models of the premises, and they are not a result of forgetting premises or of importing additional information. In the absence of generally agreed criteria for assessing logical error, it might be argued that any error in reasoning can always be explained away in Henle's terms. If so, the hypothesis of impeccable rationality is irrefutable, that is, it has no testable empirical content. We reject this view because it does not explain why errors tend to characterize subsets of the possible models of the premises. The hypothesis that subjects never make errors in reasoning has empirical content. It is false.

Another sort of argument in favour of rationality appeals to natural selection. Organisms with irrational patterns of thought will not survive; we have survived; *ergo* we are rational. Many theorists have made this assumption, for example, it underlies Cosmides' (1989) account of the selection task (see p. 198). Fodor (1980) goes still further to make the case that logical principles must be innate because they could not be learned (for a counter-argument, see Johnson-Laird, 1988: 134). While it is possible that deductive competence has evolved as a result of natural selection, it is also possible that it has not, and that it confers no real selective advantage, being merely a by-product of the evolution of some other mental capacity. No-one has measured the selective advantage of deductive competence, and no-one is likely to – one needs to show that it improved our chances as a group of surviving and reproducing in comparison, say, with a group of Neanderthals incapable of making valid inferences (see Lewontin, 1990). All that we can assert is that the *future* of humanity is likely to depend on its ability to think rationally – a point to which we will return at the conclusion of this chapter.

Still another argument for impeccable rationality is based on Goodman's (1965) analysis of how principles of inference can be justified. He argued that they are justified provided that they conform to accepted deductive practice. A principle of inference is amended if it conflicts with accepted practice; and practice is amended if it conflicts with an accepted principle. These mutual adjustments culminate in an equilibrium between principles and practice. Hence, Cohen (1981) argues that it is impossible for an individual's logical competence to be at fault because its basis – the internalized principles that govern the process of reasoning – can be ascertained only by collecting reasoners' intuitions and bringing them into equilibrium with their practice. As Cohen writes:

> Where you accept that a normative theory has to be based ultimately on the data of human intuition, you are committed to the acceptance of human rationality as a matter of fact in that area, in the sense that it must be correct to ascribe to normal human beings a cognitive competence – however often faulted in performance – that corresponds point by point with the normative theory.
>
> (Cohen, 1981: 321)

Stich rejects this argument on the cogent grounds that individuals may have erroneous intuitions about principles of inference. 'It is generally all too easy', he writes, 'to imagine circumstances in which a set of inferential rules that we would not categorize as rational satisfies the conditions of the proposed analysis' (Stich, 1990b). Stich, however, goes on to reject conceptual analyses of rationality, to reject the notion that truth *per se* has an intrinsic value, and thus implicitly to reject its maintenance as a method of evaluating patterns of inference. Instead, he favours the evaluation of patterns of inference in terms of their ability to satisfy an individual's goals, and so he comes to defend the notion of relativism (see pp. 204–5).

Granted that all the strong arguments for impeccable rationality fail, what conclusion can we draw? In our view, the only way out is to make a significant modification to the competence–performance distinction. The original notion hinged on the idea that competence is based on impeccable rules of inference, which, like the rules of grammar, are sometimes inadequately reflected in actual performance. The new notion of deductive competence depends instead on a meta-principle: *an inference is valid provided that there is no model of the premises in which its conclusion is false.* Individuals who have no training in logic appear to have a tacit grasp of this meta-principle, but they have no grasp of specific logical principles, and no systematic or comprehensive procedures for drawing conclusions according to the meta-principle. They have no principles for valid thinking, i.e. for searching for models that refute conclusions. Hence, they make mistakes in reasoning. Is competence of this sort rational or irrational? It certainly does not guarantee the validity of inferences. And to argue that errors arise as a result of performance factors is misleading because it suggests a failure to put into practice correct rules, whereas there are no rules to put into practice, only a higher-order meta-principle. Yet, this meta-principle is defensible as a rational requirement for any system of deductive inference. It provides a rational meta-competence. We are cutting the competence–performance cake at a different place to Cohen: rules of inference are not part of competence, and so real failures in valid reasoning can occur. This account is compatible with the observations of deductive failure, and the arguments against impeccable rationality.

AGAINST INTRINSIC IRRATIONALITY

Many psychologically naïve individuals believe that their conscious feelings, judgements, and intentions determine their behaviour. A major attack on this view was made by Freud, who wrote that the triumph of psychoanalysis was to show that common acts of normal individuals – slips of the tongue, parapraxes, and so on – were akin to neurotic symptoms because they, too, owed their origins to unconscious conflicts (Freud, 1963/1922). Whatever the empirical status of these claims, studies in social psychology have shown that the true causes of choices are not always available to introspection (see, for example, Nisbett and Wilson, 1977;

Nisbett and Ross, 1980). The claim is particularly apposite in the case of acts of creation (see Johnson-Laird, 1993), and, perhaps for this reason, certain artists of a Romantic cast of mind have viewed human life as fundamentally irrational (see Dostoyevsky, 1972/1864, for an archetypal expression of this point of view). If you contemplate the follies and foibles of the human condition, then you might be tempted to conclude that Dostoyevsky was right.

Curiously, certain psychologists seem to have reached the same conclusion for very different reasons. They have proposed theories of reasoning that implicitly render human reasoners irrational (e.g. Erickson, 1974; Revlis, 1975; Guyote and Sternberg, 1981). Even if a reasoner draws a valid conclusion, the underlying thought process is intrinsically irrational because these theories preclude a full representation of premises. Still more curiously, a number of psychologists have argued that logically untrained individuals are incapable of seemingly simple sorts of deduction. According to these authors, the subjects in certain experiments do not reason, but instead perform under the influence of various biases and heuristics (see, for example, Evans, 1972, 1977, 1989; Wetherick and Gilhooly, 1990; Greene, 1992). The task of deduction is beyond humanity – at least in the laboratory setting, and even, say some of these sceptics, in the world at large. Because the experiments are often precisely those that we have used to corroborate the theory of mental models, we will examine these arguments carefully to determine whether they have any substance.

Wason's selection task

In Wason's selection task, four cards that each bear a single symbol are put in front of subjects, for example:

A   B   2   3

and they know that every card has a letter on one side and a number on the other side. Their task is to select those cards that need to be turned over to find out whether the following conditional rule is true or false:

If a card has an A on one side then it has a 2 on the other side.

Nearly all subjects select either the A and the 2 card, or the A card alone (Wason, 1966, 1983). What is striking is their failure to select the 3 card (corresponding to the negated consequent of the conditional) because if this card has an A on its other side, the rule would be false. In a different experiment, Wason told the subjects the right answer, and then asked them to explain why the selections were correct. They all gave the correct reasons (see Wason and Johnson-Laird, 1972: 173–4) – a fact which suggests that they grasp the logic of the conditional rule (cf. Fetzer, 1990). Likewise, the use of a more realistic content enables subjects to gain insight into the task (Wason and Shapiro, 1971; Johnson-Laird *et al.*, 1972). The effects are labile, but significantly more subjects select the card corresponding to the negated consequent with the following more realistic assertion:

If a person is drinking beer then the person must be over 18.

Subjects tend to choose the card representing a person drinking beer, and the card representing a person less than 18 years in age (Griggs and Cox, 1982; Cheng and Holyoak, 1985). This difference in performance, as Manktelow and Over (1987) argue, is difficult to account for in terms of a theory of reasoning based on formal rules.

But, are subjects reasoning when they carry out the selection task? One major investigator, Evans (1989), has implied that they may not be, and that instead they are guided by a 'matching' bias. What led him to this view was an observation that he and his colleagues made: subjects often ignore the presence of negations in constructing instances that falsify a conditional or in making responses to the selection task (Evans and Lynch, 1973). They merely match their selections to the cards mentioned in the conditional. In particular, more than half the subjects were correct with such a conditional as:

If there's an S on one side of a card, then there is not a 9.

They chose the S card and the 9 card. Because they are correct in this case, but not in the case of an affirmative consequent, Evans concluded that in both cases subjects are merely matching their responses to the (unnegated) items in the rule: S and 9 (see Evans, 1989: 33). He allowed that in other tasks the effect can be overridden by another, more powerful, linguistic factor: 'The use of if invites one to entertain the supposition that the antecedent condition is true . . . the listener is strongly invited to consider the hypothesis (mental model, possible world) in which the antecedent and consequent conditionals are actually fulfilled' (Evans, 1989: 32).

If subjects were merely selecting cards according to whether or not they matched the unnegated items in conditional rules, they would be wholly irrational. But, as Evans hints, the bias can be reconciled with the model theory. This *rapprochement* is based on the claim that negations are typically used to deny misconceptions, and so they are likely to call to mind the notion that is negated (Wason, 1965). Hence, conditionals with negative constituents should elicit models of the unnegated items. The antecedent of a conditional is exhaustively represented, and so a conditional with a negated antecedent:

If there is not an A then there is a 2

should yield the models:

[¬A]   2
 A

That is why this conditional has a very natural paraphrase as a disjunction, 'There's either an A or a 2'. A conditional with a negated consequent:

If there's an A then there is not a 2

should yield the models:

    [A]   ¬2
           2
     . . .

Because the consequent is not exhausted, a further implicit possibility has to be left open in the model (as indicated by the three dots). This conditional cannot be paraphrased by a disjunction because there could be neither an A nor a 2.

Given these representations, the theory explains the phenomena without having to postulate intrinsic irrationality. First, reasoners consider only those cards that are explicitly represented in their initial models of the conditional rule. This assumption applies *mutatis mutandis* to any form of deduction: one can reason only on the basis of what one has represented. Second, reasoners sensibly select only those cards from within the represented set that bear on the truth or falsity of the rule. It follows that in the cases above, the card corresponding to the false consequent will be selected provided that the models of the conditional represent it explicitly.

Other tasks show that what matters are initial models rather than responses that merely match premises. As an example, consider the following problem (in a form known as modus tollens):

If there's a circle then there's a triangle.
There's not a triangle.
What, if anything, follows?

A characteristic error in such deductions is to respond that nothing follows. The error is explicable in terms of the initial models of the conditional:

    [O]   △
     . . .

The second premise eliminates the first model to leave only the implicit model, and so it seems that nothing follows. If the models are fleshed out explicitly as a weak conditional:

    [O]   [△]
    [¬O]   [△]
    [¬O]   [¬△]

or as a strong biconditional:

    [O]   [△]
    [¬O]   [¬△]

then the second premise eliminates any model containing a triangle, and so the only remaining model is:

[¬ O] [¬△]

Subjects can now draw the correct conclusion:

There is not a circle.

Several hypotheses purport to explain why a realistic conditional may elicit the correct response in Wason's selection task. One view is that the content triggers a recall of specific counter-examples (Griggs and Cox, 1982); another is that it may suggest useful analogies (e.g. Manktelow and Evans, 1979); another is that realistic materials trigger 'pragmatic reasoning schemas', which are rules of inference governing such matters as causation, permission, and obligation (Cheng and Holyoak, 1985); and yet another view is that human evolution has led to a specific inferential module concerned with violations of social contracts (Cosmides, 1989).

The trouble with all of these hypotheses is that there is no evidence to support them outside the selection task, yet they account for only some of its phenomena. In contrast, the model theory predicts that people will tend to select the card falsifying the consequent whenever they flesh out their models of the conditional with an explicit representation of that card. There are many ways in which subjects may be led to flesh out their models, and a number of them have been successfully manipulated in experiments. Thus, a realistic rule (Wason, 1983), a deontic framework (Manktelow and Over, 1991), or a rule concerning an unsatisfactory outcome relevant to a goal (George, 1991), brings to mind alternative possibilities. They will be explicitly represented in the subjects' models of the conditional, and so negated consequents are more likely to be selected. A rather different manipulation is to reduce the load on working memory and thereby improve the chances of considering the false consequent. Wason and Green (1984) investigated this possibility by using a rule that concerned only a single entity, such as, 'All circles are black'. It improved performance. If the cards are labelled with explicit negations, then the subjects should be more likely to represent such negations in their models. Jackson and Griggs (1989) report that this manipulation improved performance. Finally, the task itself can be changed so as to increase the chances that the subjects envisage all the alternatives explicitly. Methods that have worked include reducing the choice to one between the consequent and the negated consequent (Wason and Green, 1984), and instructing subjects to test for violations of the rule (Valentine, 1985). No theory about content alone, such as a memory for counter-examples or pragmatic-reasoning schemas, can account for all of these phenomena.

The atmosphere effect and other 'matching' hypotheses

There is a long tradition of claims that subjects in experiments on syllogistic reasoning are prey to irrational 'atmosphere' effects in which they choose conclusions that match premises in a purely superficial way. Recently, as we shall see, researchers have claimed that reasoning can be explained by similar 'matching' hypotheses without the need to postulate either mental models or even any process of reasoning at all. To set the scene, however, we will begin with the original atmosphere effect.

Sells (1936) and Woodworth and Sells (1935) proposed a number of principles to capture the 'atmosphere' created by premises, but the succinct version of the hypothesis is due to Begg and Denny (1969):

1 Whenever at least one premise is negative, the most frequently accepted conclusion will be negative; otherwise it will be affirmative.
2 Whenever at least one premise is particular (i.e. based on 'some'), the most frequently accepted conclusion will be particular; otherwise it will be universal.

In fact, most of the *valid* conclusions to syllogisms correspond to these predictions, and so a purely logical procedure would look as though it were susceptible to the atmosphere effect. In fairness to Woodworth and Sells, however, they did not intend the atmosphere hypothesis to be a complete account of reasoning. They suggested instead that subjects have a genuine deductive ability that is sometimes vitiated by the atmosphere effect. In an analogous way, some recent theories of syllogistic reasoning postulate that atmosphere governs the initial formulation of tentative conclusions but that this stage is followed by tests of validity (see Madruga, 1984; Inder, 1987; Polk and Newell, 1988).

Marvin Levine (pers. com.) has made a more radical assumption: 'the untrained college student doesn't know how to draw inferences from standard two-premise syllogisms'. According to Levine, the subjects in our experiments use two heuristics. The first heuristic is similar to the atmosphere effect: if there is a premise based on 'all', then the conclusion has the same mood as the other premise. For example, given premises of the form:

Some of the A are B
All of the B are C

the subjects should draw the conclusion:

Some of the A are C

or its converse:

Some of the C are A.

The second heuristic is that when subjects get confused they respond that there is 'no valid conclusion', and they get confused by negative premises and by certain figures (those which Johnson-Laird and Bara (1984) had predicted cause difficulty).

Wetherick and Gilhooly (1990) have proposed a similar variant on the atmosphere hypothesis. They suggest that some responses to syllogisms are based on logical thinking – a view that at one time Levine also accepted – but if the logic of a syllogism is not apparent to subjects, they select a conclusion that matches the mood of one or other of the premises. These authors suggest that subjects match the more 'conservative' of the two premises, but their main analyses are based on a simple match with one or other of the two premises.

If individuals were spontaneously and invariably to adopt a matching strategy, several deeply puzzling questions would inevitably arise: Why do they adopt this strategy? Where does it come from? Why should speakers regularly use quantified assertions from which neither they nor their listeners are able to draw deductively valid conclusions? In fact, contrary to the claims for irrational matching, we believe that the best explanation is that subjects are reasoning, and that they are using mental models in order to do so. Of course, some subjects may sometimes draw a conclusion because it matches the mood of a premise. It is plainly impossible to rule out this weak version of the atmosphere hypothesis. We can show, however, that all the different forms of matching hypotheses – from Woodworth and Sells to Wetherick and Levine – are implausible as general accounts of syllogistic reasoning. The essential manoeuvre of these theorists is to devise a matching strategy that yields valid conclusions for just those syllogisms that happen to be easy. They can then argue that difficult problems are merely those for which the matching response happens to be wrong. There are, however, empirical observations that run counter to all of the matching hypotheses.

First, although some predictions of the model theory are the same as those of the matching hypotheses, there are important divergencies. In particular, all one-model syllogisms have correct responses that match the mood of at least one premise, but there are multiple-model problems where the correct response also matches the mood of at least one premise. If matching is the decisive factor then these two sets of problems should be equally easy, but if the number of models is the decisive factor then the one-model problems should be easier than the multiple-model problems. In fact, the percentages of correct responses (from four independent experiments that produced highly correlated responses, see Table 6.1 of Johnson-Laird and Byrne, 1991) were as follows:

Seventy-six per cent correct for the one-model problems with 'matching' conclusions;

Forty-two per cent for the multiple-model problems with 'matching' conclusions.

The difference is highly reliable (Mann-Whitney's $U = 0.5$, $p < 0.01$). Matching cannot explain the difference, and so the number of models appears to be decisive.

Second, in addition to matching the mood of a premise, a conclusion must also contain the two end terms. For example, premises of the form:

All the A are B
All the B are C

yield two possible matching responses:

All the A are C

or:

All the C are A.

If subjects are merely matching, there is no reason to expect one of the conclusions to occur any more frequently than the other. If subjects are reasoning, then the first of these conclusions, which is valid, should be much more frequent than the second, which is invalid. A similar argument applies to conclusions of the form: Some of the X are not Y. In short, if subjects are reasoning, then we can predict that these two sorts of conclusion, which do not imply their converses, should tend to occur in their valid form rather than in their invalid form. This prediction is borne out by the results of the experiments. A matching strategy yields a valid 'All the X are Y' conclusion for two problems and a valid 'Some of the X are not Y' conclusion for 12 problems, and the converse conclusion is invalid in all of these problems. In an experiment in which subjects were allowed as much time as they needed to frame their own conclusions, 94 per cent of their conclusions to these problems were correct and only 6 per cent were incorrect (Experiment 3, Johnson-Laird and Bara, 1984). This striking difference is contrary to the thesis that subjects are generating these conclusions solely by matching.

Third, if subjects adopt a matching strategy, then those conclusions that they draw should match the mood of premises (according to the specific recipe devised by the theorist). Even if the subjects get confused by a difficult syllogism, the conclusions that they do draw (as opposed to their responses that nothing follows from the premises) should still match the mood of premises. In fact, no such uniformity occurs. The greater the difficulty of a syllogism, the greater the variety of conclusions that subjects draw. The cause of difficulty, we believe, is that the premises support multiple models, and this account immediately explains the diversity of conclusions. The subjects draw different conclusions depending on the particular models that they construct. The vast majority of conclusions are precisely those that the model theory predicts (see, for example, Johnson-Laird and Bara, 1984). In general, matching fails to explain why the variety of conclusions increases with the more difficult problems. This phenomenon counts against the atmosphere hypothesis, and both Levine's and also Wetherick and Gilhooly's variants of it, but corroborates the model theory.

Fourth, matching cannot explain why subjects respond, 'there is no valid conclusion' to certain syllogisms. Wetherick and Gilhooly offer no account of this response in their experiment (in which subjects did not formulate their own responses, but merely selected one from a set of alternatives). They write: 'This response was very much underemployed. It was used (correctly or incorrectly) in 38.3 per cent of cases by our subjects . . . but was the correct response in 60 per cent of cases.' Levine is not so ready to brush these responses aside. As we mentioned earlier, he argues that they occur when subjects get confused by negative premises or by the more difficult figures. Once again, although subjects may sometimes become confused and claim that there is no valid conclusion, this account fails as a general explanation for the response. By the end of an experiment in which subjects had been tested on a variety of syllogisms, some subjects pointed out that they had noticed that there was never a valid conclusion for certain sorts of syllogism, e.g. those where both premises were based on 'some' (see Galotti et al., 1986). Far from being a sign of confusion, the response 'no valid conclusion' in this case shows the beginnings of a grasp of certain formal principles. Similarly, when subjects respond, 'no valid conclusion', they are much more likely to be correct than incorrect. In the study reported by Johnson-Laird and Steedman (1978), for example, there were 137 'no valid conclusion' responses to problems in the easiest figure (A–B, B–C), and 132 of them were correct. It is hard to believe that this distribution of responses would occur if subjects respond, 'no valid conclusion', only when they are confused.

Finally, the proponents of matching have overlooked a striking failure to demonstrate it in a study of 'only' as a quantifier (Johnson-Laird and Byrne, 1989). With two premises that both contained the quantifier 'only', for example:

Only the athletes are bakers.
Only the bakers are canoeists.

All the different matching hypotheses concur that the likeliest conclusion should be one containing 'only'. Yet, subjects were singularly reluctant to draw such conclusions. Only 16 per cent of the conclusions were based on 'only', whereas 45 per cent of them were based instead on 'all'. Likewise, when one premise contained 'only', just 2 per cent of conclusions were based on it. The model theory postulates that the meaning of 'only' contains a negative component, and so a premise such as 'Only the athletes are bakers' calls for a model that is explicit about the sets and their complements:

```
a      [b]
a      [b]
[¬a]   ¬b
[¬a]   ¬b
 . . .
```

Hence, the theory predicts that such premises will be harder to cope with than those of the form, 'All the bakers are athletes', which have the same truth conditions. The greater difficulty of 'only' was corroborated by our experiments, and, of course, it explains the subjects' preference for conclusions based on 'all'.

Matching hypotheses reflect one profound psychological truth. When reasoners interpret premises, they tend to leave as much as possible implicit – they represent explicitly only those states of affairs that are overtly mentioned in the premises (see, for example, the representation of conditionals). They also tend to make mistakes if their initial models are not the only possible models of the premises. Their premature conclusions will be invalid, but, as our results show, they will be true for at least some models of the premises. Moreover, because the initial models tend to represent the information that occurs explicitly in the premises, inferences based on them yield conclusions that match the content of the premises. This apparent match seems to have misled theorists into arguing that subjects are relying on a matching strategy. But the matching strategies themselves, in our view, are largely chimerical – they have been devised *post hoc* by theorists who noticed the match between many conclusions that subjects draw and the mood of one or other of the premises. These theorists have overlooked the phenomena that strongly suggest that subjects are using models to reason. Matching seems a more accurate account of its own origins as a theory than of the deductive performance of logically untrained individuals.

In defence of rationality in principle

We have now reviewed all the major arguments for irrational factors in deductive performance. As we remarked earlier, we can never eliminate the possibility that subjects sometimes fail to reason and instead use an irrational heuristic, but we have shown that theories of performance in terms of matching or atmosphere do not do justice to the phenomena. In fact, subjects *are* reasoning. They are rational, but not impeccable. They have no systematic way of discovering all possible models of premises; they have no rules guaranteed to lead them to valid conclusions. In other words, some people – logicians perhaps, though we doubt it – may reason validly all of the time; all people reason validly some of the time; but no-one reasons invalidly all of the time.

RATIONALITY VERSUS RELATIVISM

When anthropologists and historians examine thinking in cultures remote from our own, they are sometimes tempted to describe it as primitive, pre-logical, or irrational (e.g. Levy-Bruhl, 1966/1910). Doubtless, people in many cultures hold beliefs that are false, and make inferences that are invalid. A classic example concerns witchcraft in an African tribe, the Azande (see Evans-Pritchard, 1937). They used a ritual called the 'poison oracle' to determine whether an accused individual was a witch – the decision depended on whether poisoned fowls live or die. They also believed that witchcraft was inherited and therefore common to all members of a clan, and that a post-mortem examination of the intestines yielded decisive information about witchhood. However, they refused to accept Evans-Pritchard's suggestion that a few well-chosen post-mortems would settle once and for all which clans were guilty. He therefore charged them with inconsistent thinking. In reaction to this claim, others have argued that the Azande were not irrational: there are no universal criteria for rationality, and so the criteria themselves must be *relative* to a culture.

The resulting debate is similar to the arguments about intrinsic rationality that we discussed earlier. It has led to a split between rational-ists, who argue for a core of rational principles common to all cultures, and relativists, who argue for principles of inference that are local to a culture, or even to an individual, and for the incommensurability of the beliefs of different groups – even those of scientists of different theoretical persuasions. If rationalism is right, the principles of thinking are universal, and so they can be revealed by psychological studies. If relativism is right, then the principles of deduction differ from one society to another and perhaps from one epoch to another, and so psychological studies are of only parochial interest. In fact, the debate has been conducted with scant regard for psychological evidence.

In defence of rationalism, Hollis (1970) asserts that the modus-ponens form of deduction:

If A then B
A
Therefore, B

is universally compelling. In defence of relativism, Barnes and Bloor (1982) retort that there is no evidence for this claim and that if modus ponens were accepted by all cultures then its universal validity would call for explanation. Following a famous argument by Lewis Carroll (1895), they claim that there is no way to justify modus ponens without presupposing its own validity. And they conclude that no account of deductive competence justifies a unique system of logical rules. We are back at the position in which Goodman attempted to justify rules by progressively bringing them into alignment with deductive practice, and that position leads ineluctably to relativism: different rules for different practices.

The solution to our difficulties should, by now, be obvious. There *is*, we claim, a central core of rationality common to all cultures, but it is not a set of rules of inference. It is the deductive competence that has at its core the meta-principle of validity: an inference is valid provided that there is no model of the premises in which its conclusion is false. Reasoners imagine the situation characterized by the premises or observations, seek a conclusion that makes explicit some new proposition, and search for an alternative model of the situation in which the premises hold but the conclusion fails to hold. They lack any systematic method to make this search for counter-examples.

A corollary of this theory of deductive competence is that certain *forms* of argument may be valid, and these forms could be specified by formal rules of inference. It is a capital mistake, however, to suppose that these rules are themselves cognitive universals. Rationality is problematical if it is supposed to be founded on rules such as modus ponens. As we showed earlier (pp. 185–190), theories of deductive performance that appeal to formal rules are unable to explain the errors in inference that most of us make from time to time. Rules make relativism attractive because systematic error suggests that some people possess illicit rules of inference (cf. von Domarus, 1944; Jackendoff, 1988).

On our account, the Azande were guilty of an inconsistency, but the propensity to err is not unique to so-called 'primitive' cultures. Logicians have devised inconsistent systems of logic; scientists have accepted inconsistent sets of beliefs – they failed to notice, for example, that the existence of polywater was not compatible with the laws of thermodynamics; and most of us have been guilty of similar invalid thinking in daily life. The model theory, however, does not need to sacrifice rational competence in explaining mistakes. Human beings need logic because they are not impeccably rational, but they can invent it because they are not intrinsically irrational. They are rational in principle, but err in practice.

CONCLUSIONS

At the outset we identified two fundamental precepts: to believe what is true (rational belief), and to infer what is valid (rational thinking). We have argued that the precept of rational thinking is reflected in a meta-principle of validity: an inference is valid only if its conclusion is not falsified by a model of the premises. This meta-principle is, we believe, part of universal human deductive competence. But what justifies the rational precept? In our view, it seeks to maintain truth, and truth has an intrinsic value that must be taken for granted. Any argument has to take something for granted, and we take the value of truth as such an assumption. One reason for this step is the difficulty of formulating a satisfactory and non-circular argument on behalf of truth. The very activity of trying to frame such an argument seems already to presuppose the value of truth: no-one would ever argue: 'I know my conclusion is false but it is useful for you to believe it because it will fulfil your current goals.' Conversely, the thesis that truth has no intrinsic value, so ingeniously defended by Stich (1990a), leads to the self-referential thought: if Stich's argument leads to a true conclusion, then this conclusion may have no intrinsic value, for it itself asserts that a truth may have no intrinsic value. These matters, however, are outside the domain of cognitive science, and we thankfully leave them to the metaphysicians.

Yet life without the rational precepts is unthinkable. Their importance is more obvious in the breach than in the observance. And they are breached whenever beliefs fly in the face of facts, or conclusions patently do not follow from their premises. We do not need to look far for well-attested instances. The engineers in charge at Chernobyl, for example, refused to believe that the reactor had been destroyed until many hours after the disaster – despite much evidence to the contrary, including the reports of two young probationary engineers whom they had sent to examine it and who paid with their lives for their observations. Likewise, the engineers in charge had persisted in trying to carry out the experiment even when it was easy to deduce that it was impossible to complete (Medvedev, 1990). The human cost of these instances of irrationality was high: the deaths of many people, and the release of radiation ten times that of the bomb dropped on Hiroshima. The future of the species will depend on its capacity to act rationally.

ACKNOWLEDGEMENTS

We are grateful to James Fetzer, Eldar Shafir, Stephen Stich, and the editors of this volume, for valid and useful criticisms of an earlier version of this essay.

REFERENCES

Anderson, J.R. (1990) *The Adaptive Character of Thought*, Hillsdale, NJ: Erlbaum.

Barnes, B. and Bloor, D. (1982) 'Relativism, rationalism, and the sociology of knowledge', in M. Hollis, and S. Lukes (eds) *Rationality and Relativism*, Oxford: Blackwell.

Begg, I. and Denny, J. (1969) 'Empirical reconciliation of atmosphere and conversion interpretations of syllogistic reasoning', *Journal of Experimental Psychology* 81: 351–4.

Braine, M.D.S. (1978) 'On the relation between the natural logic of reasoning and standard logic', *Psychological Review* 85: 1–21.

Braine, M.D.S., Reiser, B.J., and Rumain, B. (1984) 'Some empirical justification for a theory of natural propositional logic', *The Psychology of Learning and Motivation*, vol. 18, New York: Academic Press.

Byrne, R.M.J. (1989) 'Suppressing valid inferences with conditionals', *Cognition* 31: 61–83.

Byrne, R.M.J. and Johnson-Laird, P.N. (1989) 'Spatial reasoning', *Journal of Memory and Language* 28: 564–75.

Carroll, L. (1895) 'What the tortoise said to Achilles', *Mind* 4: 278–80.

Cheng, P.N. and Holyoak, K.J. (1985) 'Pragmatic reasoning schemas', *Cognitive Psychology* 17: 391–416.

Cherniak, C. (1986) *Minimal Rationality*, Cambridge, MA: MIT Press.

Cohen, L.J. (1981) 'Can human irrationality be experimentally demonstrated?' *Behavioral and Brain Sciences* 4: 317–70.

Cosmides, L. (1989) 'The logic of social exchange: has natural selection shaped how humans reason? Studies with the Wason selection task', *Cognition* 31: 187–276.

Davidson, D. (1975) 'Thought and talk', In S. Guttenplan (ed.) *Mind and Language*, Oxford: Oxford University Press.

Dennett, D.C. (1978) *Brainstorms*, Cambridge, MA: MIT Press.

Dostoyevsky, F.M. (1972/1864) *Notes from Underground*, trans. J. Coulson, Harmondsworth: Penguin.

Erickson, J.R. (1974) 'A set analysis theory of behaviour in formal syllogistic reasoning tasks', in R. Solso (ed.) *Loyola Symposium on Cognition*, vol. 2, Hillsdale, NJ: Erlbaum.

Evans, J.St B.T. (1972) 'Interpretation and "matching bias" in a reasoning task', *Quarterly Journal of Experimental Psychology* 24: 193–9.

—— (1977) 'Toward a statistical theory of reasoning', *Quarterly Journal of Experimental Psychology* 29A: 297–306.

—— (1989) *Bias in Human Reasoning: Causes and Consequences*, Hillsdale, NJ: Erlbaum.

Evans, J.St B.T. and Lynch, J.S. (1973) 'Matching bias in the selection task', *British Journal of Psychology* 64: 391–7.

Evans-Pritchard, E.E. (1937) *Witchcraft: Oracles and Magic among the Azande*, Oxford: Oxford University Press.

Fetzer, J.H. (1990) 'Evolution, rationality, and testability', *Synthese* 82: 423–39.

Fodor, J.A. (1980) 'Fixation of belief and concept acquisition', in M. Piattelli-Palmarini, (ed.) *Language and Learning; The Debate between Jean Piaget and Noam Chomsky*, Cambridge, MA: Harvard University Press.

Freud, S. (1963/1922) 'Psychoanalysis', in P. Rieff (ed.) *Character and Culture*, New York: Collier Books, Macmillan, 1963.

Galotti, K.M., Baron, J., and Sabini, J.P. (1986) 'Individual differences in syllogistic reasoning: deduction rules or mental models?' *Journal of Experimental Psychology: General* 115: 16–25.

Gardner, M. (1982) *Logic, Machines and Diagrams*, 2nd edn, Chicago: University of Chicago Press.

George, C. (1991) 'Facilitation in the Wason selection task with a consequent referring to an unsatisfactory outcome', *British Journal of Psychology* 82: 463–72.

Goodman, N. (1965) *Fact, Fiction and Forecast*, Indianapolis: Bobbs-Merrill.

Greene, S.B. (1992) 'Multiple explanations for multiply-quantified sentences: are multiple models necessary?' *Psychological Review* 99: 184–7.

Griggs, R.A. and Cox, J.R. (1982) 'The elusive thematic-materials effect in Wason's selection task', *British Journal of Psychology* 73: 407–20.

Guyote, M.J. and Sternberg, R.J. (1981) 'A transitive-chain theory of syllogistic reasoning', *Cognitive Psychology* 13: 461–525.

Hacking, I. (1975) *The Emergence of Probability*, Cambridge: Cambridge University Press.

Hamill, J.F. (1990) *Ethno-logic: The Anthropology of Human Reasoning*, Urbana, IL: University of Illinois Press.

Henle, M. (1962) 'The relation between logic and thinking', *Psychological Review* 69: 366–78.

—— (1978) 'Forward' in R. Revlin and R.E. Mayer (eds) *Human Reasoning*, Washington, DC: Winston.

Hollis, M. (1970) 'Reason and ritual', in B.R. Wilson (ed.) *Rationality*, Oxford: Blackwell, pp. 221–39.

Inder, R. (1987) 'Computer simulation of syllogism solving using restricted mental models', PhD thesis, Cognitive Studies, Edinburgh University.

Inhelder, B. and Piaget, J. (1958) *The Growth of Logical Thinking from Childhood to Adolescence*, London: Routledge & Kegan Paul.

Jackendoff, R. (1988) 'Exploring the form of information in the dynamic unconscious', in M.J. Horowitz (ed.) *Psychodynamics, and Cognition,* Chicago: University of Chicago Press.

Jackson, S.L. and Griggs, R.A. (1989) 'The elusive pragmatic reasoning schemas effect', *Quarterly Journal of Experimental Psychology* 42A: 353–73.

Johnson-Laird, P.N. (1983) *Mental Models*, Cambridge, MA, Harvard University Press and Cambridge: Cambridge University Press.

—— (1988) *The Computer and the Mind*, Cambridge, MA: Harvard University Press and London: Fontana.

—— (1993) *Human and Machine Thinking*, Hillsdale, NJ: Erlbaum.

Johnson-Laird, P.N. and Bara, B. (1984) 'Syllogistic inference', *Cognition* 16: 1–61.

Johnson-Laird, P.N. and Byrne, R.M.J. (1989) '*Only* reasoning', *Journal of Memory and Language* 28: 313–30.

—— (1991) *Deduction*, Hillsdale, NJ: Erlbaum.

Johnson-Laird, P.N. and Steedman, M. (1978) 'The psychology of syllogisms', *Cognitive Psychology* 10: 64–99.

Johnson-Laird, P.N., Legrenzi, P., and Legrenzi, M.S. (1972) 'Reasoning and a sense of reality', *British Journal of Psychology* 63: 395–400.

Johnson-Laird, P.N., Byrne, R.M.J., and Tabossi, P. (1989) 'Reasoning by model: the case of multiple quantification', *Psychological Review* 96: 658–73.

Johnson-Laird, P.N., Byrne, R.M.J., and Schaeken, W. (1992) 'Propositional reasoning by model', *Psychological Review* 99: 418–39.

Levy-Bruhl, L. (1966/1910) *How Natives Think*, New York: Washington Square Press.

Lewontin, R.C. (1990) 'The evolution of cognition', in D.N. Osherson and E.E. Smith (eds) *Thinking: An Invitation to Cognitive Science*, vol. 3, Cambridge, MA: MIT Press.

Macnamara, J. (1986) *A Border Dispute: The Place of Logic in Psychology*, Cambridge, MA: MIT Press.

Madruga, J.A.G. (1984) 'Procesos de error en el razonamiento silogistico: doble procesamiento y estrategia de verificacion por', in M. Carretero and J.A.G. Madruga (eds) *Lecturas de psicologia del pensamiento*, Madrid: Alianza.

Manktelow, K.I. and Evans, J. St B.T. (1979) 'Facilitation of reasoning by realism: effect or non-effect?' *British Journal of Psychology* 70: 477–88.
Manktelow, K.I. and Over, D.E. (1987) 'Reasoning and rationality', *Mind and Language* 2: 199–219.
—— (1991) 'Social roles and utilities in reasoning with deontic conditionals', *Cognition* 39: 85–105.
Medvedev, Z.A. (1990) *The Legacy of Chernobyl*, New York: Norton.
Newell, A. (1990) *Unified Theories of Cognition*, Cambridge, MA: Harvard University Press.
Nisbett, R.E. and Ross, L. (1980) *Human Inference: Strategies and Shortcomings of Social Judgement*, Englewood Cliffs, NJ: Prentice-Hall.
Nisbett, R.E. and Wilson, T.D. (1977) 'Telling more than we can know: verbal reports on mental processes', *Psychological Review* 84: 231–59.
Oakhill, J.V., Johnson-Laird, P.N., and Garnham, A. (1989) 'Believability and syllogistic reasoning', *Cognition* 31: 117–40.
Osherson, D.N. (1974–6) *Logical Abilities in Children*, vols. 1–4, Hillsdale, NJ: Erlbaum.
—— (1975) 'Logic and models of logical thinking' in R.J. Falmagne (ed.) *Reasoning: Representation and Process in Children and Adults*, Hillsdale, NJ: Erlbaum.
Piaget, J. (1928) *Judgment and Reasoning in the Child*, London: Routledge & Kegan Paul.
Polk, T.A. and Newell, A. (1988) 'Modeling human syllogistic reasoning in Soar'. In *Tenth Annual Conference of the Cognitive Science Society*, Hillsdale, NJ: Erlbaum, pp. 181–7.
Pollock, J. (1989) *How to Build a Person: A Prolegomenon*, Cambridge, MA: MIT Bradford Books.
Quillian, M.R. (1968) 'Semantic memory', in M. Minsky (ed.) *Semantic Information Processing*, Cambridge, MA: MIT Press.
Quine, W.V.O. (1960) *Word and Object*, Cambridge, MA: MIT Press.
Revlis, R. (1975) 'Two models of syllogistic reasoning: feature selection and conversion', *Journal of Verbal Learning and Verbal Behavior* 14: 180–95.
Rips, L.J. (1983) 'Cognitive processes in propositional reasoning', *Psychological Review* 90: 38–71.
Sells, S.B. (1936) 'The atmosphere effect: an experimental study of reasoning', *Archives of Psychology* 29: 3–72.
Shafir, E. (1991) 'Choosing versus rejecting: why some options are both better and worse than others', unpublished ms, Department of Psychology, Princeton University.
Simon, H.A. (1957) *Models of Man*, New York: Wiley.
—— (1982) *Models of Bounded Rationality*, vols 1–2, Cambridge, MA: MIT Press.
Stich, S. (1990a) *The Fragmentation of Reason: Preface to a Pragmatic Theory of Cognitive Evaluation*, Cambridge, MA: MIT Press.
—— (1990b) 'Rationality', in D.N. Osherson and E.E. Smith (eds) *Thinking: An Invitation to Cognitive Science*, vol. 3, Cambridge, MA: MIT Press.
Tversky, A. and Shafir, E. (1991) 'The disjunction effect under uncertainty', unpublished ms, Department of Psychology, Stanford University.
Valentine, E.R. (1985) 'The effect of instructions on performance in the Wason selection task', *Current Psychological Research and Reviews* 4: 214–23.
von Domarus, E. (1944) 'The specific laws of logic in schizophrenia', in J.S. Kasinin (ed.) *Language and Thought in Schizophrenia*, Berkeley: University of California Press.

Wason, P.C. (1965) 'The context of plausible denial', *Journal of Verbal Learning and Verbal Behaviour* 4: 7–11.

—— (1966) 'Reasoning', in B.M. Foss (ed.) *New Horizons in Psychology*, Harmondsworth: Penguin.

—— (1983) 'Realism and rationality in the selection task', in J.St B.T. Evans (ed.) *Thinking and Reasoning: Psychological Approaches*, London: Routledge & Kegan Paul.

Wason, P.C. and Green, D.W. (1984) 'Reasoning and mental representation', *Quarterly Journal of Experimental Psychology* 36A: 597–610.

Wason, P.C. and Johnson-Laird, P.N. (1972) *Psychology of Reasoning: Structure and Content*, London: Batsford and Cambridge, MA: Harvard University Press.

Wason, P.C. and Shapiro, D. (1971) 'Natural and contrived experience in a reasoning problem', *Quarterly Journal of Experimental Psychology* 23: 63–71.

Wetherick, N. and Gilhooly, K. (1990) 'Syllogistic reasoning: effects of premise order' in K. Gilhooly, M.T.G. Keane, R. Logie, and G. Erdos (eds) *Lines of Thought: Reflections on the Psychology of Thinking*, vol. 1, London: Wiley.

Wilkins, M.C. (1928) 'The effect of changed material on the ability to do formal syllogistic reasoning', *Archives of Psychology* 16: 102.

Woodworth, R.S. and Sells, S.B. (1935) 'An atmosphere effect in formal syllogistic reasoning', *Journal of Experimental Psychology* 18: 451–60.

Chapter 8

Rationality, deduction and mental models

E.J. Lowe

The design of the following treatise is to investigate the fundamental laws of those operations of the mind by which reasoning is performed . . . and upon this foundation to establish the science of logic and construct its method.

(Boole, 1958/1854: 1)

Logic is concerned with the laws of truth, not with the laws of holding something to be true, not with the question of how men think, but with the question of how they must think if they are not to miss the truth.

(Frege, 1979: 149)

God has not been so sparing to Men to make them barely two-legged Creatures, and left it to *Aristotle* to make them Rational. . . . He has given them a Mind that can reason without being instructed in Methods of Syllogizing: The Understanding is not taught to reason by these Rules; it has a native Faculty to perceive the Coherence, or Incoherence of its *Ideas*, and can range them right, without any such perplexing Repetitions.

(Locke, 1975: 671)

FORMAL LOGIC AND THE PSYCHOLOGY OF REASONING: A PHILOSOPHICAL PERSPECTIVE

Boole and Frege represent fundamentally opposed traditions concerning the relationship between the science of logic and the psychology of reasoning: the former holding that the empirical study of mental inference reveals the content of logical laws, the latter that logical laws are *a priori* principles which provide norms for human reasoning rather than descriptions of it. The view that I shall be defending runs counter to both of these traditions because it denies that our basic logical competence consists in an ability to employ general logistical methods of the kind studied by formal logicians like Boole and Frege and their modern descendants. Such methods provide only a variety of techniques for extending our powers of inference beyond their normal range, and as such are neither revealed by how we *do* reason nor constitutive of how we *should* reason in basic cases. Historically, this alternative view represents a third tradition, traceable at least back to Locke, which seeks to deflate the pretensions of logicians to describe or prescribe rational thought processes. To the extent that modern psychologists are sometimes too much in awe of the achievements and claims of logicians, this third tradition holds lessons for them as well.

Cognitive psychologists have been much exercised in recent years by questions about how ordinary folk reason and whether they are naturally prone to commit certain logical fallacies (see Evans, 1989). Thus there is hot debate over whether people employ a formal 'mental logic' or, alternatively, so-called 'mental models' in tackling reasoning tasks, or whether they exploit instead essentially non-logical 'heuristic' strategies whose results coincide with those of more 'logical' methods only in some of their applications (see Johnson-Laird and Byrne, 1991). And there is even hotter, and at times acrimonious, debate over whether the performance of ordinary folk in the reasoning tasks devised by psychological researchers is consistently 'bad' enough to call into question the basic rationality of human beings (see Evans, 1989).

Speaking as a philosophical logician confronted only fairly recently by much of this literature, I have to confess to some puzzlement as to what all the fuss is about, but also to some disquiet about what appear to be confusions in these debates. That people are prone to commit logical fallacies is a commonplace in philosophical circles, and indeed provides professional philosophers with one of their chief defences for being paid public money to teach logic to their students. The names of many of the standard fallacies – affirming the consequent, begging the question, and so forth – are traceable back to antiquity or at least to medieval times, testifying to their stability across languages and cultures (see Hamblin, 1970). At the same time, the very fact that philosophers have had some success in remedying fallacious reasoning by teaching logic suggests that the basic rationality of ordinary people is not seriously in question. And, after all, philosophers and logicians themselves are just ordinary people who have learnt or developed certain technical skills to a particularly high degree.

We need, of course, to be careful about just what we mean by 'logic', which is a term with many different subtly related uses. In its broadest sense, logic is the science of consequence relations: entailment relations in the case of deductive logic, probabilistic support relations in the case of inductive logic. These are relations between propositions, the bearers of truth values. Restricting ourselves for present purposes to deductive logic, a *valid* argument is one in which the premises entail the conclusion, and accordingly in which it is impossible for the conclusion to be false given the truth of the premises. But propositions are expressed in language by means of sentences, and since language is the public vehicle of thought and communication, it is useful to be able to specify conditions in which the sentences of a given language express propositions standing in consequence relations. This is the task of *formal* logic, which for practical purposes has to operate upon some suitably regimented fragment of natural language or some specially designed artificial symbolism. The task may be executed in many different ways: for instance, by adopting the axiomatic approach as classically exemplified by *Principia Mathematica* (Whitehead and Russell, 1910–13) or by adopting the 'natural deduction' approach favoured by many modern textbooks (see, for example, Lemmon, 1965). These two are 'syntactic' (or 'proof-theoretic') approaches, in as much as they characterize a valid argument purely in terms of formal properties and relations of sentences expressing it, without regard to the actual or possible meanings of those sentences. But there are also 'semantic' (or 'model-theoretic') approaches, which characterize validity in terms of possible interpretations of the sentences expressing an argument. Truth-table methods, for instance, and the method of 'semantic tableaux' (see, for example, Beth, 1962; Hodges, 1977; and Jeffrey, 1981) belong to this class.

A simple illustration may help at this point. Suppose someone contemplating how to entertain a guest reasons as follows:

(1) Either I'll take him to the museum or I'll take him to the theatre; I won't take him to the museum (it's closed today); so I'll take him to the theatre.

This is a deductively valid argument. The premises entail the conclusion. To know that, one doesn't need to know anything about formal logic: one simply has to grasp the fact that it is impossible for the premises to be true and the conclusion false – and that is a fact graspable by anyone who can understand the propositions in question. But there is a pattern discernible in this argument which is discernible in others like it. We can represent this pattern symbolically in the form:

(2) P or Q
Not P
Therefore, Q

A formal logician seeking to codify this and other valid argument patterns systematically may do so in any of a variety of ways. He may simply characterize the above argument pattern as exhibiting the application of a primitive inference rule, the rule of 'disjunctive syllogism'. Alternatively, he may treat the argument pattern as derivative from the application of some more basic inference rules (see, for example, Lemmon, 1965: 59). Or, yet again, he may resort to a 'semantic' approach and point out that the truth table for the conjunction of premises of these forms is such that there is no possible interpretation of the premises for which they can turn out true while the conclusion turns out false:

(3) | (P | or | Q) | and | (not | P) | Q |
|---|---|---|---|---|---|---|
| T | T | T | F | F | T | T |
| F | T | T | T | T | F | T |
| T | T | F | F | F | T | F |
| F | F | F | F | T | F | F |

I should stress here that there is nothing particularly *in*formal about such a 'semantic' approach: it is quite wrong to suppose that 'formal' logic is exclusively concerned with 'syntactic' or 'proof-theoretic' characterizations of logical consequence. To use a truth-table approach, as above, to exhibit the validity of an argument is just as 'formal' a procedure as it is to appeal to an inference-rule like the rule of disjunctive syllogism. I shall return to this point later, as there seems to be some confusion about it in the psychological literature.

Another thing I should emphasize is that formal logic, whether conducted in a 'syntactic' or in a 'semantic' style, is no substitute for basic logical insight and understanding: rather, it provides us with a set of useful tools for extending the range of application of that understanding (this, in part, is the point that Locke is making in the passage quoted at the beginning of this chapter). It would be absurd, for instance, to suppose that someone reasoning along the lines of (1) above could only do so by recasting his argument in the schematic form (2) and applying the rule of disjunctive syllogism or constructing a truth table as in (3). (Indeed, to carry out such formal methods correctly requires more logical acumen than is involved in grasping the validity of (1) in the first place.) Logical understanding *begins*, rather, with the immediate grasp of the validity of simple arguments like (1), and the science of formal logic merely builds upon this by discovering and codifying valid argument patterns which subsequently can be applied to more complex propositions and combined to form chains of reasoning which outstrip our unaided logical powers.

Before I turn to the psychological literature on reasoning and rationality, there is one more point I should make about that slippery term 'logic'. This is that where *formal* logic is concerned, pluralism is rife. Only the most naive of philosophers would contend that there is just one 'correct' system of formal logic. This is not just because, as we have already noted, there are many different approaches to the codification of argument patterns and so different ways of packaging what is at bottom the 'same' logic (for instance, classical truth–functional logic, or classical first-order predicate logic with identity). It is also because different logicians are interested in codifying different areas of reasoning (modal logics, conditional logics, deontic logics, epistemic logics, quantum logics, and so on) and because logicians often frankly disagree about the details of such codification (as well as about more fundamental principles, such as the law of excluded middle) (see further, Haack, 1974). Such pluralism and rivalry amongst formal logicians should not, however, lead us to lose sight of the fact that underlying and presupposed by all this academic activity is the basic logical competence of ordinary human beings, our native rationality. This consists in an ability to grasp simple consequence relations between propositions and is inseparable from the very ability to grasp propositional meaning at all. No creature could be said to understand propositions if it could not also be said to grasp at least some of their entailment relations and exercise that grasp in simple acts of reasoning (cf. Davidson, 1984: 155–70).

With these remarks in place, let us now see how they bear upon some aspects of the psychological literature on reasoning and rationality. I shall focus on two prominent issues by way of illustration: the Wason selection task and its implications for human rationality, and the rivalry between advocates of 'mental logic' and proponents of 'mental models'. (As regards the issue of human rationality, it will emerge that I am in substantial agreement with many of L. J. Cohen's conclusions (see Cohen, 1981), though I by no means wholly sympathize with the way in which he arrives at them.)

WASON'S SELECTION TASK AND THE SEMANTICS OF 'IF': THE PROBLEM OF INTERPRETATION

Consider, first, then, the so-called 'abstract' versions of the Wason selection task (supposedly the most 'difficult'), in which, for instance, each of the four cards has a letter on one side and a numeral on the other, the exposed faces displaying, say, 'A', '3', 'D', and '6', and subjects are asked to state which cards need to be turned over in order to discover whether the following conditional statement is true or false of the four cards in question: 'If a card has A on one side, then it has 3 on the other side' (see, for example, Evans, 1989: 53 ff). Most subjects, it appears, choose either both the 'A' card and the '3' card, or else just the 'A' card alone. But the 'correct' choice to make, according to the researchers setting the task, is the 'A' card and the '6' card, for only by turning over these can the conditional statement in question be shown to be false. The usual presumption here is that the 'if' statement being tested has the truth conditions of a *material* conditional of the form 'P $\rightarrow$ Q', or, equivalently, '$\neg$ (P & $\neg$Q)', that is, 'Not (P and not Q)'. That in itself is a presumption which most philosophical logicians would regard as highly questionable, in view of long-standing controversy in philosophical circles over whether indicative conditionals in natural language are truth-functional statements and, indeed, over whether they even have truth conditions at all (see further,

Jackson, 1991). However, inasmuch as it can be agreed that an indicative conditional of the form 'If P, then Q' *entails* the material conditional 'P → Q', perhaps the presumption looks harmless enough, since whatever falsifies a statement also falsifies any statement entailing it.

But some further preliminary remarks are in order here. First, it should be appreciated that the Wason selection task does not present subjects with a problem involving reasoning *with* statements so much as a problem concerning reasoning *about* statements: in short, with a *meta*logical problem. The subjects are not required to *use* the conditional statement at issue in a piece of reasoning, but rather to reason about its truth conditions. It should hardly surprise us that logically untutored subjects may find such a task difficult, and the fact that many of them appear to do so need in no way impugn their basic logical competence. (It will in any case become clear that the logic of the task is far from simple, and seems to have caused many of the researchers themselves a good deal of confusion.)

Second, given the tenacity with which some subjects adhere to their choice of cards, and in particular to their refusal to choose the '6' card, researchers would do well to consider whether there is not an interpretation of the conditional statement in question which would render the selection of these subjects appropriate: this would be to adopt a principle of 'charity' in interpreting the subjects' understanding of the conditional in the light of their attitude towards its potential falsifiers (on 'charity', see further Davidson, 1984: 136–7, 152–3, 168–9). Indeed, philosophical logicians are bound to regard the researchers' attitude as strangely dogmatic, because it is standard practice amongst philosophical logicians to treat with considerable respect the entrenched logical intuitions of ordinary language-users, since these provide a major source of data for the construction of systems of formal logic (for instance, systems of conditional logic (see, for example, Lowe, 1983; 1990)).

Nor is it in fact hard to find a non-standard truth table which will do the trick in the present case. We have only to suppose (a) that the subjects interpret the statement: 'If a card has A on one side, then it has 3 on the other side' as a *bi*conditional (so that the 'if' is interpreted as meaning 'if and only if') – not an uncommon phenomenon in ordinary language – and (b) that 'if' and 'and' have the following three-valued truth tables, where 'I' denotes a third value which we may call 'irrelevant' or (in the loose and popular sense) 'meaningless' (cf. Haack, 1978: 207):

	If P, then Q		
Q	T	I	F
P			
T	T	I	F
I	I	I	I
F	I	I	I

	Q	*P and Q*		
		T	I	F
P				
T		T	I	F
I		I	I	I
F		F	I	F

According to these truth tables, 'If P, then Q' is 'irrelevant' when it has a false antecedent, irrespective of the truth value of its consequent (coinciding, incidentally, with a commonplace intuition amongst ordinary speakers where indicative conditionals are concerned); and 'P and Q' is 'irrelevant' when either of its conjuncts is 'irrelevant'. Consequently, the biconditional 'P if and only if Q' (equivalent to '(if P, then Q) and (if Q, then P)') is 'irrelevant' when either 'P' or 'Q' is false.

Given this interpretation, clearly, a subject observing one of the cards displaying a '6' knows without more ado that the (bi-) conditional 'If (and only if) this card has A on one side, it has 3 on the other side' is neither true nor false but rather 'irrelevant' (because it is *false* that the card has 3 on the side displaying a numeral), whence it is perfectly rational for the subject not to select that card since turning it over can tell him nothing that he does not already know (and the same holds for the 'D' card). According to these semantics for 'if and only if', the only cards it makes any sense to turn over are the 'A' card and the '3' card. (Note: the *general* conditional 'If (and only if) a card has A on one side, it has 3 on the other side' is true of *all four* cards just in case the *particular* conditional 'If (and only if) *this* card has A on one side, it has 3 on the other side' is true of *each* card. So by the present account the general conditional is known *not* to be true purely by inspection of the displayed faces: so why turn over *any* card? Possible answer: because the subject, exercising 'charity' in respect of the researcher who has set the task, interprets it as a non-vacuous one, and the simplest way to do this is to assume that the question is really about whether or not the general conditional is true of the 'A' and '3' cards, since it is known already not to be true of the others.)

I do not necessarily want to claim that subjects who refuse to choose the '6' card *must* be implicitly adopting something like these semantics for 'if and only if', only that that is a legitimate hypothesis. But a further question is this: what *does* determine what semantics for a logical connective are being adopted by a speaker if not the pattern of inferences which that speaker is prepared to sanction in respect of occurrences of that connective? It is not at all clear what else could constitute a speaker's understanding of a logical connective other than his preparedness to put it to use in logical inferences in certain characteristic ways (see further, Hacking, 1979; and Cohen, 1986: 151ff.). This is not to say that it is impossible for a speaker to be *mistaken* about the logical behaviour of a connective under the interpretation of it that he is adopting – for we need only take as evidence for his interpretation his *firm* and *replicable* intuitions about its logical behaviour in relatively *simple* contexts, and this leaves plenty of scope for errors of various sorts elsewhere. I should remark though, that in view of my earlier observations about the *metalogical* nature of the Wason selection task, we cannot directly construe the choices of subjects undertaking it as revealing their intuitions about the logical behaviour of 'if' in certain contexts. It is relevant to note here that many subjects who make what the researchers regard as a 'mistaken' choice on 'abstract' versions of the selection task subsequently agree with the evaluations of the researchers when the hidden faces of the cards are revealed (Manktelow and Over, 1990: 117). This may suggest that these subjects are not in fact adopting some non-classical semantics for 'if' but rather that the metalogical nature of the task is causing them difficulty – though in view of the highly context-sensitive character of conditionals in ordinary language (see below), it is also conceivable that the change in context induced by revealing the hidden faces triggers an alteration in these subjects' interpretation of 'if' (but see also below for another, and in my opinion better, explanation of what is going on here).

One other comment on the Wason selection task that I must make concerns the so-called 'realistic' versions of the task, in which less abstract subject matter is introduced, sometimes with the result that subjects make a much higher proportion of (what the researchers regard as) 'correct' choices (see Evans, 1989: 80ff.). I would only point out that it is now a commonplace in philosophical and linguistic circles that conditional statements are highly context-dependent and consequently that the subject matter and background implications of a conditional can – at least according to some theories – affect the semantic interpretation of the conditional connective it contains (see further many of the papers in Traugott *et al.*, 1986; and also Lowe, 1990). It would be wrong, then, to assume that 'if' has a fixed interpretation, even for a single speaker, across all conversational contexts. Consequently, the 'content effects' produced by introducing more 'realistic' material into the selection task cannot be presumed to show that subjects are not processing conditionals at the level of 'logical form', because logical form itself may change with context and subject matter (thus, for instance, 'deontic' conditionals appear to have certain distinctive logical characteristics exclusive to themselves (see further, Manktelow and Over, 1990: 80–1, 156)).

These remarks have a bearing on 'abstract' versions of the selection task as well: for precisely because the conditionals and contexts involved in such versions of the task are highly 'unnatural', it is only to be expected that bemused subjects will seek to model the task on one drawn from some more familiar context which imposes its own distinctive logical constraints – for instance, the context of nomological hypothesis testing. Thus, if a subject models the task on the empirical testing of a taxonomic hypothesis such as 'If something is a raven, then it is black', it should be as unsurprising (and as little indicative of 'irrationality') that the subject should neglect to choose the '6' card as it is that he should neglect to test the hypothesis just mentioned by examining non-black things (cf. Cohen, 1986: 156). This could also explain why many subjects should get (what the researchers deem to be) the 'right' answer in 'abstract' versions of the task in which the conditional being tested has a *negated consequent* (see Evans, 1989: 57) – for, by analogy, it is perfectly appropriate to test such a nomological hypothesis as 'If something is made of gold, then it is not magnetic' by examining magnetic things, since these (unlike non-black things) are relatively scarce in normal human environments. It could likewise explain why, as mentioned earlier, many subjects who do make the 'wrong' choice in 'abstract' versions of the selection task (where there is not a negated consequent) subsequently agree with the researchers' evaluations when the hidden faces of the cards are revealed: for, again by analogy, although one would (quite properly) not *examine* non-black things to test the hypothesis 'If something is a raven, then it is black', if one were actually *presented* with a non-black thing which turned out to be a raven, one would undoubtedly recognize that it served to falsify that hypothesis. By this account, indeed, such subjects cannot be accused (as the researchers often assume) of displaying any *inconsistency* between their original selections and subsequent evaluations, even if they experience difficulty in defending their behaviour when interrogated by the researchers: for in their subsequent evaluations they are no longer addressing the original question as to which of the cards *ought to be* turned over in order to verify or falsify the conditional, but rather the logically quite distinct question as to which of the cards that *have been* turned over verify or falsify it.

If the performance of at least some subjects on 'abstract' versions of the selection task is indeed to be explained along lines like these, the lesson would be that such subjects are not exhibiting any real failure of rationality but can at most be convicted of importing elements of (impeccable) inductive reasoning into what is intended (by the researchers) to be purely a problem of deductive logic. Given the abstruse nature of the task in its 'abstract' form, it would hardly be surprising if some subjects do indeed react to it in this way. It should also be unsurprising that they should find difficulty in explaining and defending what they are doing, for that is a second-order problem of reasoning *about* reasoning.

An important general point which emerges from all this is that conditionals constitute an extremely complex logico-linguistic pheno-menon which is still only very imperfectly understood even after many decades of intensive study by logicians, philosophers, and linguists. In this respect 'if' is very unlike the other elementary sentential connectives with which it is commonly grouped – 'and', 'or', and 'not' – and it is consequently (a) unsurprising if ordinary subjects untutored in logic have difficulty with metalogical problems involving conditionals (heaven knows, even the experts do!); and (b) inappropriate for the psychological researchers to focus on conditionals for the purpose of examining the basic reasoning powers of ordinary folk.

'MENTAL MODELS' VERSUS 'MENTAL LOGIC': A DISTINCTION WITHOUT (MUCH OF) A DIFFERENCE?

Leaving the somewhat unfruitful topic of the preceding section, I turn now to the dispute between proponents of 'mental models' and advocates of 'mental logic', to provide my second object lesson (see Evans, 1989: 11–12; and Johnson-Laird and Byrne, 1991: 23ff.). As earlier remarks of mine may have indicated, I am far from sure that there is much of real substance to be debated here. In the first place, I should repeat and expand upon the point that 'semantic' methods in logic are not to be contrasted with 'syntactic' methods on account of the *formal* or *non-formal* nature of the procedures involved: both approaches are equally 'formal' – it's just that syntactic approaches characterize logical consequence purely in terms of formal properties and relations at the level of the *object* language (the language in which the argument is expressed) whereas semantic approaches characterize logical consequence at least partly in terms of formal properties and relations at the level of the *meta*language (the language in which semantic values, such as truth, are assigned to object-language sentences). Thus, in the case of argument-pattern (2):

P or Q
Not P
Therefore, Q

A 'syntactic' approach might state that the conclusion follows from the premises by a simple application of the rule of disjunctive syllogism:

A or B, Not A ⊢ B

by virtue of the fact that the premises and conclusion of (2) exhibit the forms specified by the rule. (Alternatively, one might supply a longer derivation of (2)'s conclusion from its premises using more basic inference rules (see, for example, Lemmon, 1965: 59), though nothing much hinges on which course is chosen since it is often fairly arbitrary whether a rule is treated as 'primitive' or as 'derived'.) A 'semantic' approach employing truth tables would on the other hand seek to show that there is no way of assigning the value 'false' to 'Q' while assigning the value 'true' to both 'P or Q' and 'Not P': but that is done just by showing that a certain *formal* relation obtains between the possible truth-value assignments of premises and conclusions *of these forms* – namely, that wherever 'T' appears under both 'P or Q' and 'Not P' in the appropriate truth table (see (3) on p. 214), it also appears under 'Q'. As a logistical procedure, constructing such a truth table and discerning that it exhibits the desired relationship between truth-value assignments is quite as much a 'formal', rule-governed exercise as is the procedure of deriving one formula from another using 'syntactic' rules of inference. In neither case is the logician interested in what the sentential symbols 'P' and 'Q' might actually *mean*, so that to this extent it is in fact misleading to describe model-theoretic methods as 'semantic', for it is only the meaning of the logical operators that is held constant by such methods, and in that respect they are not significantly different from 'syntactic', proof-theoretic methods, in which the inference rules themselves constrain the meanings of the logical operators. (It is perhaps worth noting here that E.W. Beth, the inventor of semantic tableaux, quite explicitly states that '(closed) semantic tableaux [may be] considered as a method of formal deduction' (Beth, 1962: 115).)

Indeed, 'semantic' or model-theoretic procedures often effectively just replicate, at a metalinguistic level, proof-theoretic procedures conducted at the object-language level. (It is even arguable that model theory in general is really parasitic upon proof-theoretic methods and so ultimately redundant (see Tennant, 1986).) Consider, thus, the method of attempted falsification to show the validity of the conditional corresponding to the inference from 'P or Q' and 'Not P' to 'Q'. In symbolic notation, this conditional is '{(P ∨ Q) & ¬P} → Q', and the method proceeds as follows. First, one assigns T and F to the antecedent and consequent respectively [1], which in turn requires one to assign T to each conjunct in the antecedent [2], and then one discovers that 'P' has to be assigned inconsistent values [3]:

$$\{(P \lor Q) \ \& \ \neg P\} \to Q$$
$$\begin{array}{ccccccc} T & T F & T & T & F & F & F \\ 3 & 2 \ 1 & 1 & 2 & 2 & 1 & 1 \end{array}$$

But this just replicates a reductio ad absurdum proof using 'natural deduction' rules:

(1)	1. (P ∨ Q) & ¬P	(Assumption)
(2)	2. ¬Q	(Assumption)
(1)	3. P ∨ Q	(1. & elimination)
(1)	4. ¬P	(1, & elimination)
(1, 2)	5. P	(2, 3, disjunct. syll.)
(1)	6. Q	(2, 4, 5, reductio)
	7. (P ∨ Q) & ¬P) → Q	(1, 6, conditional proof)

Lines 1 and 2 correspond to the initial truth-value assignments [1]. Lines 3 and 4 correspond to the second round of truth-value assignments [2] and line 5 to the final round [3]. Lines 6 and 7 replicate the conclusion that the conditional in question is logically true. Essentially the same train of reasoning is involved in both methods. (Note, incidentally, that at line 5 of the proof the rule of *disjunctive syllogism* is invoked – and a similar step is made when T is assigned to 'P' in round [3] on the grounds that T has already been assigned to '(P v Q)' and F to 'Q'. This shows that it would be idle to think of either method as *explaining* the validity of inferring 'Q' from 'P or Q' and 'Not P', since just such an inference is used in both demonstrations.)

Despite such facts, advocates of 'mental models' tend to suggest (a) that 'formal' logic is exclusively associated with 'syntactic' methods; and (b) that 'semantic' methods are not 'formal', or, sometimes, that they are not even 'logical'. By thus idiosyncratically construing 'logic' and 'formal' in unduly narrow ways, they make the gap between themselves and their perceived opponents appear larger than it actually is, if indeed it really exists at all.

Another preliminary point to make is this. As I urged earlier on, it really is preposterous to suppose that ordinary human subjects use formal logic (whether in the guise of syntactic/proof-theoretic approaches or in the guise of semantic/model-theoretic approaches) to draw elementary inferences of the sort illustrated by (1) earlier. This *ought* really to be obvious simply by virtue of the fact that most ordinary folk have never had the least exposure to the methods of formal logic, which is mostly only taught to philosophy and mathematics students at university level (again, this is part of the point of Locke's remarks quoted at the beginning of this paper). But, bizarrely enough, this does not deter some theorists from supposing that ordinary folk *do* none the less employ formal logical methods, but *unconsciously* – because their brains have been genetically programmed to process information in this way. What needs to be emphasized, though, is that you simply *don't need to know* (even 'tacitly') any formal logic in order to grasp that an inference like (1) is valid: you just need an adequate grasp of the truth conditions of the sentences involved (that is, know what they mean) in order to grasp that the conclusion can't be false given that the premises are true. Formal logic was not developed to help us to see the validity of arguments like this: if we hadn't been able to see that already, indeed, a discipline of formal logic could never have emerged in the first place. Rather, as I remarked earlier, the purpose of formal logic is to build upon our basic logical competence by constructing a set of tools which will enable us to *extend* our grasp of logical relationships beyond simple cases like (1) to complex cases involving numerous compound propositions and complicated chains of reasoning – rather in the way that formal arithmetical pencil-and-paper methods extend our basic powers of 'mental' arithmetic.

The point of these remarks is this: first, that we should expect all normal human beings to have a basic logical competence that is *not* grounded in the application of any formal methods but simply in a capacity to understand the meanings of sentences and the logical connectives they contain. Second, that when it comes to *extending* that logical competence beyond the range of our unaided logical powers, one should expect people to be thoroughly *opportunistic* and *pragmatic* in their choice of tools to aid them – especially if they have had no training in the methods of formal logic. Some may use diagrams, others may try to construct analogies with more familiar patterns of inference or to reorganize the syntax of sentences along more familiar lines, yet others may dabble in symbolism, and some may just resort to guessing: we should expect little uniformity or consistency in practice even with a single subject. Nor, of course, should we expect a great deal of success: that, after all, is why formal logic has been developed – to meet a need that ordinary folk are ill-equipped to cope with by relying on their own resources. None of this, however, in any way impugns their rationality and basic logical competence, for reasons that I have already made clear.

All this being so, though, it is surely just ludicrous to suppose, as some cognitive psychologists appear to, that ordinary folk are somehow unconsciously equipped with logic programs duplicating textbook presentations of formal logical methods, whether in a 'natural-deduction' format or in a 'semantic-tableau' style or whatnot. It really is grotesque to imagine that formal techniques, many of which have only been invented through much effort and ingenuity during the last hundred years, have somehow been secretly known to our genes for millennia, unconsciously guiding the reasoning processes of human beings from infancy. (Indeed, if there *is* a 'natural' logic, it is much more likely to be one along the lines of Sommers (1982) than anything resembling standard textbook formulations.) Just because *we* would now equip a computer with such a logic program if we wanted it to emulate aspects of human reasoning provides not the slightest reason to suppose that this is what *nature* has done to *us* to enable *us* to reason. (Nor should any spurious analogies with our alleged 'tacit' grasp of grammatical rules of natural language, as envisaged by linguists of Chomsky's persuasion, be allowed to ensnare us here: the two domains are simply not relevantly comparable. For one thing, basic logical competence is a property of 'central systems' (in the terminology of Fodor (1983)) whereas grammatical parsing ability plausibly has a modular organization (see Fodor, 1983: 50ff.).)

But let me turn now expressly to the dispute between proponents of 'mental models' and advocates of 'mental logic'. I want in particular to focus on the recent claim of Johnson-Laird and Byrne to have discovered a 'theory of propositional reasoning based on mental models' (Johnson-Laird and Byrne, 1991: 43). They illustrate the theory by attempting to show how:

a disjunctive deduction of the form:

> p or q
> not p
> Therefore, q

can be made by using the meanings of the premises to construct and eliminate models. There is no need for formal rules of inference.

(Johnson-Laird and Byrne, 1991: 44)

The theory works like this. According to Johnson-Laird and Byrne, people 'build mental models' to represent various propositions. For instance, the conjunctive proposition:

(4)   There is a circle and there is a triangle

used to state what is depicted on some blackboard, might be represented by a single model like this:

○   △

A disjunctive proposition such as:

(5)   There is a circle or there is a triangle

might be represented by means of two alternative models, thus:

○

△

where (as Johnson-Laird and Byrne put it) 'we adopt the notational convention of putting separate models on separate lines' (1991: 43). Suppose now that a reasoner adopts (5) as a premise and subsequently adds the further premise:

(6)   There isn't a circle

then this 'eliminates' the first (uppermost) of the two models representing (5), but at the same time enables the reasoner to supplement the second model, to give:

¬○   △

where '¬' is 'a propositional-like tag representing negation' (ibid, 1991: 44). This revised model represents the proposition:

(7)   There is not a circle and there is a triangle.

Since the first conjunct of (7) has already been affirmed as (6), it is now dropped as superfluous to leave:

(8)   There is a triangle.

This conclusion is then declared to be 'valid because no other model of the premises falsifies it' (ibid) (though quite what work this last remark is supposed to do is rather obscure, a point to which I shall return later). So here we have, it is alleged, an account of how the inference from (5) and (6) to (8) is made according to which '[t]here is no need for formal rules of inference' (ibid).

It should be clear by now that my own main objection to this account of how we infer (8) from (5) and (6) is not that it involves no formal rules of inference (though we shall see in a moment that the claim that this is so is questionable in any case), since I am happy to allow that we need rely on no such rules in the case of simple inferences like this: an understanding of the propositions involved is sufficient to ensure a grasp of the relationship of logical consequence obtaining between them. Rather, my objection to the account is its presumption that any sort of quasi-mechanical *procedure* is needed to execute the inference at all. (That this presumption is characteristic of Johnson-Laird and Byrne's theory of reasoning in general is demonstrated by the fact that they themselves have endeavoured to implement it in computer programs (1991:183ff.).) However, setting this objection aside for the present, let us see why Johnson-Laird and Byrne's claim that their account of the inference from (5) and (6) to (8) *invokes no formal rules of inference* is at least questionable. It is true enough that their procedure does not explicitly appeal to, say, the rule of disjunctive syllogism:

$A \vee B, \neg A \vdash B$

But one may still suspect that syntax and formal rules are tacitly being appealed to (cf. Rips, 1986: 278–9, commenting on Johnson-Laird's earlier work on syllogistic reasoning). In effect (it may be urged), what Johnson-Laird and Byrne have done is to invent their own little ideographic language, with the following translation manual into English:

O	=	There is a circle
$\triangle$	=	There is a triangle
* +	=	and
* +	=	or
–*	=	not

where '*' and '+' are place-holders for sentences of the language. In other words, writing sentence-symbols side-by-side on the same line amounts to forming their conjunction, writing them on successive lines amounts to forming their disjunction, and prefixing '–' to a sentence-symbol forms its negation. (Incidentally, it won't do to object that Johnson-Laird and Byrne are only using these symbols for the purpose of *conveying their theory*, and don't suppose tokens of them to occur 'in the heads' of reasoners: for advocates of 'mental logic', equally, don't suppose that the logical symbols like '&' and 'V' which they use to convey their theories are literally tokened 'in the heads' of reasoners, even if they adhere to some version of the 'language of thought' hypothesis.)

In addition, Johnson-Laird and Byrne could be said to have implicitly adopted the following inference-rules:

[R1] *

    $+, -^* \vdash -^* +$

[R2] * $+ \vdash +$

In more familiar notation, these could be written as:

<R1> A v B, ¬A ⊢ ¬A & B

<R2> A & B ⊢ B

The deduction then apparently proceeds as follows. First the English premise (5) is translated to give as the initial line of our proof:

(1) 1. ○ (Assumption)

    △

The second premise (6) translates to give as our second line:

(2) 2. –○ (Assumption)

Applying rule [R1] to these two lines we derive:

(1, 2) 3. –○ △ (1, 2, [R1])

Applying rule [R2] to this we finally derive our conclusion:

(1, 2) 4. △ (3, [R2])

which is translated back into English as (8).

No doubt Johnson-Laird and Byrne would object that this is a grotesque misrepresentation of their account. (In particular, they may urge that I ignore the claim that their method hinges on the principle that 'no other model of the premises falsifies [the conclusion]' (1991: 43), which shows that their approach really *is* 'semantic' and 'model-theoretic'. I shall return to this later.) But is my reading of their procedure really such a distortion? What, after all, do they mean when they say, for instance, that the information provided by the second premise, (6), 'eliminates the first model, which contains a circle [b]ut . . . can be added to the second model' (1991: 44)? This is their explanation of the move from:

○

  △

and

–○

to

–○ △

that is, the move made from lines 1 and 2 to line 3 of the little proof laid
out above. But what *licenses* the 'elimination' and the 'addition' involved
here? If it is supposed to be somehow just obvious to any reasonably
intelligent person that this move is valid, then why not simply concede
from the start that anyone reasonably intelligent can grasp without more
ado that (the propositions expressed by) (5) and (6) entail (the proposition
expressed by) (8), since that is patently no more taxing an intellectual task?
But if that (to *my* mind perfectly acceptable) answer is rejected (as it must
be by Johnson-Laird and Byrne if their account is not to become
redundant), then what can be said but that some sort of *rule of inference*
is being applied – a *formal* rule, moreover, inasmuch as it involves no
reliance on the particular *meanings* of the tokens '○' and '△' in the
representations, but solely upon their identity and combination (that is ,
upon the logical forms of the propositions being represented)?

But what about the objection that I ignore the model-theoretic aspect
of Johnson-Laird and Byrne's approach? All I can say is that it doesn't
emerge from their chosen example. Their remark that 'no other model of
the premises falsifies [the conclusion]' appears to be just a piece of window-
dressing tacked on to the end of their account, since it isn't at all clear
what additional work it does, or how. But even supposing that their
method really is meant to proceed by exhaustion of models, as this remark
suggests, that would only make it akin to the procedure of attempted
falsification by truth-value assignments discussed earlier – and, as we saw,
that is itself just a formal method which effectively replicates at a
metalinguistic level a proof-procedure at the object-language level. (I
would again emphasize, however, that it is in fact not at all apparent that
Johnson-Laird and Byrne's method *as they themselves illustrate it* really
does effectively make use of attempted falsification or exhaustion of
models as opposed to the direct proof which I have just attributed to
them.)

Another objection which Johnson-Laird and Byrne might raise against
me is that I overlook the fact that their account of propositional reasoning
differs importantly from standard model-theoretic accounts (accounts
exploiting such devices as truth tables and semantic tableaux) inasmuch as
the models that it invokes are typically partial or incomplete – a feature
which, they argue, is necessary given the limitations of human working
memory. As they put it: 'The essence of the theory is . . . that people use
models that make explicit as little information as possible, and in this way,
they overcome the unwieldy bulk of truth tables' (Johnson-Laird and Byrne,
1991: 52; see also pp. 42–3). But as far as the dispute between 'mental
models' and 'mental logic' is concerned, this feature of Johnson-Laird

and Byrne's account is not as significant as it might seem, since advocates of 'mental logic' make similar departures from standard natural-deduction systems to accommodate the practical constraints of human information-processing – they do not, for instance, invoke the full panoply of Gentzen's rules (a fact which emerges from Johnson-Laird and Byrne's own description of some of the leading 'mental-logic' theories (1991: 28–31); for Gentzen's rules, see Kneale and Kneale, 1962: 538ff.).

What I have just argued is that it is far from clear that Johnson-Laird and Byrne's account of how we reason from (5) and (6) to (8) is not indistinguishable, to all intents and purposes, from what would be offered by the sort of 'mental-logic' theory which they are so keen to oppose. But this should provide no comfort for advocates of 'mental logic'. For if I am right, not only is there little or nothing of substance in the dispute, but also *both* schools of thought are guilty of trying to press modern logical theory and practice into inappropriate service. They both commit the fundamental error of trying to explain our basic logical competence in terms of quasi-mechanical logistical procedures which human beings – exercising, of course, that very logical competence – have themselves invented precisely in order to *extend* our reasoning ability beyond its normal range of application. This is rather like trying to explain how people can whistle a tune by appealing to the way in which they play a written musical score on an orchestral instrument. As Locke himself eloquently puts it: 'Some eyes want Spectacles to see things clearly and distinctly; but let not those that use them therefore say, no body can see clearly without them' (Locke, 1975: 678).

'SO HOW DO WE DO IT?': A BRIEF SPECULATION BY WAY OF A CONCLUSION

I can well imagine any cognitive psychologist who has persisted thus far with this paper protesting frustratedly at this point:

> You've poured scorn on two of the foremost current approaches to explaining how humans reason – mental models and mental logic – but you don't offer anything substantive to put in their place. You say, indeed, that 'No creature could be said to understand propositions at all if it could not also be said to grasp at least some of their entailment relations and exercise that grasp in simple acts of reasoning'. But that doesn't tell us *how* we perform such acts. On that question you are silent, apart from denying that we perform them by executing 'quasi-mechanical logistical procedures' – in other words, by following a sequence of rule-governed formal transitions in the manner of a computer program. So how *do* we do it? By magic?

Of course, I could try to dodge this question by pleading professional disqualification: it is not the business of philosophers to indulge in armchair science. But that would be disingenuous given that (informed) speculation is the life blood of philosophy. So there follows a brief bit of speculation, which I confess doesn't propose anything particularly original.

If we put together a number of considerations which surfaced during the course of the chapter, they collectively seem to point in the direction of a 'connectionist' response to the question that has been posed. Some of these considerations are: (a) the fact that basic logical competence is plausibly a property of 'central systems' rather than having an 'encapsulated', modular organization (in the terminology of Fodor, 1983: see especially pp. 101ff.); (b) the 'holistic' nature of propositional understanding and consequently of our grasp of the logical connectives and operators (cf. Davidson, 1984); and (c) the 'particularist' conception of logical inference favoured by my account, which implies that general argument patterns or schemata are properly to be seen as abstractions parasitic upon the multitude of particular inferences (individuated by the propositions constituting their premises and conclusions) which those schemata help us to codify. All of these considerations, I suggest, are consistent with a psychological theory of rational thought processes which regards them as implemented within a highly plastic connectionist architecture involving widely distributed representations (see Clark, 1989, especially pp. 121ff.). Such a theory could be expected to dispense with the sequential, rule-following approach of logic programs in its account of human inference (at least as far as basic, untutored reasoning is concerned), while escaping the charge that it represents our ability to reason as being somehow 'magical'. I am happy to hang on to the coat-tails of any such theory in order to escape that charge myself, though I really can plead professional disqualification if pressed to say in more detail how a theory of that type might ultimately look: that is the business of cognitive psychologists.

ACKNOWLEDGEMENT

I am most grateful to David Over both for his encouragement and for some very helpful suggestions for improvements to an earlier draft of this paper.

REFERENCES

Beth, E.W. (1962) *Formal Methods*, Dordrecht: Reidel.
Boole, G. (1958/1854) *An Investigation of the Laws of Thought*, New York: Dover.
Clark, A. (1989) *Microcognition: Philosophy, Cognitive Science and Parallel Distributed Processing*, Cambridge, MA: MIT Press.
Cohen, L.J. (1981) 'Can human irrationality be experimentally demonstrated?' *Behavioral and Brain Sciences* 4: 317–70.
—— (1986) *The Dialogue of Reason: An Analysis of Analytic Philosophy*, Oxford: Clarendon Press.
Davidson, D. (1984) *Inquiries into Truth and Interpretation*, Oxford: Clarendon Press.

Evans, J.St B.T. (1989) *Bias in Human Reasoning: Causes and Consequences*, Hove: Erlbaum.

Fodor, J.A. (1983) *The Modularity of Mind*, Cambridge, MA: MIT Press.

Frege, G. (1979) 'Logic' (1897), in H. Hermes *et al.* (eds) *Gottlob Frege: Posthumous Writings*, trans. P. Long and R. White, Oxford: Blackwell.

Haack, S, (1974) *Deviant Logic*, Cambridge: Cambridge University Press.

—— (1978) *Philosophy of Logics*, Cambridge: Cambridge University Press.

Hacking, I. (1979) 'What is logic?' *Journal of Philosophy* 76: 285–319.

Hamblin, C.L. (1970) *Fallacies*, London: Methuen.

Hodges, W. (1977) *Logic*, Harmondsworth: Penguin.

Jackson, F. (ed.) (1991) *Conditionals*, Oxford: Oxford University Press.

Jeffrey, R.C. (1981) *Formal Logic: Its Scope and Limits*, 2nd edn, New-York: McGraw-Hill.

Johnson-Laird, P.N. and Byrne, R.M.J. (1991) *Deduction*, Hove: Erlbaum.

Kneale, W. and Kneale, M. (1962) *The Development of Logic*, Oxford: Clarendon Press.

Lemmon, E.J. (1965) *Beginning Logic*, London: Nelson.

Locke, J. (1975) *An Essay Concerning Human Understanding* (1690), P.H. Nidditch (ed.), Oxford: Clarendon Press.

Lowe, E.J. (1983) 'A simplification of the logic of conditionals', *Notre Dame Journal of Formal Logic* 24: 357–66.

—— (1990) 'Conditionals, context and transitivity', *Analysis* 50: 80–7.

Manktelow, K.I. and Over, D.E. (1990) *Inference and Understanding: A Philosophical and Psychological Perspective*, London: Routledge.

Rips, L.J. (1986) 'Mental muddles', in M. Brand and R.M. Harnish (eds) *The Representation of Knowledge and Belief*, Tucson: University of Arizona Press.

Sommers, F. (1982) *The Logic of Natural Language*, Oxford: Clarendon Press.

Tennant, N. (1986) 'The withering away of formal semantics?' *Mind and Language* 1: 302–18.

Traugott, E.C., ter Meulen, A., Reilly, J.S., and Ferguson, C.A. (eds) (1986) *On Conditionals*, Cambridge: Cambridge University Press.

Whitehead, A.N. and Russell, B. (1910–13) *Principia Mathematica*, Cambridge: Cambridge University Press.

Chapter 9

Rationality, utility and deontic reasoning

D.E. Over and K.I. Manktelow

INTRODUCTION

In this chapter, we are interested in one extremely important type of deontic reasoning, which takes place when people try to find out which actions they ought to perform or may perform. This type of reasoning has traditionally, in philosophy, been called 'practical reasoning' and distinguished from 'theoretical reasoning', which has the object of trying to discover, or to describe correctly, objective matters of fact. It is sometimes said that the difference between these two is that between trying to infer what one should (or may) *do* as opposed to trying to infer what one should (or may) *believe*. The latter does not have to be 'theoretical' in the scientific sense, and could be directed towards ordinary facts which are highly relevant to practical questions about what one should or should not do, for example, facts about what is healthy or unhealthy. Practical reasoning depends, in part, on some degree of theoretical reasoning, but goes beyond it to conclusions about actions. As with so much in the study of reasoning, Aristotle was the first to discuss practical reasoning systematically, and yet we still face many difficulties in specifying generally what it is for this reasoning to be rational, though we can often recognize that it has this property in particular cases. (See Audi, 1989, on practical reasoning and the history of its study.)

Cognitive psychologists have for some time investigated ordinary people's use and evaluation of Aristotelian syllogisms in theoretical reasoning (from Wilkins (1928), to Johnson-Laird (1983), and Johnson-Laird and Byrne (1991)). But until recently, little or no empirical work was done on deontic inference as such, whether on what Aristotle called practical syllogisms, which have (at least implicitly) deontic conclusions, or on more general deontic argument forms. It is difficult to understand why this should have been so. Ordinary people have always had to devote much time and energy to practical thought in order to survive at all; and they often think about what they should or should not do in pursuit of their own interests, or in light of social agreements, regulations, and laws.

This ordinary deontic reasoning affects behaviour in many ways, and we shall present experimental evidence that, in some contexts at least, people tend to be reasonably good at it. On evolutionary grounds, it is indeed hard to see how this reasoning directed towards satisfying our basic needs and desires could tend to be anything other than fairly rational. Even so, many normative and descriptive problems arise from its general study, and there are great difficulties in assessing the exact extent to which it is rational overall, as we hope to illustrate. We shall also support the view that there should not, in fact, be a unique standard of what it is for this reasoning to be rational, although that is far from meaning that anything goes in it.

Of course, some psychologists have tried to describe how ordinary people make decisions about possible actions or options they are presented with, often with the object of seeing how rational these decisions are. Here the relevant normative theory has been taken to be decision theory, combining as it does the normative theories of probability and of utility, and yielding a notion of rationality as maximizing the utility expected from an option. (See Baron, 1988, for a review of both normative and descriptive decision theories.) Deductive logic has not been considered to be directly relevant to this interest although, of course, it is presupposed and made use of in all these theories. Yet as we shall try to show, this work and that on deontic reasoning, to which deontic logic and its concept of validity obviously are relevant, should be directly related to each other. What ultimately links decision making and deontic reasoning is the mental state of preference, from which we get the technical definition of subjective utility. In fact, without preferences, decision making and deontic reasoning have no point. Bringing the study of these closely related mental processes together, and seeing how they are grounded in preferences, should help us to understand both how they ought to function and how they actually do so.

THE DEONTIC SELECTION TASK

Before we say more about bringing work on decision making and deontic reasoning together, we should explain how cognitive psychologists have recently come to the study of the latter. It has been research on Wason's selection task that has led psychologists to propose theories of how people understand and perform deontic inferences. (For a more complete account of this task, see Manktelow and Over, 1990a.)

The first experiments on this used 'abstract' tasks and indicative conditionals, of the form: 'If a card has a vowel on one side then it has an even number on the other side'. These revealed that subjects tended not to turn over a card showing, say, 7 on one side in order to see if there was a vowel on the other side. Since the subjects were asked to turn over just the cards needed to see whether the conditional was true, this tendency seemed illogical and so irrational; and some philosophers and psychologists used these results as evidence that people do tend to be generally irrational. But further research revealed that subjects did much better on the task when certain realistic conditionals were used, such as: 'If any purchase exceeds £30 then the receipt must have the signature of the department manager on the back'. Subjects were asked to imagine that they were the manager of a department store who had the job of making sure that store workers did not violate this rule. In this case, most subjects did make the rational choices, and in particular turned over an unsigned receipt to see if it was for a purchase of over £30.

Eventually, some researchers came to realize that the latter type of task calls for deontic reasoning. In these cases, subjects are not asked to find out whether an indicative conditional is true or false as a matter of fact. They are rather asked whether someone has performed an action violating what is properly called a rule, i.e. a deontic conditional, the point of which is to govern or guide behaviour. Cheng and Holyoak (1985) took the decisive step in recognizing the deontic nature of many realistic selection tasks, and all experimental studies of these tasks must come to terms with their work. They considered rules like this:

(1) If one is to drink alcohol, then one must be over eighteen.

Subjects do well in a selection task based on this deontic conditional. In our view, they do so partly because they grasp, either through their knowledge of the world or through a background story they are given in the task, that drinking alcohol and being over eighteen is much to be preferred to drinking alcohol and being under eighteen. On this basis, the subjects realize that it is important to find violators of the rule, i.e. underage drinkers. Preferences can be based on perceived benefits or costs, but in this example the possible costs seem decisive. Underage drinking is against the law, and breaking the law can get one into trouble with the authorities, and anyway may be seen as intrinsically undesirable by law-abiding people. Moreover, underage drinking can damage one's health. Though the exact details of the subjects' reasoning in this case remain to be investigated empirically, such reflections make sense of the rule and of the task of looking for its violators. This explanation makes use of the semantics of deontic conditionals, as we shall bring out below, but Cheng and Holyoak themselves try to give a purely non-semantic explanation of deontic selection tasks.

According to Cheng and Holyoak, people employ a so-called *permission schema* when they encounter such conditionals. This schema consists of four production rules:

Rule 1 If the action is to be taken, then the precondition must be
          satisfied;

Rule 2 If the action is not to be taken, then the precondition need not be satisfied;

Rule 3 If the precondition is satisfied, then the action may be taken;

Rule 4 If the precondition is not satisfied, then the action must not be taken.

In example (1) the action to be taken is drinking alcohol and the precondition is being over eighteen. Rule 4, for example, is supposed to be applied in a selection task containing this conditional in the following way. A card stating or implying that someone was not over eighteen would evoke this rule by making its antecedent true, and then the subjects would employ the rule to infer that the other side of the card must not state or imply that the action was taken.

This schema is clearly only intended as an account of how people reason with one particular type of deontic conditional; it does not apply to other types nor, of course, to non-conditional deontic reasoning. Cheng and Holyoak also recognize that it does not fully apply even to that one particular case. They themselves point out that there can be more than one precondition for an action in some contexts. In some American states, another precondition for drinking alcohol could be, to use their example, that one does not have a recent drink-driving violation. In these contexts, we should *not* infer, using Rule 3, that the action may be taken if one precondition is satisfied. But that means that it is unclear what Cheng and Holyoak expect to happen in these other cases, which after all are quite common. Is a more complex schema to be evoked, or a combination of schemas?

The schema itself contains deontic terms such as 'must' and 'may', which we are not told the meanings of, nor the function of in a mental or computational system based on the schema. Cheng and Holyoak (1985) state that the rules in the schema give rise to 'useful heuristics rather than strictly valid inferences' (p. 397). But in order to get straight about the meanings of deontic terms, and to provide a concept of validity for deontic reasoning, we need more than *pragmatic* schemas – we need a semantics. Cheng and Holyoak could rightly say that the whole point of their work is to account for the pragmatics of violating deontic conditionals. It certainly could be argued that the notion of violation is, in a sense, a pragmatic one, in that it rests on a concept of truth or acceptability for deontic statements, and is highly context-sensitive. Only people can violate deontic statements by their behaviour in particular contexts. Someone must think of these statements as true for the possibility of a violation to arise, but exactly what one says about a possible violation can depend on whether there is an excuse or mitigating circumstance for the behaviour in the given context. The fact that this pragmatic level rests on a semantic one is all the more reason to get down to the underlying level.

Another reason for studying the semantics of deontic discourse is to take the first, and most important, step towards an account of rational deontic inference, and an answer to the question of whether ordinary people's deontic reasoning is generally rational. Without at least starting to get clear about this semantics, we could not, for one thing, even hope to answer the question of whether any heuristics people might have for deontic reasoning are basically rational.

Unfortunately, there is no generally accepted normative theory of deontic reasoning. There is not even a generally accepted deontic logic, occupying the role for deontic reasoning that classical propositional logic occupies for extensional reasoning. Indeed, we doubt that there is just one 'correct' deontic logic, to be applied to all types of practical reasoning in any context. Trying to settle all the controversies in this area is way beyond the scope of this chapter. But we hope to indicate the general framework we intend to use to compare how people should conduct their deontic reasoning with how they actually do so. (See Chellas, 1980; Jackson, 1985; and Åqvist, 1986, for a range of deontic logics and their semantics. Again, we doubt that just one of these is the 'correct' one to be applied in all circumstances.)

Of course, empirical work on deontic reasoning should not be held up until all controversies are resolved in the normative theory of it, if that ever happens, which is unlikely. How people reason deontically is of independent interest, whether they do so well or badly. We are anyway able to recognize, with some understanding of the basic semantics, that certain instances of deontic inference are rational, and investigate if people perform these when it is appropriate to do so (Manktelow and Over, 1991). And as has always been the case in research on reasoning, however informal, investigating how people actually reason can sometimes help us to see how they should reason.

DEONTIC SEMANTICS

We have indicated elsewhere the basic semantic framework we intend to use to guide our research on deontic reasoning (Manktelow and Over, 1990a, b). There is much work to do, and controversies to try to settle, in the detailed semantics of deontic discourse. Our object is not to discuss the details, as yet, nor even to introduce the semantics directly, but rather to explain its psychological interest. For it suggests a way people might try to determine whether a deontic statement about actions is to be taken as true or acceptable in some sense. Not all deontic statements are, in fact, about actions, but we shall restrict ourselves to these, which could hardly be of greater importance. We shall not discuss, in this chapter, deontic conjunctions, disjunctions, or, for the most part, negations, about which there are special controversies, and shall also primarily consider here deontic thought about whether or not to perform a single action, rather than one out of a range of actions. The best way to introduce our general framework is to consider first an example of a simple non-conditional deontic statement:

(2) Alcohol should be totally banned.

Let us imagine a State legislature in America in which this statement is made. Some legislators might shout 'true', others 'false'. There are philosophers who hold that ordinary people should not say that deontic statements are true or false; what apparently could be said is these statements are, say, 'acceptable' or 'unacceptable'. But people do actually use 'true' and 'false' in this way, and it does not really matter in the semantics which words we use to mark the distinction which undoubtedly exists.

The general sort of semantics we accept suggests the following procedure for trying to decide whether or not we ourselves find (2) true (or acceptable). We imagine a relevant state of affairs in which alcohol is banned and compare it with one in which it is not banned. There is potentially just as much drinking in the former, we may think likely, as in the latter, but much more crime. On that basis, we prefer the latter to the former, and conclude that (2) is false (or unacceptable). It may be that other people prefer the former to the latter, perhaps on purely religious grounds. But it is our preferences which determine what we say and how we act.

Clearly, the point of the kind of semantics we are relying on is not to establish that there are objective deontic facts. It is perfectly consistent with the view that deontic statements are true or false only in a subjective sense, based on preferences which do not correspond to any physical relationship. Of course, in a proper presentation of the semantics itself for a normative theory of deontic logic, we would insist that the preference relation satisfy certain conditions, for example, that it be transitive. But the preference relation of ordinary people may, at times, not be transitive, and that would make their deontic judgements subjective in an even more radical sense. Some psychologists, particularly Tversky (1969), have investigated the preference relation of ordinary people and found it to be intransitive in some cases. This work has been done in the context of studying ordinary decision making, and it is not known how this apparent lack of transitivity may affect ordinary deontic reasoning. This is one point where research on this reasoning must be related to that on actual decision making.

Technically, we say that people are expressing subjective *utility* judgements when they indicate their preferences (whether or not their preference relation satisfies the conditions it should); and we say that people who indicate their degree of confidence or belief in a proposition, such as that drinking alcohol will damage their health, are expressing subjective *probability* judgements. Psychologists have also studied ordinary people's subjective probability judgements, and how these combine with their subjective utility judgements to affect ordinary decision making. *If* these degrees of belief and preferences satisfy certain standard normative principles, such as consistency in the case of belief and transitivity in that of preference, then their strengths can be represented by numbers, on a ratio and an interval scale, respectively, and some normative decision theory can be applied to work out which decisions should be taken.

People can be said to be rational, relative to this normative theory, when their beliefs and preferences satisfy the principles. They will then make rational decisions by acting to maximize expected utility, which is what one gets by multiplying the subjective utility of a possible outcome by its subjective probability. For example, we will rationally decide whether to get drunk or stay sober by taking into account how likely we think we are to get sick in the former case, and how much we prefer not to be sick, i.e. by taking into account the expected utility of our becoming sick. But when these normative principles are *not* fully satisfied by people's beliefs and preferences, psychological research is necessary to give us a descriptive theory of their probability and utility judgements and resulting decision making, which may not always maximize expected utility as defined in the normative theory. By comparing the normative theory with an account of people's actual behaviour, we can hope to assess how rational they tend to be in their decision making.

An obvious question at this point is how far people's ordinary deontic reasoning helps them to maximize expected utility, or at least to achieve reasonably satisfying outcomes. Parallel to this descriptive question, there is also the normative one of the relation between valid deontic reasoning about actions and maximizing utility in the choice of them. These are very large questions which we can only hope to clarify and stress the importance of in this chapter. We can do this by comparing further rational decision making and valid deontic reasoning; and to do that, we must say more about the general semantics of deontic statements and people's understanding of it. Once we have specified a deontic notion of truth, we can define a valid deontic argument as one which preserves truth in this sense; and then we can start to discuss logical relationships properly.

As an example, consider the logical relation between obligation and permission statements. Suppose that we compare a relevant state of affairs in which we have a social drink with one in which we do not drink alcohol at all. We decide (as might have been predicted by those who know us) that we do *not* prefer the latter to the former. A social drink is more pleasurable than abstinence, and is unlikely to make us sick or otherwise damage our health. Following the broad type of semantics we are using, we would then conclude that we *may* have a social drink. This permission statement logically implies that a certain obligation statement does *not* hold, namely, that we should abstain from social drinking. Given a certain kind of preference relation, this type of semantics makes permission and obligation operators *duals* (in the technical sense) of each other, and also ensures that what is obligatory is permissible.

The logical relation of duality is fundamental in most deontic logics, but whether ordinary people always conform to it in their deontic reasoning, and how this affects the rationality of their decision making, has not been tested in proper empirical research, as far as we know. To do so would mean seeing how negation and the deontic concepts were used together, which would anyway be interesting. One might even ask whether obligation and permission should be taken as duals in *all* contexts – this is a question which comes up in connection with moral dilemmas, which we discuss briefly below. But we must leave these questions to future empirical and normative research, and move on to the logical relation between conditional permission and obligation. This is necessary to assess fully the work of Cheng and Holyoak, and to discuss properly whether people perform rational inferences when confronted with deontic conditionals.

Consider (1) again, and suppose that we want to decide whether to assert it is true, given the type of semantics we are presupposing. We begin with a relevant state of affairs in which people drink alcohol, and then compare a more fully specified possible state in which only people over eighteen drink with one in which younger people drink as well. We find that we prefer the former to the latter, perhaps on health grounds, or perhaps because of the law of the land, and so decide that (1) is true. The procedure used here is essentially the same as we would use for this example:

(3) If you start to feel ill when drinking alcohol, then you must stop immediately.

We now begin with a possible state of affairs in which people feel ill when drinking alcohol, and go on to compare a further one in which they stop drinking immediately with one in which they do not do this. We prefer the former to the latter, on health grounds or because there is a law against being drunk, and thus decide that (3) is true. Both (1) and (3) are conditional obligations, with essentially the same semantics, and yet Cheng and Holyoak would call (1) a permission statement and (3) an obligation statement, and claim that there are different mental schemas for their interpretation. (See also Cheng *et al.*, 1986.)

The following is an example of what is properly called a conditional permission:

(4) If alcohol is prescribed for you by a doctor, then you may drink it.

For the evaluation of this, the first possible state of affairs to consider is obviously one in which people are prescribed alcohol by a doctor. From that point, we compare a further possibility in which people take the alcohol so prescribed with one in which they do not. We do *not* prefer the latter to the former, as no laws are broken in either, and the people's health tends to be at least as good in the former as the latter – on that basis, we agree that (4) is true. The semantics we have relied on here clearly distinguishes (4), the conditional permission, from (1) and (3), the conditional obligations.

Rule 3 in Cheng and Holyoak's permission schema is a proper conditional permission, but as we have pointed out, they themselves admit, in effect, that it does logically follow from what they call a 'permission statement', which is really a conditional obligation. The semantics we have sketched explains why this is so. We might accept the truth of (1), but some people who are over eighteen do not satisfy other conditions we think important for drinking alcohol, and we would actually prefer them not to drink. That would mean that we took the instance of Rule 3 in this case to be false. Cheng and Holyoak, we do admit, wish to work at the pragmatic level, but a complete and accurate classification of deontic conditionals and their logical relations requires a semantics.

Cheng and Holyoak and their collaborators do give reasons for distinguishing, at some point, the likes of (1) and (3). They point out that conditionals like (1) could be thought of as having the form 'If action A is to be taken then precondition B must be satisfied', which could be expressed using the form 'Action A is to be taken only if precondition B is satisfied'. We can say that one is to drink alcohol only if one is over eighteen, and there is certainly something wrong with saying that one is to feel ill when one is drinking alcohol only if one is to see a doctor. But this is a distinction to be accounted for in a combined semantics for deontic concepts, tense, terms referring to actions, and the various conditional forms of natural language, including the grammatical difference one should note between the antecedents of (1) and (3). We would add that whether a consequent expresses a precondition can be a highly contextual matter, as in this example (after one in the classic paper of Johnson-Laird *et al.*, 1972):

If a letter is sealed, then a 5d stamp must be on it.

Cheng and Holyoak (1985) themselves say that a deontic conditional can be what they call a 'permission' or an obligation, depending on whether the antecedent refers to a desired action under the control of the agent or to a condition independent of the agent's will. For the latter, one could imagine a kind of assembly line where letters are passed sealed or unsealed to a worker, who then has to decide which denomination of stamp to place on them. For the former, there is the standard case in which people want to seal their own letters, for the sake of privacy, and are willing to pay for it by satisfying a monetary precondition. (But one might ask why they cannot put the stamp on after they seal the letter and before they post it. The distinction is just hard to apply in some cases.) This distinction is, then, a pragmatic one, and yet that between a conditional permission and a conditional obligation is semantic.

DETACHMENT

One point in Cheng *et al.* (1986) calls for close study, which it has yet to receive. They hold that, in deontic selection tasks, even fewer subjects make the mistake of failing to choose a card showing that the antecedent of the conditional is true than in the abstract tasks. In our example of the latter, a few subjects fail to choose a card showing a vowel, in order to see if there is an even number on the other side. But in our first example of a deontic selection task, significantly fewer subjects would fail (if Cheng *et al.* are right) to turn over a receipt for over £30, to see if it were signed on the back. Cheng *et al.* take this as indicating that fewer people fail to apply, or even fail to accept the validity of, modus ponens in deontic selection tasks than in abstract ones.

On the face of it, this would be a curious result, since philosophers and deontic logicians have for a long time argued about the standing of modus ponens, or 'detachment' as it is generally called, in deontic reasoning. In other words, if many philosophers and logicians are right, there should be a *greater* tendency for people *not* to apply modus ponens, or detachment, with deontic conditionals than with indicative conditionals. This view of deontic conditionals compares them closely with conditional probability. We may be aware of the general truth that, given that you smoke, you are probably damaging your health. But when we learn that you are someone who smokes, we might not, with justice, infer that you are probably damaging your health. It depends on what else we know or have learned about you. If we know, for instance, that you may have been lucky in your genes, in that your parents and grandparents were heavy smokers who lived to a ripe old age, then we perhaps should not conclude that you are probably damaging your health. If we learned this fact about your genes after inferring the conclusion, then we would perhaps withdraw it and our advice to you to give up smoking. We would, however, still hold on to the general truth, which can be given good support by sampling the reference class consisting of all smokers.

It is important to investigate when ordinary people use detachment in probabilistic reasoning, and to discuss whether they do so rationally or not. The latter is a particularly tricky question, as it is open to debate exactly when they should use detachment in that reasoning. We can hardly be satisfied with merely saying, quite vaguely, that they should do so when they have taken into account all the relevant information they have or could reasonably acquire. This is one of the places in this chapter where we have to admit that we know neither exactly how people should reason nor how they actually do reason. But here we want to develop further some points we have made before about deontic reasoning and detachment (Manktelow and Over, 1990a). Consider the following argument:

If you continue to smoke, then you ought to smoke cigars.
You will continue to smoke.
You ought to smoke cigars.

The logical and semantic question about detachment is whether the conclusion above is always true given the premises. This is *not* the same as the 'pragmatic' question whether there is necessarily a violation of the first premise when it and the second premise are true, but the designated person continues to smoke cigarettes. Note that the conclusion has to be true for there to be a violation of it; there is no violation if it is false that the person ought to smoke cigars.

As we have also pointed out above, what we say about a possible violation can depend on the context. Accepting the two premises above, *and* inferring the conclusion, we may still not blame some people in some cases for continuing to smoke cigarettes – perhaps they are very young and being encouraged, or even forced, to smoke cigarettes by their peers. For this reason, subjects may not always be so keen to spot violators in a deontic selection task, *pace* Cheng and Holyoak. This could happen when the background story for the task suggests that possible violators have a good excuse for not doing what they should, perhaps as a result of the excuse changing the perceived utilities. Normative theorists would have to admit that they do not have a full account of when apparent violators have good excuses for not conforming to deontic rules. But then cognitive psychologists, as descriptive theorists, have not yet investigated at all when ordinary people tend to infer that apparent violators have good excuses.

Inference about violation is a very important case of non-monotonic reasoning which has received little attention from cognitive scientists. We may use the above argument to infer that some man ought to smoke cigars; and if he carries on smoking cigarettes, we may infer further that he is a violator in serious breach of what he ought to do. But then suppose we acquire more information about him: he is elderly and has been heavily addicted to cigarette smoking for many years. Perhaps that supplies a good excuse for his behaviour, and we 'take back' our inference that he is a serious violator. According to classical extensional logic, there is no justification for withdrawing conclusions when more information is added to the premises: this is what it means to say that this logic is monotonic. But deontic reasoning about violation does not have this property, and conclusions about violations can be withdrawn, or at least somehow 'softened', when more information is added to the premises.

Notice that we have just shown above, in a similar way, that probabilistic reasoning is also non-monotonic; and there is all the more reason to study this aspect of it as it is so intimately connected with deontic reasoning. Of course, we are never so free with excuses as when our own behaviour is in question, and we certainly do not like to think of ourselves in serious breach of our obligations. This tendency to make excuses for ourselves is connected with the traditional moral problem of 'weakness of the will' – our failure to do what we ought to because of some weakness (in some sense which has to be explained) on our part. How this tendency of dubious rationality affects our ability to maximize expected utility in our behaviour needs to be investigated scientifically. (See Johnson-Laird and Byrne, 1991, for one psychological theory of non-monotonic reasoning, though they do not cover deontic reasoning; and Audi, 1989, on weakness of the will.)

Let us now take up the distinct logical and semantic question about the above argument and detachment. Some philosophers and logicians have claimed that people may rightly reject the above conclusion as false even though they continue to accept the premises. They might accept these, but still insist that what you really ought to do is to give up smoking completely. However, in our view, it is essential to identify the proposition that is expressed by the conclusion: if that is not the same as what is expressed by the consequent in the first premise, then there is equivocation and so no counter-example to detachment. To evaluate the first premise, we would assume you were a smoker and then ask whether your smoking cigars was to be preferred to your smoking cigarettes. The answer to that question is 'yes' if the first premise is true. Now to evaluate the conclusion given this *and* the assumption that you will continue to smoke, we must ask again whether smoking cigars is to be preferred to smoking cigarettes. The answer will be 'yes' given the premises, and this in no way conflicts with the claim that not smoking at all is to be preferred even to smoking cigars.

We can consistently accept the proposition expressed by the conclusion above given the premises, and the proposition that no-one should smoke at all. Deontic sentences can be used to express preferences, but which preferences they express depend, in part, on what assumptions are made. The assumptions help to determine which possible states are compared for the purpose of expressing, in effect, a preference in a deontic proposition. As there is no conflict between saying that cigar smoking is preferred to cigarette smoking, but not smoking at all is preferred to both, there is no conflict between holding the above conclusion under its assumptions and asserting at the same time, under no assumptions, that no-one should smoke at all. There is thus no need, in our view, to reject detachment as a valid rule for the propositions expressed in inferences. But this view implies that one and the same deontic *sentence*, such as the conclusion we have just referred to, may express different deontic *propositions* depending on whether or not it is used under assumptions.

One problem this view leaves us with is how we take account of this distinction in deontic logic. We cannot have detachment as a valid inference form in such a logic for sentences, in which we cannot distinguish the different propositions expressed by the same deontic sentence under varying assumptions. Without detachment as a valid form in the logic, we would have to try to state principles for applying the logic and using detachment in some contexts but not others, just as we must do for conditional probability.

The application of this logic for deontic sentences would then be non-monotonic, since we might withdraw an instance of detachment as a result of learning more about some context, for example, taking back the *sentence* 'You ought to smoke cigars' on learning that someone can easily give up smoking completely. On the other hand, it may be possible to set up a deontic logic in which the *propositions* expressed by deontic sentences can be distinguished, and hence in which detachment is a valid form. Going along with this is the problem of how people actually distinguish and keep track of the different propositions expressed by deontic sentences under different assumptions. These problems are ones for future work. What we want to do now is to raise questions about detachment and rationality.

An obvious point is that one cannot both smoke cigars and give up smoking completely. What advice should we give someone who is trying to choose between these actions? Should we assume that he is going to carry on smoking something, and advise him to smoke cigars? Or should we not make this assumption and press him to give up smoking completely? To put the matter another way, should we use detachment or give up the second premise as the basis of our advice? By doing the latter, we are refusing to make the assumption that the person will continue to smoke, perhaps because we think he can give up smoking easily and intend to press him to do so. If we accept the normative principle that having an obligation to do something implies having the ability to do it, then we will not say that this man ought to give up smoking completely when he definitely cannot do so. But whether an ability exists, and to what degree it exists, can be far from a cut-and-dried matter. It might be extremely costly for the man to give up smoking completely, in terms of suffering withdrawal symptoms, and so best for him to smoke cigars. Even if giving up completely would maximize his expected utility, perhaps we should not expect such a high degree of rationality from him, but should accept that he would be fairly rational by smoking just cigars.

The problem can appear even more acute from the man's subjective view. Does he himself accept the above argument, or ask seriously whether he *should* continue to make the second premise true, i.e. carry on smoking? Reasoning about the latter question could conceivably lead him to consider more and more arguments and premises about which he has to ask similar questions (on this sort of problem, see Smith, 1991). As his time and energy are no doubt of some utility to him, he should perhaps cut the process short and smoke cigars as the reasonable course of action. In more technical terms, he would put a bound on the amount of reasoning he would be willing to devote to the problem, giving him what has been called 'bounded rationality'. (We say more about this subject below, but see Simon, 1957, 1983, for his important notion of bounded rationality.)

Note, as well, that there is a difficulty here about the connection between valid deontic reasoning and maximizing expected utility. Validly inferring that he should smoke cigars (rather than cigarettes) given certain assumptions may not maximize his expected utility if he should not make those assumptions, but look for other options which might have greater utility for him. Only how does he infer whether he should invest the time and energy looking for or considering other possible options? We should certainly try to get a better idea of how people should reason, and do tend to reason, in this kind of case, but it seems most unlikely that we shall be able to justify a unique answer to the normative question. At best, we can only hope to supply generally useful heuristics for deciding roughly how long one should think about a deontic problem.

RATIONALITY IN DEONTIC SELECTION TASKS

Before going further into the great difficulties of constructing adequate normative and descriptive theories of deontic reasoning, let us return to the relative simplicity of the selection task. We have reported that people do seem to make rational decisions in certain deontic selection tasks. Taking up yet again our first example of such a task, most subjects choose the cards indicating that a purchase has exceeded £30 and that a receipt has not been signed on the back. In other words, subjects seem to be looking for violators of the rule that, if a purchase exceeds £30, then the receipt for it must have the appropriate signature on the back. Given this rule, subjects do choose a receipt indicating a purchase of, say, £75, at least implicitly using detachment to infer that there must be a signature on the back of it. Moreover, given the rule and an unsigned receipt, they apparently infer that this card should also be chosen to see if it records a purchase for more than £30 on the other side. These are just the cards which should rationally be selected on any reasonable analysis of the task. Even for someone who has doubts about the use of detachment sometimes for deontic conditionals, these are just the cards which will reveal any violations of the rule in this particular context, and the scenario of that context in no way suggests that there could be any excuse for violations.

Why are subjects so good at this type of deontic selection task? We can explain our view more fully, and in a more general way, by referring to a fairly abstract deontic selection task devised by Cheng and Holyoak (1985). They found that subjects do reasonably well in this task, in which the rule merely states the requirement of an 'authority' that a 'precondition P' must be satisfied if an 'action A' is to be taken. The important point here is the reference to authority – authorities are associated with legitimacy or power, and are often people who can apply sanctions if we do not do what they require of us. Many subjects grasp, in our view, that action A with P is to be preferred to A without P, because of what the 'authority' says, and this helps their performance on this selection task, in which they are asked, as usual, to find violations of the rule. These are cases of A without P, which are what the subjects generally tend to look for. From the context, the subjects know that these are cases in which one may fall foul of an 'authority' and thus suffer some cost. That makes these cases salient; and in more technical terms, being able to discover such cases, which would be the first step towards correcting them, would be necessary for maximizing utility, or at least avoiding expected costs of a serious nature. In summary, people can make sense of a deontic task by representing subjective utilities in quite an abstract way, and this can improve the rationality of their practical reasoning.

Rather than presenting the semantics for deontic statements directly, we have described how people may try to discover that such statements are true, given this semantics. This approach strongly suggests that people use what Johnson-Laird (1983) calls mental models for this purpose. If so, then when considering whether action A ought to be performed, people construct a mental model of the result of performing A and also one of the result of not doing so. If they prefer the former state or outcome to the latter, perhaps out of self-interest, or on wider moral grounds, they conclude that they ought to perform A. Given a conditional of the general form we have discussed in the last paragraph, people construct a mental model of the result of doing A with P satisfied and one of doing A without P satisfied. If they prefer the former to the latter, perhaps because of what an authority has said, or for any other reason, then they will conclude that P must be satisfied if they are to perform action A. (We cannot pursue here the point that the deontic 'must', at least in some uses, seems stronger than 'ought to', but we hold that this difference in use depends on how strongly an outcome is preferred.)

Such preferences allow us to speak of differences in subjective utility among outcomes. Our view is that grasping clear differences of this type can help subjects to construct appropriate mental models for deontic reasoning. In opposition to this, Johnson-Laird and Byrne (1992) doubt that subjects are ever helped to solve deontic selection tasks, in particular, because such differences are expressed in the scenarios; and they present their own account of how mental models are used in deontic reasoning. This is based on the idea that people classify possible situations in deontic reasoning as either permissible or impermissible. But their proposal is incomplete, in that it does not explain why people make this classification.

To provide this explanation, in our view, one must take account of the fact that people have preferences, leading them to represent some states of affairs as permissible and others as impermissible. Unless people prefer one outcome to another, say, out of self-interest or respect for an authority, they will not make this distinction. We can also show that the presence or absence of definite differences of subjective utility can be important in deontic selection tasks. Consider the following conditional permission:

(5) If your number is 75 then you may write a G on your card.

This rule can be embedded in two different deontic selection tasks which we call ones of weak preference and of strong preference. For a task of weak preference, we simply tell the subjects that some people have been given (5) as a rule about which numbers are allowed to appear with which letters on cards. There is no reference to an authority who has laid down (5) as a rule, nor is any other explicit reason given in a scenario for preferring some number and letter combinations to others. Merely from the presupposed fact that someone has gone to the trouble of asserting (5), one might infer that someone or other has some reason or other for preferring some combinations to others; but this is a weak conclusion to come to.

The subjects are presented with representations of cards showing 75, 55, G, and N, and asked which of these would have to be turned over to see whether anyone has broken the rule. What should they do from the normative point of view, assuming only that (5) is taken to be true by some person or other, whose point of view they are asked to take? One can only conclude, given the semantics of conditional permission, that a card with a 75 on one side and an N on the other is *not* preferred by that person to one with a 75 on one side and a G on the other. Of course, from this information alone one may not infer that any cards should be turned over, and indeed we find no significant pattern in the subjects' responses (see Manktelow and Over, 1992). In contrast, Johnson-Laird and Byrne would hold that (5) makes impermissible a state of affairs in which there is not a 75 on a card but a G on it. This cannot be right semantically, as there could be other ways of getting permission to place a G on a card, and is not upheld in subjects' responses in the task of weak preference we have just described.

In a task of strong preference, we tell the subjects that one side of a card shows how high a score a student has got on a test, and that a G on the other side means that the student is eligible for a prize. The subjects are told further that students have been given (5) as a rule for writing letters on their cards, but that they may have cheated when doing this. Thus the *context* suggests that the only way the students can get permission to put a G on their cards is by getting a 75. The subjects are again asked to indicate which cards would have to be turned over to see whether anyone has broken the rule. Now with this richer context, more can be said from the normative point of view, especially with background information about people's general preferences.

Most people obviously greatly prefer not to be cheated in ordinary contexts. Cosmides (1989) has given evolutionary reasons why this is perhaps a universal fact about people, and has shown experimentally that subjects are keen to spot cheaters. Moreover, we must distinguish two social roles or perspectives in this kind of case, as we have shown in a previous paper (see Manktelow and Over, 1991; also Gigerenzer and Hug, 1992, on cheating and perspectives). There is the role of the 'agent' who lays down the rule, and that of the 'actor' who is supposed to conform to it. In our present example, some school authority is presupposed as the agent, and the students are the actors. The authority has its preferences, and the students theirs; and these must be adequately represented and kept separate if the example is to be properly understood.

From the point of view of the authority, students who do not have a score of 75 on one side of their cards, but still write G on the other side, are cheaters. The authority cannot maximize utility, in this simple example, if it cannot spot cheaters. Our prediction was that, when cued to the view or role of the authority, subjects would look for this combination by choosing a card without a score of 75 on it and one with a G showing on it. By doing this, they have a chance of uncovering cheaters and preventing the cost of giving them prizes they do not deserve. This prediction was clearly upheld in the results, marking a significant difference between this case of strong preference and the above weak one. Johnson-Laird and Byrne do not predict this difference between the two cases, and could only account for it by extending their mental models with representations of social roles and associated subjective utilities. (For more on this, see Johnson-Laird and Byrne, 1992; and Manktelow and Over, 1992.)

RATIONAL PREFERENCES

In the type of deontic selection task so far studied, subjects tend to perform rational inferences and make rational choices, given an appropriate question about a scenario expressing strong preferences. That does not mean, of course, that subjects will always combine valid deontic reasoning and acting to maximize the subjective utility of a view they are asked to take in any deontic task, given an appropriate question. There is already some evidence that subjects are more sensitive to possible costs than to possible benefits in these tasks (Manktelow and Over, 1990b). We do not yet know how subjects will perform when a scenario is less straightforward, as when it raises the possibility that 'violators' may have good excuses for doing what they do, or when it appears that the points of view in the task may have incoherent preferences. We have already suggested that the former kind of case needs to be studied, and so does the latter. As we have also said above, some research implies that people sometimes fail, for example, to have transitive preferences: they say that they prefer x to y and y to z but not x to z.

There are other ways people are supposed to violate the principles of normative utility theory, and of the probability calculus, and various descriptive accounts of actual preferences and decision making have been proposed. (Kahneman and Tversky, 1979, is a classic example.) People may still perform valid deontic inferences when they, or the views they are asked to adopt in an experiment, have preferences which are unclear, confused, or even inconsistent. But little is known about ordinary deontic reasoning in these circumstances.

Two further points should be made about this issue, however. The fact that people sometimes fail to have consistent or coherent preferences among *objective* states of affairs is one which has to be taken account of in all theories of actual deontic reasoning. People in this unfortunate position will surely also fail to have a consistent or coherent idea of which objective states should be considered permissible or impermissible. It then is hard to see how Johnson-Laird and Byrne's account, as it stands, could be applied. Some schemas may well be invoked in deontic reasoning at some stage, including the pragmatic, but we are not told how this happens when people are confused in this way. For us, this difficulty supports our view that *subjective* mental models must be used at the deepest level in a complete account of actual preferences, deontic discourse, and deontic inference.

The second point is the need for some caution in interpreting results that are sometimes taken to show that people can be highly inconsistent or incoherent in their preferences. Kahneman and Tversky discuss a famous experiment in which they asked subjects to:

> Imagine yourself on the way to a Broadway play with a pair of tickets for which you have paid $40. On entering the theater you discover that you have lost the tickets. Would you pay $40 for another pair of tickets? Now imagine you are on your way to the same play without having bought tickets. On entering the theater you realise that you have lost $40 in cash. Would you now buy the tickets?
>
> (Kahneman and Tversky, 1982)

Kahneman and Tversky claim that, from the objective point of view, these two questions should be answered in the same way, but find that subjects tend to say that they would prefer to buy the tickets in the second case but not in the first. They infer that subjects have two different representations, or as we might say, mental models, of what should be treated as the same in objective terms: in both cases one has to decide whether to spend $40 to see a play after losing $40. But is this really so? After all, in the former case, one is arguably being cheated by the theatre – it is getting the benefit of (your) $80 for tickets which are only worth $40. One could at least claim that the theatre is being unfair in making an excessive profit, and in not fulfilling its obligation to give you seats for the $40 you paid.

In this respect, this example is like another described by Kahneman and Tversky (1982). Subjects tend to say that they would make a 20-minute drive to another store to save $5 on a calculator costing $15, but not to save $5 on a jacket costing $125. Kahneman and Tversky do not, in fact, claim that it is irrational to act in this way, but they do not note a possible rational reason for making the distinction. A store which charges $15 for an item on sale elsewhere for $10 may be making an unfair profit, and this could probably not be said about a store charging $125 for something on sale elsewhere for $120. It might not maximize utility to deal generally with a supplier of goods or services who would be unfair in this way; and by not dealing with such suppliers, it might be possible to change their pricing policy. Anyway, possible cheating or unfairness, and not just money, are relevant in such examples, as so far investigated. Further manipulations might, of course, remove these possibilities, but might also reveal interesting facts about how such choices are made in ordinary dynamic affairs, in which people have different perspectives and stand to gain or lose in different ways.

Research on the selection task has rightly moved away from conditionals about static states of affairs, as in the early abstract tasks, to rules embedded in scenarios about dynamic activities where there are different social relationships. Some of these even concern monetary gains and losses, and provide a kind of bridge between research on reasoning and that on decision making of the sort we have just discussed (Manktelow and Over, 1991). For these scenarios, we have referred to three standards of rationality: valid deontic inference; maximizing subjective utility in decision making; and at the deepest level, which links the other two, rational preference. The deepest problems arise when we try to say what rational preference is. The question of what properties the preference relation should have, as defined for each individual, is deeply connected with serious controversies among deontic logicians. (See, for example, Åqvist, 1986; and Almeida, 1990.)

There is also controversy among decision theorists about exactly what normative utility theory should or should not require of the preference relation. Kahneman and Tversky (1982), for example, conclude their paper by saying that it is unclear whether the tendencies they have observed 'should be treated as errors or biases or whether they should be accepted as valid elements of human experience'. More generally, to hold that people should *always* get themselves into a position in which they know of all the options completely within their power, and coherently order these in some way, is to set an impossibly high standard. It is indeed as unreasonable as assuming that people could devote unlimited time to trying to work out which of those options maximized expected utility. *If* this were possible, then perhaps we could recommend that people use, in all circumstances, just one deontic logic and one effective procedure for decison making. As that is an irrationally high ideal, we must work with the notion of bounded rationality, and even doubt that, in any given context, there is just one bound or limit which must, or may, be set on the time spent in practical reasoning. On this point we do not have to appeal to evidence from artificial experiments such as those we have reviewed so far: support can be given to this view by considering problems of deontic reasoning in fully dynamic activities and social settings.

DEONTIC CONFLICTS AND DILEMMAS

Cognitive psychologists have, in general, gone beyond the restricted study of abstract reasoning, and towards experiments calling for ordinary reasoning about realistic matters. But in one respect at least, the scenarios of experiments on deontic reasoning have remained unrealistic, being too neat and tidy, without a hint of conflicting desires, and so of reasons or excuses for not conforming to given rules. It is extremely important, however, to understand deontic conflicts and dilemmas, and not just for theoretical reasons, as we shall see. Most of the work on these problems has been done by social psychologists, philosophers, economists, and others generally interested in decision making and game theory. We can only discuss here some examples relevant to what we have said above about deontic reasoning.

Let us look at two broad examples of individual conflict or dilemma: the 'cost-spiral' conflict, and the potential clash between short-term and long-term utility. The former goes under various names: entrapment in escalating conflicts (Brockner and Rubin, 1985), the sunk-cost trap (Baron, 1988), the Concorde fallacy (Dawkins and Carlisle, 1976), or colloquially, throwing good money after bad. The last two reveal the nature of the problem: people are inclined to commit more resources to a project to the extent that they have already committed resources. Thus the British and French governments in the 1960s continued to fund the development of their supersonic airliner, Concorde, long after it became apparent that it was, to put it mildly, not going to be an economic proposition. There is no reason to be smug about this – any of us might continue for too long to pay out for repairs on a troublesome car.

People thus become caught in a spiral of escalating cost, and incur greater losses than they would have if they had cancelled the project earlier. This becomes a cognitive 'trap' when certain properties are apparent: there are repeated, irretrievable investments, uncertainty as to the achievement of the goal of these investments, and crucially, a choice between continuing and curtailing investments (Brockner and Rubin, 1985). The word 'investment' here refers generally to what has utility, and not just to money: other sorts of investment are possible, such as in time, effort, or emotional commitment. There are investments of time and energy in reasoning, and so this conflict is closely related to a problem we discussed above. How much time and energy should we invest in trying to infer what we should do? Any of us can become like Hamlet if we continue to throw good reasoning time after bad.

At first blush, this looks like a prima-facie case of irrationality: people are clearly acting in ways which diminish rather than enhance utility, as costs pile up and a point is reached at which these costs will outweigh any subsequent gains which result from achieving the goal. But however irrational this behaviour is in particular cases, there remains the normative problem of stating general rules, if only of thumb, for avoiding or breaking out of it. Moreover, psychological research in this area shows that one has to be careful about what the subjective utilities are.

A factor which we have not considered hitherto emerges in this context: Brockner and Rubin present convincing empirical evidence that subjective utility *changes* as the conflict deepens. For instance, the tendency to persist in fruitless investment is powerfully influenced by social factors such as self-presentation: people will act in such a way as to show themselves in what they consider to be their best light in front of others. They will try to save face, in other words. Of course, this can sometimes promote escape from the sunk-cost trap, if the perceived prevailing social value is for escape rather than persistence. In addition, it seems that social approval rapidly becomes more important than economic outcome as the trap proceeds: people increasingly prefer the former to the latter, perhaps out of a felt need to rationalize their conduct. Note as well that people who expend much effort on reasoning about what they ought to do have a kind of limited excuse for making the wrong decision: they did at least try hard.

Consistent with what we have said above, however, persistence in the trap is often characterized by a lack of accurate representation of what its costs actually are; in the argot of Johnson-Laird and Byrne's (1991) theory of mental models, people do not 'flesh out' their model of what is happening to compute explicitly the costs of persistence and failure. They forget what their limits are and tend to focus on the present rather than the future (a theme to which we shall shortly return). Escape can be facilitated by counteracting these tendencies, i.e. by promoting a fully fleshed-out model of the utility structure. This could be done by encouraging people to set limits on investment, providing role models of prudent and imprudent behaviour, making explicit the precise cost of investments, and establishing the socially desirable value of escape as opposed to persistence. Recent consumer-credit legislation in the UK seems to be based on such considerations, presumably in response to horror stories about people becoming trapped in irresolvable debt spirals: credit offers have to quote the actual annual percentage rate of interest, and the full credit purchase price along with the cash price. But on an individual basis, it is not so easy, as we have pointed out, to set a bound on how much reasoning time one should invest in some deontic problem.

Mention of credit brings us to a second and very powerful form of individual utility trap, which also poses real problems for the ascription of rationality. This is the conflict between short-term and long-term benefits and costs; the conflict, and potential dilemma, occurs when subjective utility dynamically shifts over time. This can be in either direction: an action producing short-term benefit can give rise to longer-term costs, but equally, an action extracting short-term costs can yield benefits in the longer term. As we have seen, sunk-cost traps have some of these qualities, but not all utility-shift dilemmas are sunk-cost traps. (For psychological reviews of these problems, see Platt, 1973, and Edney, 1980.)

Consumer debt spirals are partly an example of this problem; indeed, a major British credit card was introduced to the market in the early 1970s with the slogan that it 'takes the waiting out of wanting'. Access to immediate benefit was thus presented as an unalloyed virtue. The problem is that it is only a virtue in the absence of potential costs in the longer run. These occur when the time comes to pay off the accumulated debt and people find they cannot afford to do so, and thus incur quite steep interest charges, which in turn further increase the debt. Other real-world situations have similar properties, and in some cases can literally be a matter of life and death: Platt (1973) gives the example of the use of addictive drugs, including tobacco, where increments of a short-term 'high' eventually lead to economic and medical debilitation. There are also problems when utilities shift the other way: people sometimes tend not to submit themselves to a short-term cost for the promise of a long-term benefit. Some of us 'forget' our dental appointments, or to make a will, take out a pension plan, or save up for Christmas. Both types occur in their purest form when we think we have definite preferences but act against them, as when a man thinks that he definitely prefers an increased chance of good health to the pleasure of a cigarette, but even so carries on smoking cigarettes.

Scientific explanations of these dilemmas are even more sketchy than for sunk-cost traps, but some ideas have been voiced, ranging from the Skinnerian (Platt, 1973) to the game-theoretic (Colman, 1982). Philosophers have written about these dilemmas since Plato, usually under the heading of weakness of the will, which we referred to above; and for a purely cognitive theory of them, there is perhaps still nothing better than the one given by Plato in the *Protagoras*. The thought expressed there is that such dilemmas result from what would now be called cognitive illusions, closely analogous to visual illusions – benefits and costs are supposed to appear smaller than they really are when distant in time, just as physical objects seem smaller than they actually are when distant in space.

Of course, drug addiction can hardly be thought of as a *purely* cognitive problem, and Aristotle was surely on the right track when he suggested that these dilemmas, in general, result from a combination of faults in practical reasoning and weakness of *willpower* in some sense (see Audi, 1989, for this interpretation). One might wonder how far we have advanced beyond Aristotle in identifying the cognitive faults which, sometimes at least, help to give rise to weakness of the will, and in giving advice on how to avoid or escape from this unhappy state. Baron (1988) quotes the work of Ainslie on self-control as a way of doing this. Ainslie gives four general strategies: extrapsychic devices (e.g. remove the tempting item, commit oneself to a savings scheme); control of attention (to 'take one's mind off it'); control of emotion (trying not to become excited or fearful about some imminent event); and personal rules (cf. New Year resolutions). All these and similar prescriptions seem to have at their core the manipulation of cognitions of utility. The first simply remove or reduce access to the short-term option, while the latter have to do with altering the representation of utility when the option of whether or not to act still exists.

It is unreasonable to demand that people have absolute self-control, even if they do not have a problem as serious as drug addiction. As a matter of fact, we do accept excuses, more generally, from people who are not acting as they should because of weakness of the will, and by doing so we are, in effect, sometimes admitting that these people are reasonably rational. To put the matter in a combination of formal and informal terms, we apparently think it reasonable for people to place a bound on the amount of time and energy they devote to resisting temptation. But we do not have a good normative theory of how this bound ought to be set, and of when excuses referring to it should be given or accepted. Equally, we do not have a good descriptive, scientific account of how such bounds are set, nor of when such excuses are actually given or accepted.

As we have already argued, it is also unreasonable to assume that people can always order the options they have before them in a unique way. Relevant to this point is the topic of moral dilemmas. Suppose some terrorists threaten to shoot an innocent person unless we give them money, which we consider wrong in itself and a potential threat to life in the future. Should we prefer the shooting of the innocent person to giving the money, giving the money to the shooting of the innocent person, or be indifferent between these options? Of course, deontic logic could not give us a specific answer to this question, nor should we expect more general reflections on rationality to do so. The *content* of preferences at this level is surely not the same for all rational people. But can we even insist, in the semantics of deontic logic and so in its formal principles, that this question have an answer? Can we insist in normative decision theory that it have an answer?

Some people might refuse to answer the question, or be unable to in the time they are given to do so. They may say that they do not prefer either option, and cannot even say that one is as good as the other, or hold that they cannot answer the question in the time the terrorists have given them. Just because people cannot state a preference between options, we cannot conclude that they are indifferent in the technical sense. (Note the reluctance of Savage, 1954, Ch. 2, to conclude this.) It is hard to see how logic or decision theory alone can condemn these people as irrational. This is so even if they go so far as to say that they have an obligation to help the innocent person, and an obligation in this case not to do so (as that would mean giving money to terrorists). People in this unfortunate position may need a special deontic logic and decision theory, based on a preference relation which is a partial ordering, to help them in their practical reasoning. Even the relation between obligation and permission may have to be modified in these cases. (See what Chellas (1980) says about moral dilemmas and minimal deontic logic, and Almeida (1990), for an extreme view of the problems moral dilemmas pose for deontic logic.)

SOCIAL DEONTIC CONFLICTS AND DILEMMAS

Individual dilemmas are sometimes closely related to a similar set of dilemmas whose dynamics are inherently social, i.e. their nature comes from social interaction. The sunk-cost trap, for instance, has formal similarities to the 'dollar auction dilemma' expounded by Shubik (1971) as an analogue of certain real-world traps, such as the arms race. In a game version of this dilemma, a banknote is auctioned to the highest bidder. The auction is like the familiar kind, except that there is an additional condition: when the bidding stops, the auctioneer is paid not only the winning bid but also the next highest.

For people playing this game, there are three dilemmas. The first is whether to enter the bidding at all: entering is the way to make a gain, but not entering is the only certain way to avoid loss. The second is when a bid reaches half the value of the note: another bid will lead the auctioneer to make a profit out of the two bidders (this resembles the case of the theatre cheating you by having you buy extra tickets; see p. 248). The third, of course, is when the bid reaches the full value of the note. If the second bidder bids again, he will sustain a loss even if that becomes the winning bid, since the note is now worth less than the bid, but if he declines to bid further, he loses his entire bid – and the other bidder loses nothing.

The connection between this dilemma and the sunk-cost trap should be clear, as should the influence of the competitive social element.

The comparison with Kahneman and Tversky's theatre problem leads one to doubt how close this artificial dilemma actually is to any in the real world. An actual auctioneer who tried this trick would presumably be identified quickly as a potential cheat, who was trying to get something for nothing from the bidders. Outside artificial restrictions, the bidders could quickly agree counter-measures among themselves. It is interesting to compare this dilemma with what could *theoretically* happen to people without transitive preferences, or whose degrees of belief do not satisfy the principles of the probability calculus; such people are easy to find according to some research we have mentioned. In artificial set-ups, it should be possible to turn these people into 'money pumps', or to make a 'Dutch Book' against them. This means that they could be systematically enticed to give up what had utility for them, or into bets which they could not possibly win. But it does not seem easy (though it is not impossible) to get ordinary people to behave like this in dynamic states of affairs in the real world. Part of the explanation of this must lie in the fact that people are usually quick to spot instances of cheating, in which they suffer a cost for nothing in return. (On Dutch Books and cheating, see Manktelow and Over, 1990a; and on money pumps, preference, and descriptive accounts of decision making, see Machina, 1991.)

The most famous game-theoretic dilemma of all, the prisoner's dilemma, can be played in a dynamic or iterated way in a fully social context. A good example of this general form is the commons problem as basically set out by Hardin (1968). Suppose there is a patch of common land available to an agricultural community, i.e. a place where everyone can graze their animals freely. The more animals that use it, the lower will be the benefit to each, since each will have a smaller share of the pasture; if use is unrestricted, the land will be exhausted and everyone will be worse off. An individual farmer has a choice every summer: she can limit her use of the common to the benefit of all, or try to maximize her personal gain by grazing her animals as much as possible. It is sometimes said naïvely that this sort of problem would not arise if only people were more altruistic. But in the abstract form of the dilemma, nothing is said about how the utilities arise: they can come from either selfish or altruistic preferences. The latter do not *necessarily* help, as can be shown in the commons problem. Just suppose that the farmer, out of altruism, prefers to overgraze her neighbour's cows on the common rather than her own, and proceeds to do so. The common land will become just as quickly exhausted if all the other farmers are similarly altruistic.

The shift in utilities here is tied to social perspective: do you act purely as a utility-maximizing individual, or do you act to promote the overall utility of the group, however that is defined, and sublimate your own preferences? There are disputes about what rationality really means in game-theoretic cases, making the normative position even more unclear than we have so far indicated. Though game theory can be said to be part of decision theory in the widest sense, there is controversy about the relation between utility maximization as the basis of rationality and what has been specifically proposed in game theory. This is based on the notion of an *equilibrium* of choices by the players of a game, from which no player can do better by making another choice unilaterally. (On this issue, see Skyrms, 1990.)

More micro-level social situations are also prey to dilemmas of this general sort, as Platt (1973) shows. For instance, there are well-known cases of 'bystander apathy', where someone suffers a misfortune (sometimes even murder) in full view of other people, none of whom does anything to help, or when inconvenience to a large number of people could be removed by one individual act, e.g. removing an obstruction from the road which is causing a traffic jam. Platt calls these cases instances of a 'missing-hero' trap. Loss of utility on the part of an individual is required to secure gain for the group; but if nobody 'acts the hero', each individual can lose, through increasing crime or in endless traffic jams.

One way to try to solve these dilemmas is through explicit agreements or contracts, expressed in rules with sanctions for violators; in other words, to alter the utility structure. The farmers could, for example, agree on a rota for using the common moderately, with fines for those who cheat on this arrangement. When no explicit agreement is possible, because of an inability to communicate or for some other reason, an implicit one may dynamically develop. A farmer could use the common moderately one summer and see what happened, and then try to adjust her behaviour accordingly the next year, retaliating in some way against those who were not so moderate. Initial moderation may be a good idea; but it is not completely clear what overall strategy someone with this sort of problem should adopt, and there may be no uniquely best one.

Little is known, as well, about the cognitive side of actual strategies adopted, in real dilemmas like this, for trying to achieve explicit or implicit agreements. We can predict, however, that these strategies will depend on people's ability to understand rules, and their facility at detecting violators and especially cheaters. Even so, until more is known about these strategies, it will not be possible to assess the extent to which they are rational. (See Axelrod (1984) on the problem of finding good strategies for solving these problems. He discusses the notion of an evolutionarily stable strategy, which is relevant to Cosmides' work on cheating and evolution.)

Moderation is a virtue of much more general importance in deontic reasoning. We have shown in a range of examples how people need to place a bound on this reasoning; to devote too much time and energy to it in the attempt to maximize utility is itself irrational. We should be moderate in our reasoning time as well as our goal, not always attempting to infer what will maximize our subjective utility. We should rather, sometimes at least, try to infer what will satisfy our preferences to a reasonable degree, that is, our modest goal should then be 'satisficing' as it has been called. (See Slote (1989) on this, and for an argument that people often do pursue moderate goals and think of this as rational.) Of course, moderation comes in degrees, and we cannot assume that there will be just one answer to the question of how moderate we should be in any context. It is also true that pious statements about moderation do not get us much closer to good normative and descriptive theories of bound setting.

CONCLUSION

Cognitive psychologists should have a great deal to contribute to the study of practical reasoning, possibly even to a solution of some of the many normative problems which arise for it. This will mean, however, combining research on deontic inference with that on decision making and subjective utility and probability. In our view, it will be necessary to use mental models to get the basic semantics of deontic discourse right, and to explain how people represent preferences, their own and other people's. This will need to be combined with a cognitive account of probability judgements to give us a theory of human decision making in all its individual and social forms. Until we make more progress toward this goal and that of solving, in so far as this is possible, the normative problems, we cannot fully assess the extent to which people are rational in their practical reasoning. There is already experimental evidence, which can be supplemented by evolutionary arguments, that people tend to be fairly good at certain types of deontic inference, especially when performing the right inference can help them to avoid a serious cost, such as might result from getting a serious illness or from being cheated. By finding out *how* people engaged in deontic reasoning set up mental models and other mental representations, flesh them out, manipulate them, and cut the whole process short to try to reach reasonable conclusions efficiently, we might just get some good ideas about how this process *ought* to be conducted. We also know already that ordinary practical reasoning can often be improved, but we will probably not find that there is always just one reasonable way to do this.

REFERENCES

Almeida, M.J. (1990) 'Deontic logic and the possibility of moral conflict', *Erkenntnis* 33: 57–71.
Åqvist, L. (1986) 'Some results on dyadic deontic logic and the logic of preference', *Synthese* 66: 95–110.
Audi, R. (1989) *Practical Reasoning*, London: Routledge.

Axelrod, R. (1984) *The Evolution of Cooperation*, New York: Basic Books.

Baron, J. (1988) *Thinking and Deciding*, Cambridge: Cambridge University Press.

Brockner, J. and Rubin, J.Z. (1985) *Entrapment in Escalating Conflicts*, New York: Springer-Verlag.

Chellas, B.F. (1980) *Modal Logic: An Introduction*, Cambridge: Cambridge University Press.

Cheng, P.W. and Holyoak, K.J. (1985) 'Pragmatic reasoning schemas', *Cognitive Psychology* 17: 391–416.

Cheng, P.W., Holyoak, K.I., Nisbett, R.E., and Oliver, L.M. (1986) 'Pragmatic versus syntactic approaches to training deductive reasoning', *Cognitive Psychology* 18: 293–328.

Colman, A.M. (1982) *Game Theory and Experimental Games*, Oxford: Pergamon Press.

Cosmides, L. (1989) 'The logic of social exchange: has natural selection shaped how humans reason? Studies with Wason's selection task', *Cognition* 31:187–276.

Dawkins, R. and Carlisle, T.R. (1976) 'Parental investment, mate desertion, and a fallacy', *Nature* 262: 131–3.

Edney, J.J. (1980) 'The commons problem: alternative perspectives', *American Psychologist* 35: 131–50.

Gigerenzer, G. and Hug, K. (1992) 'Domain-specific reasoning: social contracts, cheating, and perspective change', *Cognition* 43: 127–71.

Hardin, G.R. (1968) 'The tragedy of the commons', *Science* 162: 1243–8.

Harrison, R. (ed.) (1979) *Rational Action: Studies in Philosophy and Social Science*, Cambridge: Cambridge University Press.

Jackson, F. (1985) 'On the semantics and logic of obligation', *Mind* 94: 177–96.

Johnson-Laird, P.N. (1983) *Mental Models*, Cambridge: Cambridge University Press.

Johnson-Laird, P.N. and Byrne, R.M.J. (1991) *Deduction*, Hove, Sussex: Erlbaum.

—— (1992) 'Modal reasoning, models, and Manktelow and Over', *Cognition* 43: 173–82.

Johnson-Laird, P.N., Legrenzi, P., and Legrenzi, M.S. (1972) 'Reasoning and a sense of reality', *British Journal of Psychology* 63: 395–400.

Kahneman, D. and Tversky, A. (1979) 'Prospect theory: An analysis of decision under risk', *Econometrica* 47: 263–91.

—— (1982) 'The psychology of preferences', *Scientific American* 264: 160–73.

Machina, M.J. (1991) 'Dynamic consistency and non-expected utility', in M. Bacharach and S. Hurley (eds) *Foundations of Decision Theory*, Oxford: Blackwell.

Manktelow, K.I. and Over, D.E. (1990a) *Inference and Understanding*, London: Routledge.

—— (1990b) 'Deontic thought and the selection task', in K.J. Gilhooly, M. Keane, R.H. Logie, and G. Erdos (eds) *Lines of Thinking*, vol. 1, Chichester: Wiley.

—— (1991) 'Social roles and utilities in reasoning with deontic conditionals', *Cognition* 39: 85–105.

—— (1992) 'Utility and deontic reasoning: a reply to Johnson-Laird and Byrne' *Cognition* 43: 183–8.

Platt, J. (1973) 'Social traps', *American Psychologist* 28: 641–51.

Savage, L.J. (1954) *The Foundations of Statistics*, New York: Wiley.

Shubik, M. (1971) 'The dollar auction game', cited in A.M. Colman (1982) *Game Theory and Experimental Games*, Oxford: Pergamon Press.

Simon, H. (1957) *Models of Man: Social and Rational*, New York: Wiley.

—— (1983) *Reason in Human Affairs*, Stanford: Stanford University Press.

Skyrms, B. (1990) *The Dynamics of Rational Deliberation*, Cambridge: Harvard University Press.

Slote, M. (1989) *Beyond Optimizing*, Cambridge, MA: Harvard University Press.

Smith, H. (1991) 'Deciding how to decide: is there a regress problem?' in M. Bacharach and S. Hurley (eds) *Foundations of Decision Theory*, Oxford: Blackwell.

Tversky, A. (1969) 'Intransitivity of preferences', *Psychological Review* 76: 31–48.

Wilkins, M.C. (1928) 'The effect of changed material on the ability to do formal syllogistic reasoning', *Archives of Psychology* 102.

Chapter 10

Intuitions about rationality and cognition

E. Shafir

The fundamental distinction between normative and descriptive theories of decision making is accepted by most students of human behaviour. The normative theory, which has emerged from a logical analysis of games of chance, describes the rules according to which an idealized, superrational individual should make decisions. Descriptive theories, which emerge from psychological analyses of value, risk, and uncertainty, describe the ways in which real people make decisions. While the theoretical distinction between the two accounts is clear, the normative theory has been widely applied throughout the social sciences as part of a descriptive analysis. In effect, the axioms of the rational theory are so intuitively appealing that many have considered it likely that a theory derived from these axioms would provide an acceptable, if somewhat idealized, account of actual behaviour. von Neumann and Morgenstern, the founders of modern expected utility theory, hoped to show that 'it is possible to describe and discuss mathematically human actions in which the main emphasis lies on the psychological side'. There are, they concluded, 'many – and most important – aspects of psychology which we have never touched upon, but the fact remains that a primarily psychological group of phenomena has been axiomatized' (von Neumann and Morgenstern, 1944: 76–7). The rational theory captures strong psychological intuitions and has led many researchers to hope for a symbiotic analysis, one that will meet the normative desiderata while at the same time describing how we actually go about making decisions.

Our intuitions about rational behaviour, however, do not always correspond to the ways in which we behave. Our behaviour is the outcome not of intuitive principles, but of mental processes largely confined to a particular, albeit remarkable, 3lb machine! Naturally, our cognitive mechanisms, the ways in which we process information, have a decisive influence on the decision behaviours that we exhibit. Many theorists are not concerned with cognitive process; they simply assume that we make decisions conforming to the rational theory. However, to suppose that a single theory can serve as both a normative guide and a descriptive model of decision making requires that the cognitive processes that guide behaviour conform with our desire to reach rational decisions.

The compelling nature of the normative theory of rationality notwithstanding, social and behavioural scientists are generally interested in theories of behaviour that appear psychologically feasible. Even those who suppose an exceedingly high degree of rationality on the part of individuals have typically regarded their assumptions to be plausible, if somewhat idealized. While they cannot deny the relevance of our mental lives, these theorists adopt a naïve account of mental processes that, if approximately correct, would yield observed behaviours very much in line with those predicted by the normative theory. They often attribute decision errors to inappropriate training, lack of motivation, or a momentary lapse of attention. Errors of reasoning and decision are often considered embarrassing because there is the feeling that we could, and should, have done better.

This paper focuses on our intuitions about rational behaviour and cognitive process. It makes use of well-known probability paradoxes to illustrate how particular patterns of rational behaviour that seem unavoidable if one account of mental process is adopted, may be expected to fail if other – equally plausible – processes are assumed. Specifically, the paper begins by describing a compelling axiom of the rational theory of decision under uncertainty, known as Savage's sure-thing principle. It then addresses the hypothetical implications to the sure-thing principle of a well-known paradox from statistics, known as Simpson's paradox. Recent empirical findings are then reviewed, which bear on the foregoing discussion. These studies document actual violations of the sure-thing principle, which are attributed not to rare patterns that exhibit Simpson's paradox, but rather to people's natural tendency to rely on compelling reasons for making decisions under conflict. Intuitions about rational behaviour as they relate to the cognitive processes that underlie reasoning and decision making are discussed in the concluding section. It is argued that an intriguing aspect of the study of rationality are the cognitive processes that underlie people's decisions, for a reliance on intuition about rational behaviour, with insufficient attention paid to cognitive process, risks leaving us with inadequate theories about the kinds of behaviour that people are likely to exhibit.

TWO WAYS TO MAKE A DECISION

Imagine that you have just taken a tough exam and that you feel equally likely to have passed or failed. Imagine, furthermore, that you now have to decide whether or not to go on vacation for the holidays. You will find out about the exam before you go, but right now you hope to make the decision that's most likely to make you happy given the exam's currently unknown outcome. As an experienced student, who has taken many exams and gone on many vacations, how should you make your decision?

There are many ways to make this choice. One reasonable strategy is to consider each of the possible future outcomes – failing and passing the exam – and to predict to what extent each option – staying or going – would make you happy given each outcome. Then, depending on your anticipated feelings given the outcomes, you would have to determine which option has a higher expected happiness (or 'utility') for you. Another reasonable strategy is not to trust your ability to predict your future feelings for each option given each outcome but, instead, to rely on your previous experience: to ask yourself how often in the past you were happy when you stayed, and how often you were happy when you went. Of course, you may choose to trust neither your simulation of future feelings nor your memories of feelings past, and opt instead for the tossing of a coin. Alternatively, you may simply try to think of good reasons or justifications for choosing to stay or for choosing to go. What strategy you use may depend, among other things, on your previous experience with such choices and on your confidence in being able to anticipate future feelings or to infer from past ones.

Consider now a special situation, in which the occurrence of some binary event X is uncertain and in which you are asked to choose between option a and option b. The situation is special for you because, as it turns out, you would prefer a to b if X obtains, and you would also prefer a to b if X does not obtain. What do you think you would choose when you do not know whether or not X obtains? In terms of the exam scenario above, imagine a student who would go on vacation if he were to pass the exam and who would also go if he were to fail. What would the student choose to do when the exam's outcome is unknown?

Predicting preference and the sure-thing principle

Most people have a clear intuition regarding this kind of problem. The intuition was captured by Savage in an analogous scenario:

> A businessman contemplates buying a certain piece of property. He considers the outcome of the next presidential election relevant to the attractiveness of the purchase. So, to clarify the matter for himself, he asks whether he would buy if he knew that the Republican candidate were going to win, and decides that he would do so. Similarly, he considers whether he would buy if he knew that the Democratic candidate were going to win, and again finds that he would do so. Seeing that he would buy in either event, he decides that he should buy, even though he does not know which event obtains. . . . It is all too seldom that a decision can be arrived at on the basis of the principle used by

this businessman, but, except possibly for the assumption of simple ordering, I know of no other extralogical principle governing decisions that finds such ready acceptance.

(Savage, 1954: 21)

Savage calls this principle the sure-thing principle (STP). According to STP, if a person would prefer a to b knowing that X obtained, and if he would also prefer a to b knowing that X did not obtain, then he definitely prefers a to b (ibid: 22). In the context of the exam problem, STP asserts that if the student would prefer to go on vacation if he were to pass the exam, and if he would also prefer to go if he were to fail, then the student definitely prefers to go on vacation, and would choose to do so even when the exam's outcome is unknown.

STP has a great deal of both normative and descriptive appeal; it is one of the simplest and least controversial principles of rational behaviour (although see, for example, McClennen (1983) for discussion). It is an important implication of 'consequentialist' accounts of decision making, in that it captures a fundamental intuition of what it means for a decision to be determined by the anticipated consequences.[1] It is a cornerstone of 'expected utility theory', and it holds in other models which impose less stringent criteria of rationality. It is intuitively very compelling. Do we have reason to expect a rational and attentive decision maker ever to violate STP?

Remembering past experience and Simpson's paradox

Let us now return to the above vacation problem (pp. 261–2). Savage envisions that upon encountering this problem the student will consider the possible events and their consequences, as illustrated in Figure 10.1. The student will ask himself whether he would want to go on vacation if he were to pass the exam, and whether he would want to go if he were to fail. Seeing that he would want to go in either case, the student would decide to go.

But now suppose that the student employs a somewhat different strategy. Feeling insecure about his ability to predict his future desires (and aware that we are often weak at such predictions, cf. Kahneman and Snell (1990)), the student may decide to rely instead on his vast previous experience. He may simply ask himself how often in the past was he happy when he went, and how often was he happy when he stayed. An experienced student, he recalls his fifty previous exams, equally divided between staying and going, remarkably well (see Table 10.1).

Of the twenty-five times in which he went on vacation following an exam, the student was happy on 40 per cent of those occasions and unhappy on the remaining 60 per cent. Of the twenty-five times in which

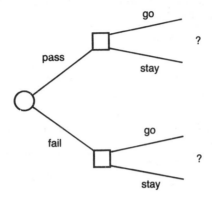

Figure 10.1 A tree diagram illustrating the vacation problem, as envisioned by Savage

Table 10.1 Hypothetical outcome distribution of vacation decisions following previous exams

	Stayed	Went
unhappy	10	15
happy	15	10
% happy	60	40

he had chosen to stay behind, he was happy on 60 per cent of those occasions and unhappy on the remaining 40 per cent. Since, in the past, he has been happier more often when he stayed than when he went on vacation, the student decides to stay.

Now what would he have done had he failed the exam? Following his current strategy, the student would recall all the previous cases in which he had taken an exam and failed. In the past, has he been happier when he went on vacation after failing an exam or when he stayed behind? The student has no trouble recalling all twenty-five cases (a subset of those in Table 10.1) in which he had failed the exam (see Table 10.2). As would be expected, the student has usually not been very happy after failing his exams. In an attempt to forget his troubles, he has often gone on vacation following his failures. In fact, having failed an exam, he has managed more often to feel happy when he went on vacation than when he stayed behind. Thus, having failed, the student decides to go.

And what about having passed the exam? What would the student have done then? Having had no trouble recalling all his exams so far, he is naturally able to recall the twenty-five exams (from the original fifty in Table 10.1) which he passed (see Table 10.3). Not surprisingly, the student has generally been much happier after passing his exams. Often in the past

Table 10.2 Hypothetical outcome distribution of vacation decisions following previously failed exams

	Stayed	Went
unhappy	6	14
happy	1	4
% happy	14	22

Table 10.3 Hypothetical outcome distribution of vacation decisions following previously passed exams

	Stayed	Went
unhappy	4	1
happy	14	6
% happy	78	86

he has felt no particular need to go on vacation, but the few times that he did decide to go, the pleasure of vacationing after having passed the exam has almost always made him happy. Since, having passed his exams in the past, he has tended to be happier when he went on vacation than when he stayed behind, the student definitely decides to go.

This student's vacation history yields the following pattern: when all previous exams are considered, the student has been happier when he did not go on vacation than when he went (60 per cent versus 40 per cent of the time, respectively); but going on vacation rather than staying behind has made the student happy more often when he passed his exams (86 per cent versus 78 per cent of the time), and also when he failed (22 per cent versus 14 per cent of the time). Based on his past experience, the student exhibits the following pattern of preferences: He decides to stay behind when he does not know whether he has passed or failed the exam, but he decides to go once he finds out that he passed and also once he finds out that he failed. This, in violation of STP.

Naturally, this hypothetical student's contrived vacation history, as well as the assumption that previous vacations are recalled with such selective precision, are unlikely to characterize most people's decisions. None the less, the above scenario serves to capture an interesting hypothetical counter-example to STP that merits further consideration. The pattern of frequencies exhibited in the tables above portrays a state of affairs known as Simpson's paradox (Simpson, 1951). The particular relationship between Savage's sure-thing principle and Simpson's paradox was first illuminated by Blyth (1972a). Simpson's paradox can arise when weighted averages are computed in situations where acts and events are not independent. In the example above, the student has gone on vacation more often after failing the exam than after passing and, having failed, he often felt unhappy. Conversely, he has chosen to stay behind more frequently after passing than after failing, and passing has generally made him happier. It is interesting to note the subtle distinction between the causal and diagnostic implications of the student's experience. If asked: 'Do you want to stay or go?', the student should choose to go for, regardless of whether he passes or fails, going tends to make him happier than staying. But if asked 'Are you more likely to be happy given that you went or given that you stayed?', the student would be correct in predicting that he is more likely to be happy given that he stayed. This is true simply because, for this student, staying is diagnostic of having passed the exam, and passing tends to make him happier.

When the exam's outcome is unknown, the student need not merge all previous experience, as in Table 10.1. The student could, in theory, partition his past experience into those cases in which he failed and those in which he passed. This strategy, however, is often neither intuitive nor simple, nor does it guarantee adherence to STP. The logic inherent in STP advises that we partition the set of possible events into mutually exclusive and jointly exhaustive situations, and look for an act that seems to be preferred, or at least acceptable, in all these situations. Partitioning of the event space, however, is often difficult because the 'correct' partitions are not easily identifiable. Any observed ordinal relationship between two variables faces the possibility of being reversed through a third variable such that within each level of this third variable, the relationship between the two initial variables is the opposite of the original relationship. (In the aforementioned problem, for example, the relationship between going on vacation and being happy is reversed once we distinguish between passing and failing the exam.) Of course, a fourth variable can then be introduced which re-reverses the reversed relationship, etc. Messick and van de Geer (1981) review the logic of such reversal in some detail and demonstrate that almost any 2 by 2 contingency table can be decomposed, as was done above, into two additive subtables in such a way that the direction of the relationship in the original table is reversed in both subtables.

Such reversals, moreover, are not restricted to merely hypothetical examples. Certain analyses in memory research, for instance, have been questioned on the grounds that they are based on contingency tables that may incorporate Simpson-paradoxical patterns (see Hintzman, 1980, and the reply by Martin, 1981). For another example, a study of sex bias in graduate admissions at the University of California at Berkeley in 1973, found that female applicants for graduate admissions had a higher probability of being denied admission than did male applicants, although a department-by-department analysis failed to reveal this bias, and in many departments female applicants had a lower probability of being denied (Bickel et al., 1975).[2] While the bias disappeared at the departmental level, it is conceivable that a further, intradepartmental partitioning of, say, applicants for Masters degrees and for PhDs, would have re-revealed the previously observed (or another) bias.

Precisely at what level to partition the space of events in order to achieve the ideal level for our purposes is an unresolved problem, both normatively and descriptively.[3] Philosophers of science have addressed the tension between our intuitive and our scientific levels of partitioning the state space (see, for example, Cartwright, 1979; Hardcastle, 1991; and references therein). Related problems have proven very difficult to model in the area of artificial intelligence (see, for example, the 'frame problem'; McCarthy and Hayes, 1969). The question of how best to parse our environment gets to the heart of our inductive practices; as Goodman (1979: 82) pointed out in his now famous work on the topic, 'regularities are where you find them, and you can find them anywhere'.

The partitioning of classes of events is not always intuitively compelling. When we ask ourselves whether we have enjoyed going to discotheques, we do not normally separate our remembered disco experiences into those that took place on weekends and those that took place on weekdays; or into those that occurred in winter as opposed to summer. Our failure to partition certain naturally occurring categories may occur in cases where a partitioning along certain dimensions seems recommendable. When in the process of selecting a surgeon, for example, most of us would undoubtedly opt for surgeon A if her mortality rates were half those of surgeon B. Good surgeons, however, tend to get the more difficult cases. A surgeon's mortality rates reflect her skills as well as the nature of her cases. It is quite possible that surgeon B outperforms surgeon A on every possible type of operation, and at the same time has higher mortality rates due to a practice heavily weighted by severe cases.[4]

Numerous studies have shown that people often do not decompose categories into their relevant subcategories. In certain inferential contexts, for example, subjects rate the probability that every member of a category has a given property to be greater than the probability that every member of a respective subcategory has it. Thus, having been told that: 'Robins have an ulnar artery', subjects rate it more likely that all birds have an ulnar artery than that ostriches have it (Osherson *et al.* (1990); see also Shafir *et al.* (1990)). A precondition for such judgement is the failure to take account of the fact that the category 'birds' consists of subcategories, like 'robins', 'sparrows', and 'ostriches'. Along similar lines, most subjects estimate the frequency, on a typical page, of seven-letter words that end in -ing (----ing) to be greater than the frequency of seven-letter words that have the letter n in the sixth position (-----n-) (Tversky and Kahneman, 1983). When asked to make these estimates, subjects focus on the particular category under consideration: because instances of the former category are more easily available than instances of the latter, subjects erroneously conclude that they are more frequent. They do not extensionally decompose the latter category into some of its constituent subcategories (i.e. seven-letter words that end in -ing, seven-letter words that end in -ent, seven-letter words that end in -ine, etc.). Similarly, when presented with a description of a young woman 'who is 31 . . . outspoken . . . and concerned with issues of discrimination and social justice' subjects estimate the likelihood that she is a feminist bank teller to be greater than the likelihood that she is a bank teller. Again, people would not be prone to commit this fallacy were they to decompose the category 'bank tellers' into its constituent subcategories of feminist and non-feminist bank tellers.

When thinking about a familiar category, people are not compelled to break it down into its constituent subcategories. Similarly, when envisioning hypothetical scenarios, people tend to reason using the simplest and most available scenario, in which many factors are not seen to vary. Findings along these lines have been documented in work on deduction (for example, Johnson-Laird, 1983; Rips, 1988; see also Legrenzi *et al.*, 1992, for discussion), counter-factual reasoning (Kahneman and Miller, 1986; Kahneman and Tversky, 1982a; Tversky and Kahneman, 1973), causal reasoning (Shaklee and Fischhoff, 1982; Tversky and Kahneman, 1980; see also Shustack, 1988, for a review), hypothesis testing (Bruner *et al.*, 1956; Wason, 1960), and contingency judgements (Beyth-Marom and Fischhoff, 1983; Einhorn and Hogarth, 1978). When the category 'bank tellers' is considered, subjects focus on that category; they are not likely to break it down into its various constituents.

When evaluating the admissions policy of a university, we investigate the university's record; we do not feel compelled to investigate separately each of its departments. Similarly, when contemplating whether to go on vacation following an exam, we ask ourselves how we felt when we went on vacation following previous exams. When contemplating whether to go on vacation having passed, we are likely to ask ourselves how we felt when we went after passing, and when considering whether to go having failed, we would ask ourselves how we felt when we went after failing. Inferring preferences in this fashion could lead us to delve into a database that exhibits Simpson's paradox and, as a result, to violate STP.

Savage's businessman revisited

What if, instead of forecasting his preferences for the acquisition of property as envisioned by Savage, the businessman chose to base his decision on his previous experience, as in the case of the hypothetical student above? Suppose that, a seasoned veteran, the businessman had made property-acquisition decisions during numerous (twenty-one to be precise) past elections, roughly equally won by Republicans and Democrats. Due to greater economic optimism, the businessman has tended to buy more often following a republican than a democratic victory. The

Table 10.4 Hypothetical outcome distribution of previous property-acquisition decisions

	Republican elected		Democrat elected	
	Bought	Did not buy	Bought	Did not buy
unhappy	5	2	1	3
happy	3	1	2	4
% happy	38	33	67	57

Table 10.5 Hypothetical outcome distribution of all previous property-acquisition decisions (Republican or Democrat elected)

	Bought	Did not buy
unhappy	6	5
happy	5	5
% happy	45	50

optimism, however, has proved to be unwarranted. As it turns out, the businessman has been happier following the latter rather than the former. His personal history is as shown in Table 10.4.

When he considers whether to buy after a republican has won, the businessman, based on his previous experience, decides he should; historically, following a republican victory, he has been happier when he bought than when he did not buy. Similarly, when he considers whether to buy following a democratic election, he again decides he should, for similar reasons. Now what does the businessman decide to do when he does not know the outcome of the election? A natural thing to do, since he does not know whether it is going to be a Democrat or a Republican, is simply to base his decision on all his previous election-time property-acquisition experience, for Democrats and Republicans combined (see Table 10.5). Now, contrary to his originator's STP, the businessman will decide not to buy. After all, in the past he has been happier when he did not buy than when he bought.

A prisoner's dilemma game

For another example, imagine facing a non-repeated prisoner's dilemma game as presented in Figure 10.2. The cell entries indicate the number of points that you and another player receive contingent on your chosen strategies. For example, if you both co-operate, you each receive 75 points, whereas if the other co-operates and you compete, you receive 85 points while the other receives 25. What characterizes the prisoner's dilemma game is that regardless of the opponent's choice, each player fares better by competing than by co-operating; yet, if you both compete you do less

OTHER

co-operates   competes

	co-operates	competes
co-operate	You: 75 Other: 75	You: 25 Other: 85
compete	You: 85 Other: 25	You: 30 Other: 30

YOU

Figure 10.2 A typical 'prisoner's dilemma'
Note: The cell entries indicate the number of points that you and the other player receive contingent on your choices.

well than if you had both co-operated (for more on the prisoner's dilemma, see Rapoport and Chammah, 1965). Do you choose to compete or to co-operate?

Suppose that you have played this game one hundred times in the past. You have always experienced a tension between your desire to accumulate points and your wish to do the ethical thing and co-operate. Altogether, you have chosen to compete – which, no matter what the other does, brings you more points – more often than you have co-operated. Suppose, in addition, that you always found out how the other had played and that, apart from the points earned, the strategies the two of you had chosen also had an impact on how you felt. In fact, when you think of your previous games, summarized in Table 10.6, you realize that you have felt happy more often after co-operating than after competing. Thus, you decide to co-operate.

Now, what would you have done had you known that the other had chosen to compete? To make this decision, you think of all the previous cases (in Table 10.6) in which the other had competed. These are summarized in Table 10.7(a). In a few of these cases you had co-operated, and while occasionally you felt happy for having done the ethical thing, you were usually upset for having been taken advantage of. In most other

Table 10.6. Hypothetical outcome distribution of previously played prisoner's dilemma games

	You co-operated	*You competed*
unhappy	14	49
happy	11	26
% happy	44	35

Table 10.7(a) Hypothetical outcome distribution of prisoner's dilemma games in which other competed

Table 10.7(b) Hypothetical outcome distribution of prisoner's dilemma games in which other co-operated

	You co-operated	You competed	You co-operated	You competed
unhappy	4	45	10	4
happy	1	20	10	6
% happy:	20	31	50	60

cases you had competed, and felt a little better for having obtained equal (albeit small) payoffs. Given your previous experience with competitors, you decide to compete.

Alternatively, what would you have done had you known that the other had chosen to co-operate? To make this decision, you think of all the previous cases (the remaining games of Table 10.6) in which the other had co-operated. These are summarized in Table 10.7(b). Not surprisingly, playing against people who eventually co-operated with you, you have had a greater tendency to co-operate. In those cases, you were equally likely to feel happy about obtaining mutual co-operation as you were to feel unhappy about failing to take advantage of the situation. In fact, on those occasions in which you had competed against a co-operator, you sometimes felt guilty for not reciprocating, but more often felt happy for having obtained the maximum number of points. Given your previous experience with co-operators, you decide to compete. Thus, you prefer to compete both when the other competes and when the other co-operates, but you decide to co-operate when the other's decision is not known, contrary to STP.

It is interesting to observe that the prisoner's dilemma game has been used extensively to model interactions among non-human animals as well as humans (see, for example, Dawkins, 1989; Krebs and Davies, 1987; Maynard Smith, 1982, and references therein). Since animals are less likely to be able to deliberate in the consequentialist manner envisioned by Savage's STP, it seems quite plausible that these animals would employ some variant of the memory-based strategy outlined above. Field crickets, for example, have been shown to have a memory for what happened in previous fights. Using a model cricket to fight against real crickets, Alexander (1961) has shown that a cricket that has recently won a large number of fights becomes more hawkish, and a cricket with a recent losing streak becomes more dovish. Given this general strategy, one is tempted to ask whether these animals could be induced to violate STP. For example, a situation could be created (using the model cricket) wherein a cricket won more often by being aggressive than passive when fighting either males or females, but won more often by being passive than aggressive overall. Various stimulus–response associations could substitute for the hypothetical 'memories' hypothesized in the preceding examples, leading to violations of STP in animal behaviour.

EXPERIMENTAL EVIDENCE AND REASONS FOR CHOICE

The foregoing use of Simpson's paradox is meant as an illustration of how plausible decision-making processes could in theory lead to violation of some of the most basic principles of rational choice, in this case STP. The above accounts, of course, are hypothetical. Violations of STP resulting from patterns that exhibit Simpson's paradox are rarely observed. While these contrived patterns may occasionally characterize people's decisions, they are unlikely to occur with great frequency. Many decisions are not of the sort for which we have accumulated a rich database, and even if we had such data, only very particular distributions would yield effects of the Simpson's-paradox type. Moreover, even if our memory for an event consisted of just this kind of distribution, it is not clear that we would base our decision on just a selective retrieval of past experience, with no attempt to predict our future feelings, as Savage suggests. In light of this, can real STP violations actually be documented? As it turns out, reliance on past experience is not required in order to produce violations of STP, nor does a forward outlook ensure its observance. As suggested below, other, more realistic, decision-making processes may produce actual STP violations with non-negligible frequency.

The making of decisions is a difficult matter involving uncertainty and conflict. We are usually uncertain about the precise consequences of our decisions, and we often experience conflict about what matters to us most (for example, savings or leisure) and, consequently, how much of one attribute to trade off in favour of another. We often arrive at a decision problem not with well-established and clearly ranked preferences as assumed by the classical theory, but rather with the need to determine our preferences as a result of having to decide. Preferences, as many have argued, are actually constructed – not merely revealed – during their elicitation, and the construction of preference is guided partially by the attempt to formulate coherent reasons or justifications for choosing one option rather than another (see Shafir et al., 1993, for discussion). As a result, violations of STP may be predicted to occur when we are able to produce a convincing argument for a particular action when we consider each outcome in isolation, but fail to construct a convincing argument when the precise outcome is unknown. Conversely, we may violate STP when uncertainty about the outcomes provides a seemingly compelling argument for action, which then dissipates once the uncertainty is resolved (see Shafer, 1986, for a similar point).

Actual violations of STP in contexts similar to those described above have recently been documented in experiments conducted by Shafir and Tversky (1992) and Tversky and Shafir (1992a). In a variant of the vacation problem, for example, we have shown that many people who chose to purchase a vacation to Hawaii if they were to pass an exam *and* if they were to fail, decided to postpone buying the vacation when the exam's outcome was not known (Tversky and Shafir, 1992a). Once the outcome of the exam is known, we have argued, the student has good – albeit different – reasons for going to Hawaii: having passed the exam, the vacation is seen as a time of celebration following a successful semester; having failed the exam, the vacation becomes a consolation and time of recovery. Not knowing the outcome of the exam, we suggest, the decision maker lacks a clear reason for going. He may feel it is inappropriate to reward himself with a trip to Hawaii while the exam's outcome is still pending and, as a result, may prefer to postpone the decision, contrary to STP. We call the above pattern of decisions a *disjunction effect*. Evidently, a disjunction of conflicting reasons (reward in case of success or consolation in case of failure) is often less compelling than either definite reason alone, and may lead people to refrain from action in situations of uncertainty, contrary to the logic which underlies STP.

We have also documented disjunction effects in one-shot prisoner's dilemma games played for real payoffs (Shafir and Tversky, 1992). Subjects (*n*=80) played a series of prisoner's dilemma games (as in Figure 10.2) on a computer, each against a different unknown opponent supposedly selected at random from among the participants. The rate of co-operation was 3 per cent when the subjects knew that the opponent had defected, and 16 per cent when they knew that the opponent had co-operated. However, when subjects did not know whether their opponent had co-operated or defected (as is normally the case in this game), the rate of co-operation rose to 37 per cent. Contrary to STP, one-quarter of the subjects defected when they knew their opponent's choice – be it co-operation or defection – but co-operated when their opponent's choice was not known.

The prisoner's dilemma (PD) game is characterized by the fact that an individually rational decision by each player results in an outcome that is not optimal collectively. Our subjects seem to exhibit a change of perspective that may be described as a shift from collective to individual rationality. In the disjunctive condition, when the opponent's choice of strategy is unknown, all four cells of the table are in play. The outcome of the game depends on the collective decision of both players, and the collectively optimal decision is for both to co-operate. Once the other's strategy is known, on the other hand, a player is 'on her own'. Only one column of the PD table is relevant (that which corresponds to the strategy chosen by the other), and the outcome of the game depends on her and her alone. The individually rational strategy, of course, is to compete.

Thus, the violation of STP observed in the prisoner's dilemma game may be explained, in part at least, by the greater tendency to adopt the collective perspective in the disjunctive version of the game. The collective incentive to co-operate, which seems appealing while the outcome is uncertain, loses much of its force once the uncertainty is resolved.[5]

As discussed earlier, the hypothetical Simpson's paradox violations of STP, due to their specific nature, are seldom likely to characterize people's actual decisions. In contrast, the above experimentally demonstrated violations of STP are attributed to relatively mundane constructs, such as our reasons for making one or another decision, and appear to occur with some regularity. These demonstrations highlight the tension between our intuitions about rationality and observed violations of rationality explained by intuitively compelling mechanisms.

CONFLICT AND THE REGULARITY CONDITION

A straightforward implication of the classical theory of choice is that adding a new alternative to a choice set can never increase the 'market share' of an option that was there all along. At the individual level, this condition, called *regularity*, states that adding a new alternative can never increase the probability of choosing an old one. Like STP, this is a compelling intuition; it plays a central role in microeconomic theorizing and has been widely used in marketing to model consumer choice. Regularity stems from the standard assumption that each alternative has a utility or subjective value for the decision maker, and that the decision maker selects the alternative with the highest subjective value. Added alternatives, as long as they do not provide relevant new information, are not expected to change the value of ones that were already available.

Consider, however, a somewhat different account. Imagine, for example, that you regularly buy your pens and pencils at a local store. You usually go there with $1.50 and, for that price, you either buy a pen, or a two-pencil set. On a subjective (ordinal) scale, where higher numbers indicate greater satisfaction, each time you bought a pen you have enjoyed it at a '3' level. Your satisfaction with the pencils, on the other hand, has been more varied: 50 per cent of the times that you bought the pencils you have enjoyed them at level '2', 40 per cent at level '4', and the remaining 10 per cent at level '6'. Finally, the times that you chose to keep the money rather than buy pens or pencils, it has brought you a satisfaction of '5' and '1', 40 per cent and 60 per cent of the time, respectively. These are summarized below:

Pen	Pencils	Money
100%: 3	50%: 2	60%: 1
	40%: 4	40%: 5
	10%: 6	

Your aim is to choose the alternative that has the best chance of bringing you more satisfaction than either of the other two. Now, suppose that only the pens are available. Do you buy a pen or do you keep the money? Judging from your previous experience, you are bound to derive a satisfaction of '3' from the pen, while there is a 60 per cent chance that you will get less enjoyment from the money (level '1') and only a 40 per cent chance that you will enjoy the money more (level '5'). Thus, you decide to buy the pen.

But what if the pencils were also available? Since there is a 50 per cent chance that you will enjoy the pen more than the pencils (a sure '3' versus a 50 per cent chance of '2'), and a 60 per cent chance that you will enjoy the pen more than the money (a sure '3' versus 60 per cent chance of '1'), there is a 30 per cent chance that you will enjoy the pen more than either the pencils or the money. That is:

P(Pen > Money, Pencils): 0.60 * 0.50 = 0.30

Similar calculations yield the following:

P(Pencils > Money, Pen): 0.10 + (0.40 * 0.60) = 0.34
P(Money > Pen, Pencils): 0.40 * 0.90 = 0.36

The money, as it turns out, is the alternative that has the best chance of bringing you more satisfaction than either of the other two. Hence, you decide to keep the money. Thus, you prefer the pen when money is the only alternative, but you prefer the money when the pencils are also made available, contrary to regularity.

Note that this example involves a somewhat different decision rule than simple utility maximization – you are here assumed to be conducting a 'contest' between the options under consideration, and such contests are known for their proneness to intransitive patterns. None the less, the above account (after Blyth, 1972b; see also Gardner, 1976) presents a hypothetical scenario in which the regularity condition may be seen to fail. Of course, few people are likely to make their choices in the manner described by this example, and even then, rarely would their preferences exhibit the above reversal. As with Simpson's paradox, this example provides a contrived illustration of how, in principle, a compelling intuition may be violated. But can actual violations of the regularity condition be observed? In what follows, the intuitive notion of decisional conflict is used to account for violations of regularity, and actual violations of the regularity condition are described.

The regularity condition is based on the intuition that each option has an inherent value for the decision maker. When new options are added, they are not expected to alter the value of the options that were already there: if we preferred one of two previous options, we should not now prefer the other. The addition of new options, however, may increase the conflict that people experience when making a decision, and greater conflict enhances people's tendency to resort to the status quo, or retain the default option (Tversky and Shafir, 1992b). The conflict generated by the need to make decisions plays no role in the classical theory but, like the arguments purported to guide decisions in the previous section, decisional conflict can have a significant, sometimes counterintuitive, effect on people's choices.

A pattern of preferences much like the one – involving the pen and pencils – described above has been documented by Tversky and Shafir (1992b). Princeton University undergraduates agreed to fill out a questionnaire for $1.50. Then, one half of the subjects were offered the opportunity, instead of the $1.50, to receive one of two prizes: a metal pen, or a set of two plastic pens. The other half of the subjects were only offered the opportunity to choose the metal pen instead of the money. The prizes were shown to the subjects, who were informed that each cost a little over $2.00. Subjects actually received the option that they chose. The results were as follows. When only the metal pen was offered, 75 per cent of the subjects took advantage of the opportunity to exchange the default payment for a prize of greater value. But when both the metal pen and the set of plastic pens were offered, only 47 per cent opted for either of these options, while the majority chose to retain the default payment, contrary to regularity ($p<0.05$). When the metal pen alone is available, it looks like a 'good buy'. It can be easily justified, since it is worth more than the $1.50. The same may be true for the set of plastic pens. But when both options are available, there may not be a clear reason to choose one over the other. The decision maker faces increased conflict, which enhances his tendency to retain the default payment, thus violating the otherwise very intuitive regularity condition.[6]

CONCLUDING REMARKS

Fundamental to research into reasoning and decision making has been the contrast between observed behaviour and our intuitions about human rationality. This contrast has generated a collection of well-documented errors and biases which are of interest for at least two reasons. First, they expose some of our intellectual limitations and thus may contribute to the improvement of our decision-making practices. Second, they shed light on the cognitive mechanisms and the heuristic procedures that underlie our judgements and decisions. The focus on human error is not limited to the study of reasoning and decision making. Research on memory, for example, is inseparable from studies of forgetting; work on language investigates production and comprehension errors; and research on perception explores perceptual illusions (see Kahneman and Tversky (1982b) for discussion).

The cognitive processes uncovered by research on decision making, while often effective, have been shown to lead to violations of simple normative rules in certain situations. For example, the representativeness heuristic (Kahneman and Tversky, 1973) is effective when items' typicality co-varies with their likelihood, but produces erroneous judgement whenever typicality and likelihood are uncorrelated. As discussed earlier, this can lead to the well-known conjunction fallacy, wherein P(A&B) is judged to be higher than P(A), contrary to the conjunction rule, which states that the probability of a conjunction cannot exceed the probabilities of its constituents (Tversky and Kahneman, 1983; Shafir *et al.*, 1990). Prior to the documentation of representativeness and related judgemental heuristics, people were not expected systematically to violate the very basic and intuitive conjunction rule of probability. While occasional errors would be expected, people were assumed to evaluate probabilities roughly along extensional lines and, as a result, to adhere to this compelling rule. Since the exposure of the representativeness heuristic, violations of the conjunction rule have come to be regarded as an integral part of the intuitive ways in which the human mind processes information. Processes such as those that underlie the representativeness heuristic have important implications for our intuitions about human rationality. The judgement that P(A&B) is greater than P(A) has evolved in the last twenty years from a curious and unexpected violation of rational thought into a predictable human error.

The descriptive adequacy of several normative assumptions of decision theory, such as cancellation (or independence), dominance, invariance, and transitivity, has been questioned by recent empirical research (for reviews, see Hogarth and Reder, 1986; Slovic *et al.*, 1989; Tversky and Kahneman, 1986, and references therein). All these point to the fact that the normative theory is irreconcilable with the ways in which people make choices. As a consequence of this tension, several alternative theories have been developed that try to effect a synergy between the normative and the descriptive; these theories retain some of the more normatively appealing principles, like dominance and invariance, while relaxing others, like independence and transitivity (for reviews, see Camerer, 1990; Machina, 1982; Schoemaker, 1982). It is not clear, however, who these theories are about. They are not about superrational agents, because *they* behave in conformity with all the principles and have no good reason to give up any. After all, we see no reason to revise our normative theories of ethics in light of the fact that people steal, nor do we revise our mathematics when we find out that people make systematic errors of arithmetic. At the same time, these revised theories are not about real people because we, it appears, systematically violate all the principles, including some of the normatively indispensable ones, like dominance, invariance, and STP. The normative theory, with its elegance and mathematical sophistication, helps to crystallize our views about what is genuinely rational, and to set standards that are provably superior to (or, as some would argue, at least different from) what we observe in everyday life. The normative account is illuminating in a number of ways, but is only truly predictive so long as it is used to make predictions in the same domain that it describes. Instead, throughout the social sciences, one encounters legal, political, sociological, and economic analyses purporting to explain and make predictions about human beings, that are based on assumptions about superrational agents.

What seems commonplace or surprising about behaviour is largely a function of how we think the organism processes information and interacts with its environment. Aware of the sonar capabilities of bats, for example, we are less likely to be astonished at their remarkable ability to manoeuvre in the dark. To the extent that we have a good understanding of the navigational and communicative skills of the honeybee, we can predict some truly remarkable feats as well as some very simple errors; the fact that a navigating bee, unperturbed by strong winds, cloudy skies, and various obstacles along its course, should be thrown off when outfitted with a tiny drag-producing tinfoil flap, is an outcome not so much of what the bee *can* do, as of precisely how it does what it can.[7]

As Simon (1957) has argued, the classical conception of rationality, based on unlimited memory and computational capacity, needs to be replaced by a more realistic conception, informed by our limited information processing abilities, before it can be applied to interpret and predict our behaviour. A more realistic portrayal of our computational abilities, however, may none the less be instantiated in a variety of ways. It is not only *how much* we can do that will determine the rationality of our behaviour, but exactly how we do what we can. 'Just imagine the banner headlines', writes Dawkins (1989: 239), 'if a marine biologist were to discover a species of dolphin that wove large, intricately meshed fishing nets, twenty dolphin-lengths in diameter! Yet we take a spider web for granted, as a nuisance in the house rather than as one of the wonders of the world.' Our marvel at the dolphins would not stem from the intellectual abilities that we attribute to these creatures – clearly most of us think that dolphins are smarter than spiders. Our presumed surprise regarding the dolphins, and lack thereof in the case of the spiders, stems from what we consider 'natural' or 'built into the system' in the two cases. The larvae of Caddis flies, to use another of Dawkins' examples, build themselves what amount to mobile houses at the river bottom, meticulously put together of sticks, dead leaves, and stones, each rotated to achieve the best fit. That impresses us less than if we were to discover chimpanzees building their own well-insulated houses. Again, this is not a reflection of what we otherwise think of these creatures; most of us expect chimpanzees to be able to grasp the notion of a house better than Caddis flies. Yet, while their intellectual grasp may be superior, we know that building houses just isn't part of what chimpanzees naturally do. Similarly, while most of us find the rational principles of the normative theory of decision making compelling upon reflection, these apparently do not form an integral part of the ways in which we naturally process information about our environment.

It is worth keeping in mind that the term 'rational' is accorded here a much more specific meaning than its general dictionary significance of 'agreeable to reason; of sound mind; sane'. These latter terms, of course, may apply to us even if the normative theory fails to describe our behaviour (see Simon (1978) for related discussion). It is also possible, however, that some of our behaviours are really not 'of sound mind'. Arguments about natural selection and adaptation notwithstanding, some of our ways of making decisions may be truly 'maladaptive'. According to the more generous current estimates, humanity started – somewhere between Lucy and *Homo habilis* – about 2.5 million years ago. Dinosaurs, on the other hand, not normally regarded as the paradigm of intellectual sophistication, dominated the earth for well over 100 million years. Biological assumptions of optimality notwithstanding, most biologists would not find it incredible if horses were to systematically make some maladaptive decisions; yet, the horse family has been around for more than 60 million years. It is interesting to note, in this context, the commonly perceived contrast between, on the one hand, economists and other social scientists who are assumed to hold a laudatory view of people as highly rational, and, on the other, many psychologists (and others) who presumably degrade us with theories of less-than-perfect rationality. This characterization is rather misleading. Psychologists recognize the inescapable fact that we are limited biological creatures who may not always do things exactly as suggested by our own intuitive theories. Economists, on the other hand, guided by an idealized set of assumptions, suppose that decisions that conform to the rational account typically characterize our behaviour, and attribute our persistent failures to a lack of understanding, confusion, distraction, meanness towards experimenters, or a simple failure to be moved by insufficient incentives.

The principles underlying the rational theory are compelling, originating as they do from strong intuitions about rational behaviour that most of us share. Indeed, numerous studies have shown that many principles that are systematically violated when their applicability goes undetected are generally satisfied when it is made transparent. It thus appears that both normative and descriptive accounts capture important aspects of human competence. Osherson (1990) has termed this the *coexistence thesis*.[8] The coexistence thesis recognizes the compelling nature and intuitive appeal of the principles of rationality, while at the same time acknowledging their systematic violation.

The discovery and explication of systematic errors contribute to our understanding of the ways in which the mind processes information. At the same time, the cognitive processes that characterize our mental apparatus have important consequences for our intuitions about human rationality. Of course, the normative status of rational desiderata will not be affected by whether or not they are adhered to by humans or any other organism. But their status as assumptions upon which social and behavioural hypotheses are adduced may well be affected. As we learn more about how people make decisions, our intuitions about human rationality may change and, with them, the theories we propose in the social and behavioural sciences.

ACKNOWLEDGEMENT

This work was supported by US Public Health Service Grant No. 1-R29-MH46885 from the National Institute of Mental Health, and has benefited from the comments of Philip Johnson-Laird, Daniel Osherson, Edward Smith, and Amos Tversky.

NOTES

1 The notion of consequentialism appears in the philosophical and decision theoretic literature in a number of different senses. See, for example, Hammond (1988), Levi (1991), and Bacharach and Hurley (1991) for a technical discussion. See also Shafir and Tversky (1992) for a discussion of non-consequential decision making.
2 The explanation was that proportionally more women applied to more selective departments.
3 A famous illustration is 'Bertrand's paradox', described in Ross (1988: 161–2).
4 This example is taken from Bar-Hillel (1990) who provides further discussion of the relation between base rates and Simpson's paradox.
5 A related interpretation – in terms of arguments that are overlooked when outcomes are considered in isolation – has been suggested to account for the well known Allais paradox, which can also be seen as a violation of STP (see Shafer, 1986). See also Hurley (1991) for a 'collective action' interpretation of co-operative behaviour in one-shot prisoner's dilemma games.
6 For other violations of regularity, see Huber *et al.* (1982), Simonson and Tversky (1992), and Tversky and Shafir (1992b).
7 For more on honeybee navigation and communication, see Gould (1982) and references therein.
8 Osherson's discussion of the coexistence thesis centres around people's adherence to Bayesian principles of judgement, rather than on the rational theory of choice.

REFERENCES

Alexander, R.D. (1961) 'Aggressiveness, territoriality, and sexual behaviour in field crickets', *Behaviour* 17: 130–223.
Bacharach, M. and Hurley, S. (1991) 'Issues and advances in the foundations of decision theory', in M. Bacharach and S. Hurley (eds) *Foundations of Decision Theory: Issues and Advances*, Oxford: Blackwell, pp. 1–38.

Bar-Hillel, M. (1990) 'Back to base rates', in R.M. Hogarth (ed.) *Insights in Decision Making: a Tribute to Hillel Einhorn*, Chicago: University of Chicago Press, pp. 200–16.

Beyth-Marom, R. and Fischhoff, B. (1983) 'Diagnosticity and pseudodiagnosticity', *Journal of Personality and Social Psychology* 45: 1185–95

Bickel, P.J., Hammel, E.A., and O'Connell, J.W. (1975) 'Sex bias in graduate admissions: data from Berkeley', *Science* 187: 398–404.

Blyth, C.R. (1972a) 'On Simpson's paradox and the sure-thing principle', *Journal of the American Statistical Association* 67: 364–6.

—— (1972b) 'Some probability paradoxes in choice from among random alternatives', *Journal of the American Statistical Association* 67: 366–73.

Bruner, J.S., Goodnow, J.J., and Austin, G.A. (1956) *A Study of Thinking*, New York: Wiley.

Camerer, C.F. (1990) 'Recent tests of generalizations of expected utility theory', in W. Edwards (ed.) *Utility: Theories, Measurement and Applications*, Boston: Kluwer Academic Publishers.

Cartwright, N. (1979) 'Causal laws and effective strategies', *Nous* 13: 419–37.

Dawkins, R. (1989) *The Selfish Gene*, new edn, Oxford: Oxford University Press.

Einhorn, H.J. and Hogarth, R.M. (1978) 'Confidence in judgment: persistence of the illusion of validity', *Psychological Review* 85: 395–416.

Gardner, M. (1976) 'On the fabric of inductive reasoning and some probability paradoxes', *Scientific American* March, 234 (3): 119–22.

Goodman, N. (1979) *Fact, Fiction, and Forecast*, Cambridge, MA: Harvard University Press.

Gould, J.L. (1982) *Ethology: the Mechanisms and Evolution of Behavior*, New York: Norton.

Hammond, P. (1988) 'Consequentialist foundations for expected utility', *Theory and Decision* 25: 25–78.

Hardcastle, V.G. (1991) 'Partitions, probabilistic causal laws, and Simpson's paradox', *Synthese* 86: 209–28.

Hintzman, D.L. (1980) 'Simpson's paradox and the analysis of memory retrieval', *Psychological Review* 87: 398–410.

Hogarth, R.M. and Reder, M.W. (eds) (1986) 'The behavioral foundations of economic theory', *Journal of Business* 59 (4), Part 2.

Huber, J., Payne, J.W., and Puto, C. (1982) 'Adding asymmetrically dominated alternatives: violations of regularity and the similarity hypothesis', *Journal of Consumer Research* 9: 90–8.

Hurley, S.L. (1991) 'Newcomb's Problem, Prisoner's Dilemma, and collective action', *Synthese* 86: 173–96.

Johnson-Laird, P.N. (1983) *Mental Models*, Cambridge, MA: Harvard University Press.

Kahneman, D. and Miller, D.T. (1986) 'Norm theory: comparing reality to its alternatives', *Psychological review* 93: 136–53.

Kahneman, D. and Snell, J. (1990) 'Predicting utility', in R.M. Hogarth (ed.) *Insights in Decision Making: a Tribute to Hillel Einhorn*, Chicago: University of Chicago Press, pp. 295–310.

Kahneman, D. and Tversky, A. (1973) 'On the psychology of prediction', *Psychological Review* 80: 237–51.

—— (1982a) 'The simulation heuristic', in D. Kahneman, P. Slovic, and A. Tversky (eds) *Judgment under Uncertainty: Heuristics and Biases*, New York: Cambridge University Press, pp. 201–8.

—— (1982b) 'On the study of statistical intuitions', *Cognition* 11: 123–41.

Krebs, J.R. and Davies, N.B. (1987) *An Introduction to Behavioral Ecology*, 2nd edn, Oxford: Blackwell Scientific Publications.

Legrenzi, P., Girotto, V., and Johnson-Laird, P.N. (1992) 'Focussing in reasoning and decision making', Unpublished Manuscript, Princeton University.

Levi, I. (1991) 'Consequentialism and sequential choice', in M. Bacharach and S. Hurley (eds) *Foundations of Decision Theory: Issues and Advances*, Oxford: Blackwell, pp. 92–122.

McCarthy, J. and Hayes, P. (1969) 'Some philosophical problems from the standpoint of Artificial Intelligence', in B. Meltzer and D. Michie (eds) *Machine Intelligence*, New York: American Elsevier.

McClennen, E.F. (1983) 'Sure-thing doubts', in B.P. Stigum and F. Wenstop (eds) *Foundations of Utility and Risk Theory and Applications*, Dordrecht: Reidel, pp. 117–36.

Machina, M.J. (1982) '"Expected utility" analysis without the independence axiom', *Econometrica* 50: 277–323.

Martin, E. (1981) 'Simpson's paradox resolved: a reply to Hintzman', *Psychological Review* 88: 372–4.

Maynard Smith, J. (1982) *Evolution and the Theory of Games*, New York: Cambridge University Press.

Messick, D.M. and van de Geer, J.P. (1981) 'A reversal paradox', *Psychological Bulletin* 90: 582–93.

Osherson, D.N. (1990) 'Judgment', in D.N. Osherson and E.E. Smith (eds) *An Invitation to Cognitive Science*, Vol. 3, Cambridge, MA: MIT Press.

Osherson, D.N., Smith, E.E., Wilke, A., Lopez, A., and Shafir, E. (1990) 'Category based induction', *Psychological Review* 97 (2): 185–200.

Rapoport, A. and Chammah, A. (1965) *Prisoner's Dilemma*, Ann Arbor: University of Michigan Press.

Rips, L.J. (1988) 'Deduction', in R.J. Sternberg and E.E. Smith (eds) *The Psychology of Human Thought*, New York: Cambridge University Press, pp. 116–54.

Ross, S. (1988) *A First Course in Probability*, London: Macmillan.

Savage, L.J. (1954) *The Foundations of Statistics*, New York: Wiley.

Schoemaker, P.J.H. (1982) 'The expected utility model: its variants, purposes, evidence, and limitations', *Journal of Economic Literature* 20: 529–63.

Shafer, G. (1986) 'Savage revisited', *Statistical Science* 1: 463–85.

Shafir, E. and Tversky, A. (1992) 'Thinking through uncertainty: nonconsequential reasoning and choice', *Cognitive Psychology* 24(4): 449–74.

Shafir, E., Smith, E.E., and Osherson, D.N. (1990) 'Typicality and reasoning fallacies', *Memory & Cognition* 18 (3): 229–39.

Shafir, E., Simonson, I., and Tversky, A. (1993) 'Reason-based choice', *Cognition* (forthcoming).

Shaklee, H. and Fischhoff, B. (1982) 'Strategies of information search in causal analysis', *Memory & Cognition* 10: 520–30.

Shustack, M.W. (1988) 'Thinking about causality', in R.J. Sternberg and E.E. Smith (eds) *The Psychology of Human Thought*, New York: Cambridge University Press, pp. 92–115.

Simon, H. (1957) *Models of Man*, New York; Wiley.

—— (1978) 'Rationality as process and as product of thought', *Journal of the American Economic Association* 68: 1–16.

Simonson, I. and Tversky, A. (1992) 'Choice in context: tradeoff contrast and extremeness aversion', *Journal of Marketing Research* (in press).

Simpson, E.H. (1951) 'The interpretation of interaction in contingency tables', *Journal of the Royal Statistical Society* Ser. B, 13 (2): 238–41.

Slovic, P., Lichtenstein, S., and Fischhoff, B. (1989) 'Decision making', in R.C. Atkinson, R.J. Herrnstein, G. Lindzey, and R.D. Luce (eds) *Steven's Handbook of Experimental Psychology*, 2nd edn, New York: Wiley.

Tversky, A. and Kahneman, D. (1973) 'Availability: a heuristic for judging frequency and probability', *Cognitive Psychology* 4: 207–32.

—— (1980) 'Causal schemas in judgments under uncertainty', in M. Fishbein (ed.) *Progress in Social Psychology*, vol. 1, Hillsdale, NJ: Erlbaum, pp. 49–72.

—— (1983) 'Extensional versus intuitive reasoning: the conjunction fallacy in probability judgment', *Psychological Review* 90: 293–315.

—— (1986) 'Rational choice and the framing of decisions', *Journal of Business* 59 (4), pt. 2: 251–78.

Tversky, A. and Shafir, E. (1992a) 'The disjunction effect in choice under uncertainty', *Psychological Science* 3(5): 305–9.

—— (1992b) 'Choice under conflict: the dynamics of deferred decision', *Psychological Science* 3(6): 358–61.

von Neumann, J. and Morgenstern, O. (1944) *Theory of Games and Economic Behavior*, Princeton, NJ: Princeton University Press.

Wason, P.C. (1960) 'On the failure to eliminate hypotheses in a conceptual task', *Quarterly Journal of Experimental Psychology* 12: 129–40.

Chapter 11

The bounded rationality of probabilistic mental models

G. Gigerenzer

Imagine you are a subject in a psychological experiment. In front of you is a text problem, and you begin to read:

> Linda is 31 years old, single, outspoken and very bright. She majored in philosophy. As a student, she was deeply concerned with issues of discrimination and social justice, and also participated in antinuclear demonstrations. Which of two alternatives is more probable?
> (a) Linda is a bank teller.
> (b) Linda is a bank teller and is active in the feminist movement.

Which alternative would you choose? Assume you chose (b), just as most subjects in previous experiments did. The experimenter explains to you that (b) is the conjunction of two events, namely that Linda is a bank teller *and* is active in the feminist movement, whereas (a) is one of the constituents of the conjunction. Because the probability of a conjunction of two events cannot be greater than that of one of its constituents, the correct answer is (a), not (b), the experimenter says. Therefore, your judgement is recorded as an instance of a reasoning error, known as the *conjunction fallacy*. You may be inclined to admit that you have committed a reasoning error. The experimenter now explains that these reasoning errors are like visual illusions: once the error is pointed out, people like you show insight, but this knowledge does not necessarily help. People see the same illusion again, or continue to reason in the same way, despite showing insight. Therefore, in analogy to visual illusions, stable reasoning errors such as the conjunction fallacy have been labelled *cognitive illusions*.

Cognitive illusions, and their explanations, cognitive heuristics, are the stock-in-trade of a research programme known as the heuristics-and-biases programme (for example, Tversky and Kahneman, 1974, 1983). Cognitive illusions 'seem reliable, systematic, and difficult to eliminate' (Kahneman and Tversky, 1972: 431). Stable cognitive illusions are not the first assault on human rationality by psychologists. Sigmund Freud's attack on human rationality is probably the best-known: the unconscious desires and wishes of the Id are a steady source of intrapsychical conflict that may manifest itself in all kinds of irrational fears, beliefs, and behaviour. But the cognitive-illusion assault is stronger than the psychoanalytic. It does not need to invoke unconscious wishes or desires to overwhelm human rationality. Cognitive illusions are seen as a straightforward consequence of the laws of human reasoning. Humans do not possess the proper mental algorithms.

Paleontologist Stephen J. Gould, referring to the 'Linda problem', puts the message clearly: 'Why do we consistently make this simple logical error? Tversky and Kahneman argue, correctly I think, that our minds are not built (for whatever reason) to work by the rules of probability' (Gould, 1992: 469). The purpose of this chapter is to evaluate this claim and to provide an alternative. In the first part, I will draw the reader's attention to the fact that both proponents and opponents of rationality tend to focus on the same single psychological concept: algorithms in the mind. Second, I will extend this focus by conceptual distinctions drawn from philosophy, statistics, and cognitive science, and argue that these distinctions are not just the province of philosophers and statisticians but have quite tangible implications for understanding the cognitive processes in reasoning and for the rationality debate. Third, I demonstrate that these implications are so powerful that they can make apparently stable cognitive illusions disappear. Finally, I will present a model of bounded rationality, the theory of *probabilistic mental models*, as an alternative to traditional explanations in terms of the heuristics-and-biases programme. Using the overconfidence effect as an illustration, I will show that this theory explains both the old data (cognitive illusions), predicts new phenomena, and provides a fresh look at what rational probabilistic reasoning means.

RATIONALITY: WHAT KIND OF MENTAL ALGORITHM?

In his *Movements of Animals*, Aristotle described a *practical syllogism* as one that guides practical rationality:

> For example, when you conceive that every man ought to walk and you yourself are a man, you immediately walk; or if you conceive that on a particular occasion no man ought to walk, and you yourself are a man, you immediately remain at rest.
>
> (Aristotle, 1945: 701a)

The foundation of present-day theories of rationality, however, was laid in the mid-seventeenth century with the classical theory of probability (Daston, 1988). In contrast to syllogisms, probability could deal with degrees of beliefs, weights of evidence, expectations, and other forms of uncertainty that are characteristic of everyday affairs – from weighing the evidence in a law court to calculating insurance premiums. Probability theory and rational reasoning came to be seen as two sides of the same coin; probability theory is 'nothing more at bottom than good sense reduced to a calculus' (Laplace, 1951/1814: 196). For instance, in his famous treatise of 1854, the mathematician George Boole set out to demonstrate that the laws of logic, probability and algebra can in fact be derived from the laws of human reasoning.

> There is not only a close analogy between the operations of the mind in general reasoning and its operations in the particular science of Algebra, but there is to a considerable extent an exact agreement in the laws by which the two classes of operations are conducted.
>
> (Boole, 1958/1854: 6)

Bärbel Inhelder and Jean Piaget echo this belief a century later: 'Reasoning is nothing more than the propositional calculus itself' (Inhelder and Piaget, 1958: 305).

According to these views, the laws of probability or logic are the algorithms of the mind, and they define rational reasoning as well. According to some critics of these views, the laws of probability are not the algorithms of the mind, but the laws still *define* rationality. Rather, mental algorithms are non-statistical heuristics causing cognitive illusions. Defenders and detractors of human rationality alike have tended to focus on the issue of algorithms. Only their answers differ. Here are some prototypical arguments in the current debate.

Statistical algorithms

For philosophers such as L. Jonathan Cohen, the assumption that human intuition is rational is absolutely indispensable for legitimizing their own profession. If intuition were not rational, this would 'seriously discredit the claims of intuition to provide – other things being equal – dependable foundations for inductive reasoning in analytical philosophy' (Cohen, 1986: 150). Cohen (1983: 511) assumes that statistical algorithms (Baconian and Pascalian probability) are in the mind, but distinguishes between not having a statistical rule and not applying such a rule, that is, between competence and performance. Cohen's interpretation of cognitive illusions parallels J.J. Gibson's interpretation of visual illusions (Gigerenzer, 1991): illusions are attributed to non-realistic experiments using impoverished information, to experimenters acting as conjurors, and to other factors that mask the subjects' competence: 'unless their judgment is clouded at the time by wishful thinking, forgetfulness, inattentiveness, low intelligence, immaturity, senility, or some other competence-inhibiting factor, all subjects reason correctly about probability: none are programmed to commit fallacies or indulge in illusions' (Cohen, 1982: 251). Cohen does not claim, I think, that people carry around the collected works of Kolmogoroff, Fisher, and Neyman in their heads, and merely need to have their memories jogged, like the slave in Plato's *Meno*. But his claim implies that people do have at least those statistical algorithms in their competence that are sufficient to solve all reasoning problems studied in the heuristics-and-biases literature, including the Linda problem.

The Enlightenment view that human reasoning is in part probability theory does *not* imply that humans make no mistakes in reasoning. Nobody would deny that, even Cohen. According to Boole, for instance, errors in reasoning 'are due to the interference of other laws with those laws of which *right* reasoning is the product' (Boole, 1958/1854: 409). The message of the heuristics-and-biases programme, however, is stronger than reminding us that emotions, desires, and the like make us err in reasoning.

Non-statistical algorithms: heuristics

Proponents of the heuristics-and-biases programme seem to assume that the mind is not built to work by the rules of probability:

> In making predictions and judgments under uncertainty, people do not appear to follow the calculus of chance or the statistical theory of prediction. Instead, they rely on a limited number of heuristics which sometimes yield reasonable judgments and sometimes lead to severe and systematic errors.
>
> (Kahneman and Tversky, 1973: 237)

A few more quotations illustrate the claim that the mind lacks statistical algorithms and, therefore, rationality. In a paper on biases in bargaining, Bazerman and Neale say, 'The biases of framing and overconfidence just presented suggest that individuals are generally affected by systematic deviations from rationality' (Bazerman and Neale, 1986: 317). The human mind lacks 'the correct programs for many important judgmental tasks' (Slovic *et al.*, 1976). 'We know that our uneducated intuitions concerning even the simplest statistical phenomena are largely defective' (Piattelli-Palmarini, 1989: 9). The experimental demonstrations have 'bleak implications for human rationality' (Nisbett and Borgida, 1975: 935), and 'For anyone who would wish to view man as a reasonable intuitive statistician, such results are discouraging' (Kahneman and Tversky, 1972/1982: 46).

Cognitive illusions are explained by non-statistical algorithms, known as cognitive heuristics. For instance, the standard explanation for the conjunction fallacy in the Linda problem is that the mind assesses the probability by calculating the similarity between the description of Linda and each of the alternatives, and chooses that alternative with the highest similarity. Because the description of Linda was constructed to be representative of an active feminist and the conjunction contains the term 'feminist', people judge the conjunction more probable – so the explanation goes. Judging probability by similarity has been termed the *representativeness heuristic*. This heuristic was only vaguely defined when first proposed in the early 1970s, and it still is. It has not yet been linked to any of many existing theories of similarity, nor has it been spelled out how exactly similarity or representativeness is calculated.

Statistical and non-statistical heuristics

So far we have two research programmes. Cohen assumes that statistical algorithms are in the competence of humans, and one should explain cognitive illusion by identifying performance-inhibiting factors. Tversky and Kahneman assume that mental algorithms are non-statistical heuristics, which cause stable cognitive illusions. Proponents of a third position do not want to be forced to choose between statistical and non-statistical algorithms, but want to have them both. Fong and Nisbett (1991: 35) argue that people possess both rudimentary but abstract intuitive versions of statistical principles, such as the law of large numbers, *and* non-statistical heuristics such as representativeness. The basis for these conclusions are the results of training studies. For instance, the experimenters first teach the subject the law of large numbers or some other statistical principle, and subsequently also explain how to apply this principle to a real-world domain such as sports problems. Subjects are then tested on similar problems from the same or other domains. The typical result is that more subjects reason statistically, but transfer to domains not trained in is often low. Evans (1984) has proposed a similar interpretation of deductive reasoning, assuming both a mental logic and non-logical heuristics.

To summarize: I have briefly sketched three positions in the present debate on the rationality of probability judgement. My point is that the discussion between these three positions focuses on the kind of mental algorithm – is it probability, heuristics, or both? I now invite you to look beyond algorithms, to different questions and new kinds of experiments. Let me start with three ideas and distinctions.

THERE IS MORE THAN MENTAL ALGORITHMS

The distinction between algorithms and information representation

Information needs representation. In order to communicate information, it has to be represented in some symbol system (Marr, 1982). Take numerical information. This information can be represented by the Arabic numeral system, by the binary system, by Roman numbers, or other systems. These different representations can be mapped in a one-to-one way, and are in this sense equivalent representations. But they are not necessarily equivalent for an algorithm. Pocket calculators, for instance, generally work on the Arabic base-10 system, whereas general-purpose computers work on the base-2 system. The numerals 100000 and 32 are representations of the number thirty-two in the binary and Arabic system, respectively. The algorithms of my pocket calculator will perform badly with the first kind of representation but work well on the latter.

The human mind finds itself in an analogous situation. The algorithms most western people have stored in their minds – such as how to add, subtract, or multiply – work well on arabic numerals. But contemplate for a moment division in Roman numerals, without transforming them first into Arabic numerals.

There is more to the distinction between an algorithm and a representation of information. Not only are algorithms tuned to particular representations, but different representations make explicit different features of the same information. For instance, one can quickly see whether a number is a power of 10 in an Arabic numeral representation, whereas to see whether that number is a power of 2 is more difficult. The converse holds with binary numbers. Finally, algorithms are tailored to given representations. Some representations allow for simpler and faster algorithms than others. Binary representation, for instance, is better suited to electronic techniques than Arabic representation. Arabic numerals, on the other hand, are better suited to multiplication and elaborate mathematical algorithms than Roman numerals – possibly one of the reasons for the superior development of mathematics in the early Arabic cultures as opposed to Roman culture.

The distinction between algorithms and information representation is central to David Marr's (1982) analysis of visual information processing systems. From vision to reasoning, I argue, understanding of cognitive processes needs to take account of both algorithms *and* information representation. I now connect this distinction with another conceptual distinction prominent in philosophy and probability theory.

The distinction between subjective degrees of belief and objective frequencies

The classical probabilists of the Enlightenment slid with breathtaking ease and little justification from one sense of probability to another: from objective frequencies to physical symmetry (today referred to as 'propensity') to subjective degrees of belief. Lorraine Daston (1988) has argued that this ease was a consequence of the associationist psychology of these days, of the belief, advanced *inter alia* by John Locke and David Hartley, that the matching of objective frequencies to subjective belief was rational. Only when associationist psychology shifted its emphasis to illusions and distortions introduced by passion and prejudice, did the gap between objective and subjective probabilities become evident. Philosophers and mathematicians now drew a bold line between the first two objective meanings on the one hand and subjective probabilities on the other. The unity of belief and frequency crumbled in the first half of the nineteenth century. After the fall of the classical interpretation of probability the frequency interpretation emerged as the dominant view in the nineteenth and twentieth centuries.

For proponents of the frequency view such as Richard von Mises (1957/1928) and Jerzy Neyman (1977), probability theory is about frequencies, and does *not* deal with degrees of belief in single events. In the subjective ('Bayesian') interpretation that re-emerged in this century, however, degrees of belief are what probability means. Others wanted to have it both ways, or have proposed alternative interpretations of probability. The question, What is probability about? is still with us.[1]

My intention here is not to take sides in this debate, but to liken the conceptual distinction between single-event probabilities and frequencies to the concept of information representation. This leads us to distinguish two kinds of representations: frequency information or single-event probabilities. Finer distinctions can be made, but this will suffice for a start.

Monitoring of event frequencies

The third idea is an evolutionary speculation that links with the above distinctions. Bumblebees, birds, rats, and ants all seem to be good intuitive statisticians, highly sensitive to changes in frequency distributions in their environments, as recent research in foraging behaviour indicates (Gallistel, 1990; Real and Caraco, 1986). From sea snails to humans, as John Staddon (1988) argued, the learning mechanisms responsible for habituation, sensitization, and classical and operant conditioning can be described in terms of statistical inference machines.

Assume that some capacity or algorithm for statistical reasoning has been built up through evolution by natural selection. What information representation would such an algorithm be tuned to? Certainly not percentages and single-event probabilities (as in the typical experiments on human reasoning), since these took millenia of literacy and numeracy to evolve as tools for communication. Rather, in an illiterate world, the input representation would be *frequencies* of events, sequentially encoded, such as 3 out of 20 (as opposed to 15 per cent or p = 0.15). Such a representation is couched in terms of discrete cases. Moreover, frequencies such as 3 out of 20 contain *more* information than percentages such as 15 per cent. These frequencies contain information about the sample size (here: 20), which allows one to compute the *ambiguity* or precision of the estimate.

The notion that the mind infers the structure of the world through monitoring event frequencies is an old one. Locke and Hartley assumed that the mind is a kind of counting machine that automatically registered frequencies of past events, an assumption that is now called *automatic frequency processing* (Hasher and Zacks, 1979). David Hume thought the mind was very sensitive to small differences in frequency: 'When the chances or experiments on one side amount to ten thousand, and on the other to ten thousand and one, the judgement gives the preference to the latter, upon account of the superiority' (Hume, 1975/1739: 141).

Now we can put these three ideas together. First, to analyse probabilistic reasoning, information representation and algorithms have to be distinguished. Second, there are (at least) two kinds of representations, frequencies and single-event probabilities. Finally, if evolution has selected some kind of algorithm in the mind, then it will be tuned to frequencies as representation.

In the next section I will show that these ideas, still rather general, are powerful enough to make several apparently stable cognitive illusions disappear.

HOW TO MAKE COGNITIVE ILLUSIONS DISAPPEAR

Cognitive illusions have become a hard currency in many debates. When Stephen Stich argued against Donald Davidson's philosophy of language and Daniel Dennett's philosophy of mind, he pointed out that these two systems are inconsistent with the psychologists' 'evidence for extensive irrationality in human inference' (Stich, 1990: 11). When I discuss with colleagues the actual evidence underlying such claims, the *conjunction fallacy* is often thrown in as *the* truly convincing and replicable demonstration of irrational reasoning.

So let us first see what the distinction between algorithm and information representation, and between frequency and single-event format, does to this cognitive illusion.

Conjunction fallacy

Tversky and Kahneman (1983) reported that 85 per cent of 142 undergraduates indicated that the conjunction 'Linda is a bank teller and is active in the feminist movement' (T&F) is more probable than 'Linda is a bank teller' (T). They and others have shown that this judgement is replicable and stable – not only with statistically naïve undergraduates but with 'highly sophisticated respondents' such as doctoral students in the decision science programme of the Stanford Business School who had taken advanced courses in probability, statistics, and decision theory (Tversky and Kahneman, 1983: 298).

The conjunction fallacy and the conclusion that the mind is not programmed by the laws of probability but by non-statistical heuristics (albeit only very loosely defined ones) has become the accepted wisdom in much of cognitive and social psychology, philosophy of mind, and beyond. The conjunction fallacy has been proposed as the cause of various kinds of human misfortune, such as US security policy, where 'the conjunction fallacy . . . lends . . . plausibility to highly detailed nuclear war-fighting scenarios' (Kanwisher, 1989: 671).

Stephen J. Gould, explaining the Linda problem to his audience, writes:

> Tversky and Kahneman's 'studies have provided our finest insight into "natural reasoning" and its curious departure from logical truth . . . I am particularly fond of [the Linda] example, because I know that the [conjunction] is least probable, yet a little homunculus in my head continues to jump up and down, shouting at me – "but she can't just be a bank teller; read the description".'
>
> (Gould, 1992: 469)

Gould should have trusted his homunculus. In what follows, I will discuss the claim that the judgement called 'conjunction fallacy' is an error in probabilistic reasoning. I will argue that this claim is not tenable, and Gould's homunculus will be vindicated. Thereafter I will show what the distinction between algorithm and information representation can do to the conjunction fallacy.

Cognitive illusion illusory?

Is the conjunction fallacy a violation of probability theory? Has a person who chooses T&F violated probability theory? The answer is no, if the person is a frequentist such as Richard von Mises or Jerzy Neyman; yes, if he or she is a subjectivist such as Bruno de Finetti; and open otherwise.

The mathematician Richard von Mises, one of the founders of the frequency interpretation, used the following example to make his point:

> We can say nothing about the probability of death of an individual even if we know his condition of life and health in detail. The phrase 'probability of death', when it refers to a single person, has no meaning at all for us. This is one of the most important consequences of our definition of probability.
>
> (von Mises, 1957/1928: 11)

In this frequentist view, one cannot speak of a probability unless a reference class has been defined. The relative frequency of an event such as death is only defined with respect to a reference class, such as 'all male pub-owners fifty-years old living in Bavaria'. Relative frequencies may vary from reference class (pub-owners) to reference class (HIV-positives).

Since a single person is always a member of many reference classes, no unique relative frequency can be assigned to a single person. As the frequentist statistician G.A. Barnard put it, if one wants to evaluate subjective probabilities of single events, one 'should concentrate on the works of Freud and perhaps Jung rather than Fisher and Neyman' (Barnard, 1979: 171). Thus, for a strict frequentist, the laws of probability are about frequencies and not about single events such as whether Linda is a bank teller. Therefore, in this view, no judgement about single events can violate probability theory.

From the frequency point of view, the laws of probability are mute on the Linda problem, and what has been called a conjunction fallacy *is not* an error in probabilistic reasoning – probability theory simply doesn't apply to such cases. Seen from the Bayesian point of view, the conjunction fallacy *is* an error. Note that the experimental subjects were neither told that the Linda problem is meant to be a Bayesian probability textbook problem, nor did the experimenters try to persuade and commit their subjects to the Bayesian view.

How shall we evaluate this situation? The frequency view has been dominant since the nineteenth century, and teaching in statistics departments today as well as in undergraduate psychology courses is still predominantly frequentist in philosophy. Therefore, we cannot expect psychology undergraduates to carry around a Bayesian superego in their minds. One should be careful not to evaluate reasoning against some norm, unless subjects have been committed to that particular norm. Thus, choosing T&F in the Linda problem is *not* a reasoning error. What has been labelled the 'conjunction fallacy' here does *not* violate the laws of probability. It only looks so from *one* interpretation of probability.

How to make the conjunction fallacy disappear

We apply now the distinction between single-event and frequency information representation to the Linda problem. We just change the format from single event to a frequency representation (see italicized passage), leaving everything else as it was.

> Linda is 31 years old, single, outspoken and very bright. She majored in philosophy. As a student, she was deeply concerned with issues of discrimination and social justice, and also participated in antinuclear demonstrations.
> *There are 100 people who fit the description above. How many of them are*:
> *bank tellers?*
> *bank tellers and active in the feminist movement?*

Subjects are now asked for frequency judgements rather than for the probability of a single event. If one focuses on mental algorithms, this change appears irrelevant. If the mind solves the Linda problem by using a representativeness heuristic, changes in representation should not matter, because they do not change the degree of similarity. The description of Linda is still more representative of (or similar to) the conjunction T & F than of T. Subjects therefore should still exhibit the conjunction fallacy. Similarly, if one assumes with Cohen that the laws of probability are in the mind, but that subjects have been misled by the experimenter into bad performance, changes in representation should not matter either. For instance, subjects may have been misled by assuming that the description of Linda is of any relevance to the solution, whereas it is completely irrelevant to finding the solution. This irrelevancy argument is not altered by the frequency format.[2]

However, if there is some statistical algorithm in the mind *that is tuned to frequencies* as information representation, then something striking should happen to this stable cognitive illusion. Violations of the conjunction rule should largely disappear.

The experimental evidence available confirms this prediction. Klaus Fiedler (1988) reported that the number of conjunction violations in the Linda problem dropped from 91 per cent in the original, single-event representation to 22 per cent in the frequency representation ($n = 44$). The same result was found, when he replaced 'There are 100 people' by some odd number such as 'There are 168 people'. The drop in the number of conjunction violations here was from 83 per cent to 17 per cent ($n = 23$). Fiedler reported similar results for other standard problems from which the conjunction fallacy has been inferred as a stable cognitive illusion. Tversky and Kahneman (1983: 308–9) reported similar phenomena.

To summarize: The debate between Cohen and Tversky and Kahneman has centred on the question of algorithm. I have argued that in order to understand probabilistic reasoning, one should distinguish between algorithms and information representation. The philosophical and statistical distinction between single events and frequencies clarifies that judgements hitherto labelled instances of the 'conjunction fallacy' cannot be properly called reasoning errors in the sense of violations of the laws of probability. The conceptual distinction between single event and frequency representations is sufficiently powerful to make this allegedly stable cognitive illusion disappear. The conjunction fallacy is not the only cognitive illusion that is subject to this argument.

Base-rate fallacy

Casscells *et al.* (1978) presented sixty staff and students at Harvard Medical School with the following problem:

If a test to detect a disease whose prevalence is 1/1000 has a false positive rate of 5%, what is the chance that a person found to have a positive result actually has the disease, assuming you know nothing about the person's symptoms or signs?

If one inserts these numbers into Bayes' theorem, the posterior probability that the person actually has the disease is 0.02, or 2 per cent (assuming that the test correctly diagnoses every person who has the disease – a piece of information that is missing). However, almost half of the sixty staff and students at Harvard Medical School estimated this probability as 0.95, or 95 per cent, not 2 per cent. Only eleven participants answered 2 per cent. Note the variability in the judgements of physicians about the probability of the disease! The modal answer of 0.95 was taken as an instance of the *base-rate fallacy*. This term signifies that the base rate of the disease (1/1000) is neglected, and the judgement is based only (or mainly) on the characteristics of the test (the false-positive rate). Tversky and Kahneman (1982) used the results of this study to illustrate the generality and stability of the base-rate fallacy, a cognitive illusion that has been widely discussed and given much prominence. 'The failure to appreciate the relevance of prior probability in the presence of specific evidence is perhaps one of the most significant departures of intuition from the normative theory of prediction' (Kahneman and Tversky, 1973: 243). Little is known about how the participants made these judgements, and why these were so variable. It just seems that students and staff did not get effective training in statistical reasoning at Harvard Medical School.

How to make the base-rate fallacy disappear

I will now apply the same argument to the Harvard Medical School problem as I did to the Linda problem. Assume there is some kind of algorithm for statistical reasoning that works on frequency representations. Therefore, if we change the information representation in the Harvard Medical School problem from percentages and single-event probabilities to frequencies, then the base-rate fallacy should also disappear. As a consequence, the large variability in judgements should disappear. This is a testable prediction.

When I made this prediction during luncheon discussions at the Center for Advanced Study in the Behavioral Sciences, two of the other fellows, Leda Cosmides and John Tooby, got up from the table and went down the hill to Stanford University, where they tested the prediction with 425 undergraduate subjects (Cosmides and Tooby, 1991). They constructed a dozen or so versions of the medical problem as controls; of chief interest here is the frequency version:

> One out of 1000 Americans has disease X. A test has been developed to detect when a person has disease X. Every time the test is given to a person who has the disease, the test comes out positive. But

sometimes the test also comes out positive when it is given to a person who is completely healthy. Specifically, out of every 1000 people who are perfectly healthy, 50 of them test positive for the disease. Imagine that we have assembled a random sample of 1000 Americans. They were selected by a lottery. Those who conducted the lottery had no information about the health status of any of these people. How many people who test positive for the disease will actually have the disease? ____ out of ____.

In this version, the representation of the input information is changed from percentages, such as 5 per cent, to frequencies such as '50 out of 1000'. The representation of the output information is changed from a single-event probability ('What is the probability that a person . . .?') to a frequency judgement ('How many people . . . ?'). This made the proportion of Bayesian answers skyrocket from 12 per cent (in a replication using the original representation) to 76 per cent (and to 92 per cent, if subjects were instructed to visualize frequencies in a graphical display).

If only the representation of the input information was changed into frequencies, but not that of the output information, or vice versa, the effect of the change in information representation was halved. All other changes, such as adding the missing information about the false-negative rate and the explicit information about random sampling, had little effect on the judgements, as the control versions showed.

We have the same result as for the Linda problem. Judgements labelled 'base-rate fallacy' largely disappear in the Harvard Medical School problem when we change the information representation from single events to frequencies. The effect is about as strong as in the Linda problem.

Results in the same direction have been obtained on other reasoning problems when information representation was only partially changed into a frequency format, such as using sequential monitoring of frequency information and random sampling from a collective (e.g. Borgida and Brekke, 1981; Gigerenzer *et al.*, 1988; McCauley and Stitt, 1978).[3]

It is also instructive that some researchers tend to change their own information representation when they turn away from the subject and explain the correct solution to the reader. An early example is Hammerton, who used single-event probabilities to communicate information to his subjects:

1. A device has been invented for screening a population for a disease known as psylicrapitis. 2. The device is a very good one, but not perfect. 3. If someone is a sufferer, there is a 90% chance that he will be recorded positively. 4. If he is *not* a sufferer, there is still a 1% chance that he will be recorded positively. 5. Roughly 1% of the population has the disease. 6. Mr. Smith has been tested, and the result is positive. The chance that he is in fact a sufferer is: ____.

(Hammerton, 1973: 252)

When the author explains the correct answer to his readers, he switches, without comment, into a frequency representation:

> Out of every 100 persons tested, we expect 1 to have the disease; and the device is nearly certain to say that he has. Also, out of that 100, we expect the machine to say that 1 healthy person has the disease. Thus, in the long run, out of every 100 persons tested, we expect 2 positive results, one of which will be correct and the other incorrect. Therefore the odds on any positive result being valid are roughly even.
>
> (ibid: 252)

The frequency format is easily digested by Hammerton's readers. However, Hammerton's subjects not surprisingly failed on the single-event representation. Their median response was not one-to-one (i.e. 50 per cent), but 85 per cent.

Thus far, we have seen how to make two cognitive illusions, the conjunction fallacy in the Linda problem and the base-rate fallacy in the Harvard Medical School problem, largely disappear. I will now turn to a third prominent illusion.

Overconfidence bias

Confidence in one's knowledge is typically studied with questions of the following kind:

Which city has more inhabitants?
(a) Hyderabad
(b) Islamabad
How confident are you that your answer is correct?
50%, 60%, 70%, 80%, 90%, 100%

Imagine you are an experimental subject: your task is to choose one of the two alternatives. Possibly you chose Islamabad, as most subjects in previous studies did. (If your choice was indeed Islamabad, you agree with the majority of subjects but are, regrettably, wrong.) Then you are asked to rate your confidence that your answer 'Islamabad' is correct. Fifty per cent confident means guessing, 100 per cent confident means that you are absolutely sure that Islamabad is the larger city. After many subjects answer many questions, the experimenter counts how many answers in each of the confidence categories were actually correct.

The major finding of some two decades of research is the following: in all the cases where subjects said, 'I am 100 per cent confident that my answer is correct', the relative frequency of correct answers was only about 80 per cent; in all the cases where subjects said, 'I am 90 per cent confident' the relative frequency of correct answers was only about 75 per cent; when subjects said 'I am 80 per cent confident' the relative frequency of correct

answers was only about 65 per cent, and so on (Lichtenstein *et al.*, 1982).
Values for confidence were systematically *higher* than relative frequencies.
This systematic discrepancy has been interpreted as an error in reasoning
and has been named 'overconfidence bias'. Quantitatively, overconfidence
bias is defined as the difference between mean confidence and mean
percentage correct.

Consistent with the general research strategy of the heuristics-and-biases
programme, the explanandum is a *discrepancy* (overconfidence bias)
between a confidence judgement and a norm (frequency), not the confidence
judgements by themselves (there are some exceptions, e.g. May (1987)).
Little, however, has been achieved in explaining this discrepancy. A
common proposal is to explain 'biases' by other, deeper mental flaws. For
instance, Koriat *et al.* (1980) propose that the overconfidence bias is caused
by a 'confirmation bias'. Here is their explanation. After one alternative
is chosen (e.g. Islamabad), the mind searches for further information that
confirms the answer given, but not for information that could falsify it.
This selective information search artificially increases confidence. The key
idea is that the mind is not a Popperian. Other deficiencies in cognition
and motivation have been suggested as explanations: Fischhoff, Edwards,
and others proposed that subjects are insensitive to item difficulty (von
Winterfeldt and Edwards, 1986: 128). Dawes suggested the tendency of
humans in the western world to overestimate their intellectual powers,
which 'has been reinforced by our realization that we have developed a
technology capable of destroying ourselves' (Dawes, 1980: 328). Others
have proposed motivational reasons such as 'fear of invalidity' or 'illusion
of validity'. Note that in all these explanatory attempts the experimental
phenomenon is seen as a 'cognitive illusion', that is, an error in probabilistic reasoning, that has to be explained by some deeper flaw in our
mental or motivational programming.

Similar to the conjunction fallacy, overconfidence bias has been suggested as an explanation for human disasters of many kinds, including
deadly accidents in industry (Spettell and Liebert, 1986), errors in the legal
process (Saks and Kidd, 1980), and systematic deviations from rationality
in negotiation and management (Bazerman and Neale, 1986).

Checking the normative yardstick

Is overconfidence bias really a 'bias' in the sense of a violation of
probability theory? Let me rephrase the question. Has probability theory
been violated if *one's average degree of belief (confidence) in a single event*
(i.e. that a particular answer is correct) is different from the *relative
frequency* of correct answers in the long run? From the point of view of
the frequency interpretation, the answer is 'no', for the reasons already
discussed. Probability theory is restricted to frequencies; it does not apply

to single-event judgements like confidences. Therefore, no statement about confidences can violate the laws of probability. Even for Bayesians, however, the answer is not 'yes', as it was with the conjunction fallacy. The issue here is not internal consistency or coherence, but the relation between subjective probability and external (objective) frequencies, which is a more complicated issue and depends on conditions such as exchangeability (for a discussion related to overconfidence see Kadane and Lichtenstein, 1982).

To summarize: a discrepancy between confidence in single events and relative frequencies in the long run is not an 'error' in the sense of a violation of probability theory, contrary to the claims in the heuristics-and-biases literature. It only looks that way from the perspective of a narrow interpretation of probability theory that blurs the fundamental distinction between single events and frequencies.

How to make overconfidence bias disappear

Many experiments have demonstrated the stability of the overconfidence phenomenon despite various 'debiasing methods' (Fischhoff, 1982). In our own experiments, we have also confirmed the stability despite *those* methods (Gigerenzer *et al.*, 1991). We warned subjects, prior to the experiment, of overconfidence, or gave them monetary incentives – this did not decrease overconfidence. We tried it with a bottle of French champagne as an incentive – to no avail. To quote von Winterfeldt and Edwards (1986: 539): 'Overconfidence is a reliable, reproducible finding.' And they conclude, with a tone of regret 'Can anything be done? Not much' (Edwards and von Winterfeldt, 1986: 656). Let's see.

I will now apply to the overconfidence bias the same argument as before to the conjunction fallacy and base-rate fallacy. Assume an experiment in which you present subjects with fifty general-knowledge questions of the Hyderabad–Islamabad type and ask them for confidence judgements, as usual. Here is where this experiment diverges from earlier work. You also ask the same subjects about judgements of the frequency of correct answers: 'How many of these fifty questions do you think you have answered correctly?' Assume your subjects' mean confidence judgements are, just like in earlier studies, systematically higher than their relative frequency of correct answers. That is, you replicate the earlier findings and get a typical overconfidence bias of about 15 per cent. What do you guess how your subjects' frequency judgements will compare with the true frequency of correct answers?

If confidence in one's knowledge were truly biased due to confirmation bias, wishful thinking, or other deficits in cognition, motivation, or personality, then the difference between a single-event and a frequency representation should not matter. Overestimation should remain stable, just as it does with warnings and French champagne.

Table 11.1 Overestimation disappears in judgements of frequency

Difference between	Experiment 1 (n = 80)	Experiment 2 (n = 97)
Mean confidence and true relative frequency of correct answers (overconfidence)	+13.8	+15.4
Estimated frequency and true frequency of correct answers	−2.4	− 4.2

Ulrich Hoffrage, Heinz Kleinbölting and I have performed this and related experiments (for details see Gigerenzer *et al.*, 1991). Table 11.1 shows the results of two experiments with 80 and 97 subjects, respectively. Only averages are shown here, because individual results conformed well to averages. In both experiments, the stable discrepancy between mean confidence and the true relative frequency of correct answers could be replicated. This is necessary for control, but no surprise. Overconfidence bias, expressed in percentage (by multiplying the difference by the factor 100) was 13.8 per cent and 15.4 per cent, respectively. What about the frequency judgements? When we compared subjects' estimated frequencies with their true frequencies, overestimation *disappeared*. In both experiments subjects showed a tendency towards underestimation. In Table 11.1, the differences between estimated and true frequencies are also expressed in percentages, for comparison. For instance, in Experiment 1, the average estimated frequency of correct answers (in a series of 50 questions) was 1.2 lower than the true frequency of correct answers, which corresponds to −2.4 in 100 questions, or −2.4 per cent. Negative signs denote underestimation, positive signs overestimation.

To summarize: I have argued that the discrepancy between mean confidence and relative frequency of correct answers, known as 'overconfidence bias', is not an error in probabilistic reasoning. It only looks that way from a narrow normative perspective, in which the distinction between single-event confidence and frequencies is blurred. If we ask our subjects about frequencies instead of single-event confidences we can make this stable phenomenon disappear.

It is easy to see how my argument, illustrated here by three prominent examples, can be extended to and tested for other cognitive illusions. The philosophical distinction between single-event probabilities and frequencies teaches us that the irrationality claim, at least as based on these examples, is premature. The normative yardstick does not stand up to closer examination. The distinctions between algorithm and information representation, and between single event and frequencies, combined with the notion of the mind as a frequency-monitoring device, teaches us how to make apparently stable cognitive illusions disappear. This is of course good news for those who would like to believe in human rationality, or for those biologically minded people who wonder how a species so bad at statistical reasoning could have survived so long, and also for those unfortunate souls charged with teaching undergraduate statistics.

Earlier explanations of reasoning in terms of a general representativeness heuristic or a general confirmation bias cannot account for these striking results. We have to look for a fresh understanding of cognitive processes that explains both the old and new facts. What follows is a brief introduction into the theory of probabilistic mental models (Gigerenzer *et al.*, 1991). The theory explains both the old facts (the robust overconfidence and hard–easy effects of the last two decades) the new facts (the disappearance of overconfidence) and makes several other novel predictions.[4]

PROBABILISTIC MENTAL MODELS

I will illustrate the theory of probabilistic mental models (for short, PMM theory) by the following problem:

Which city has more inhabitants?
(a) Heidelberg
(b) Bonn
How confident are you that your answer is correct?
50%, 60%, 70%, 80%, 90%, 100%

Assume that subjects do not know the answer, but have to make an inference under uncertainty. How is that inference made?

Before I start outlining the theory, a general remark on explanatory strategy is helpful. Our explanandum is confidence and choice, and not overconfidence bias. That is, we attempt to explain judgement, not the deviation of judgement from some controversial norm. As a consequence, we do not need to invoke deeper-level biases (such as confirmation biases) or error-prone heuristics as explanations. This contrasts with the heuristics-and-biases programme. Nor do we invoke explanations that assume perfect knowledge and unlimited computational and attentional capacities, as in traditional rational-choice theories. Instead, PMM theory postulates cognitive mechanisms that work well given limited knowledge, limited attention, and limited computational capacities. In these respects, PMM theory is a model of 'bounded rationality' (Simon, 1955).

PMM theory assumes that a frame of inference is constructed to solve a particular problem such as the Heidelberg–Bonn problem. This frame of inference is called a *PMM*. A PMM generalizes the two alternatives, Heidelberg and Bonn, to a reference class, such as 'all cities in Germany'. And it generalizes the target variable, number of inhabitants, to a network of probability cues that co-vary with the target. Thus, a PMM consists of

Table 11.2 Probability cues for solving tasks of the Heidelberg–Bonn type. Examples given are for the reference class 'cities in Germany'

Probability cues
1 Soccer-team cue (one city's soccer team plays in the soccer 'Bundesliga', the other city's team does not).
2 State capital cue (one city is a state capital, the other city is not).
3 Industrial cue (one city is located in the 'Ruhrgebiet', the other in rural Bavaria).
4 Licence-plate cue (the letter code that identifies a city on a licence plate is shorter for one city than for the other).
5 Familiarity cue (one had heard of one city, but not of the other).
6 Capital cue (one city is a capital, the other city is not).

a reference class (that contains the two alternatives), a target variable, and probability cues.

Table 11.2 shows examples of probability cues for population size in the reference class 'German cities'. Take the soccer-team cue. Large cities are likely to have a team playing in the Soccer Bundesliga, in which the eighteen best teams compete. The *ecological validity* of this cue can be determined by checking all pairs in which one city has a team in the Bundesliga but the other does not. For instance, one finds that in 91 per cent of these cases the city with the Bundesliga team has more inhabitants (calculated for 1988/89, for what then were West German cities with more than 100,000 inhabitants). Thus, the ecological validity of the soccer cue is 0.91 in this reference class. Note that it is defined as a relative frequency, not as a Pearson correlation as in Brunswik's (1955) framework. Ecological validity is defined on the environment, whereas *cue validity* is the corresponding concept in a subject's PMM. I will call a PMM well-adapted if the cue validities correspond well to the ecological validities.

Note, however, that the soccer team cue cannot be *activated* for the Heidelberg–Bonn problem: neither city has a team in the Bundesliga; so the cue does not differentiate. In fact, only the last cue in this list can be activated, and this *capital cue* does not have a particularly high cue validity – because it is well known that Bonn is not exactly London or Paris. (The low cue validity may change soon, however, because Bonn's days as capital are numbered.)

PMM theory assumes when activation rates are low or time pressure occurs, as is typical for studies of general knowledge, that the *first* cue that can be activated determines choice (here: Bonn) and that *confidence equals cue validity* (Table 11.3). This algorithm is 'satisficing' (Simon, 1982) in the sense that it produces good, but not necessarily optimal, performance. The algorithm is a variant of bounded rationality (Simon, 1955) in so far as it is designed to work on limited knowledge and on the first cue activated. The latter avoids computationally complex integrations of many cues.

Table 11.3 PMM algorithm for choice and confidence

Task:	Choose the correct alternative, *a* or *b*, and give confidence judgment.
Algorithm:	
Step 1:	Generalize *a* and *b* to a reference class *R*, where *a, b* ∈ *R*.
Step 2:	Generate cue C_i highest in cue validity.
Step 3:	Generate values of *a* and *b* for cue C_i. If one or both values are unknown, go back to step 2 and generate the cue next highest in cue validity.
Step 4:	Test whether values of *a* and *b* differ, i.e., whether C_i can be activated. If yes, denote this as aC_ib. If not, go back to step 2.
Step 5:	Choose *a* if $p\,(a|aC_ib;R) > p\,(b|aC_ib;R)$. (For example, let aC_ib stand for '*a* has a soccer team in the Bundesliga but *b* does not'. Then $p\,(a|aC_ib;R)$ is the probability that *a* has the larger population given aC_ib, for all *a,b* ∈ *R*. This probability is the cue validity, and *R* is the reference class.)
Step 6:	Confidence = $p(a|aC_ib;R)$. (The confidence that the choice *a* is correct is equal to the cue validity of the activated cue C_i.)

Source: Gigerenzer *et al.* (1991).
Note: Knowledge of cues can be limited, i.e. only a subset of all ecological valid cues may be available from memory (step 2). Knowledge of values can be limited, too. Cues have binary values (yes/no; see Table 11.2), but knowledge is tertiary (yes/no/unknown; see step 3).

Table 11.4 Probabilistic mental models for single-event (confidence) and frequency tasks

PMM	Confidence task	Frequency task
Target variable	Number of inhabitants	Number of correct answers
Reference class	Cities in Germany	Similar sets of general-knowledge questions in similar testing situations
Probability cues	E.g. soccer team cue, state capital cue	E.g. base rates of previous performance

Now consider a frequency task. Subjects answer several hundred questions of the Heidelberg–Bonn type. After each group of fifty questions they are asked: 'How many of the last fifty questions do you think you have answered correctly?' The point is that according to PMM theory, confidence and frequency judgements are based on different cognitive processes, because different PMMs have to be constructed (Table 11.4).

The target variable in the confidence task is number of inhabitants, whereas in the frequency task it is number of correct answers. As a consequence, reference class and probability cues are different, too. A soccer cue, for example, no longer helps. A task that involves judgements of frequencies of correct answers has a different reference class: sets of general knowledge questions in similar testing situations. And base rates of earlier performance in such testing situations are an example of a probability cue for frequency judgements. Note that both single-event confidence and frequency judgements are explained by reference to experienced frequencies. However, these experienced frequencies relate to different reference classes, which are in turn part of different PMMs.

PMM theory can be quantitatively simulated; for the present purpose, however, qualitative predictions are sufficient. In the following sections, I will derive several novel predictions from PMM theory, some of them being counterintuitive and therefore surprising. First, however, we will see how PMM theory explains the stable overconfidence bias.

Explaining old facts: overconfidence bias

PMM theory explains the stable overconfidence effect in the following way. Assume that subjects' PMMs are, on the average, well adapted. This means that although subjects' knowledge about some domain (such as about German urban centres) may be limited, it should not be systematically biased. This implies that cue validities roughly correspond to ecological validities, but it does not imply that subjects know all the relevant cues. If the general-knowledge questions were a representative sample from the knowledge domain, zero overconfidence would be expected. For instance, if the soccer cue has an ecological validity of about 0.9, and the cue validity matches this, it follows from PMM theory that confidence would be around 0.9 in those cases where the soccer cue can be activated. From the definition of the ecological validity it follows that the relative frequency of correct answers would be 0.9, too. However, general-knowledge questions typically are not representative samples from some domain of knowledge, but are selected to be difficult or even misleading. The Hyderabad–Islamabad question is an example for a misleading question. Here, a usually valid cue, the capital cue (Islamabad is a capital, Hyderabad is not), leads to a wrong choice: Hyderabad has a much larger population.

Selecting difficult and misleading questions decreases the number of correct answers, and 'overconfidence bias' results as a consequence of selection, not of some deficient mental heuristic. To the best of my knowledge, all previous studies that have demonstrated overconfidence in general knowledge have used selected questions: this explains the stability of the phenomenon against warning, monetary incentives, and French champagne. Here are several novel predictions.

Novel predictions

Prediction 1. Confidence and representative sampling

Assume (1) well-adapted PMMs as above, and (2) use a *representative* sample of questions from some knowledge domain. Then, PMM theory predicts that overconfidence will disappear. We have tested this prediction using random samples from the reference class 'all cities in Germany with more than 100,000 inhabitants' (Gigerenzer *et al.*, 1991). In Experiment 1, 'overconfidence bias' decreased from 13.8 per cent in a set of selected questions to 0.9 per cent in a representative sample; in Experiment 2 this decrease replicated from 15.4 per cent to 2.8 per cent. Juslin (in press, a) independently confirmed this novel prediction using random samples from several other domains of knowledge.

Prediction 2. Frequency judgements and selected sampling

Recall that PMM theory implies that frequency judgements such as 'How many of the last fifty questions do you think you got right?' are solved by a PMM with a different reference class (e.g. other general-knowledge tests). Assume (1) that the PMMs for a frequency task are well adapted and (2) use a set of questions that are representative for *this* reference class. Because the typical sets of general-knowledge questions used in earlier research are representative for this reference class, frequency judgements should be accurate. We have tested and confirmed this novel prediction (see Table 11.1).

The crucial point is that confidence and frequency judgements refer to different kinds of reference classes. The same set of questions can be representative with respect to one reference class, and at the same time selected with respect to the other class. Thus a set of fifty general-knowledge questions of the city-type may be representative for the reference class 'general-knowledge questions', but not for the reference class 'cities in Germany' (because city pairs have been selected for being difficult or misleading). Asking for a confidence judgement summons up a PMM based on the reference class 'cities in Germany'; asking for a frequency judgement summons up a PMM based on the reference class 'sets of general-knowledge questions'.

Prediction 3. Underestimation in frequency judgements

We use here the situation of prediction 1 to deduce a condition in which frequency judgements *underestimate* the true frequency of correct answers. If a PMM for frequency judgement is well adapted to its reference class (i.e. sets of selected items), but the actual set of questions is not selected, then we expect frequency judgements to be underestimations of true frequencies. We have tested and confirmed this novel prediction (Gigerenzer *et al.*, 1991). In Experiment 1, the difference between estimated and true frequency of correct answers decreased from −2.4 per cent (set of selected items, see Table 11.1) to −11.8 per cent; and from −4.2 per cent (see Table 11.1) to −9.3 per cent in Experiment 2.

Further novel predictions can be derived from quantitative simulations of PMM theory. Here is one last example. The prediction is about percentage correct, that is, about correct choice rather than about confidence or frequency judgements, on which we have focused so far.

Prediction 4. When little knowledge is as good as good knowledge

Recall that in the experiments just reported, our subjects were German, and they were answering questions about German cities. Their mean percentage of correct answers varied between 70 per cent and 75 per cent (for representative samples of cities). Assume we take a new sample of German students who are just as good as the earlier ones – they are familiar with German cities and know the relevant probability cues. We do the same kind of experiment; the only difference is that we give them questions about an environment which is highly unfamiliar to them: cities in the USA. More precisely, we take the 75 largest cities in the USA, draw a random sample of 100 pairs, and give these 100 questions to our German subjects. What would you predict?

All theories of overconfidence I am aware of are mute on the issue of percentage correct. All the people I have asked so far concluded that percentage correct will be much lower when subjects answer these 100 questions about foreign cities. From our simulations with PMM theory, we derived a quite different and surprising prediction: subjects will do just as well with American as with German cities. That is, their percentage correct will be the same for German and US cities. I will deduce this prediction here by a simplified calculation.

We take the 75 largest cities in the USA. Assume that our German subjects have not even heard of half of these, such as Mesa, Mobile, and Shreveport, and that they know nothing about the other half, except that they have heard of these cities. Thus, their PMM is poor; the only probability cue it can generate is the familiarity cue, that is whether one has heard of a city or not. This familiarity cue is of high cue validity, but it plays almost no role in judgements about German cities, because most of our subjects have heard of all these German cities. Thus, it can rarely be activated. The point is that for judgements about US cities, the familiarity cue has a high activation rate. To be precise, if half of the US cities are familiar, the activation rate is 50.7 per cent.[5] What is the validity of the cue? Pretests have shown that the cue validity is around 0.90.[6] Thus, we have about 50 per cent of questions where the familiarity cue can be activated, and 50 per cent where it cannot (because either the names of both cities are known or both unknown). For the first group, we expect 90 per cent correct – given a cue validity of 0.90 – that is, in absolute terms, 45 per cent correct answers. In the other group, we expect by mere guessing an additional 25 per cent correct answers, that is, altogether, 70 per cent correct answers. This value is counterintuitively large. Note that this value is in the range of the percentage correct for German cities (70–75 per cent), although it has been calculated on the assumption of no specific knowledge. Any such knowledge (e.g. that New York is larger than Boston) will add on to this estimate.

Thus, PMM theory makes a counterintuitive prediction: in the situation described, German subjects will get about the same percentage correct in judgements about unfamiliar US cities as in judgements about German cities.

Horst Kilcher, Ulrich Hoffrage, and I conducted an experiment. Fifty-six subjects each answered 200 questions of the Heidelberg–Bonn type, 100 being a random sample of city pairs from the 75 largest US cities, the other 100 being a random sample from the 75 largest German cities. Half of the subjects got the questions about the German cities first, the other half those about US cities. Consistent with our earlier experiments, mean percentage correct was 75.6 per cent for German cities. But what was the percentage correct for judgements about US cities?

Table 11.5 shows that mean percentage correct for US cities was 76 per cent, that is, about the same as for the German cities about which our subjects had considerably more knowledge. This result follows from PMM theory. Here, we have an interesting situation, where quite limited knowledge (but not *no* knowledge) produces the same good performance (percentage correct) as quite good knowledge.

To summarize my second part: I have briefly presented PMM theory, which specifies the cognitive processes underlying choice, confidence, and frequency judgements. The theory implies conditions under which overconfidence appears: either a PMM for a task is not properly adapted to a corresponding environment (for example, cue validities do not correspond to ecological validities), or the set of objects used is not a representative sample from the corresponding environment, but is selected for difficulty. In our experiments, overconfidence disappeared when random samples instead of selected samples were used, which is consistent with the latter explanation. Thus, the source of overconfidence seems to be in the relation between the sample of objects used in the task and the reference class in a corresponding environment. Overconfidence does not seem to be located in the relation between PMMs and corresponding environments (that is, in a low correspondence between cue validities and ecological validities).

Table 11.5 Mean percentage of correct answers

	US	*German*
Mean percentage correct	76.0	75.6
	$(SE_m=0.7)$	$(SE_m=0.9)$
Mean confidence	72.3	79.5
	$(SE_m=1.0)$	$(SE_m=0.8)$

PMM theory specifies conditions under which the 'robust' overconfidence effect of the last fifteen years appears, disappears, and even inverts. One can no longer speak of a general overconfidence bias, in the sense that it relates to deficient processes of cognition or motivation. I have not dealt here with how the theory explains the second robust finding in the literature – the hard–easy effect (that is, overconfidence increases with item difficulty). I will simply mention that the theory also provides an explanation for the hard–easy effect on the same principles, and specifies conditions under which it disappears or even inverts. Juslin (in press, b) has tested and confirmed a prediction from PMM theory that specifies conditions that make the hard–easy effect disappear (Gigerenzer *et al.*, 1991: 512). Simulations with PMM theory have led us to explain several anomalies in the literature, and to integrate earlier explanatory attempts into a comprehensive theoretical framework. For instance, Koriat's and colleagues' (1980) results testing the confirmation bias explanation can be fully integrated into PMM theory (Gigerenzer *et al.*, 1991). PMM theory seems to be the first theory in this field that offers a coherent explanation not only of the effects previously reported in the literature on judgement under uncertainty, but also for the new results we have obtained in our experiments.

CONCLUSIONS

Since the Enlightenment, probability theory has been seen as the codification of human rationality. Consequently, recent experiments suggesting that human reasoning systematically violates the laws of probability have been widely cited as evidence for human irrationality. Here are the arguments of this chapter.

1 I have argued that the cognitive illusions I have dealt with are not genuine illusions, contrary to the assertions in the heuristics-and-biases literature. They only look like errors from a narrow normative view about what is right and wrong in reasoning, a view that blurs the philosophical distinction between single-event probabilities and frequencies.

2 I have linked this philosophical distinction with Marr's (1982) distinction between algorithms and information representation, and with the evolutionary idea that the mind's algorithms are tuned to frequency information. This framework suggests how to make apparently stable cognitive illusions disappear. I have demonstrated this using three cognitive illusions, widely cited as evidence for human irrationality. The new facts cannot be accounted by the old explanations invoking heuristics such as representativeness.

3 I introduced the theory of probabilistic mental models (PMM theory) as

an alternative explanation of intuitive reasoning, using confidence in one's knowledge as an example. The theory explains both old and new facts. PMM theory postulates a mental algorithm that processes frequency information from the environment. This algorithm works well given only limited knowledge, limited attention, and limited computational capacities, and is a variant of bounded rationality. The theory describes reasoning and performance in terms of relations between a PMM, an environment, and an experimental task. Focusing on mental algorithms alone, whether they seem to be good or bad ones, turns out to be too narrow for understanding the mind, and also, for discussing rationality.

ACKNOWLEDGEMENT

This chapter is based on a lecture delivered at Harvard University, 2 October 1991. I wrote this chapter under a fellowship at the Center for Interdisciplinary Research, University of Bielefeld, Germany, and with the support of the *Fonds zur Förderung der wissenschaftlichen Forschung* (*P 8842-MED*), Austria. I am grateful to Lorraine Daston, Ralph Hertwig and Ulrich Hoffrage for many helpful comments.

NOTES

1 The debate between the frequentists and Bayesians was particularly lively before the 1970s. Today, both sides know each other's arguments well and the vital debate has turned into sterile, well-rehearsed argument. The two sides seem to have quit listening. As Glenn Shafer (1989) complained, statistics departments no longer provide a forum for the debate, and the main divisions over the meaning of probability now follow disciplinary lines: frequentists dominate statistics and experimental social sciences, Bayesians predominate in artificial intelligence and theoretical economics. 'Conceptually and institutionally, probability has been balkanized' (Shafer, 1989: 15).

2 The attentive reader will have noticed that the frequency version of the Linda problem asks for a quantitative judgement, whereas the single-case version asks for a comparative judgement. The latter, however, is an accidental feature of our choice of example. Single-case versions asking for quantitative judgements ('What is the probability that Linda is . . . ?') are known to give about the same amount of conjunction errors as comparative judgements (Tversky and Kahneman, 1983).

3 In some studies widely cited as demonstrating base-rate neglect, subjects were not informed about random sampling. In the 'Tom W.' Problem (Kahneman and Tversky, 1973), the crucial information about how the personality sketch of Tom W. was selected, whether randomly or not, is missing. The same holds for the Gary W. and Barbara T. problems that Ajzen (1977) used. Several studies have demonstrated that it can make a difference to subjects' reasoning when they learn about random sampling (e.g. Ginossar and Trope, 1987; Grether, 1980; Hansen and Donoghue, 1977; Wells and Harvey, 1977), or, even better, when they can actually watch random sampling. For instance, the neglect of base

rates in the engineer–lawyer problem (Kahneman and Tversky, 1973) largely disappears when subjects themselves *do* the random sampling (Gigerenzer *et al.*, 1988). For general critical discussions of the evidence see Berkeley and Humphreys (1982), Gigerenzer and Murray (1987, Ch. 5), Lopes (1991), Lopes and Oden (1991), Macdonald (1986), and Scholz (1987).

4 Other proposals have been made in the literature to explain the old facts, that is, the cognitive illusions. I cannot discuss these here, but only mention a few: the role of conversational principles in the experimenter–subject interaction (Adler, 1991); the evolutionary idea that there are domain-specific reasoning mechanisms (e.g. cheating detection) that reflect our inherited social intelligence rather than a domain-general logic (e.g. Cosmides, 1989; Gigerenzer and Hug, 1992), and the idea that category judgements such as in probability revision problems and in the Linda problem can be modelled by connectionist architectures (e.g. Gluck and Bower, 1988).

5 There are 75 cities, 38 are familiar, 37 not (or 37 familiar, 38 not, which leads to the same result). If two familiar cities are compared, or two unfamiliar ones, the familiarity cue cannot be activated; it can only be activated if one city is familiar but the other is not. The number of such familiar–unfamiliar pairs is 38×37, and the number of all possible pairs is $75 \times 74/2$. Thus, the activation rate is 38×37 divided by $75 \times 74/2$, which is 38/75 or 50.7 per cent. The activation rate can be determined in this way for each individual separately depending on the number of familiar and unfamiliar cities. For instance, if not one-half, but only one-third of the cities were familiar, the activation rate would change slightly, from 50.7 per cent to 45 per cent.

6 The cue validity of the familiarity cue can be calculated for each individual from the set of familiar–unfamiliar pairs. The relative frequency in which the familiar city actually has the larger population is the cue validity.

REFERENCES

Adler, J.E. (1991) 'An optimist's pessimism: conversation and conjunction', *Posnan Studies in the Philosophy of the Sciences and Humanities* 21: 251–82.

Ajzen, I. (1977) 'Intuitive theories of events and the effects of base-rate information on prediction', *Journal of Personality and Social Psychology* 35: 303–14.

Aristotle (1945) *Movements of Animals*, trans. E.S. Foster, Cambridge, MA: Harvard University Press.

Barnard, G.A. (1979) 'Discussion of the paper by Professors Lindley and Tversky and Dr. Brown', *Journal of the Royal Statistical Society*, (A), 142: 171–2.

Bazerman, M.H. and Neale, M.A. (1986) 'Heuristics in negotiation', in H.R. Arkes and K.R. Hammond (eds) *Judgment and Decision making: An Interdisciplinary Reader*, Cambridge: Cambridge University Press, pp. 311–21.

Berkeley, D. and Humphreys, P. (1982) 'Structuring decision problems and the "bias heuristic"', *Acta Psychologica* 50: 201–52.

Boole, G. (1958) *An Investigation of the Laws of Thought on which are Founded the Mathematical Theories of Logic and Probabilities*, New York: Dover (original work published in 1854).

Borgida, E. and Brekke, N. (1981) 'The base rate fallacy in attribution and prediction', in J.H. Harvey, W. Ickes, and R.F. Kidd (eds) *New Directions in Attribution Research*, vol. 3, Hillsdale, NJ: Erlbaum, pp. 63–95.

Brunswik, E. (1955) 'Representative design and probabilistic theory in a functional psychology', *Psychological Review* 62: 193–217.

Casscells, W., Schoenberger, A., and Grayboys, T. (1978) 'Interpretation by physicians of clinical laboratory results', *New England Journal of Medicine* 299: 999–1000.

Cohen, L.J. (1982) 'Are people programmed to commit fallacies? Further thoughts about the interpretation of experimental data on probability judgment', *Journal for the Theory of Social Behavior* 12: 251–74.

—— (1983) 'The controversy about irrationality', *Behavioral and Brain Sciences* 6: 510–17.

—— (1986) *The Dialogue of Reason*, Oxford: Clarendon Press.

Cosmides, L. (1989) 'The logic of social exchange: has natural selection shaped how humans reason? Studies with the Wason selection task', *Cognition* 31: 187–276.

Cosmides, L. and Tooby, J. (1991) 'Are humans good intuitive statisticians after all? Rethinking some conclusions from the literature on judgment under uncertainty', manuscript submitted for publication.

Daston, L. (1988) *Classical Probability in the Enlightenment*, Princeton, NJ: Princeton University Press.

Dawes, R.M. (1980) 'Confidence in intellectual judgments vs. confidence in perceptual judgments', in E.D. Lantermann and H. Feger (eds) *Similarity and Choice: Papers in Honor of Clyde Coombs*, Bern, Switzerland: Huber, pp. 327–45.

Edwards, W. and von Winterfeldt, D. (1986) 'On cognitive illusions and their implications', in H.R. Arkes and K.R. Hammond (eds) *Judgment and Decision Making*, Cambridge: Cambridge University Press, pp. 642–79.

Evans, J. St B.T. (1984) 'Heuristic and analytic processes in reasoning', *British Journal of Psychology* 75: 451–68.

Fiedler, K. (1988) 'The dependence of the conjunction fallacy on subtle linguistic factors', *Psychological Research* 50: 123–9.

Fischhoff, B. (1982) 'Debiasing', in D. Kahneman, P. Slovic, and A. Tversky (eds) *Judgment under Uncertainty: Heuristics and Biases*, Cambridge: Cambridge University Press, pp. 422–44.

Fong, G.T. and Nisbett, R.E. (1991) 'Immediate and delayed transfer of training effects in statistical reasoning', *Journal of Experimental Psychology: General* 120: 34–45.

Gallistel, C.R. (1990) *The Organization of Learning*, Cambridge, MA: MIT Press.

Gigerenzer, G. (1991) 'On cognitive illusions and rationality', *Poznan Studies in the Philosophy of the Sciences and the Humanities* 21: 225–49.

Gigerenzer, G. and Hug, K. (1992) 'Domain-specific reasoning: social contracts, cheating, and perspective change', *Cognition* 43: 127–71.

Gigerenzer, G. and Murray, D.J. (1987) *Cognition as Intuitive Statistics*, Hillsdale, NJ: Erlbaum.

Gigerenzer, G., Hell, W., and Blank, H. (1988) 'Presentation and content: the use of base rates as a continuous variable', *Journal of Experimental Psychology: Human Perception and Performance* 14: 513–25.

Gigerenzer, G., Hoffrage, U., and Kleinbölting, H. (1991) 'Probabilistic mental models: a Brunswikian theory of confidence', *Psychological Review* 98: 506–28.

Ginossar, Z. and Trope, Y. (1987) 'Problem solving in judgment under uncertainty', *Journal of Personality and Social Psychology* 52: 464–74.

Gluck, M.A. and Bower, G.H. (1988) 'Evaluating an adaptive network model of human learning', *Journal of Memory and Language* 27: 166–95.

Gould, S.J. (1992) *Bully for Brontosaurus. Further Reflections in Natural History*, Harmondsworth: Penguin.

Grether, D.M. (1980) 'Bayes rule as a descriptive model: the representativeness heuristic', *The Quarterly Journal of Economics* 95: 537–57.

Hammerton, M. (1973) 'A case of radical probability estimation', *Journal of Experimental Psychology*, 101: 252–4.

Hansen, R.D. and Donoghue, J.M. (1977) 'The power of consensus: information derived from one's own and others' behavior', *Journal of Personality and Social Psychology* 35: 294–302.

Hasher, L. and Zacks, R.T. (1979) 'Automatic and effortful processes in memory', *Journal of Experimental Psychology: General* 108: 356–88.

Hume, D. (1975) *A Treatise of Human Nature*, Oxford: Clarendon Press (original work published 1739).

Inhelder, B. and Piaget, J. (1958) *Growth of Logical Thinking: From Childhood to Adolescence*, New York: Basic Books.

Juslin, P. (in press, a) 'The overconfidence phenomenon as a consequence of informal experimenter-guided selection of almanac items', *Organizational Behavior and Human Decision Processes*.

—— (in press, b) 'An explanation of the hard–easy effect in studies of realism of confidence in one's general knowledge', *European Journal of Cognitive Psychology*.

Kadane, J.B. and Lichtenstein, S. (1982) *A Subjectivist View of Calibration*, Report No. 82–86, Eugene, OR: Decision Research.

Kahneman, D. and Tversky, A. (1972) 'Subjective probability: a judgment of representativeness', *Cognitive Psychology* 3, 430–54. Reprinted in D. Kahneman et al. (1982) (eds) *Judgment under Uncertainty: Heuristics and Biases*, Cambridge: Cambridge University Press, pp. 32–47.

—— (1973) 'On the psychology of prediction', *Psychological Review* 80:237–51.

Kanwisher, N. (1989) 'Cognitive heuristics and American security policy', *Journal of Conflict Resolution* 33: 652–75.

Koriat, A., Lichtenstein, S., and Fischhoff, B. (1980) 'Reasons for confidence', *Journal of Experimental Psychology: Human Learning and Memory* 6: 107–18.

Laplace, P.S. (1951) *A Philosophical Essay on Probabilities*, New York: Dover (original work published 1814).

Lichtenstein, S., Fischhoff, B., and Phillips, L.D. (1982) 'Calibration of probabilities: the state of the art to 1980', in D. Kahneman, P. Slovic, and A. Tversky (eds) *Judgment under Uncertainty: Heuristics and Biases*, Cambridge: Cambridge University Press, pp. 306–34.

Lopes, L. (1991) 'The rhetoric of irrationality', *Theory & Psychology* 1: 65–82.

Lopes, L. and Oden, G.C. (1991) 'The rationality of intelligence', *Posnan Studies in the Philosophy of the Sciences and the Humanities* 21: 199–223.

McCauley, C. and Stitt, C.L. (1978) 'An individual and quantitative measure of stereotypes', *Journal of Personality and Social Psychology* 36: 929–40.

Macdonald, R.R. (1986) 'Credible conceptions and implausible probabilities', *British Journal of Mathematical and Statistical Psychology* 39: 15–27.

Marr, D. (1982) *Vision: A Computational Investigation into the Human Representation and Processing of Visual Information*, San Francisco: Freeman.

May, R.S. (1987) *Realismus von subjektiven Wahrscheinlichkeiten*, Frankfurt/Main: Lang.

Neyman, J. (1977) 'Frequentist probability and frequentist statistics', *Synthese* 36: 97–131.

Nisbett, R.E. and Borgida, E. (1975) 'Attribution and the psychology of prediction', *Journal of Personality and Social Psychology* 32: 932–43.

Piattelli-Palmarini, M. (1989) 'Evolution, selection and cognition: From "learning" to parameter setting in biology and in the study of language', *Cognition* 31: 1–44.

Real, L. and Caraco, T. (1986) 'Risk and foraging in stochastic environments: theory and evidence', *Annual Review of Ecology and Systematics* 17: 371–90.

Saks, M. and Kidd, R.F. (1980) 'Human information processing and adjudication: trial by heuristics', *Law and Society Review* 15: 123–60.

Scholz, R.W. (1987) *Cognitive Strategies in Stochastic Thinking*, Dordrecht, Holland: Reidel.

Shafer, G. (1989) *The Unity and Diversity of Probability*, inaugural lecture, 20 November 1989, University of Kansas.

Simon, H.A. (1955) 'A behavioral model of rational choice', *Quarterly Journal of Economics* 69: 99–118.

—— (1982) *Models of Bounded Rationality*, 2 vols. Cambridge, MA: MIT Press.

Slovic, P., Fischhoff, B., and Lichtenstein, S. (1976) 'Cognitive processes and societal risk taking', in J.S. Carroll and J.W. Payne (eds) *Cognition and Social Behavior*, Hillsdale, NJ: Erlbaum.

Spettell, C.M. and Liebert, R.M. (1986) 'Training for safety in automated person-machine systems', *American Psychologist* 41:545–50.

Staddon, J.E.R. (1988) 'Learning as inference', in R.C. Bolles and M.D. Beecher (eds) *Evolution and Learning*, Hillsdale, NJ: Erlbaum.

Stich, S.P. (1990) *The Fragmentation of Reason*, Cambridge, MA: MIT Press.

Tversky, A. and Kahneman, D. (1974) 'Judgment under uncertainty: heuristics and biases', *Science* 185: 1124–31.

—— (1982) 'Evidential impact of base rates', in D. Kahneman, P. Slovic, and A. Tversky (eds) *Judgment under Uncertainty: Heuristics and Biases*, Cambridge: Cambridge University Press.

—— (1983) 'Extensional versus intuitive reasoning: the conjunction fallacy in probability judgement', *Psychological Review* 90: 293–315.

von Mises, R. (1957) *Probability, Statistics, and Truth*, London: Allen & Unwin (original work published in 1928).

von Winterfeldt, D. and Edwards, W. (1986) *Decision Analysis and Behavioral Research*, Cambridge: Cambridge University Press.

Wells, G.L. and Harvey, J.H. (1977) 'Do people use consensus information in making causal attributions?', *Journal of Personality and Social Psychology* 35: 279–93.

Name Index

Subject Index